John Hammond On Record

John Hammond On Record

An Autobiography With Irving Townsend

SUMMIT BOOKS | NEW YORK

RIDGE PRESS

Copyright © 1977 by John Hammond
All rights reserved, including the right of reproduction in whole or in
part. Prepared and produced by The Ridge Press.

Library of Congress Cataloging in Publication Data
Hammond, John, 1910-
   John Hammond on record.

   Discography: p.
   Includes index.
   1. Hammond, John, 1910-   2. Impresarios—
United States—Biography. 3. Jazz music. I. Town-
send, Irving. II. Title.
ML429.H26A3   77-8789
ISBN 0-671-40003-7

To Esmé

Picture Credits

Preface

Almost everyone closely associated with me in the course of a long life in music—and in a changing America—has a place in the pages which follow. I hold them all in affection and respect, and I have tried to make this evident in the text.

I must offer a special salute, however, to several of my oldest companions on the journey: Fletcher Henderson, Bill Basie, Benny Goodman, and Teddy Wilson.

I have always been grateful to the late Goddard Lieberson, the brilliant president of Columbia Records, for his unfailing friendship and support. He was the conscience of the record business and its boldest innovator. My gratitude, as well, to Bob Altshuler, the head of Columbia Records' public relations, for tirelessly touting my successful records and minimizing my failures.

I want to acknowledge the unstinting assistance of Frank Driggs and Michael Brooks, who for years have done much of the legwork for which I received credit.

Of my many wonderful cousins not already mentioned, Shirley Burden and Watson Webb have been of enormous help. And so has John Berg, the fine art director of Columbia Records.

Thanks, too, to my old friend Willis Conover, who encouraged me to reminisce on tape some twenty years ago and gave me the notion that there might be a story in my unstructured life. By the fortunate coincidence that Irving Townsend and I retired from Columbia Records at about the same time, a man who knows me as well as any in the world was able to help make this book a reality. For patiently and skillfully untangling the facts of my life, Irving, many thanks. Any errors which may crop up, of course, are mine.

Finally, an appreciative nod to Adie Suehsdorf, the most knowledgeable and creative editor in my experience. The fact that he is also a lover of jazz made our collaboration even more of a pleasure.

—JH

I

Late in the afternoon of December 15, 1910, John Henry Hammond left his downtown law offices for the recently built, eight-story mansion which was his home, just off Central Park at 9 East 91st Street. Although he was aware that the birth of his fifth child was imminent, he saw no reason to hurry. Children are seldom born at the cocktail hour; if there were to be a cocktail hour for him, and a toast to his newest child, he would not be able to enjoy it at home anyway. His wife did not approve. Nor had he any doubts about either the baby's safe arrival or the mother's well-being. There were sixteen servants in help at home and the best doctors on call. At forty he had sired four daughters, all of whom were by then healthy girls between two and ten years old. Confident that all was well, he stopped off at one of his clubs, the Knickerbocker, and enjoyed his cocktail. Although he usually traveled to work by subway, that day he continued home by taxi, repeating to himself the name of the newest Hammond heiress. He had long since given up hope of fathering a boy, and was so certain that the next child would be another girl he had already chosen her name: Esther.

When he reached home about six o'clock, the butler met him at the door. "There's a gentleman to see you, sir," he announced, with a small smile.

And so in an upper bedroom I joined the Hammond family, a late and welcome surprise. Although my father's father was also named John Henry Hammond, I was christened John Henry Hammond, Jr., and immediately entered at St. Paul's, Groton, and St. Mark's, college preparatory schools for the sons of the wealthy destined to follow their fathers into business or the law. The Hammond son's future was decided. His path would be smoothed by inherited wealth (Mother's share of the hundreds of millions accumulated by *her* mother's Vanderbilt forebears and of her father's mercantile fortune), and by a tradition of accomplishment whose momentum had been well begun four generations before him.

Life in the 91st Street mansion resumed its normal, oppressively regulated routine, and until two or three years old I was my mother's special, pampered treasure in long golden curls.

My father, whom I hardly saw during my earliest years, had been born in Louisville, Kentucky, in 1870, the son of the youngest Union general in the Civil War. Soon after my father's birth the family moved to St. Paul, Minnesota, where the general became a land speculator. More often poor than rich, Grandfather Hammond now and then hit a bonanza, and it must have been during one of his flush moments that he developed the city of Superior, Wisconsin, one of the dreariest places in the country. But General Hammond had his memories. He had been Sherman's chief of staff and was said to have been Sitting Bull's only white friend. My grandfather liked Indians, but his tolerance did not extend to blacks. My father shared his prejudices. Grandmother Hammond, whose maiden name was Wolfe, I loved dearly. Although she died when I was twelve, I remember her as a fanatical Presbyterian who had raised six children, all of whom received excellent educations despite the ups and downs of her husband's fortunes. My father's older brother, Ogden, married a Stevens of the Stevens Institute family and at one time was the United States ambassador to Spain. His older sister, Mary, married and divorced another diplomat, Lincoln MacVeagh, a failure which broke my grandmother's heart. There were also three younger sisters: Sophie, who became Mrs. Burnside Foster; a delightful aunt of mine, Hattie —Harriet King Hammond—who never married and who died in 1974 at the age of ninety-nine after years of devotion to my family; and, finally, Peggy, the baby, who died relatively young at the age of eighty-two. The women on both sides of my family outlived their men by a quarter century or more.

Father grew up in St. Paul, but he came east to attend Phillips Exeter Academy in New Hampshire, went on to Yale, and received his law degree from Columbia, one of the finest law schools in the country. A man of many interests and talents, he became a banker, a railroad executive, and a successful lawyer. But as I came to know him better I realized that his greatest achievement was his fifty-year marriage to my mother, a union founded in deep mutual love, yet often frustrating and difficult for my father. Being married to a Vanderbilt often must have been an even greater burden than being born one.

At the point in my life when I began to understand and to appreciate my father he was in his fifties and sixties, a fine-looking man, an inch under six feet and sandy haired, although I remember him as being practically bald. He used a preparation called Herpicide on his hair, though to no avail. As the advertisements used to say, he was "too late for Herpicide." He wore a neatly trimmed mustache, and although he developed a rather considerable pot late in life—a "corporation" was the favored term in those days—he was never fat. The forty-year disparity in our ages while I was growing up prevented the close father-son relationship I wish we had had, and our rare attempts to create such a relationship were, I'm afraid, disappointing to each of us. My father was a fine golfer, so I tried to impress him by playing golf, but an eight-year-old on the golf course succeeded only in spoiling the game. At my grandmother's house in Lenox, Massachusetts, where our family often visited, I tried to learn to ride a bicycle on the broad lawns around the house. My father tried to help, but after I fell off the bike eight or nine times, bawling loudly, after seeing disgust on his face at my clumsy failures, and hearing him cry at last, "You rotten mutt," I admitted crushing defeat. I wanted his sympathy, his friendship, and, as his only son, his love. I received it all and more in time, but not until we both were men. Like many fathers, mine improved with age. Mine, not his.

The Hammonds never had money. They married it. My father married Emily Vanderbilt Sloane, the daughter of Emily Thorne Vanderbilt and William Douglas Sloane. Emily T. V. Sloane, my maternal grandmother was the eldest daughter of William H. Vanderbilt and granddaughter of the pater familias, the first Cornelius Vanderbilt, the railroad tycoon. She was a swinger for her day. Her husband, Mr. Sloane, was one of the most attractive men I ever knew, a second or third-generation American whose ancestors came from Dunfermline, Scotland, also the starting point of another of the Land of Opportunity's multimillionaires, Andrew Carnegie. Grandfather's family founded W. & J. Sloane, a high-class, high-priced, and very famous furniture store located in a beautiful building at the southeast corner of Fifth Avenue and 47th Street. Branch stores were later opened in many parts of the country. More recently the company was sold; there are no Sloanes left at Sloane's. The original site is now occupied by a Korvette's discount store.

Grandfather and Grandmother Sloane were happily married until 1915, when he died. Young as I was, I remember him well. He used to sit next to me at the Welte-Mignon player piano in Lenox, reading aloud the words on the roll, and allowing me to play with his wonderful pocket watch which, if you pulled a little lever, chimed each quarter hour. He left me that watch, but somehow it was lost. My grandmother Emily was a stunning woman. She was extremely proud of her bosom and very daring for her day about revealing it. She loved clothes and dressed beautifully, and while I was growing up she made her house a haven for my sisters whenever they needed to escape the rigid restrictions imposed at home.

My mother was born in 1874 on East 44th Street, between Madison and Fifth Avenues, but before my great-grandfather, William H. Vanderbilt, died, he built twin mansions on Fifth Avenue between 51st and 52nd Streets for my Great-Uncle William K. Vanderbilt and Grandmother Emily. Her house, where De Pinna's store was later located, was built with the appalling taste that only a vast American fortune looking for ways to expend itself could command. Cupids flew across ceilings, a carriage entrance on 52nd Street led to an ornate doorway, and the kitchen rivaled that of the Waldorf Astoria (then, of course, at 34th and Fifth Avenue). We Hammond children rarely saw the bedrooms. We were not allowed to venture above the first two floors. But we were always welcome. It was in this house that my mother grew up, surrounded by wealth thoroughly enjoyed at a time in America's history when evidence of depression and poverty lay no farther away than Lexington Avenue to the east, 96th Street to the north, Sixth Avenue and 42nd Street to the west and south. She lived on a golden island and was not quite comfortable about it.

Mother was sent to Sunday school early on at the Fifth Avenue Presbyterian Church. There she discovered religion and the relief she needed from the embarrassment of riches. She took her Sunday-school lessons seriously and believed it obscene to wallow in wealth when grinding poverty and distress were so close at hand. She was both fascinated and repelled by the high society which was her natural station, and she soon fashioned her own way of living with it. It was not possible for her to rebel politically as a young girl, and she knew little of politics anyway. But through religion she could rebel socially. She would not flaunt wealth as her mother did. Instead she would impose, first upon herself and later upon her family, a code of moral behavior and responsibility which would serve as an example to her small world of the duties of the blessed. She was a beautiful woman, tall for her time, and with the erect bearing the nineteenth century required of elegant ladies. There was no arrogance in it, simply evidence of good breeding. Vanity was lavished only on her hair and ankles. She had her hair—a woman's "crowning glory"—cared for regularly by the only Jewish woman she knew, Mrs. Block, whom she described as a Hebrew. She cared little for clothes, never wore a dab of powder in her life, and would not allow lipstick to be brought into her house. Her only formal education was private tutoring by Miss Spence; her parents did not approve her mixing with even the uncommon herd in private schools. Like all Vanderbilt women, with the exception of my sister Adele, she did not go to college.

While the careers of Cornelius and William H. Vanderbilt revealed little evidence of compassion or concern for the public they ostensibly served, they did value education and sought to be remembered as founders of Vanderbilt University and financial props of Yale. They were savage money makers, controlling utilities and the New York Central Railroad, among other holdings, but, unlike my father's parents, they saw little value in educating Vanderbilt daughters. Trust funds were quite sufficient to assure their children the continuing place at the top of society they prized so highly.

My mother felt otherwise about society. She believed most of the young men thrust upon her while she was growing up to be quite useless, and, already a reformer, she tried to change them, which did not make her popular. If her escort smoked in her presence he was told not to. If he drank she never saw him again. Until she met my father, when she was twenty-four, she must have led a miserable life, her convictions rejected by her contemporaries, her self-appointed role as the conscience of the wealthy repúdiated. Like many legatees of American millionaires, she inherited more than their millions. She inherited the guilt they never felt themselves.

My mother and father were married April 7, 1899, and both were alive to celebrate their fiftieth wedding anniversary. By the time she married, Mother was a prodigious woman, considered odd by her friends, terribly earnest, and undaunted by any challenge. When she wanted to do something, she did it even though it was often difficult and sometimes strongly resented. She loved poetry, memorized an enormous amount of it, and there were whole chapters of the Bible she could recite at will. The "at will" came much too often for us children, who were expected to learn complete Psalms and chapters of Genesis. Mother took it all very seriously and felt that having wealth required responsible behavior by her and her family. She led the good life herself. She intended to see to it that we did, too.

If Mother had been exposed to the political realities of her time, and if she had not met my very conservative father, she might well have become a political radical. As it was, she did not hesitate to march to protest alcohol and other sins, but she never came across anybody who was other than a Republican conformist. Democrats she could not approve of. Socialists she had never heard of. In any event, I think it would have been a miracle for her to have decided, with very little education and even less exposure to opposing opinion, that her mission should include political protest. The social order she found was the one she accepted. Racial minorities were beyond her reach. Blacks were porters and laundresses. The poor existed and were to be helped, yet even the dispensation of charity must begin, if not at home, within the circumference of familiar territory.

From the Bible Mother knew what was right and wrong. She knew it was wrong to smoke, to drink, to have extramarital affairs. Yet when her friends were guilty of such lapses and excesses, she found it easy and obligatory to forgive them, realizing that there were temptations which did not come to her, but which others could not resist. The Bible taught her to forgive, "for they know not what they do."

My mother's compulsion to save the world took many forms. She founded the Three Arts Club, a place where girls from good white Christian families could live in New York while they pursued careers in music, the theater, and the dance. The girls received two meals a day for $14 a week, the club's annual deficit being made up by Mother and her friends. But the boarders had to be in their rooms by midnight, even if they were in the theater. Men visitors were not allowed above the ground floor, and the inevitable shenanigans which went on from time to time Mother forgave, even though she would have had difficulty forgiving such conduct in her own children.

She had extraordinary energy, as all reformers do, and very disciplined work habits. She arose each morning between six and six-thirty, a habit which forced my father to sleep in a separate room, and wrote letters for an hour before breakfast. She was a compulsive letter writer, and although she avoided ostentation in most things, her letters had the Hammond crest in raised silver at the top of each page and her stationery came either from Tiffany's or Cartier's. Mother was not one to hide her wealth completely, although she was careful never to reveal its extent. She would never allow my father to sell any of her securities, even to advantage, for fear someone would find out how much she had.

Mother was influenced by various ministers in her early life and believed as they did that the ills of this world would be solved in the next. She was totally convinced of a hereafter and that in order to reach Paradise one must lead as good a life on earth as possible. She really tried to live as uncorrupted a life as anyone ever did, and when she made up her mind she was right, nobody could budge her. This made life difficult for her, while her two sisters, who were much more adjusted to their high and fortunate position, lived well and without doubts. Mother also had a brother, Malcolm, who in family parlance was "sickly." This meant that after he graduated from Yale, where he became involved with "the wrong people," he was never encouraged to work. Instead, he drank. He belonged to the Racquet Club, caroused, and married a beautiful Southern belle, Eleanor Lee from Virginia. Malcolm drank himself to death when I was about twelve or thirteen, confirming Mother's convictions about the evils of alcohol, but she was not content to leave the lesson at that. I was told that Uncle Malcolm died because he smoked while he drank, burned his fingers, and died of blood poisoning. I found out much later from my sisters that he had not died so dramatically at all. It simply suited Mother's purpose to combine alcohol and tobacco into one horror story which would keep her highly inhibited son on the straight and narrow.

And she succeeded. I did not smoke or drink, nor did I understand why anybody would. My father once promised me $2,000 if I foreswore these indulgences until I was twenty-one. I thought this a totally unacceptable proposition, a bribe I could not accept because no one should be rewarded for refraining from habits not good for him. One evening my school friend Billy McCampbell and I were taken to the theater by his beautiful and worldly sister. Afterward she took us to a speakeasy called Frank and George's, on 58th Street, for oysters, which I loved. I purposely ordered and drank a sidecar and smoked one cigarette so I would be ineligible to accept my father's reward. I was so brainwashed by my mother that I believed her warning that if I kissed a girl I might catch a venereal disease. I could look, and I often did, but I could not touch.

Mother played the piano at least an hour each day and studied most of her life with a succession of teachers. Her technique was never what it should have been, considering the amount of effort she devoted to her playing, though she had an enormous repertoire and she loved chamber music. I began piano lessons at four, but because of double-jointed thumbs which curl backward, making it difficult to strike piano keys cleanly, I switched to the violin, equally satisfying to Mother because we could play sonatas together. We played Mozart, Handel, early Beethoven, and Dvořák, and Mother always believed she was giving pleasure to her friends with our recitals. I knew better. My playing never gave much pleasure to anyone, but all Mother's friends gushed over us. I was always suspicious of anyone who told me how good I was. Mother, on the other hand, took compliments as her due. She had worked hard and she loved flattery. I suppose I do, too, even though I was taught long ago by my father to be suspicious of it.

Mother, for all her inhibitions and self-denials, was warm-hearted, very affectionate, and physically quite stunning. It is not unusual for people who become fanatics as she did to have some physical insecurity to compensate for. Not my mother. She never danced, she never went swimming. She was reluctant to expose her extremely good figure and never did. She loved to hear the trials and falls from grace of others and would always be helpful and understanding—except where my sisters were concerned. They never confided in her, sure of her disapproval, except for my sister Alice, who told only a fraction of the truth. Although I loved Mother dearly, I too confided in her only to a degree. I came to love show business, including the bawdiest of burlesque. I could not have explained why to my mother, so I never tried. I felt that what she didn't know wouldn't hurt her; at the same time, I could not lie to her.

My mother had many sycophantic friends, and she had what was known in our household as a payroll—regular support for deserving people she felt she must maintain in the style to which they would like to become accustomed. I remember one wonderful old party, "Tante" Hope, from Montgomery, Alabama, who cultivated ladies with lots of money. "Tante" Hope lived quite comfortably on allowances she received from my mother and one or two other wealthy women, and when she died she left quite a fortune. Mother was annoyed that someone with several hundred thousand dollars had been taking money from her all those years to live in a studio apartment at the Croyden with summers in Bar Harbor with my Aunt Alice Morris. We all loved her just the same.

Not long before I was born my youngest sister, Rachel, developed a serious ear infection. A friend of Mother's suggested she go to a Christian Science practitioner to see whether prayer and direct talk with God would cure Rachel's affliction. Mother took the advice, refused to have Rachel's ear operated on, and, lo and behold, the abscess, if that is what it was, disappeared. Mother immediately became an absolute captive of Christian Science, leaving the rest of the family, except me, to continue attending St. Bartholomew's with my grandmother and the Madison Avenue Presbyterian Church with my father. The pastor of the Madison Avenue Church was Henry Sloane Coffin, my mother's first cousin, who later became the head of Union Theological Seminary and moderator of the Presbyterian Church. Cousin Henry was to have a profound effect upon my life, but during the first World War he was a pacifist, a stand my father considered treasonable, so he stopped attending Cousin Henry's church.

Father once confessed to me that his father had been an agnostic and not to tell Mother, but he was something of a free thinker himself. He was by no means master of his own house, exercising his authority only occasionally and otherwise accepting the house rules laid down by my mother. Although he belonged to several private clubs where he could have a drink, he could not drink or smoke at home except in his library. Mother would not tolerate cigars, and when father smoked his pipe in the car he had to ride in front with the chauffeur. When he married my mother he received from her father an excellent wine cellar, which he prized, for he liked brandy and good wines, but with the advent of Prohibition, when liquor became illegal, as well as immoral in my mother's view, she dumped every bottle of wine into the gutter in front of our 91st Street house. Father came home from the office to find his lovely cellar in ruins, with only a small quantity of champagne left for future weddings and a few bottles of sweet, after-dinner wine. That was a day when his ego, as well as his palate, suffered cruelly.

Father had his own strange economies, as well as his expensive indulgences. He rode the subway to work every morning because, he said, close contact with subway crowds would help to immunize him from common diseases which even the sheltered rich were heir to. He also hated to spend money on expensive cars. We drove Pierce-Arrows and Cadillacs handed down to us by my grandmother and always painted dark maroon, the Vanderbilt color. He would not accept my grandmother's Rolls Royces, but for years we rode in second-hand cars with two chauffeurs on permanent staff. Despite his successful career as a respected banker, chairman of several railroads, and member of one of New York's finest law firms, it was my mother who had the money and called the shots. He had married a very rich woman whose annual income made his own insignificant by comparison. Like all such men, he paid with his freedom and often with his self-esteem.

Meanwhile, I went with my mother to all her Christian Science churches, and I cannot describe how dreadful they were. I believed because she believed, but the services were agonizing. The only thing I can say for them is that they did have quite good singers. I remember one named Nevada Vanderveer, who sang at the First Church of Christ, Scientist, at 96th Street and Central Park West, an area of Manhattan only religion could have persuaded my mother to visit. Nevada sang well, and she was also a Columbia recording artist, which impressed me very much. In 1943, when I was casting *Carmen Jones* for Billy Rose, I visited the Cleveland Institute of Music and found that the head of the vocal department was none other than Nevada Vanderveer. I told her I was an old fan of hers, dragged to church where she sang. She led me to believe that her Sunday solos had not been inspired by Mary Baker Eddy's teachings.

For the first ten or twelve years of my life I accepted my mother's faith in Christian Science as my own. When my dog was lost, I prayed hard. I went to a Science practitioner, and when I came home—it seems unbelievable, but it happened—the dog would be there. I read *Science and Health* every day and believed, as Mother did, that the mind can exert superiority over the ills of the body. I found Christian Scientists to be supremely self-centered, certain of complete power over themselves, and while, like my mother, they were extremely kind, thoughtful people, they believed they alone had the key to the mechanism of the universe. I believed it also. Hopelessly.

The fact that my mother had turned to Christian Science before I was born did trouble me in one way. I was the only member of my family who had not been baptized at birth, and this exception bothered me. Finally, at thirteen, I went to Henry Sloane Coffin to be baptized and to become a member of his Presbyterian Church. By that time I had developed growing suspicions about my mother's religion, although certainly not about the power of religion itself. Baptized, I felt better. I varied my Sunday church attendance between my grandmother's Episcopal church, Cousin Henry's Madison Avenue church, and Mother's Christian Science, which I could still not dismiss altogether.

My first schooling was at the Froebel League on East 71st Street, a private school which included kindergarten and the first two grades. I was naturally left-handed, and the first contribution the Froebel League made to my education was to force me to become right-handed, something I am sure did little for my intellect or equilibrium. It was the only co-ed school I ever attended, and a girl in my class quickly assured me that there was no Santa Claus. I did learn good work habits, however, and did an enormous amount of reading. I had learned to read at the age of three, and, although one of my mother's dutiful pleasures was to read to me every evening—books by Albert Payson Terhune and other accepted fare for young boys—I much preferred the magazines I found for myself. I have always been a magazine freak, identifiable if for no other reason by the armful of current periodicals I carry wherever I go, and in those days I discovered the pulps and detective stories, the best reason to learn to read I knew of. My love of phonograph records also helped make me an early reader. I had been listening to records since I was two years old, and I had to read the labels to find the music I liked. Even then, music prompted me to take action.

Practically speaking, I grew up as an only child. My four older sisters ignored me if possible, occupied as they were with affairs of their own. I was Mother's special pet, and because I was also a Christian Scientist in a society where there were few Scientists, I was considered odd—like my mother—and usually left alone. In my friends' houses the fact that I had not been vaccinated, that when I had a cold I denied its reality, made me an outcast. It also made me quite independent, for—again like my mother—I was certain my way was the right way.

I think I remember my young self well enough to say I was curious, enthusiastic, full of ideas, excited by many interests. I was soon aware of the family wealth and position. Mother made clear to me the matter of status, the difference between rich and poor. Walking the streets, I could see for myself that there were multitudes living a great deal less well than I.

My parents were strict, yet I was indulged. This fostered enterprise, but the heady sense of privilege made me more prejudiced and intolerant than I knew. I thought—and I had no one to contradict me—that I was special. I had eyes that saw what others didn't see. I had ears that heard what

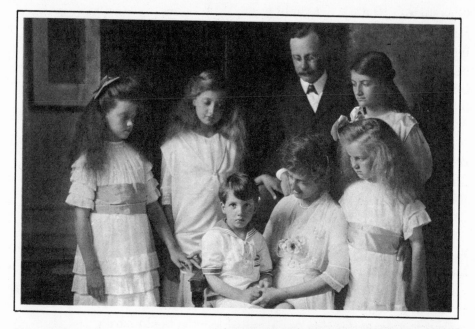

Mr. and Mrs. John Henry
Hammond and their children, c.
1915. From left: Alice, Adele,
young John Henry, Rachel,
Emily. Right: Western vacation,
1924.

others didn't hear.

Many of my attitudes were precocious. I made judgments about the many religious denominations to which I was exposed. I opted for Republicans over Democrats. I disapproved the Victor Talking Machine Company because, in my juvenile wisdom, it seemed an exploitative monopoly. I liked Szigeti, but not Heifetz. I liked Eugene Ysaye—as I live and breathe—as an innovator and intellectual, but thought his records lousy.

My first slogan, to which I subscribed wholeheartedly, yet not, I think, with full comprehension of its import, was: "A man is known by his enemies."

A boy with four older sisters is a frequent, if unwelcome witness to flaring and dying romances, to an unending procession of young suitors, and I had a front-row seat. My sisters, two brunettes and two blondes, never lacked attention and never ceased to welcome it. My oldest sister, Emily, could hardly wait to get out of the house and married the first serious suitor who came along, a Harvard Porcellian and athlete named Jack Franklin. Their courtship was carried on at my grandmother's house on 52nd Street, where she told Emily, "I understand about your mother, and any time you want to see your friends, you come right here." "At least," she added, "they can get a drink here and they can't at your house."

My second sister, Adele, the most beautiful of all, attracted men like flies. I was once caught behind a sofa fascinated by the amorous conversation taking place between Adele and one of her admirers. An early favorite of hers was Jack Emery, but when my mother discovered that Jack's mother played cards on Sunday and for money, she broke up the friendship and Jack dropped out of our life. Adele went on to attend Barnard, the only one of my sisters with even a smattering of a college education. There is a strange postscript to Adele's broken romance with Jack Emery. A few years later she married another Harvard Porcellian, John Olyphant. They remained happily married for fifty-two years, until John died in 1974. Soon afterward Adele received a telephone call. "Is this Adele Olyphant, who used to be Adele Hammond?" a man asked.

Adele said it was. "Well, this is Jack Emery and I'd like to visit you."

He arrived at Adele's house on Staten Island, by now in his mid-seventies and a prominent Cincinnati business man. Six months later they were married. Jack had never given up hope.

My third sister, Alice, was the family rebel. She had a sharp wit and a fanciful way of embroidering a narrative. She would tell the family one quarter of the truth about her escapades, a fraction so horrifying that they could not imagine anything worse. Alice, of course, fascinated me and became my favorite sister. I inherited her Reo roadster in 1927 when she, even more desperate than the others to escape, married a Tory member of the British Parliament, George Arthur Duckworth, and moved to England. Not, however, before she became engaged to Jack Speiden, a suitor disapproved of by the family, but a man destined to join it anyway.

My youngest sister, Rachel, was unusually tall for a girl in those days, which gave her a problem finding dancing partners. Rachel was the only one of my sisters at home during the early years of my life; I remember the summer of 1921, when I was sent to Lone Pine Camp. I had left behind an irreplaceable collection of piano rolls by Lem Fowler, James P. Johnson, and Fats Waller, which Rachel gave to the Salvation Army. It broke my heart, but she just didn't appreciate their value. She understood her strange little brother no better than her sisters, seeing him a confusing combination of jazz fan, vaudeville addict, and religious nut. Rachel's love affairs were also dramatic. Her second husband, for instance, turned out to be the irrepressible Jack Speiden.

Shortly before I was born my grandmother did for my mother and my Aunt Adele (Mrs. James A. Burden) what her father had done for her. She built twin houses on East 91st Street for them and their families. Built on lots fifty-five feet wide and one hundred and twenty feet deep, they were far more than mere houses. Located just east of Fifth Avenue and Central Park, they turned out to be among the most elaborate private mansions in the city. The house in which I was born had two cellars and six stories. A marble staircase led from the ground floor to a second-floor ballroom where more than two hundred guests could be seated comfortably for one of Mother's recitals. Other floors could be reached by two elevators. The household staff of sixteen servants included a butler and footman, governesses and maids, a cook and kitchen help, not to mention the two chauffeurs and various day workers. It was the family town house until shortly before my father died in the late 1940's, when it was sold to Ramon Castroviejo, a noted Spanish eye doctor, who converted it into a fine private hospital. On several occasions my wife Esmé and I have had cocktails with the Castroviejos in the very room where I was born. More recently we Hammonds have been excluded from the house; it is now the Russian consulate. A Soviet flag flutters above its elaborate front entrance.

My father strongly objected to the mansion when it was presented to him and my mother. It was one more reminder that he was married to a wealthy woman and expected to live in a house he could never have afforded to buy himself. Mother's own way of handling the conflict between living in opulence and the always nagging sin of ostentation was to furnish it as she accoutered herself, in a subdued and often tasteless fashion. It was furnished from the undistinguished but expensive stock of the family store. I don't remember a single rare antique or piece of real beauty in the house.

A few years before I was born my father bought a dairy farm in Mount Kisco, a fashionable retreat in Westchester County, as the Hammond country house. Dellwood, while equally impressive in its own way, was quite another residence from Father's point of view. It was a working farm with barns for sixty or seventy Guernsey cows, poultry houses, and vegetable gardens. It cost $50,000, a bargain in those days. Father became a breeder of prize Guernseys and the president of the New York State Guernsey Breeders' Association. Still, the main house, a hideous rambling structure which

9 East 91st Street had a domestic staff of sixteen and a ballroom seating 250. Opposite: Library (top) and music room.

leaked, required an enormous staff. I once counted fourteen bathrooms, and there was also a fifteen-room "cottage" which the family used during winter weekends because the main house was too expensive to heat. There were acres of woodland for walking and tobogganing in winter, a fine tennis court, and later a swimming pool.

The Hammond life style while I was growing up consisted of summers at Dellwood, chauffeured trips to Lenox to visit my Vanderbilt relatives, and, for longer journeys, a private railroad car which was hitched to the back of trains heading toward our destinations. The Vanderbilt children had no reason to play with toy trains. We had real ones.

We were plagued by governesses, those substitute mothers of the wealthy. How I hated this protection, an embarrassing retainer escorting me wherever I went! When I was about eleven I finally managed to persuade Father that I needed no lady companion. I remember only one governess I liked. She agreed to accompany me to the first Negro revue I ever saw. We sat in the balcony, watched scantily clad show girls and shocking skits, and I loved it all. Of course, my governess thought that I was only interested in the music, so she allowed me to stay and made a pact with me not to tell my parents.

Until I went away to school I lived the life of a coddled little rich boy, tolerant like my mother of weaknesses and sins in others, intolerant of any fall from grace in myself, ignorant as Mother was of the world beyond our island of social and financial equals, except to realize that there were people out there who were not like us. I shared her religious fervor, her prejudices, and her saintly resolve to set an example for others, then to forgive them when they failed to measure up to it. Like her, I was already the reformer, fired with her energy, certain in the right, oblivious to physical infirmities which all right-minded flesh could overcome, an inheritor of the guilt and therefore the obligations of wealth.

II

Music, especially music on records, entered my life early to become the catalyst for all that was to happen to me. In the grooves of those primitive early disks I found in my house, I discovered a new world, one I could enter easily and as often as I pleased simply by winding the handle of a phonograph. I loved it all. In the front of the house we had a Victrola and some Red Seal Victor records, mostly opera and my mother's favorite classical pieces. Records in the early years of this century were sold through exclusive franchises, which meant that a store offering Victor records was not allowed to sell any other brand. The best stores sold Victor, just as the best people bought them, but I discovered my favorite music on other records. In the rear of the house the servants had a Columbia Grafanola, a wonderful phonograph, and there I found my first favorite record, Sir Harry Lauder's "Roamin' in the Gloamin'," which I learned by heart. On the Brunswick label I heard Josef Hofmann. I immediately decided he was better than Rachmaninoff, who recorded for Victor. (I was wrong.) I listened to Paul Biese's orchestra, to early Paul Whiteman records, and to the Original Dixieland Jass Band, all on the Grafanola.

By the time I was eight I had switched from piano to the violin, and although I never practiced as hard as I should have, nor so diligently as my mother, I had a good ear and, like her and most violinists, I loved chamber music. I also loved the early jazz I heard on the Grafanola, but I never tried to play it. The fiddle is not an instrument well suited to jazz, although there have been a few jazz violinists deservedly famous. The first one I heard was Joe Venuti; I wrote two letters asking him to teach me. Not unexpectedly, he never answered, so I remained a listener to, rather than a performer of, jazz. Except for a brief and disastrous attempt to play the Stroh-viol: This was an instrument with one large horn for sound projection, a smaller horn which fitted the ear, and the regular neck, bridge, and four strings of a violin. It made a terrible noise, but for a while I played the Stroh-viol in the Society Syncopaters, the school dance band. I was bad, the instrument worse, and I never attempted to be a jazz musician again.

By the time I was twelve I had become an avid record collector. I was paid $1 a week as my allowance, and for that I could take the bus down Fifth Avenue to 37th Street, spend an hour at the Widener store listening to new Columbia and Okeh releases on which most of the early Negro and country artists appeared. Then I spent half an hour at the Hardman-Peck store, where Brunswicks were sold, and finally I stopped for a couple of minutes at Landay's Victor Records store. I could spend seventy-five cents, which would buy one ten-inch Columbia or Brunswick record, take the bus home, and have a dime left for the rest of the week. All music fascinated me, but the simple honesty and convincing lyrics of the early blues singers, the rhythm and creative ingenuity of the jazz players, excited me most. It was not long before I discovered that most of them—certainly all those I liked best—were black.

From my earliest listening the piano was my favorite instrument. The player piano at my grandmother's house in Lenox was the first I ever heard, and when I discovered that jazz rolls were available, I bought them as well as records. In 1920 our family traveled west by private railroad car to visit the Grand Canyon, whose north rim had just been opened to the public. We reached Salt Lake City and Ogden, Utah, by train, then hired two automobiles, a Chalmers and a Maxwell, to drive across the desert. Roads in that part of the country were pretty primitive—where they existed at all—and the first night we stayed in a boardinghouse in Kanab, Utah. In the parlor Mother found a piano and sat down to play Chopin, pressing the middle pedal. Suddenly, a banjo attachment gave Chopin a wild new sound. I ran to the piano to find out how this was done and discovered that the instrument had been manufactured by Wing & Son of New York. I took off the front panel and there was a row of little jangles which the piano hammers struck when the middle pedal was depressed. I thought that piano was the most intriguing instrument I had ever heard, and I never forgot Wing & Son.

When my family moved to Dellwood in the summer I lived on the top floor, as far as possible from everybody else, and there, of course, I had my own phonograph. The family Victrola was downstairs, but I wanted to play my records alone. Holidays were also celebrated at Dellwood, and I remember one Thanksgiving crisis which sent me off to my room and my records. When the turkey appeared, Adele stared at it in horror and asked whether it was not one of the Three Wise Men, a trio of ancient birds my sisters had made into pets. When Father admitted the turkey on the platter might indeed be one of the Magi, all my sisters burst into tears and refused to eat a bite. That was the last home-grown bird we had at Dellwood.

With the addition of music as one of my passions, my childhood became even less ordinary, and I even further removed from my contemporaries.

When I transferred from the Froebel League to St. Bernard's, another private elementary school, I became more conscious than ever of the difference between me and other boys my age. I used to walk to 98th Street and Madison Avenue, just beyond the fringe of our wealthy neighborhood and into a depressing area of tenements and the poor. Wearing my neat schoolboy clothes and a little cap which had "St. B" stitched on its front, I was a target to be jeered at. I used to run all the way home, duck down the alley, and enter by the servant's door so I would not be seen walking through the elaborate front door of our elaborate house.

In school I was disconcertingly different from my classmates. I read the Bible every day, and as the youngest boy in the class I was far more innocent than the rest about most things. But not about all, which made me strange to them. I managed to transfer to Browning, another private school little better in my view than St. Bernard's. There, true to my mother's example, I became the reformer—except that the boys at Browning were far more sophisticated than I. In my second year the subject of masturbation came under discussion. I knew this was regarded as a form of self-abuse, so I went to my Bible for enlightenment and a few debating points. Matthew 5:29 seemed appropriate: "And if thy right hand offend thee, cut it off, and cast it from thee."

I went back to class prepared to argue, not realizing how Draconian my solution sounded. While the teacher listened, hardly able to control his mirth, I gave my view of masturbation and my stern remedy for it. And I convinced my classmates I was right. Mother would have been proud.

As for politics, I was a dedicated Republican, proselytizing as usual. At nine I remember writing HARDING FOR PRESIDENT on the school blackboard, and, of course, in 1924 I was for Coolidge. By the next presidential election, however, my convictions were in flux. I was not in favor of Hoover, but I was not fond of Al Smith, either. Smith was connected with Tammany Hall and, worse for me, he was a Catholic. Among my earliest prejudices was strong opposition to Catholicism. I was in favor of complete separation of church and state, adamantly opposed to the role the Catholic church played in education. By then I had read about the Inquisition, the Reformation, and Martin Luther, and I believed strongly that no Catholic could hold political office entirely free of the influence of his church.

As music in all its forms absorbed me, religion, still the strongest influence in my life, seemed more and more contradictory. The teachings of Christ, sifted and interpreted by denominational bias, seemed to have been lost. My record collection demonstrated the unique talents of Negro artists, while what I saw and heard about Negroes denied my growing respect for them. In Mount Kisco, where my family attended the Episcopal church, I noticed that black servants were forced to sit in the back row and were not allowed to take communion. When I confronted my mother with this puzzling contradiction, she said, "John, you're old enough to know the facts of life. I realize that you're fascinated by colored people, and I want you to know that everybody is born alike.

"But with Negroes," she explained, "their skulls harden when they are twelve. There *is* a difference." That was what Mother had been taught. I wanted to believe her, but I simply could not.

In 1920 a shocking sight appeared on the Mount Kisco horizon. A man named Eugene Meyer had purchased hundreds of acres adjoining our farm and had built the most impressive house Mount Kisco residents had ever seen. Unfortunately, it included a water tower which would be seen above the trees for miles. For me the Meyer family immediately became enemy aliens, flaunting their wealth and spoiling the view. Although I was not to meet them until much later, Mrs. Meyer attended a few of the recitals Mother presented as a cultural courtesy each season. At these affairs Mother played the piano and recited poetry—al-fresco performances with frequent memory lapses. Mrs. Meyer came, reluctantly, I suspect, to a few of Mother's productions. I learned that she was the Republican boss of Westchester County and, according to family reports, a formidable woman.

I heard no more of the Meyers for several years, until my father happened to mention that Eugene Meyer was the head of the Reconstruction Finance Corporation and a brilliant banker. The Meyer family, water tower and all, was obviously not to be ignored. Father was at that time president of the Mount Kisco Golf and Tennis Club. He recognized that the racial and religious restrictions of the club were keeping the two most prominent families of Mount Kisco from joining: the Meyers, of course, and the Strauses. Jesse Isadore Straus was formerly the United States ambassador to France and the president of R. H. Macy and Company. Father reminded the directors of the club that funds were low and suggested that it was wrong to bar such wealthy and distinguished neighbors simply because they were Jewish. The club, he told the board of directors, should invite Mr. Meyer and Mr. Straus and their families to join.

Anti-Semitism dies hard, especially in private clubs for the rich. The directors agreed to allow the Meyers and the

Arthur Schutt, pianist for Paul Specht's Georgians, shown here at
New York's Alamac Hotel in 1923, shortly after becoming first
Hammond "discovery."

Strauses to join as honorary members, which meant that they could not bring their friends to the club. Both Mr. Meyer and Mr. Straus refused this condescending invitation, and I think my father was relieved that the directors' insulting compromise had been turned down. By the time I heard this story I wanted very much to meet the Meyers. Not only did they sound interesting, but by then I had decided that I might be part Jewish.

As I mentioned earlier, my paternal grandmother's name was Wolfe, a name which could, I thought, be Jewish. I also thought she had a decidedly Semitic cast to her profile. When I brought up the possibility, Father vociferously denied that there was any Jewish ancestry in his family. He explained that my Wolfe ancestor had been the young British general who won Canada for the Crown by defeating Montcalm and the French at Quebec in 1759. But this for me was no answer at all. Checking my history books, I found that General Wolfe had died a bachelor on the Plains of Abraham. Other Wolfe relatives, my father told me, had included a commandant of West Point and an attorney general of Kentucky, unlikely positions for Jews to have held. So the matter of my possibly Semitic background was temporarily resolved, though not to my satisfaction. By then I realized that many prominent people in show business, theater owners, agents, the stars themselves, were Jewish. I admired them as I admired the black artists on my favorite records. I wanted to be Jewish.

In 1923 I discovered a news dealer at the corner of 91st Street and Madison Avenue, Mr. A. Epstein, who sold a thick, intriguing paper called *Variety*. After that I read *Variety* every week, spending two hours over each issue, memorizing theater sizes, grosses, and vaudeville bills, and reading every review. Movies did not interest me because there was no good music in movie theaters, but all sorts of live entertainment did. Reading *Variety* made me feel like an insider in this exciting world of show business, and I read the columnists— Jack Pulaski, Jack Conway, and Sime Silverman—devouring their witty, scathing comments. I envied all who could enter a theater through the stage door.

Another magazine I found was *Black Mask*. I remember writing the editor [Edwin Baird] when I was about fourteen to tell him I thought his magazine was the best in the country and to ask where he had discovered that wonderful writer, Dashiell Hammett. My letter was printed in a subsequent issue, proving that, at least occasionally, my opinions were appreciated.

In the summer of 1923 I went to Europe for the first time. In London, while my family was otherwise occupied, I lucked upon Paul Specht's Georgians, a white Dixieland band playing downstairs at Lyons' Corner House, off Piccadilly Circus. They played the first improvised jazz I had ever heard in the flesh. And during intermissions, their twenty-year-old pianist, Arthur Schutt, played solos. Arthur was a cadaverous Pennsylvania Dutchman with a prominent nose, a fixed smile, a sardonic view of life, and a superlative piano technique. When I got back to the States I bought all the records he ever made. His music captivated me, and remembering the intensity of my response I would say that Arthur Schutt must have been my first jazz discovery.

Until I went to Cousin Henry Sloane Coffin to be baptized I believed all my mother told me. Now, at thirteen-fourteen, I was beginning to be aware of the prejudice rampant in every facet of the world I admired. Mount Kisco sermons so infuriated me that I turned to the Methodist Church, whose pastor was supposed to have been a member of the Ku Klux Klan. That did not upset me. We had a Catholic chauffeur who used to cross himself every time we passed a Catholic church. I thought this ridiculous, so my anti-Catholic prejudice allowed me to listen contentedly to the Methodist pastor's sermons for four months.

In the summer of 1925 news of the sensational trial of Richard Loeb and Nathan Leopold for the "thrill" kidnapping and murder of a young Chicago boy was spread across the front page of every paper. The Episcopalian minister's reaction to the life sentences the pair received was: "Well, what can you expect from a couple of decadent Jewish boys?" I remember turning to my mother to ask, "How can you pretend this has anything to do with Christianity?"

I was also bewildered by my father's code of behavior. In 1924, for instance, he threatened to horsewhip the editor of a society gossip magazine called *Town Topics* for printing a story about one of my sisters attending the Winter Garden Sunday Night Frolic, a comparatively innocent affair by any standards except Father's. By then I had done much worse. I had managed to sneak off to vaudeville shows without my parents' knowledge.

On my thirteenth birthday I accomplished something of a coup. Irving Berlin had opened a new theater called the Music Box, on 45th Street. The first show was called the *Music Box Review of 1923*, and it had received excellent notices. The leading dancer did what was called a "suggestive" number, which made me all the more determined to see for myself. It was banned, however, by the Parents' League, a self-appointed group dedicated to the preservation of young morals, which interposed itself between me and almost anything I wanted to see. The League was made up of Social Register parents determined to shield their children from bad taste in the theater, movies, in dress, dancing, and places to go. It issued a monthly bulletin proscribing what it did not like, but also occasionally recommending shows and books with sexual themes, vulgar language, and so forth, as long as their intentions were "serious." Mother was the League's president. Needing an ally against the formidable array of the Parents' League, I wrote to Percy Hammond, the *Tribune* critic, who was by far the wittiest reviewer of the day. He was, incidentally, an unrelated Hammond. I explained how much I wanted to see the Berlin show, to hear the score, and visit the new theater. Hammond replied, saying he knew no reason why naked girls should corrupt a boy of my age and that he was all for my seeing the show. Father was so amazed at my defiance of the League's edict that he took me and some friends of the Music Box forthwith. Mother stayed home.

On my fourteenth birthday Adele's new boy friend, John Olyphant, invited me and a friend to dinner in the grill of the Alamac Hotel, where Paul Specht's band played with my man Arthur Schutt on piano, and then to a preview of the first Broadway show in which the Marx Brothers appeared, *I'll Say She Is*. Because it was a preview I was allowed to go. When the reviews were published it was found objectionable and banned. For once the Parents' League was too late to stop me.

In my fourteenth year it was decided that I should go away to school. There was no protest from me. I was ready to leave home. My father wanted me to go to Exeter, his old school, but it was far off in New Hampshire, a region of cold winters, and I was a poor skater who also did not ski. I preferred something closer to New York, say, Hotchkiss, in Lakeville, Connecticut, two hours from the city by train. My cousins Fred and Osgood Field, sons of my mother's younger sister, had gone to Hotchkiss and told me about a marvelous English teacher there, John McChesney. I was very fond of my cousins and respected their opinions. They lived in Lenox, and I had grown up admiring them as older and very independent boys. Moreover, Henry Sloane Coffin had by then moved to Lakeville and occasionally preached a Sunday sermon in the Hotchkiss chapel. I convinced my parents that Hotchkiss was for me.

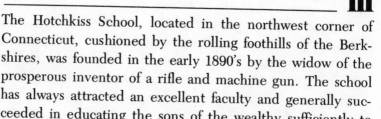

The Hotchkiss School, located in the northwest corner of Connecticut, cushioned by the rolling foothills of the Berkshires, was founded in the early 1890's by the widow of the prosperous inventor of a rifle and machine gun. The school has always attracted an excellent faculty and generally succeeded in educating the sons of the wealthy sufficiently to gain entrance to Yale, Harvard, Princeton, and other Eastern colleges. It is generously remembered by its alumni.

The first day of the new school year at a New England boarding school is one of tears and terrors for freshmen, or preps, as they are called at Hotchkiss. I arrived no better prepared for that first day than any other fourteen-year-old. We come flanked by fussing parents not quite ready to relinquish us to the care of strangers, and to an institution which in four years will make us strangers to them, our independence established, the bonds of family frayed if not snapped. Our mothers clutch us one last time, repeating instructions about laundry and letters home. Our fathers settle for a self-conscious handshake instead of the juvenile kiss good-by. The four-year difference between newcomers and seniors is enormous, obvious, belittling: We still are children made unbearably aware of our childishness, they are self-assured and mature, intent upon ignoring us, determined that we shall not ignore them. At no other time of life will any four-year span seem such an unbridgeable chasm. And to emphasize the crucial difference, freshmen at Hotchkiss are required to wear small black caps. It will be a year before we can throw them away and strut before a new class of freshmen.

My first meeting with John McChesney, the English teacher my cousins had told me about, was one of the embarrassing moments of my life. He had been expecting us and approached, smiling, to meet us. I noticed his slightly stooped posture, the result, I learned later, of arthritis of the spine. He walked with short, hurried steps, immaculately dressed in a pink Brooks Brothers shirt, expensive tweed jacket and slacks, and polished, slip-on shoes. His handsome face glowed with good health, his blue eyes twinkled as if he knew what I must be feeling and wanted to reassure me. My cousin Fred Field had been a favorite of his. He must already have planned to make me another. I took to him immediately and wholeheartedly.

Mother, remembering my alliance with the Klansman minister of Mount Kisco, as well as my generally intransigent religious views, said, "Mr. McChesney, I don't know what you'll do with my son. He's unmanageable at home and very interested in the Ku Klux Klan."

I wanted to disappear. There was nothing worse she could have said to this humane man I wanted to impress. I had made my way into several sessions of the 1924 Democratic convention in New York (at the first Madison Square Garden, off Madison Square), a convention at which the Klan supported Oscar Underwood of Alabama for President, so I knew and disapproved its power in American politics. By 1925 I had no illusions about the Klan, but I could not explain that to John McChesney on first meeting.

I need not have worried. He grinned at me, not the least bit shocked. "Oh, he'll get over that," he said blithely.

Few Hotchkiss freshman have ever arrived more innocent of the world of their contemporaries than I, or more confused about their own beliefs. The certainties which had sustained me were crumbling, and only my love of music and the confidence I felt in my musical tastes remained. Hotchkiss was not a place where they would be questioned. Rather, it was a place where they would be virtually ignored. The school itself in 1925 was as mixed up as I was. The first headmaster had died the year before, and his successor, a former Latin teacher, did not exert strong leadership. The school was floundering. It was not until my second year that leadership appeared.

One of the first shocks a new boy encounters away from home in an all-male institution is homosexuality. I had had no experience with sex of any kind, not even the innocent contact with a girl on a dance floor. True to my mother's teaching, I had looked but never come closer to the opposite sex. Homosexuality was a subject not even discussed until I arrived at Hotchkiss. The master in charge of our floor was a French teacher who, I learned from my fellow preps, was a homosexual. He used to visit each boy's room just before lights out to see that we were in bed. I was so terrified of him and what he might do to me that when he looked in on me I was always praying. Whether it was my fear or my religiosity, I can't say, but he clearly didn't like me and rather made an example of me in his French class, offering the ultimate French insult that I had a Swiss accent. Before I left Hotchkiss he was indeed caught in bed with a student and dismissed, so the rumors I had heard were true. Nonetheless, I remained as innocent of sex and its deviations as I had been when I entered the school.

I faced two other problems that year. One concerned my violin. While I wanted to continue lessons, the only teacher available was most inept. I could learn nothing from her. Hotchkiss, while academically unsurpassed, was no place for a serious student of music. I also found myself in the predicament of hating Latin, a required course, and only when I was allowed to switch to Greek did I become stimulated enough to do well. My mentor, John McChesney, taught senior English, and because I was a freshman even he remained remote from me. I was sustained that first year only by my resolve not to fail and by the lingering strength of the religious faith I had brought with me.

The changes which were to take place in me began in my second year. A new headmaster, George Van Santvoord, arrived and became my friend. Van Santvoord was one of the most remarkable scholars and educators ever to run a private school, and my admiration for him began to change my life. One of his first acts on arriving in Lakeville was to become chairman of the local Democratic party, a remarkably undiplomatic beginning in that strongly conservative Connecticut town. But George Van Santvoord, sandy haired and with hooded blue eyes which seemed to challenge disagreement, was no man to fear the opinions of others, including faculty, parents, and townspeople. His long tenure as Hotchkiss' headmaster placed the school at the top level of the academic hierarchy of New England preparatory schools, and he managed either to persuade or frighten all dissenters. His great friend when he arrived at Hotchkiss was Henry Sloane Coffin, whose influence was still so strong in my own life that I planned to attend Union Theological Seminary after graduation. Cousin Henry preached remarkable sermons in the Hotchkiss chapel under Van Santvoord's approving eye, and at Union was encouraging Negroes to enter the ministry. He more than any other man was responsible for a whole genera-

Violinist, c. 1926. Excursions from Hotchkiss to New York for lessons were first opportunities to hear jazz in Harlem.

tion of enlightened black ministers.

I found in George Van Santvoord a man who would talk to me. We spent hours discussing religion, his shrewd and sympathetic questioning helping me to penetrate the accumulating doubts and confusions about the various beliefs I carried around inside me. He examined my prejudices, exposed my biases, and finally asked me, with deadpan good humor, "Are you sure, John, that the church is ready for your point of view?" My talks with him, my own reexamination of all I was experiencing both inside and outside the church during that year at Hotchkiss, opened the first unsettling breach in my religious faith. I continued to believe in the teachings of Christ, certainly in the Golden Rule, though I could no longer accept the narrow interpretations of these teachings by the appointed agents of His word. I continued my membership in the Madison Avenue Presbyterian Church and occasionally in later years attended other churches, among them the Church of the Master in Harlem, where Dr. James Robinson was the minister, but I accepted no interpretations of Christianity other than my own. The Hotchkiss yeast was working in me.

While Van Santvoord was probing my religious beliefs, John McChesney, himself a socialist and an agnostic, affected me otherwise through his Sunday philosophy class. This was a small group of students which met at his house after chapel "to undo," he said, half seriously, "the harm of the Sunday service." It was in these informal discussions that he began to change my social and political opinions, not by imposing his own, but by urging me to read. "You must find out for yourself through reading," he told me, "if something is true." McChesney taught me to take nothing for granted. I knew I lacked the discipline of an inquiring scholar, yet I realized that the search for the truth, no matter how difficult, rested with me alone.

John McChesney was married to the delightful, soft-spoken, wealthy Molly Scoville. They disagreed about many things—sometimes jarringly to the sensibilities of a youthful outsider—but I came to know them well enough to recognize their special bond which transcended opposing viewpoints. What they had was a spiritually close relationship I had never encountered before. It was a lesson I needed to learn.

One thing bothered me, and I tackled McChesney to ask why there were no Negroes at Hotchkiss. His answer seemed pussyfooting. "Well," he said, "we have to find a Negro teacher first." The next time I saw my father I asked him if there had been Negroes at Exeter when he was there. "Sure," he told me. "There have been Negroes at Exeter since the Civil War." Hotchkiss still had a long way to go.

McChesney's answer did not shake my faith in him. He had never known any blacks, nor had he had reason, as I had through jazz, to concern himself with the problem. He could not have changed the policy of the school in any event. The man who could was George Van Santvoord. He knew my love for jazz and my admiration for black performers, of course, although somewhat academically. He agreed that jazz musicians personified the kind of social injustice he deplored, but to me jazz was a catalyst. For him it was not. It was not until long after he retired that Negroes were welcomed as Hotchkiss students.

Although Van Santvoord had no personal interest in jazz, he contributed in a roundabout way both to my musical education and to my earliest visits to Harlem, where I met many jazz players. At the beginning of my third year he allowed me to leave the school every other weekend to take violin lessons in New York. This was an unprecedented liberty. No Hotchkiss student had ever been allowed to leave school except for vacations, or to accompany his family to a nearby restaurant on Sundays. This came about through another Hotchkiss violinist, Holland Duell, a junior when I was a freshman and a much better fiddler than I. Duell told me about an excellent teacher in New York—Ronald Murat—and because I had made no progress since coming to Hotchkiss I asked Van Santvoord to let me study with the teacher Duell had recommended. Perhaps Van Santvoord's agreement illustrated his liberal administration of the school, or, more likely, he felt he could trust me not to smoke or drink or break any

Harlem, 1928-29. Lafayette
Theater, with Connie's
Inn next door. (Covan's was
behind.) Bessie Smith as
she looked at the Alhambra.
Luis Russell, whose
great band had Red Allen
and J.C. Higginbotham.

of the other rules of the school while I was away from it. His trust was warranted.

In the fall of 1927 I boarded the 1:07 train from Millerton every other Saturday afternoon, arriving in the city at 3:30. Murat lived on Tiemann Place, in the Morningside Heights area, and on the way to my first lesson I passed the Alhambra Theater. That day Bessie Smith's name was on the marquee. After my two-hour lesson I went home to dinner at 91st Street, then, telling my family I was off to play string quartets, hurried uptown to hear Bessie. I had her records by then, and I considered her the greatest blues singer I had ever heard. I still do.

That became the pattern during the rest of my Hotchkiss days. Every two weeks I traveled to New York for my lesson, then discovered the Lafayette Theater, the Club Saratoga, where Luis Russell's band played with Henry "Red" Allen (trumpet), J. C. Higginbotham (trombone), Charlie Holmes (alto sax), and Paul Barbarin (drums). I went to every theater and club in Harlem and was usually the only white person there. I would order a lemonade while I listened, and I'm sure people thought I was crazy, for these were Prohibition years and in Harlem, as everywhere else, lemonade was legal and therefore unfit to drink. I also went to classical concerts. My education became more complete and more satisfying than anyone at the school realized. I was known to be an avid record collector, but now I also knew every jazz joint and speakeasy where jazz was played. I also became a much improved violinist. Needless to add, George Van Santvoord became my Hotchkiss hero.

One thing I did not inherit from my mother was her proclivity for writing letters. Most of mine to her were brief and written on scraps of paper with a pencil stub. I did write two surprising letters while at Hotchkiss, however, both of which produced even more surprising responses. During my second year, the then-youthful *Time* magazine (nee 1923) dropped its record column. This, together with *Time*'s irritating prose style, annoyed me. I wrote a letter saying so. I had no idea that Henry Luce, *Time*'s founder and publisher, had gone to Hotchkiss, but I sent my letter anyway, signing it John H. Hammond, Jr., The Hotchkiss School, Lakeville, Connecticut. Two weeks later my letter appeared in *Time*, along with a long letter from the secretary of John Hays Hammond, Jr., explaining that he had not written the letter of protest and disclaiming any relationship with the writer. Hammond was a distinguished inventor, later a member of the board of the Radio Corporation of America, and a man I eventually came to know, but that was the first of many occasions when we have been confused. Jack Hammond also invented a quarter-tone piano which was manufactured by the Mehlin Piano Company; this compounded the confusion, for neither of us is related to the inventor of the Hammond organ. That is Laurens, no kin as far as I know. People still believe the organ is my doing and, to make matters worse, there *is* a John Hammond who is an organist and an executive of the Hammond Organ Company. When I was a boy he played at the Victoria and later the Warner Theater on Broadway.

To be frank, the sound of the organ, except when played by Count Basie or Fats Waller, is an abomination to my ears. I always loathed the Mighty Wurlitzer and have disliked the effects of the various stops ever since I used to hear Archer Gibson give organ recitals at my grandmother's house every Sunday after dinner. It was only later, when I became acquainted with Bach's preludes and fugues, that I began to like the Baroque organ as an instrument. Some of Fats Waller's small-band records of 1935 and 1936 for which he played organ are among my favorites, and Basie plays organ with the same taste and economy that distinguishes his piano. Even when Basie is sentimental at the organ I like it, but maybe that is because of all the instrumentalists in jazz Basie is my favorite.

While disposing of Hammonds let me also say that I was a bit young to be the silver-haired Colonel John S. Hammond, first president of the New York Rangers hockey club.

As my Hotchkiss years neared their end, I wrote another letter. Encouraged by John McChesney, I was seeking ways to exercise my own independence in constructive activity of some sort. In the spring of my senior year I read an article in the *New Republic* written by Silas Bent of the *Herald Tribune* called "The Battle of Portland." It told the story of a struggling newspaper in Maine run by a former managing editor of the *Tribune*, Ernest Gruening. In study hall, preparing to retake a flunked math exam, I wrote a long, barely legible letter to the embattled editor asking for a summer job on his Portland *Evening News*.

His reply had what I soon learned were his customary vigor and warm-heartedness. An old Hotchkiss boy himself, he found it astonishing that anyone at the school might read the *New Republic* or want to work for a Democratic newspaper in Maine. Since I was such a creature, I was welcome to join him. And, he said, "if you're any good, we'll pay you."

After graduation I proudly waved the letter before my parents. Father was horrified. He was board chairman of the Bangor & Aroostook Railroad, and the family had very conservative relatives who summered in Bar Harbor. He was certain I would disgrace the Hammonds and the Vanderbilts in Maine. Mother was not really opposed to my plan. Bewildered by my choice of jobs, she was still pleased that I wanted to exert my independence, and Jack Speiden, erstwhile suitor of Alice and Rachel, spoke up for me, telling Mother she should be grateful that I wanted to work at a summer job.

In June of 1929 I was a changed young man. I was convinced that there are no absolutes, that it was impossible for me as a human being to follow any line, be it a political line, a religious line, or a philosophical line. I recognized that there would always be points of view based on others' experience which must be considered, and I had learned that dogmatism is a result of insecurity, that intolerance, including my own, is always suspect. Thanks to George Van Santvoord I had heard more jazz, seen more live entertainment than any boy in my class, and I could even hold my own in string quartets. Best of all, I had made lifelong friends of Van Santvoord and John McChesney.

John and Molly never had children of their own, yet

their family was enormous and devoted, and, like my cousins Fred and Osgood, I was forever a part of it. Two generations of Hotchkiss boys taught and inspired by John McChesney revere him as I do. He passed on his love of books, his respect for our language, and, by his gentle prodding, he ignited in us the determination to search out truth for ourselves. McChesney died in 1973. To the end of his life he continued in his quiet way to fashion freethinking men out of young Hotchkiss preps.

IV

When I arrived in Portland my first stop was a barbershop. My hair had been falling out by the handful at Hotchkiss, and I was certain that, like my father, I would soon be bald. My solution was to cut it off. I instructed the first barber I found to give me a crew cut. He was not a good barber. He would not cut my hair the way I wanted it cut, so my first crew cut looked like an abandoned bird's nest. But it felt good, and I found that by brushing it, by giving up the goo I had been using on it, it stopped falling out. My dandruff disappeared. And in time my hair stood up and stayed in. I have never changed it since.

When my sisters saw my new hair style they thought it looked awful, and now and then a girl I dated would beg me to let my hair grow. My reaction was to keep the crew cut and let the girl go. I became defensive about my hair. Nobody in those days wore a crew cut—not even crewmen, as I remember—and finding reliable barbers was a problem. I found one at the Hotel Roosevelt barbershop. Then I moved to the St. Regis, which had a nonunion shop. I used to see John L. Lewis having his lion's mane cut there. He even had those famous eyebrows trimmed. I decided that if this giant of the national labor movement could patronize a scab operation for the sake of his appearance, so could I. For twenty years a most competent Swede named Carlsen Hilding cut my hair, until in 1955 he retired to raise mink on Long Island. Perhaps a lifetime of cutting hair prompted him to atone by growing fur.

My crew cut became a sort of trade mark. I doubt that I would be recognized without it. Now it is graying, but I have kept my hair, and I still like it the way it is. It seems to fit me.

Ernest Gruening proved to be all I had hoped: an excellent newspaper man, a patient teacher, and a major influence on me. He started me off as a proofreader, the best way to begin a newspaper career. Soon he had me covering the local Lions, Kiwanis, and Rotarians. I met the businessmen of Portland and learned the routine of getting out a daily paper. I had my own car, an Oldsmobile convertible, an unusual luxury in those days. Because the paper paid low salaries and few expenses, most of the reporters had no cars, so I was assigned to chauffeur a veteran to Haverhill, Massachusetts, to cover a story. My colleague, who had a very religious wife and six kids at home, decided this was the perfect opportunity to enjoy a little extracurricular sex. I wanted to impress this old newspaper hand, but I simply could not enter the seedy-looking brothel he chose. Instead I waited in the car, ashamed of my innocence though not so ashamed as I would have been of myself. Mother might as well have been riding in the right-hand seat.

Another reporter assigned to teach me the newspaper business was Bernard McQuaid, a young man my own age whose father, the former publisher of the Boston *Sunday Advertiser*, had recently died. Bernie had been forced to leave Georgetown University to go to work, and he was a full-time employee of the *Evening News*. Gruening told McQuaid to make a writer out of me, an almost impossible job in 1929, but Bernie did his best, became my friend, and he must have taught me something because I was invited back the following summer at a salary of $25 a week.

That was the summer of 1930, an election year, and I covered the Republican and Democratic headquarters in Portland and saw a Democratic governor elected, the first in this century. By my second summer I was a qualified reporter. I traveled all over the state looking for stories and got my share of scoops. I interviewed Governor Ralph Owen Brewster about the Indian problem, an issue I was very much concerned about. The Catholic church had been educating the Indian population of Maine for years, but not one had ever gotten into high school. Although the State had recently taken over, the Indians' plight was still a scandal. I visited the reservations of the Penobscot and Old Town Indians and found beautiful churches, handsome houses for priests, and not even running water and electricity for Indians. I did an exposé of the situation which made the front page of the paper, and I learned something about myself: I write best when I am angry, when protesting injustice, criticizing bad music or uncaring musicians.

In the fall I entered Yale. After my summer in Portland, returning to formal education and the society of my contemporaries was a letdown. My classmates were interested in sports, in girls, in undergraduate weekends. Once again I was the oddball in the group. I believe I am the only Yale undergraduate who never saw a Saturday football game, who never attended a postgame dance.

I moved into one of those boardinghouses on Wall Street in New Haven, with my record collection, my armful of magazines, and a growing awareness of the directions I wanted my life to take. Yale was not one of them, but my father was an Eli and I was not yet ready to disappoint him. I had two roommates. Ashley Fly Wilson was an athlete, a real jock. The other, who had best remain nameless, never took a bath and smelled something awful. Ashley usually went to bed early, about nine o'clock, and I followed by eleven. Our roomy would stagger in at three in the morning. Not surprisingly, he was dropped after the fall semester and was certainly not missed.

One evening I went to a Boston Symphony concert at Woolsey Hall. It was an important event, the American premiere of Ravel's famous "Bolero," and an even more significant occasion for me. I sat next to a tall, handsome young man with jet hair and a well-trimmed moustache. He appeared to be older than I and very well dressed. During the concert we introduced ourselves. We both liked "Bolero" and it was apparent that he was knowledgeable about all music and keenly interested in jazz. His name was Edgar Siskin, and he had arrived from Hebrew Theological Seminary in Cincinnati as the replacement for a rabbi who recently had died.

After the concert I invited Rabbi Siskin back to my room to listen to records. I had all the Louis Armstrongs, everything by Walter Gieseking and Joseph Szigeti, and more jazz than he had ever heard before. I played him "Pinetop's Boogie Woogie," Tampa Red's "How Long, How Long," many classic blues, and also records by white favorites: Frankie Trumbauer (C-melody sax), Eddie Lang (guitar), and Red Nichols (trumpet). At one point Edgar asked, "Have you ever been to a synagogue, John?"

I admitted I had not.

"Why don't you come over," he suggested. "I think the sermon this week will interest you."

The Temple Mishkin Israel was a hideous building. On the bulletin board outside was the announcement of that night's sermon, "Can We Find God in Nature?"

I went in and sat down to see what would happen. Spotlights came on, illuminating the Arc of the Covenant and, as he stepped to the pulpit, the rabbi himself. He was lit up like a vaudeville star. Later he explained that because the synagogue was so unattractive and because the services were usually at night, when no one could see a stained glass window or much of the architecture, he had hired Alexander Mc-Candless, the lighting expert of the Yale drama school to install indirect lighting. The $10,000 he had been allowed for renovation of the building was insufficient to make much improvement, so McCandless illuminated the congregation's best-looking asset—Rabbi Siskin.

Edgar was an impressive man. He was also an anthropologist who taught at the Yale School of Human Relations. He used to make field trips every summer to Nevada, and later joined Milton Herskovits at Northwestern, where he became an authority on the American Indian. He was also the table-tennis champion of New Haven and was voted the best-dressed member of the faculty by the Yale *Daily News*. Naturally, he was a prime target for mothers in his congregation with eligible daughters, and when he finally married Lillian, a Juilliard graduate from Tulsa, Oklahoma, and a fine concert pianist, Edgar was finished in New Haven. He moved to Glencoe, Illinois. A new synagogue was built for him and he served as rabbi until his retirement. Naturally, he continued his anthropological studies. I always believed that Edgar became a rabbi out of respect for a family tradition (both his father and grandfather were rabbis) and remained one out of deference to Lillian's wishes. To me he seemed to have a maverick tendency; I always thought he valued a full professorship more than the new synagogue. But certain it is that he has had many rewards in both careers.

Siskin was extremely sophisticated about both jazz and classical music. One of his great complaints was that other than Mendelssohn nobody ever wrote good music for the Jewish service. There was no heritage to compare with what Bach wrote in celebration of Protestantism, or Mozart and Monteverdi in praise of Catholicism, so Edgar minimized music in his services. If he had been able I think he would have enlisted Bach for the synagogue. His interest in music, his independent ideas, and his maturity made him a welcome friend during my first year at Yale. I could discuss problems with him, as well as enthusiasms. I invited him to spend an occasional weekend in Mount Kisco, and it was during one of his visits that he asked me, "John, how well do you know the Eugene Meyer family?"

I had to confess that I didn't know them at all, although I had long since forgiven them for their water tower and had wanted to meet them.

"That's ridiculous," Edgar said. "They're your next-door neighbors and their son Bill is at Yale. Last year he came to me with a strange request. He's an athlete who went to St. Paul's and then was sent by his father to study with Harold

Laski at the London School of Economics. But he told me he knew nothing about being Jewish. His mother is a Lutheran and his father is a Jew who never practices his religion. He asked me to tell him something about it." Edgar had been teaching Bill Meyer the history of the Jewish faith.

Soon after, through Edgar, I met the Meyers. Mr. Meyer was a short, dumpy man, a conservative Republican, a cordial host, and obviously a very important man. Agnes, the big Republican wheel in Westchester, was the most imposing female I had ever met. Everything about the Meyers was large scale. Their estate was huge, even by Vanderbilt standards. They had an indoor swimming pool of Olympic dimensions, and Agnes' collection of Brancusi statues towered over strollers in the garden. They towered over Agnes, too, but they were the only things that did. There was nothing she liked better than to argue, and since I am not notably reticent we started talking and arguing as though making up for lost years.

Thanks to Edgar I became very close to this extraordinary family. The eldest daughter, Florence, was married to Oscar Homolka, the actor. Elizabeth was married to Pare Lorentz, the masterful documentary filmmaker. Katherine was a fine tennis player, a vital, enchanting girl who immediately became my favorite. The fourth daughter was Mary. I never really knew her or brother Bill. Altogether, they were splendid people. The more I knew of their spectacular lives, the more impressive they became. I had found friends next door and I never lost them again.

While at Yale I continued my violin lessons, and through them I was fortunate enough to join a string quartet in New York. Because I was not the violinist one should be to play with professionals, I switched to the viola. Experts may disagree, but I think it is less difficult to play passably well, and because it is not so spectacular a solo instrument as the violin or cello, it has fewer practitioners. Yet it is essential to a string quartet, so it provided just the slot for me. The cellist was a young law graduate of New York University, Artie Bernstein.

Artie had paid for his education by strumming his bass in many of the white bands around New York, and the first time I heard him play I realized he was unlike any other bass I had ever heard. Instead of slapping the strings to make the thudding, Pops Foster sound—Pops being an old-timer who pioneered use of the bass in jazz—Artie provided a musical line, a harmonic foundation for the orchestra. He had played with Ben Pollack and Red Nichols while he was a student, and he knew all the working musicians in New York. Of course, in 1930 and 1931 the working musicians were white. Artie didn't know any black musicians and I didn't know any white ones.

I traveled to New York every weekend for my lesson, then for a workout with the string quartet, and finally I would take Artie to Harlem.

Often we went to Smalls' Paradise, a landmark night club at 135th Street and Seventh Avenue, where Charlie Johnson's band was a fixture for some fifteen years. In those days it included the two fabulous trombones J.C. Higginbotham and Jimmy Harrison.

Ed Smalls had his first joint—an after-hours speakeasy —somewhere on Fifth Avenue. (As early as 1925–26 he had a pianist named Basie there.) But the famous, never-to-be-forgotten Smalls' was in the basement of the Dunbar Bank building. You went downstairs, under a modest marquee, into a standard night-club setup: a room holding about two hundred and fifty persons, with a bar at one end, a bandstand at the other, and banquettes against the wall surrounding a dance floor. Ed had a line of eight girls—dark-skinned; the Cotton Club and Connie's Inn catered to whites and featured light-skinned Negroes—and had original music written for his shows. He served good Chinese food, another plus. Connie's had no kitchen and the Cotton Club menu was bad and expensive. Smalls' was popular with show people, among them George Gershwin, who had a keen and sympathetic ear for all music and musicians. He was famous for picking the pit musicians for all his shows. I could get lemonade for seventy-five cents, so Smalls' was Paradise for me, too.

Another band Artie and I heard was Elmer Snowden's,

Paradise was in the basement.
Top: Higginbotham, Roy
Eldridge (trumpet), and Dickie
Wells—all looking older
here—were bright new stars
in the rollicking 1920's.

the band that became Duke Ellington's. Elmer was a banjo player at a time when that remarkable instrument was disappearing, like the tuba, from jazz. I can remember every member of his band. The first alto saxophonist was Otto (pronounced Oh-toh) Hardwicke, the extraordinary, bald-headed genius of the first Ellington band. The third alto was an unusual man to find in a Harlem jazz orchestra, Wayman Carver, an intellectual who also played excellent flute. Carver later became a professor of music at Morris Brown College in Atlanta, and head of a Jim Crow local of the Musicians' Union —segregated being the only kind they had down there. The tenor sax was a wild and woolly soul named Al Sears, a friend of a singer whose only record was in my collection, and who I believed then and now to be one of the great singers in jazz history: Helen Humes.

The brass section had a little man who had just come out of the Middle West: Roy Eldridge. The other trumpet player was not so spectacular, but he was still pretty good: Gus Aiken. The trombone was that flower of jazz, Dickie Wells. The rhythm section had one of the all-time superlative drummers: Big Sid Catlett. Don Kirkpatrick, a veteran of many Broadway shows, was the pianist. He later wrote arrangements for Benny Goodman. The bass player was a Pops Foster slapper: Dick Fullbright. He went through all kinds of gyrations when he played, but to Artie's ear he was out of tune.

The band was glorious, the best music in New York, except for Fletcher Henderson's orchestra. And it was the jazz at Smalls', the late nights, the long weekends in New York which finally caught up with me. I flunked biology; I was feeling terrible; I found I had what was known in those days as yellow jaundice. Today it is hepatitis. I was so sick I lost twenty pounds. Never mind, after Christmas vacation I returned to Yale and continued my New York weekends. Thanks to Artie, I was finally getting to know jazz professionals as an insider, a friend, and to me this was more important than a degree from Yale, a career as a banker, or even my saffron-colored skin and precarious health.

I had a recurrence of jaundice in the winter of 1931. I had to drop out of college to recuperate and probably would have to repeat my sophomore year when I returned. Thanks, again, to Artie Bernstein I was going to recording sessions, was actually present in the studio when the records I loved were being made. I was on the edge of the music business and eager to get to the center of it. I knew for sure what I wanted, and Yale was not it.

V

My decision not to return to Yale was a blow to Father. He could have stopped me. Instead, he arranged for my recuperation at a place known as the Millionaires' Club, a golfing resort on Jekyll Island, off the coast of Brunswick, Georgia. With Billy McCampbell, whom I had known at Browning, I spent Easter vacation there, resting and playing golf. In those days you could reach the island only by small boat, and no cars were allowed. Visitors rode around in little red bugs powered by storage batteries, which usually died about a mile from the clubhouse. It was a Wasp retreat. Blacks did all the work. Jews and even Catholics were barred. But it was a place of serene isolation where I could recover, so I did not protest.

I managed an escape to the mainland, nonetheless, visited the Negro quarter of Brunswick, and returned to the club dining room with the Baltimore *Afro-American,* the Pittsburgh *Courier,* and the Chicago *Defender.* The eyes of the waiters popped as I read these Negro newspapers in the club dining room, but if any of the members objected no one could do anything about it. My father was president of the club.

I did recover my health at Jekyll Island, and I also saw for myself, for the first time, the cruelty and repression of Southern segregation. I vowed then never to join a private organization which discriminated against anyone because of race or religion. (Jekyll Island has long since become a State park, open to the public.)

I returned to New York physically recovered and emotionally enraged. The habit of discrimination was so encrusted by centuries of acceptance that both black and white knew no other way to act. I had walked through my first Southern Nigger town, the son of the president of a private club for millionaires, many of them Southern, all of them white and Protestant. To know better was no longer enough. I had to do something.

I fervently wanted to enter the record business, but I had no experience and no idea where to begin. My credentials were no more than a love for jazz, a growing acquaintance with many of its players, and a toehold as a writer for an English music publication called *Gramophone*. Already American jazz was attracting far more critical and public acclaim in England than in the United States, and anyone who could write jazz news, particularly of Negro players, was in demand. The English public drew no color line in music. Because Americans often did, few American jazz writers had ever been to Harlem or knew enough about black players to be effective correspondents. I had and did, and for this reason I had been hired by *Gramophone* after correspondence with its jazz editor, Edgar Jackson. I got one guinea a month.

In the summer of 1931 I decided to go to Europe. I wanted to visit Munich and Salzburg, where Clemens Krauss was conducting the Vienna Philharmonic. Krauss was not then the famous conductor he later became, but he had made records for Brunswick and I had them in my collection. And as a chamber music fan I loved Mozart. To attend a festival of his music in Salzburg seemed an admirable thing to do.

En route I visited Alice in London. She still was the sister I felt closest to, and she was always fascinated by my friends in music and the theater. Many of them visited her during those years in England, found her a delightful hostess, and believed she must share my musical enthusiasms. That was not really true, although she was intrigued by those who did.

I called Edgar Jackson, and through him I met Patrick

"Spike" Hughes, recording director for English Decca, a good orchestrator, and a reviewer for another British music publication, *Melody Maker*. Spike was anxious for news of jazz players in America, and one of the first people he asked me about was a clarinetist named Benny Goodman. Had I met him? What did I think of his playing?

I had, in fact, met Benny once through Artie Bernstein, who had taken me to the Woodmansten Inn, where Russ Columbo had the band. Goodman was Columbo's contractor, the orchestra member responsible for hiring and firing musicians, a sort of sub-leader who is usually paid slightly more than the rest and who, because he does the dirty work, is usually disliked by every other man in the band. Certainly Benny was. Columbo's band was a commercial group, the kind which plays the latest tunes for dancing in a corny, unimaginative style. There were two pianists, one who played the floor show and the other, in this case Joe Sullivan, whom I greatly admired, who played for dancing. Needless to say, it was an all-white band—no mixed bands played in public in 1931—but it did have some good musicians, Gene Krupa, for instance, on drums. Artie and I listened, not at all impressed, and later Artie introduced me to Goodman. Neither of us sparked the other. I could hardly tell Spike Hughes I knew Benny.

I felt that Benny was a good clarinet player, although no better than Jimmy Dorsey, and less good than several black clarinetists I could think of. He had made some jazz records with Red Nichols and one with a group called Bennie Goodman and His Boys, a satire on Ted Lewis' clarinet style. It was called "Shirt-tail Stomp" and was even a mild hit for those Depression years. He was working where he could, playing what he was paid to play, and I knew nothing of his true genius. I respected Spike Hughes' opinions, however, and I resolved to make it my business to find out more about Goodman as soon as I could.

As a result of meeting Spike, I became American correspondent for the *Melody Maker*, where, Hughes assured me, I would have more space, a much larger audience, and

Benny Moten band heard at Lafayette in 1931. Lips Page is 2nd left,
Jimmy Rushing 3rd right. Bill Basie is seated next to Jack Washington
(on arm of couch). Remnants of group formed nucleus of Basie's band
when Moten (2nd right) died in 1935. Electric-guitarist Eddie
Durham (fifth left) was an early Basie arranger.

five times the money I was receiving from *Gramophone*. It also gave me a better excuse than ever to return to Harlem, to write for an English audience about Elmer Snowden, Fletcher Henderson, and my other favorites. The magazine, Spike explained, was dissatisfied with its former American reporter because he wrote only about white musicians. He was the drummer with Adrian Rollini's California Ramblers, a man named Herbie Weil, and the same rigid segregation which prevented Artie Bernstein from knowing any black musicians prevented Weil from meeting any either. Hughes wanted to hear more about Fletcher Henderson and Don Redman, Ellington and Jimmie Lunceford, and I was in a better position to supply news of them.

I returned to America with my first assignment as a regular reporter for a music magazine, with valuable English contacts in the record business, and with the satisfaction at last of feeling like an insider in music. That small opening was all I needed to try my hand at recording.

The production of a phonograph record for sale requires the capacities and special skills, the marketing and business acumen of dozens, if not hundreds, of people. Yet of all the essential roles involved in turning a studio performance into a record-counter sale, the position of producer, or A & R (Artist and Repertoire) man, sums up the glamour and the glory everyone aspires to. There are as many paths to this sought-after job as there are men and women who have held it. Some are musicians, true artists in their own right; others can barely whistle a tune. All, however, have an ear for talent and tune, the courage and determination to hear performed what they hear in their lively imaginations, and the good fortune to be at the right place at the right time. There is no formal training school for would-be record producers, nor are there any but unorthodox means of becoming one. That is as true today as it was in 1931.

Between my trips South and to Europe that year, I had heard a piano player in Harlem who accompanied a very good blues singer named Monette Moore. This was Garland Wilson, later a favorite of Doris Duke's and not at all one of mine, but in 1931 he was playing in a Harlem joint called Covan's, a haunt I frequented because it was right behind the stage entrance to the Lafayette Theater. Show people gathered at Covan's, as well as many musicians who played the revue at the Lafayette. It was at Covan's in 1932 that I first heard Bill Basie, the second pianist in Benny Moten's band, noodling at the piano by himself. I thought he was a combination of the best Fats Waller and Earl Hines; he was a rather lowly member of Moten's group, however, and I had no inkling of his talents as a leader and a star.

I was introduced to Covan's by an artist friend of mine, Charles "Spinky" Alston, whose paintings now hang in the Whitney, the Metropolitan, and the Museum of Modern Art, as well as in my own living room. Covan himself was a sinister-looking man who must have wondered about allowing a young white into his illegal bar. He must have wondered even more when he saw me buying for the musicians and drinking lemonade myself. After that night I always made sure to stop at a men's room before I arrived at Covan's, because Covan provided only an outhouse in his backyard, a place I was determined to avoid.

I heard Garland Wilson and decided he should be recorded. I went to the Columbia Phonograph Company, which at that time was controlled by English Columbia. I had always been partial toward Columbia because its recording manager, Frank Walker, had discovered Bessie Smith and recorded her early performances. I went to see Walker and told him I was willing to pay the costs involved. Frank quoted me what I considered a stiff price, although a tiny fraction of what the recording would have cost today: $125 for four twelve-inch sides, and the obligation to buy one hundred and fifty of the finished records myself. I preferred twelve-inch to ten-inch disks because I could get nearly five minutes of music on each side and I wanted Garland to be able to stretch out as much as possible.

Wilson recorded "St. James Infirmary" and "When Your Lover Has Gone." They were not great, but Columbia was so impressed that Bob Miller, in charge of the Okeh label, did four additional sides. Frank Walker and others at Columbia must have thought I was a nut, albeit a nut with money, who should not be ignored while the company was struggling for survival.

I got my money's worth out of the venture, thanks to Hank Lollio, the studio engineer. He was an irascible Frenchman but patient enough to teach me about his equipment, including a cutter which made it possible to adjust the number of grooves per inch. Obviously, the more grooves, the more music could be recorded on a side. To me this was revolutionary. At the old 78-rpm speed we were always limited by the few minutes of music possible on the surface of a disk. Lollio convinced me that Columbia was the place to record in future.

My premiere performance as a record producer had an embarrassing conclusion. I did not know how to pay Garland Wilson for his performance, the regular union scale for recording being very low. I finally decided to present him with a Movado watch, which cost $125 in Depression money. Garland was delighted with the watch, and Garland also was gay, a fact I didn't know, although everybody in Harlem did. For weeks after our record date Garland went around showing off his new watch saying, "Look what John gave me." It took me a while to live that down.

VI

I celebrated my twenty-first birthday by moving out of the marble halls of 91st Street and into a modest apartment on Sullivan Street in Greenwich Village. At twenty-one I had come into a lump sum of money, and I already had plans to spend it. But contrary to the prevailing impression, I was not a rich young man with a bottomless wallet. Like other Vanderbilt children and grandchildren, I lived on the income from grandparental trust funds that were not under my control. My income from these trusts during the 1930's, for in-

stance, was approximately $12,000 a year, ample certainly, but not princely. Now and then, of course, a relative would depart, leaving me money over which I did have control.

The move from my parent's house was prompted as much by recognition of what I was not, as well as by what I wanted to become. I suppose I could best be described as a New York social dissident, finally free to express my disagreement with the social system I was born into and which most of my contemporaries accepted as a matter of course. Many sons and daughters of my parents' friends took my strange behavior as fear of not being accepted, as shyness, as the result of the inhibited behavioral codes instilled by my mother. In part this was true. I have never considered myself handsome, a wit, or a strong competitor for girls' attentions. I refused to go to dances—because the music was bad, I always said, overlooking my incompetence as a dancer.

(I did participate in one society affair in 1932, when a girl I knew in Mount Kisco asked me to find an orchestra for a dance at the local golf and tennis club. This I could do. I assembled a seven-piece band from New York which included Fats Waller, Frankie Newton [trumpet], Benny Carter [alto], Pee Wee Russell [clarinet], Zutty Singleton [drums], Eddie Condon [guitar], and Artie Bernstein—four Negroes out of seven, the best band ever heard in Mount Kisco, and a rather nice little combo to be heard anywhere. I provided a large jug of gin for Fats, who promptly sat down and played "Bugle Call Rag" for twenty-two minutes. The Mount Kisco socialites had never heard such music and I had the time of my life.)

My dissent from the social order started with my objection to the discrimination I saw everywhere around me. New York private schools might enroll one or two Jewish boys whose families were too prominent to ignore, not more. I had found discrimination in the churches my mother took me to. I even found discrimination in my own house. One weekend when my parents were away I invited Spinky Alston to visit me in Mount Kisco. One of my sisters ordered us to leave the house, which of course I refused to do.

I did not revolt against the system. I simply refused to

Fats Waller (piano) and Frankie Newton were two of seven jazz giants recruited for country-club dance in 1932.

be a part of it. The jazz I liked best was played by Negroes. My two best friends, Edgar Siskin and Artie Bernstein, were Jews. I had been strongly influenced at Hotchkiss by John McChesney, a socialist and an agnostic, and by George Van Santvoord, an independent liberal Democrat. I had seen Ernest Gruening in action and learned from him the power of protest.

Despite the influence of early teachers, the books I read, and what I had seen for myself in the South, the strongest motivation for my dissent was jazz. I heard no color line in the music. While my early favorites were white players, the recorded and live performances of Negroes excited me more. The fact that the best jazz players barely made a living, were barred from all well-paying jobs in radio and in most night clubs, enraged me. There was no white pianist to compare with Fats Waller, no white band as good as Fletcher Henderson's, no blues singer like Bessie Smith, white or black. To bring recognition to the Negro's supremacy in jazz was the most effective and constructive form of social protest I could think of.

I had my name removed from the Social Register. Mother, bewildered, asked why. I told her it was to keep my name off sucker lists. All wealthy socialites were constantly badgered for contributions to every imaginable cause. But the primary reason was that with a few exceptions this printed list of the elite was non-Semitic. Later it would be charged that I had been dropped for my political activities, but this was not true. I resigned, one of the all too few who ever did.

I had another reason for moving to the Village. Ever since I discovered *Variety* I had wanted to become involved in the theater, particularly the live, vaudeville theater. Ever since I sneaked off to the Alhambra to hear Bessie Smith, Negro variety theater had interested me. By 1932, when the Alhambra closed, I had come to know its owner, Milton Gosdorfer, and another aficionado of Negro vaudeville, Eddie Eliscu. Eddie was a lyricist who wrote, among many other famous songs, the words to Vincent Youmans' "Without A Song." Eddie's wife, Stella Block, used to visit the Alhambra to sketch Bessie Smith on stage. I bought one of Stella's sketches and eventually gave it to my older son as a wedding present.

Gosdorfer and Eliscu were looking for a downtown theater in which to present Negro acts. Because I had money to invest and shared their enthusiasm for such a project, I became the third partner in a venture to lease a 42nd Street house for Negro variety and stage bands playing to unsegregated audiences. In those days most of the legitimate theaters on 42nd Street were dark, victims of the Depression, and Gosdorfer had already settled on the Liberty as the place for our productions. I rejected the Liberty because its large second balcony limited seating in the orchestra and the first balcony, where vaudeville fans prefer to sit. My father had hired a lawyer, Adolf A. Berle, then a youngster, later a legal savant and Washington wheel, who tried on my behalf to take over the Apollo in the same block, the former home of *George White's Scandals* and one of the best legitimate theaters in the country. It had one balcony and 1,500 seats. I thought it was ideal for the kind of show I used to enjoy at the Alhambra and Lafayette in Harlem.

The Marc Klaw estate, which controlled the Apollo, disliked the idea of Negro shows—it would attract black audiences to 42nd Street—so the theater was made unavailable to us. And as word of what we were looking for got around, all the theaters on 42nd Street suddenly seemed to be out of reach.

There was, however, an alternative. The last legitimate theater built in New York City had been opened in 1928 by the Bank of the United States, which had gone into a scandalous bankruptcy. The Public, as it was called, was located on 4th Street and Second Avenue, a diversely ethnic neighborhood, and it had been used to present Yiddish plays. It was an 1,800-seat house with a beautifully equipped stage and an orchestra seating more than a thousand people. At first I thought the neighborhood around the Public was primarily Jewish. I had gone to the Yiddish Art Theater to see Paul Muni and John Garfield (better known on Second Avenue as

Muni Weisenfreund and Julie Garfinkel), but when I visited the neighborhood I found it a synthesis of New York's rich mixture of races and nationalities. There were Rumanians, Italians, Poles, Germans, and Chinese, as well as Jews.

We took over the Public and opened with a first week's bill that included Fletcher Henderson's orchestra, Dusty Fletcher, who was one of the funniest comedians I can remember, and a line of sixteen chorus girls. Dusty was a lively, all-purpose funnyman who danced, sang, and performed a vast repertoire of knockabout sight gags. He had one hit record before he died: "Open the Door, Richard." The important attraction for me, of course, was Fletcher's band which at the time included Bobby Stark, Red Allen, and Rex Stewart on trumpet; Sandy Williams and J. C. Higginbotham on trombone; a saxophone section of Coleman Hawkins, Buster Bailey, Edgar Sampson, and Hilton Jefferson; Fletcher on piano; Clarence Holiday, Billie's father, on guitar; John Kirby on bass; and Walter Johnson on drums.

In the first week a problem with Fletcher—Henderson, not Dusty—developed. The first show each day was scheduled to begin at one o'clock, and never were there more than one or two of the band members in the pit on time. I was very disappointed, feeling that Fletcher was letting me down and hurting himself as well, but I later encountered the same situation on record dates. In part I believe it was the discouragement Negroes felt as economic victims of the times, and perhaps it was also a small and self-defeating exercise of independence. In the second week, Luis Russell took over and every member of the band was on time.

Idealistic as usual, I hoped to create something new in show business, avoiding all the clichés of Harlem vaudeville because we had a new audience. I reckoned without the hard-nosed business views of one of my partners, who for years had made money from tried-and-true variety formats. Milton Gosdorfer fired the director, a man I thought perfect for our purpose, and hired a commercial director, Addison Carey, who had put on the shows at Connie's Inn and other New York clubs. Because Carey was a Negro I hoped he would share my aspirations for a new kind of show in which the real talents of black performers could be demonstrated, but I was wrong. Carey wanted to make our theater a New York base for traveling companies which would play the vaudeville circuit in Philadelphia, Washington, and Baltimore, the same tired fare I wanted to avoid.

Carey's policy was unacceptable to me. It forced my withdrawal from the partnership and the eventual closing of the Public Theater, yet not without valuable lessons learned and new opportunities offered. One surprising friendship established directly from my involvement with the Public happened on opening night, when Sergei Eisenstein, the Russian film director, already known for *Potemkin* and *Ten Days That Shook the World,* came to our show. Eisenstein and I spent most of one night talking and listening to jazz, and I learned some startling things about Russia. This was an era when the American Communist Party was an effective instrument of social protest, when many of my Village friends were persuaded that the Communist answer might be the only one. Eisenstein predicted that Russian taste was going to be atrocious for years to come. (True.) Until the Russian people became accustomed to their new role in world affairs, Eisenstein thought, they would show little discernment in architecture and in the arts. He was appalled by many aspects of the Stalin regime, although he felt that eventually something wholesome would emerge and he believed fundamentally in the socialist state.

Eisenstein's views interested me. Here was a man widely acclaimed for his talents, a man of obvious integrity, yet honestly persuaded that Communism was the only valid social system. Both his candor and his critical appraisal surprised me. The flirtation of the early thirties—for it could hardly be called a love affair—between American blacks and Communists, both Russian and American, was just beginning. It was important to anyone interested in the struggle for civil and social justice to understand both the lure and the dangers Communism held for Negroes. Considering that they had few friends among whites, Communist sympathy for their cause could not be ignored. But Moscow, as many Negroes discovered, was a fair-weather friend. Russia's espousal of the Negro's viewpoint, his art, and his right to equal justice coincided only with Soviet self-interest and the current Communist line. The result for most Negroes who turned to Communism in that turbulent decade was frustration, disillusionment, and final rejection.

I was witness to one such example. In 1932 a group of twenty-three Negroes was invited to the Soviet Union to make a film which the Russians promised would be "the true story of race relations in America." No such film could be made in Hollywood, so the invitation was accepted. Among those who went were Langston Hughes, Henry Moon, Ted Poston, Lauren Miller, and Wayland Rudd. Most of them were not actors, but all were talented people. Out of the entire group not more than one or two were Communists. After being in Russia for a little over six months they were told that the project had been canceled. The Soviet government had been recognized by the United States. Negro viewpoints were immediately subordinated to amicable international relations, and the group was sent home.

I was one of many people in this country who believed that this group had been double-crossed. I also felt that the place to make a film about Negroes in America was in America, even with the obvious difficulties. In his autobiography, *I Wonder As I Wander*, Langston Hughes gives a hilarious account of this trip. All realized they had been used and that even in Russia they could not tell the truth, except when truth and Communist purpose happened to coincide.

My adventure at the Public Theater led directly to another opportunity I might never have had otherwise: I became a disk jockey for radio station WEVD, whose call letters were the initials of the noted Socialist, Eugene V. Debs. In 1932 the station was owned by the *Jewish Daily Forward* and staffed almost entirely by Jews. It was located in the Broadway Central Hotel, four blocks from the Public Theater, and featured ethnic programs in Yiddish, Polish, Rumanian, and

German for that polyglot neighborhood on Manhattan's Lower East Side.

Our theater budget did not allow us to advertise in newspapers, so I decided that radio plugs on WEVD, costing $2.50 apiece, might be the most effective way to reach our local audience. I had a press agent, a youngster named Sam Friedman, who had enough influence to get us an occasional mention in Hearst's *Journal* or *American*, but no other New York paper was interested. I went to WEVD to handle the theater plug myself and found some interesting people working there. One was the house pianist, Sylvia Sapira, who as Sylvia Marlowe later became a famous harpsichordist.

Another employee was Bernard H. Haggin, who was to become my boss at the Brooklyn *Eagle*. Haggin, in my opinion, was the best music critic in America, a man of considered musical judgment and absolute integrity who managed to transmit his views clearly and honestly to his readers. If he had his musical blind spots, his standards were unassailable. When I found myself in the awkward dual role of record producer and critic, he did not let our friendship prevent him from publicly questioning my compromised position. It was uncomfortable, being called to task, but I wouldn't have expected him to do otherwise.

I started talking on WEVD about the Public Theater, writing announcements for broadcast, and, of course, emphasizing the jazz being played there. There were no jazz programs on the station, so I began playing my favorite records an hour every day. The response was good. I suggested that we add a live Saturday-night jam session between 9:30 and 10. That was fine, except that the station had no budget to pay the musicians I wanted to include. Only sponsored programs paid musicians anything at all, and even though the union wage scale was low the musicians hired were expected to kick back a third of their take to the station. It was a scandalous situation, but this was the depth of the Depression. Anything was better than nothing.

My solution was to offer each musician $10 out of my own pocket for each broadcast. I also paid transportation to

the studio, although more often than not I picked everyone up in my car, and of course New York still had the nickel subway ride. One way or another they all got there. Almost every superb jazz player I knew appeared during the nine or ten weeks we had those broadcasts, the first regular programs of live jazz, I believe, ever.

I already had Fletcher Henderson at the theater, and I brought Benny Carter and Frankie Newton down. We also had Joe Sullivan, the legendary Art Tatum, drummer Chick Webb, Sid Catlett, alto/tenor Charlie Barnet, tenor Chu Berry, Dickie Wells, and always Artie Bernstein.

A note about Chu: After Lester Young and "Bean" Hawkins he was the best. I am not alone in this opinion. Many professionals who heard his big, round, soft tone and good ideas would agree. Leon "Chu" Berry—I heard him first in 1932 at the Dunbar Palace, a dance hall on Seventh Avenue, between 140th and 141st Streets. The band wasn't much. Aside from Chu there was only Ram Ramirez, who wrote "Lover Man," on piano. I got Chu a job with Elmer Snowden at Smalls' and used him on a number of the earliest records I produced. He was just marvelous, and his death in an auto crash at the age of thirty-one was tragic. I just loved that man. And you know who else did? Joseph Szigeti. This superlative classical violinist was with me on those early visits to the Dunbar Palace and he shared my admiration and affection for Chu.

Then a big opportunity came for WEVD. It moved from the Broadway Central to the Claridge Hotel on Broadway at 44th Street, where, in return for plugging the hotel, it was given the air-conditioned penthouse as a studio. Problems immediately developed for me and the musicians. At the Broadway Central the studio had been on the mezzanine, so we could all walk up the grand staircase from street level. At the Claridge we had to use the elevators, and in the second week of our live broadcasts the hotel management decreed that musicians arriving to play in the WEVD studios must use the freight elevator.

I could understand the reason for a drummer or bass

Legendary Art Tatum (top) and Chu Berry were among jazz stars who played on WEVD radio for $10 per session.

75

player to use the freight elevator. For the rest there was no practical reason at all, and freight elevators had become for traveling Negro musicians one more insult. I told the station manager that such discrimination must not be tolerated, particularly by the management of a good Socialist radio station. "I'm sorry, John," he said. "We're at the mercy of the hotel. We're here rent-free and we can't fight them."

He may have thought that, but it was no answer for me. I went around the station protesting the segregation policy being forced on us, telling everyone to present a united front on the issue. Many agreed, and we walked out, picketing the station, proclaiming that in the enlightened year of 1932 a Socialist radio station must not participate in any type of racial discrimination.

Alas, that was the end of our broadcasts. They had been an innovation, a chance for a new audience to hear the best in jazz. I came to know many more jazz musicians than I otherwise could have, and I like to think we helped make jazz more popular in New York. If the recording equipment we have now had been available then those classic sessions could have been preserved.

I also reported all I heard in *Melody Maker*. In the years since I have often been accused of chauvinism because of my preference for Negro musicians. I suppose I must have seemed so to English readers, but I was being honest. I could not, and still cannot, compare the often stiff feeling of white jazz rhythm sections to the unbuttoned freedom and swing of a superb Negro section. As any musician will tell you, great improvisation depends on, takes off from, is inspired by the drive of proper rhythmic support. I said so again and again in print, prompting some people to call me "nigger lover," or to think I must be black.

VII

Greenwich Village in the early 1930's was a neighborhood of artists, writers, political activists, and theatrical people, a Bohemia living up to its reputation before that reputation was established. It certainly was the right place for me. I met people I could agree and disagree with—the perfect mixture for a young man who needed to learn, who loved to argue, and who occasionally found, as Lincoln Steffens did, that "it was as pleasant to change one's mind as it was to change one's clothes." Living on Sullivan Street I found myself in a circle of young people concerned with all sorts of causes, prepared to involve themselves at any risk. They were reformers given, as all reformers are, to overstatement, radicals, as all who would change the system are called. To me they were stimulating friends.

One of these was Betty Spencer, a great friend of Paul Robeson's and a very impulsive woman. Another was Charles Rumford Walker, who lived at 174 Sullivan Street on income from the Rumford Press, which published the *Atlantic Monthly*. To them and to others I suppose I was a pigeon, young, with independent means, and willing to become involved in every worthy cause. At any rate, Betty Spencer and Charles Walker took me to a fund-raising party to help the striking coal miners of Kentucky and there I met one of my heroes, the then-radical John Dos Passos, the author of *Manhattan Transfer* and *The 42nd Parallel*, the first volume of his eventual trilogy, *U.S.A.*

Two weeks before, Dos Passos and Theodore Dreiser had gone to Harlan County, Kentucky—not yet known as "bloody Harlan"—where they were promptly arrested with a group of Northern liberals. The Kentucky coal fields were unorganized and a Communist-front group called the National Miners' Union, not to be confused with John L. Lewis's United Mine Workers, had persuaded the miners to act together and strike the mines. The American Red Cross refused to send aid; its policy limited it to natural disaster, which the strike was not. So a group of Northern sympathizers decided to take food and clothing to the strikers and their families. They were turned back and beaten up by the sheriff's deputies, for in Kentucky small mining communities were company towns, the sheriff was owned by the mine owners, and the miners endured the peonage peculiar to the mining industry.

There was only one national labor-union group, the American Federation of Labor. The CIO, the Congress of Industrial Organizations, was not yet in existence. The AFL believed in organizing by craft rather than by industries as a whole, and almost all AFL unions were strictly segregationist. The largest independent union was Lewis's United Mine Workers, which was less segregationist than most, but still had not made much effort to organize Negroes in the Deep South. The Communists' answer to this was the Trade Union Unity League (TUUL), which created the National Miners' Union.

TUUL decided to organize the nonunion South, and I suspect that in doing so it put back the labor movement some twenty years, because when organizing white workers proved next to impossible it decided to organize blacks first. This enraged the whites, who made Negroes targets for further abuse. Even I, who was no expert in these matters, could see that attempting to organize the Negroes first was no answer. It simply emphasized segregation. But at least TUUL was doing something, and I think it can safely be said that the CIO grew at least to some degree out of TUUL's industry-wide concept.

When I met Dos Passos, he and others had decided to make a second trip to another Kentucky town, hoping to avoid the mistakes of the first failure, taking along the most famous people they could find to publicize the rescue mission. Dos Passos asked me if I would like to go to Pineville. This was about a month after the Public Theater closed, so I was free and ready to go anywhere.

Our caravan was a notable one. It included Edmund

Wilson and Malcolm Cowley of the *New Republic*, Quincy Howe of *Living Age*, Mary Heaton Vorse, one of the nation's best-known labor reporters, Waldo Frank, the novelist, Allan Taub, a lawyer from the International Labor Defense, and a young man fresh out of Columbia University, Alan Max. There were also reporters from the New York *Times*, the Associated Press and United Press, and a newsreel cameraman from Paramount. Again, the fact that I had my own car made me especially welcome on the journey, and it was because of the car that we achieved what little we did in Pineville.

When we reached Knoxville, Tennessee, where our headquarters were located, we bought about $1,500 worth of food, much of it milk and canned staples. We continued on to Pineville with lots of publicity in the nation's press because of what had happened to Dos Passos and Dreiser on their previous trip. We were met at the edge of town by sheriff's deputies who broke into our trucks, dumped the milk on the highway, and confiscated the food. They then arrested the members of our party. The group stood fast. Malcolm Cowley, particularly, defied the deputies and their guns and was slugged for his effort. But Malcolm had decided that the most important thing was to see that the Paramount cameraman escaped with his film, and he appointed me to get the fellow out of the state before the deputies could confiscate his negative.

The cameraman and I reached Knoxville safely. The film was processed and shown all over the country. That night in Knoxville the local papers said that blanket arrests had been made in Pineville, including—remarkably—my own. The following day's papers reported that the group had been kidnapped by masked men, taken to the state line, and dumped. The two Jews in the group, Waldo Frank and Allan Taub, had been severely beaten. They managed to reach a telephone and in a couple of hours all were driven to Knoxville.

Some forty-three years after this abortive attempt to help the miners and their families, Professor Leon Edel, the distinguished editor of the memoirs of Edmund Wilson, now dead and considered by many to have been America's finest literary critic, told me over lunch at the Century Association that he understood Wilson had turned tail and fled when the deputies showed up outside Pineville. I assured him this was untrue. "There are others who can confirm Wilson's courage that day," I told him. "One is Quincy Howe. Another is Allan Taub."

Edel had to return to the University of Hawaii, so I promised to look up Taub for him. I asked Allan how much he remembered of Edmund Wilson on our trip to Pineville. "He was wonderful, John," Allan said. "Of course, Malcolm Cowley was the most courageous of us all, but Wilson never ran."

The situation in the Kentucky mines opened my father's eyes, too. After all, he had been born in Kentucky and many of the mine owners were among his fellow members of the Jekyll Island Millionaires' Club. When I told him about the outrages I had seen in Pineville—families starving and every Government agency aligned against them, or, as in the case of the Red Cross, ignoring them—he realized that there were things going on he should find out about. One incident most upsetting to him was the dumping of milk on the highway. As a dairyman he felt this outrage keenly!

He agreed to go with me to Washington. He intended to call first on New York's Senators, Robert F. Wagner and Royal S. Copeland, both Democrats. They refused to see us. The only Senators who would talk to us were George W. Norris, the serenely liberal Nebraskan who, until then, had been anathema to my father, and William E. Borah, of Idaho, both Republicans. We had a wonderful lunch, an occasion Father enjoyed, and he left Washington realizing that there were a few inequities in our system, as well as a few blemishes on the integrity of New York's Senators.

I think Father was pleased that I had tried to do something for the Kentucky miners. Certainly, I was very proud of him for backing me up. It would not be the last time my father surprised me by his fairness and his concern for causes I would never have thought he cared about.

As a result of meeting many people involved in the struggle for social change, particularly Negro leaders in New York, I was asked to join the board of directors of the National Association for the Advancement of Colored People.

Ernest Gruening, my old boss at the Portland *Evening News*, had just become editor of *The Nation*. Naturally, he knew many Negro leaders in New York and through him I met them, too. My dedication to their cause, growing out of my love for their music, made it seem essential to understand as much as I could about their problems, the solutions they proposed, and the men who were undertaking to lead American blacks in their long fight for equal justice. One such was Walter White, the executive secretary of the NAACP, an old friend of Gruening's. A meeting was arranged at 69 Fifth Avenue, where the NAACP had had its headquarters since its founding in 1909. Walter White was a charming man, very light-skinned and soft-spoken, but clearly a fighter. I liked him immediately and gave him a sizable contribution. Perhaps as a result, I was asked to join the NAACP board, a flattering offer to a twenty-one-year-old, but I declined. I knew nothing about the organization then, although I knew enough about black groups to realize that not all were effective or sufficiently militant to bring about the changes needed.

In 1932 the NAACP was a middle-class organization with a membership of some 50,000. Its financial support came from white philanthropy, foundations, and a few liberal individuals who wanted to help the Negro help himself. Its leadership was predominantly white and liberal. Oswald Garrison Villard, who had just relinquished the editorship of *The Nation* to Ernest Gruening, the Rev. John Haynes Holmes, pastor of the Community Church, and Charles Edward Russell, a founder of the American Socialist Party, now a lively but cantankerous elder, were typical of the distinguished white members of its board. There were few Negro directors, and working-class blacks had no place or voice anywhere in the organization. The membership was mostly professional: black lawyers, doctors, academics, and, unfortunately, undertakers and preachers, who were inclined to preserve what status they had by playing Uncle Tom in the presence of whites. This is not to say that the NAACP was Uncle Tom; certainly Walter White was not. But its inclination was to be gradualist and conciliatory, it was careful of its reputation, and it moved very cautiously toward its objective of full equality for black Americans.

What I felt to be the fundamental weakness of this philosophical position was dramatically exposed during the crisis that arose over the sensational Scottsboro trials, perhaps the major civil-rights case of the 1930's.

In 1931 nine Negro boys between the ages of twelve and twenty were riding a freight train between Chattanooga and Memphis, Tennessee. Also aboard were some whites. These were the desperate days of the Depression and thousands of out-of-work Americans were hopping the freights from city to city, living a hobo existence, looking for jobs. Evidently—testimony wavered on details in the many trials which followed—the blacks, or some of the blacks, had jumped from a boxcar into a gondola in which nine whites were huddled, fought with them, and thrown six off the slow-moving train. Somewhat battered, the six made their way to a station; the station master called ahead; and at Scottsboro, Alabama, the train was stopped by a posse of waiting sheriff's deputies. A ten-minute search of the forty-two-car train yielded nine blacks, who were arrested, and three whites, two of whom turned out to be girls wearing men's caps and overalls. Some twenty minutes later one of the girls, Ruby Bates, told the Deputy Sheriff in charge that she and her friend Victoria Price had been raped by the blacks.

The Negroes were quickly indicted by a Jackson County grand jury. The judge, noting that the case could be thrown out on appeal if the defendants were not adequately represented, appointed the entire local bar—seven attorneys —to the defense. Six found reason to excuse themselves. The seventh, nearly seventy and nearly senile, agreed to serve, together with a lawyer enlisted by a Chattanooga black minister's group who had primarily done real-estate and minor police-court work, but who had at least tried from time to time to help Negroes in their tangles with the law.

In the nearly two weeks that elapsed before trial, the case was reported—and tried—in lurid and inflammatory terms in the Southern press, and there was enough lynch talk in the wide, tree-shaded streets of Scottsboro to require some thirty National Guardsmen at the courthouse. It was a classic instance of the violation of white Southern womanhood by black brutes, and it elicited a classically virulent Southern response.

The defense had less than half an hour of preparation with its clients before the trials began: four in a period of four days, first Norris and Weems, then Patterson, then Powell, Williams, poor, sick Roberson, nearly blind Montgomery, and Andy Wright, and finally Andy's little brother Roy. Trials were interrupted by the return of juries with verdicts from the preceding one, invariably a finding of guilty and a sentence of death. Only twelve-year-old Roy got the benefit of a split jury and a mistrial. Seven jurors wanted to execute him, although the prosecution had only asked for life imprisonment.

Whatever the South's outrage, this cruel and hasty justice—and the stench of frame-up—caused an uproar elsewhere in the country. The NAACP reacted cautiously. It did not want to get involved in appealing a rape case unless there was evidence that the boys were innocent or had been deprived of constitutional rights. The Communist Party was less reticent. Realizing that this was the kind of American dilemma in which it could score points, it reacted quickly and vociferously. The International Labor Defense sent representatives to Alabama, got the boys to designate them as counsel, and prepared to ask the Alabama Supreme Court for a new trial.

The Communists were opportunistic in their program for Negroes. They espoused a Leninist theory of self-determination for blacks which would result in a forty-ninth State to be gerrymandered out of territory in the Deep South, where blacks were in the majority. However unrealistic that may have been at the time, the ILD's aggressive and emotional efforts on behalf of the Scottsboro boys appealed strongly to blacks in the various Negro enclaves of America, while the temporizing of the NAACP earned it contempt. Walter White struggled to gain control of the case, and for weeks there was an unseemly squabble as the confused and ignorant boys, or their parents, switched allegiance from ILD to NAACP and back. In the end it was the NAACP whose nose was bloodied. Outmaneuvered, under attack by a scornful black press for showing more caution than humanity, it finally withdrew from the case and left the appeal to the ILD. Not notably patient myself, I was exasperated by the NAACP's whole performance.

The Alabama Supreme Court, equally exasperated by a flood of mail from Americans protesting Southern justice, not surprisingly refused to grant a new trial. The doggedly persistent ILD now petitioned the U.S. Supreme Court for a hearing and got it. Three points were argued: that Negroes were systematically barred from serving on Jackson County juries, that the defendants had been inadequately represented by counsel, and that the bias of the all-white jury and the tumultuous environment of the courthouse had infringed the defendants' right to a fair trial. The Court was persuaded. The judgment of the Alabama Supreme Court was reversed and the cases ordered retried.

Although I doubted that the boys would fare any better the second time around in the superheated atmosphere of Alabama, I rejoiced at the decision. It was a triumph—and, incidentally, one for which the ILD could, and did, take a good measure of credit. The Communist Party, new champion of the Negro, added more blacks to its central committee and one William L. Patterson became national secretary of the ILD.

Pat was one of New York City's important Negro leaders, a lawyer, of course, a Democrat, of course, and a loyal member of Tammany Hall until he found clubhouse life too humiliating for an ambitious black attorney. He was married to the sister of Paul Robeson's college roommate, and they were divorced when he changed his politics. He later married

Louise Thompson, a remarkable woman who worked actively in the Congregational Church for Negro rights.

He was a demon for work and as head of the ILD determined to raise the much-needed funds for the Scottsboro boys' new trial. In December of 1932 he asked me to arrange the entertainment for a benefit the ILD was planning for the Scottsboro Defense Committee. I knew Pat's position, just as he knew I was not a Communist sympathizer, but I was as interested in the new trial as he was, so I agreed to do what I could.

The benefit was held at the Rockland Palace at 155th Street and Eighth Avenue, underneath the elevated tracks next to the Polo Grounds. It was dingy and decrepit, but as large as the Savoy Ballroom. It would serve very well. I got Benny Carter's orchestra and Duke Ellington—solo—and the benefit was a great success. Miriam Hopkins and Tallulah Bankhead were there, and it also was the show-business debut of a fifteen-year-old singer named Martha Raye. Martha, the daughter of vaudevillians, was a protégée of Irving Mills, Ellington's manager and mentor, who had met her through another of his clients, Ina Ray Hutton, the exuberant blonde leader of an all-girl orchestra. Martha's career as comedienne and clown has overwhelmed the singer, and many of us do not know, or have forgotten, what a fine musician she was. My best memory is of the young girl singing in front of the Carter orchestra—with Duke at the piano—at this benefit. The voice was strong and pure. She was fine.

There was yet another thing Patterson wanted me to do for the cause. The Defense Fund was still short, and Pat knew I had a wealthy and important family. He asked me to write my grandmother for a contribution. I did, explaining the situation and hoping she would understand. What I forgot was that any letter to her was first read by my father, who visited her every morning. I received a very sweet note from Nanan saying she would be glad to help and enclosing a check for $50—not quite what Pat was looking for.

"I just don't understand you, John," he said in a subsequent telephone call. "You're the first white man who seems

to be straight on the race problem. Why don't you go to your father and mother?"

"Pat," I said, "you must be kidding. My father was born in Kentucky with the usual prejudices against Negroes. My mother wouldn't know what I was talking about."

Soon afterward I had an evening alone with my mother and father at Dellwood. After dinner Father asked me to come to his study. "I met two very interesting friends of yours the other day," he began. "A man named William L. Patterson and an artist named Hugo Gellert."

I was shocked. Hugo Gellert was an artist for *The New Yorker* and the *New Masses*. Obviously, Patterson had decided he did not want to tackle my father.

"Patterson," my father continued, "is the first educated black man I have ever met. I found him fascinating and an excellent lawyer."

"Father," I protested, "I told him not to go near you."

Father smiled. "You're wrong, John."

"The greatest band in the country": Fletcher Henderson's in 1932.
From left: Russell Procope, Coleman Hawkins, Edgar Sampson,
Clarence Holiday (Billie's father), Walter Johnson, John Kirby, Fletcher,
Russell Smith, Bobby Stark, Rex Stewart, J.C. Higginbotham, Sandy Williams.

"What happened?"

"Well," he said, "they stayed for two and a half hours. Patterson reviewed every aspect of the Scottsboro case. He's convinced that the trial was a frame-up devised by the attorney general of Alabama for his own aggrandizement." Father paused. "If I were a black man," he said at last, "maybe I'd have been a Communist myself. I gave him a large check, John, and agreed to contribute any advice I could in how to handle the appeal."

Again he had surprised me and I loved him for it.

VIII

In 1932 the offices of New York's music and recording industries were still scattered, neither as interdependent as they were to become, nor economically healthy enough to invest in new headquarters. One advantage to my living on Sullivan

Street in the Village was that Columbia's studios were located at the corner of Fifth Avenue and 12th Street, within walking distance of my apartment.

Columbia's recording director was Ben Selvin, an ex-band leader I had heard as a child at the Frivolity Club on Broadway at 52nd Street, where Birdland was later to be located. The Frivolity Club was a restaurant, so I could go there even when I was too young to enter night clubs. At the Hofbrau House one night in 1932 Ben Selvin introduced me to Herman Ward, who had just been made president of Columbia Records. Ben said, "John, we've been getting requests from England for jazz records. Have any ideas about what we should record?"

What a question to ask me! Perhaps my reports to English jazz fans were being read after all. "Yes, indeed," I said. "The greatest band in the country is Fletcher Henderson's. I'd like to bring Fletcher's band to your studios to make four sides. I'll make them for union scale, and I won't charge you for my services."

"I know exactly what this band can do," I continued, not giving Ben a chance to voice any doubts. "Their last records were made for Victor two years ago. Now they're better and very popular in England. You leave it to me."

I told Fletcher I wanted to record him, that there would be no more than union-scale money because Columbia was then operating in receivership. Fletcher was anxious to cooperate. Records are the best advertisement there is for a band. We were scheduled for ten o'clock on a Friday morning, a standard three-hour recording session, which meant we had to be through by one.

At ten on Friday two musicians were in the studio. At 12:15 John Kirby showed up with his bass, followed shortly by the rest of the band. We cut three sides in less than forty-five minutes, two of which were masters acceptable for release: "Underneath the Harlem Moon" and "Honeysuckle Rose." The third side, "New King Porter Stomp," we could play through only once.

Columbia, of course, was furious with Fletcher and

with me, as it had every right to be. Fletcher had once again let me down. Worse, he had missed an opportunity he badly needed. Still, the session was one of the most satisfying I have ever had anything to do with. Perhaps to make amends for their casual behavior, the musicians really put out in the short time available to us. The studio was small, the band setup intimate—the kind of conditions in which musicians can hear and feel what each man is doing. The results were superb.

The records were issued. Even "King Porter" appeared on the Okeh label backed by "Mister, Will You Serenade?" recorded by Clarence Williams and a nonunion jug band. Okeh did not pay scale to recording artists if it could be helped, and jug bands were not considered legitimate instrumentalists qualified for union membership. In fairness to Fletcher, I should add that he—and, indeed, most Negro band leaders—were discouraged, if not defeated, by the Depression. Duke Ellington and Cab Calloway were making it. No one else was.

Fletcher's records did sell in England. Best of all, I had been asked to make them. I made friends at Columbia in Ben Selvin and Harry Kruse, then head of the promotion department. I could drop in and be welcomed as a record producer.

Meanwhile, a pattern had developed in my life style, centered around jazz but also reflecting an urge I have always felt to be the first to hear a great player, see a new show, and find out what is going on in every town and city I can get to. I thought nothing of traveling hundreds of miles to visit a jazz club or a theater where rumor or a friend had told me I would find someone worth hearing. Like my mother, I was an entrepreneur at heart and like her I wanted to bring my discoveries to the world. Unlike most young men, I was mobile, neither unemployed nor regularly employed. Each year I bought a new Hudson, usually a convertible, for $300 and my old car, eventually ten Hudsons in a row and all wonderful automobiles. There were no car-rental agencies in those days and I wanted to be free to drive to every club in town. For company

Billie Holiday, aged 20 and already a bit older than she looked "when I first saw her at Monette Moore's club on 133rd Street."

I picked up hitchhikers along the way.

I had membership in a large family. My relatives were everywhere, and while few of them shared any of my interests I kept in touch with all of them on my travels. Friendships for me have been cumulative, not to be replaced but to be added to and constantly renewed.

My visits to American towns and cities included stops at variety and burlesque houses, as well as jazz clubs. I was still the voyeur, the theater buff, curious to know everything that was going on, being printed, played, or flaunted. Recording offered a unique opportunity for creative casting; the stage provided the spontaneity of live performance; the music and liberal press gave me a platform for constructive criticism. The times themselves imposed insurmountable odds, particularly for Negroes, against achieving any sort of recognition without help. The opportunities for me were clear.

American liberals of the early thirties often found themselves in a frustrating position. Although Franklin D. Roosevelt had been elected on promises of a New Deal for all Americans, neither he nor the nation was really prepared to improve the deal for blacks as well as whites. While socially progressive measures were passed to help the country out of the Depression, none really concerned the relationships between the races, and in Congress the Southern filibuster was still a powerful weapon, cocked and ready to shoot down anything that threatened the racial status quo.

Usually my involvement in political and social activism resulted from my love for jazz and the people I met who shared that enthusiasm. Walter White, for instance, had attended Atlanta University with Fletcher Henderson, which gave us a mutual friend and a common bond. And I made sure, whenever I did find a new musical talent, to drive my friends to hear it, to share my excitement, and perhaps to participate in the launching of a great career.

Early in 1933, for instance, I dropped in at Monette Moore's place on 133rd Street, a stop on my Harlem rounds. I was expecting to hear Monette, a fine blues singer. Instead, a young girl named Billie Holiday was substituting because

Monette had gotten a part in a Broadway show with Clifton Webb. Billie's accompanist was Dot Hill, and among the first songs she sang was "Wouldja for A Big Red Apple?" which I learned much later was the second song Johnny Mercer ever wrote lyrics for. Billie had come to New York from Baltimore two years before, aged fifteen. For a time she had turned to prostitution and served a term in jail. She was not a blues singer, but she sang popular songs in a manner that made them completely her own. She had an uncanny ear, an excellent memory for lyrics, and she sang with an exquisite sense of phrasing. She always loved Armstrong's sound and it is not too much to say that she sang the way he played horn. Further, she was absolutely beautiful, with a look and a bearing that were, indeed, Lady-like and never deserted her, even in the degraded final years. I decided that night that she was the best jazz singer I had ever heard.

My discovery of Billie Holiday was the kind of accident I dreamed of, the sort of reward I received now and then by traveling to every place where anyone performed: Most of the time I was disappointed, but now and then it all became worthwhile. Later, with Monette Moore's club out of business, Billie moved to the Hotcha, at 134th Street and Seventh Avenue, where there was a back room separated from the bar, a better place to listen to her. There Billie found a new accompanist, Bobby Henderson, a distant relative of Fats Waller's, with a great stride style on the piano and the same charisma Billie had. It was clear to me that Bobby also had a future. He was a good composer and his pianistic technique was limitless. I also learned that the better Billie's accompanist was, the better she sang.

Night after night I went to the Yeah Man, the Hotcha, Pod's and Jerry's Log Cabin, the Alhambra Grill, Dickie Wells', and other Harlem speakeasies to hear Billie, who moved around, living off tips and whatever salary she was offered in each place. I came to know her better, and as I did I discovered that her beauty surpassed her disposition, which could be remarkably moody. She smoked marijuana and drank a little, although not to excess then. And, of course, I brought everybody I knew to hear her, including Artie Bernstein, who realized immediately how great she was. I had found a star, and I wrote about her in *Melody Maker*.

When I first heard Billie Holiday she was seventeen and I barely twenty-two. There was little I could do for her immediately. No one would record her. She was unknown outside Harlem and, indeed, a vocalist who did not play an instrument—like Armstrong—was not even considered a jazz singer. I could not forget her, but all I could do was talk and write about her.

And a more immediate project intruded, in any event. Two friends had been after me to join them in the production of a Broadway play: Joe Losey, a persuasive young man with ambitions to become a theater director, and Irving Jacoby, whom I had met through Bernard Haggin in the WEVD days and through Alan Max, a veteran of our mission to help the Pineville coal miners. Alan had been a classmate of Irving's at Columbia. Jacoby, who was to become a lifelong friend, later became a first-class documentary filmmaker and the brother-in-law of Eddie Condon. Seldom have two more different individuals found themselves in each other's company: Condon the flashy, fast-talking salesman of jazz, Jacoby an introspective man of quiet accomplishment.

A corporation was formed, Henry Hammond, Inc., which included Losey, Jacoby, and me, and we found a script about the inmates of a reform school by a talented young playwright named Albert Bein. The title was *Little Ol' Boy*. The total investment was less than $10,000, of which I put up $8,000. It is amazing now to think that so small an amount could mount a three-set play on Broadway. We booked the Playhouse Theater on 48th Street, east of Broadway, a block which during the 1920's had six legitimate theaters. Only one remains.

Casting and rehearsals began early in 1933. The cast, considerably less well known than it would be today, included Garson Kanin, who also served as assistant stage manager, Burgess Meredith in his first Broadway role, Lionel Stander, and nearly two dozen others. *Little Ol' Boy* opened in April, a poor month for New York in the 1930's; summer heat came early and air conditioning in the theater district was poor or lacking entirely. Still we had no choice. Our option on the Playhouse was running out.

There were casting changes I would have liked to make, but I was away from New York during rehearsals, occupied with a different assignment. When I returned, I found trouble with the theater, as well as with the play. The owner of the Playhouse, William A. Brady, one of the great Broadway producers and entrepreneurs, subscribed to the New York Producers' League policy of not selling orchestra seats to Negroes. Never one to shrink from a confrontation, I told Mr. Brady that Negroes were going to sit downstairs and that, if necessary, I would sit with them. He backed off, though not entirely. When I went to get my black friends orchestra seats I had to go to the box office and pick them up myself.

Critical response was mixed. Percy Hammond of the *Herald Tribune* wrote: "An appealing heart-cry story whose sincerity and validity are not to be questioned." Walter Winchell, never noted for profundity, wrote in the *Daily Mirror:* "Tugs at the heart."

Little Ol' Boy closed after about three weeks, and I must admit I was not too sorry. But during its brief run, as a result of my name appearing in *Variety*, I received a surprising telephone call early one morning, while I was still in bed. "Is this John Henry Hammond, Jr.?"

"Yes, it is."

There was a pause. "Well, this is your Uncle Louis."

"Who?"

"Your Uncle Louis Wolfe."

I still could not understand. "How am I related to you?"

"Your grandmother was my sister."

"Well," I said, "this is a most pleasant surprise. I never knew I had any Wolfe relatives until this moment. How are you? What can I do for you?"

Uncle Louis said, "I'd love to see you. Your grandfather would never speak to me because I went into the theater. Your Aunt Georgia is the secretary of Actors' Equity. Unfortunately, I'm leaving town very soon. When can you make it?"

We agreed on a date the following week and said good-by.

That night I hurried to East 91st Street for dinner with my parents, quite upset. "What do you mean by never telling me I had an Uncle Louis?" I demanded.

Father looked shocked. "Did *he* call you?"

"Yes, he did, and I'd like to know more about him."

"He's no good," Father said. "Your grandfather banished him because he ran away from home to go into the theater. He's a gambler and, as a matter of fact, I've been helping to support him all these years."

"But you never told me," I cried. "What were you hiding?"

"John, I just didn't want you to get involved."

I had good reason to trust my father. My respect for his fairness had grown as we became closer. He had understood my concern during the Kentucky miners' strike and had done what he could to help. He had listened to and sympathized with Pat Patterson's opinions of the Scottsboro trial. If he felt that strongly, I decided, I would not try to meet Uncle Louis. Once again the curtain was drawn. My Wolfe relatives remained a mystery.

#

The second trial of the Scottsboro boys was held in Decatur, Alabama, fifty miles west of Scottsboro, in March of 1933, Circuit Judge James E. Horton, Jr., presiding.

As the trial date approached, Ernest Gruening asked whether I would report the proceedings for *The Nation*. He could pay me no more than $50—*The Nation* was nearly broke, as usual—but I had my car, enough money for expenses, and I realized that the experience was certain to be an important one. Looking back, I would say it was a turning point. It not only offered me a front-row seat at a pivotal battle in the civil-rights movement, it helped clarify and establish my own position on the issue, and it eventually led to my joining the NAACP board. The trial offered liberals an opportunity to voice their resentment of the South's perverted notions of justice, and the South an occasion to assert its doctrine of white supremacy through court action. It was a made-to-order case for Communist propagandists, a case embodying constitutional issues that would claim the attention of the U.S. Supreme Court.

I drove south with Mary Heaton Vorse of Federated Press and Selden Rodman, who was representing *Time.* The trip was difficult. Southern roads were fairly primitive in the early thirties. Outside Scottsboro, on a dirt road paralleling the Southern Railroad tracks on which the incident had taken place, I had a flat. I was not eager to have any Southern constabulary happen along as I struggled to change the tire, with my alien New York license plates gleaming, but the job was accomplished without trouble.

We arrived in Huntsville, a cotton-mill town some twenty-six miles from Decatur, which was the home of Victoria Price and Ruby Bates, about two in the morning and were lucky to get rooms in the Russel Erskine Hotel. In daylight I soon discovered that everyone's mind was hermetically sealed. In Decatur, as I later wrote in *The Nation*, things seemed calm and peaceful on the surface. Little bitterness was being expressed: "The prevailing feeling was one of annoyance at the expense of the trial. The townsfolk were fully aware of the fact that the schools of Scottsboro and Jackson County had been shut down by the cost of the original trial and appeal. The defendants, of course, were guilty. The average Southerner firmly believes that Negroes desire above everything to have intercourse with white women. But there was little animosity shown the prisoners. They would be found guilty and executed." They would die as a warning to other Negroes who might have similar intentions toward Southern white women.

In urging a change of venue, the defense had hoped

for an urban environment, perhaps Birmingham. Decatur was gritty and nondescript, the home of several hosiery mills and an iron foundry, with none of Scottsboro's gracious appearance and apparently serene atmosphere, although spiritually they were the same.

Judge Horton proved a pleasant surprise. A native Alabamian, he was tall, lean, and handsome, like a clean-shaven Abe Lincoln, some thought, although there was nothing rustic about him. More than that, his manner was reassuringly judicial: courteous but firm, moderate, decent, and—a term not then in use—unflappable.

The prosecutor was something else again. Thomas J. Knight, Jr., was the attorney general of Alabama and, at thirty-four, one of the youngest men ever to hold the office. His father was one of the Alabama Supreme Court justices who had denied the retrial about to get underway, and young Tom was hoping that convictions here would earn him a nomination for lieutenant-governor. "He is a small, nervous man," I wrote. "Even in court he had little control of himself. His behavior was that of a small and enthusiastic child. But Tom Knight is exceptionally clever. He knows his courtroom gallery and all its prejudices. . . . He is a bad cross-examiner and seems not too sure of himself, but he is well versed in legal procedure. . . . He browbeat Negro witnesses with all the thoroughness of a country solicitor."

When the defense attempted to discredit Victoria Price's image as deflowered Southern virtue, as well as the reliability of her testimony, by alleging prior arrests, Knight cried: "I don't care how often you prove she was convicted as long as you can't prove she had anything to do with niggers."

For the defense, Pat Patterson and the ILD had engaged the flamboyant New York criminal lawyer, Samuel S. Leibowitz. To many—I among them—this was a curious choice. Leibowitz was a Northerner, a Jew, a tough and abrasive man who had defended gangsters and got them off. In the recent investigation of the New York magistrate's courts by Samuel Seabury, ex-judge and a figure of towering rectitude, Leibowitz had been indicted by a grand jury on charges of subornation of perjury for having allegedly coached witnesses to give false testimony. Although the indictment was dismissed shortly after the death of the principal witness, the notoriety was unwelcome, and he seemed an odd choice to handle a delicate racial confrontation in a Southern court.

He had, in fact, been selected through the agency of Harvey Duell, managing editor of the *Daily News* and a close friend of the newspaper's publisher. Duell urged the politically ambitious Leibowitz to add a needed bit of luster to his name by finding a popular case, perhaps a civil-liberties case in which he could assume the mantle of hero, could appear before the public like that other champion of lost causes, Clarence Darrow.

Scottsboro, as it turned out, was the case. Duell called Pat Patterson to his office and made the following proposition: Leibowitz would take no fee from the ILD. In return, conduct of the case was to be left completely in his hands, he was to be given credit for all defense maneuvers, and he was to have immunity from attack by the Communist press, win, lose, or draw. Patterson accepted. Whatever his problems, Leibowitz was a high-powered attorney. The boys would have better representation than any amount of fund-raising could buy them. And given the sensitive nature of the case, and the South's habitual manipulation of the law to serve and defend its social structure, the defense was going to have to be agile and resourceful, indeed.

Leibowitz was not alone. He had two smart and aggressive ILD assistants, Joseph Brodsky and Allan Taub, as well as Colonel George W. Chamlee, a capable white lawyer from Chattanooga with an uncommon willingness—particularly for a Southern gentleman—for defending Communists and other radicals. Tom Knight had at his elbow H. G. Bailey, the circuit solicitor who had tried the original cases, and Wade Wright, a blustering bully whose frenzied oratorical style twanged every dark prejudice known to the South.

The press was well represented. Aside from hot-eyed reporters from the local papers, there were F. Raymond Daniell of the New York *Times*, unquestionably the journalistic authority on the case; Allan Raymond of the *Herald Tribune;* Hamilton Basso of the *New Republic;* William Bradford Huie of the Birmingham *Post,* a Scripps-Howard paper, which meant that he also covered for the Scripps wire service, United Press; Mary Heaton Vorse, and Tom Cassidy, a youngster from the New York *Daily News,* not a newspaper ordinarily concerned with such far-off events, but which gave this trial banner headlines. There were reporters from the Associated Press and from the *Daily Worker,* and even black newspaper men from the Baltimore *Afro-American* and the Norfolk (Virginia) *Journal and Guide.*

It was a strange, melodramatic trial. At the outset, even before a jury was selected, Leibowitz moved to quash the indictment. The arbitrary exclusion of Negroes from the jury rolls meant that the original grand jury was illegally constituted. Educated, intelligent, property-owning blacks appeared in court to testify to their qualifications for jury service. It was a stunner and had the prosecution spluttering. Judge Horton denied the motion, but the basis already was laid for an appeal to the Federal courts.

To gasps of astonishment Leibowitz called Negro witnesses "mister," and when Tom Knight started browbeating one of them, Leibowitz rose in a rage. "Now listen, Mr. Attorney General, I've warned you twice about your treatment of my witness. For the last time now, stand back, take your finger out of his eye, and *call him mister.*"

With the help of the Lionel Corporation he assembled a forty-two-car freight train, with every boxcar and gondola in proper sequence. It worked for him, too, as witnesses confused and contradicted previous testimony as to where they had been, and the defendants had been, and where the girls had been when whatever happened had happened.

He established convincingly that for at least two of the boys rape was physically unlikely, if not impossible. The youngest—twelve—was not of an age at which Southern blacks were likely to approach white women sexually, or to be accepted, even by accommodating ones. Another was so crippled by syphilis that he could barely walk unaided, let alone have sexual intercourse.

"Leibowitz," I wrote, "is a master showman. And the court is the principal place of diversion for the Southern citizen. There were often gasps of unwilling admiration for this outsider who could outsmart their own Tom Knight."

By the same token, it was Leibowitz's first trip south and he was dismayingly ignorant of the black-white relationship and the protocols governing it. However exhilarating his tactics, he ignited a slow-burning hatred that set spectators and townspeople implacably against him. The attack on the jury system was an attack on a prop of white supremacy. And no black ape on God's earth deserved to be called mister.

Where he went astray, I think, was in his aggressive treatment of Victoria Price. He went after her like a tiger, trying to crack her sullen composure, seeking the contradiction, the discrepancy, the damaging admission that would destroy her credibility with the jury. He proffered testimony that she and Ruby had engaged in sex with two white men some thirty-six hours before the alleged assault took place, which would explain why the doctors who examined them the day of the incident could find only nonmotile—inert—sperm in their bodies. In fact, the medical examinations, by two doctors, were almost *prima facie* evidence that no rape had been committed, let alone a gang rape. Neither woman had shown any sign of emotional disturbance. Neither woman's body bore any marks of physical or sexual assault.

But Victoria was tough. She stuck to her story, however implausible it seemed, and retreated behind stony-faced I-don't-knows and I-don't-remembers when she began to get out of her depth.

What Leibowitz seemed not to realize, however, was that, besmirched as she was, Victoria was Southern womanhood incarnate. Nothing he had said could dislodge that fact from the hearts and minds of the good people of Morgan County.

Even the unexpected and melodramatic appearance of Ruby Bates as a defense witness at the end of the trial to retract her earlier testimony and to absolve the Scottsboro boys of any criminal act, was a fizzle. Tom Knight squeezed admissions from her that she had been up North and that no'the'ners had bought the nice new clothes she was wearing. Obviously she was a creature of the defense. He made her a laughingstock and she retired in confusion. For what it is worth, I believed her. I had visited Ruby in New York, while she was being treated at Mt. Sinai Hospital for venereal disease. In the course of our talk she admitted to me that the case was a frame-up. But in Decatur that day, Victoria's marble image was unchipped.

I also managed to interview Haywood Patterson, who was the single defendant in this trial, in the Decatur jail. Among that sorry Scottsboro lot, undernourished in body and soul, Patterson stood out. He seemed strongest. Perhaps he was, or perhaps only the most truculent. There was no subservience in him; Southern whites invariably disliked him, immediately and intensely. He didn't unburden to me. He impressed me as a wildcat at bay. More violence and hatred emanated from him than from any Negro I have ever met.

The case lasted nearly two weeks. The jury retired at midday on a Saturday and was ready with its verdict the following morning: guilty and a sentence of death. The long deliberation had been due to a juror who held out twelve hours for life imprisonment. Jurors acknowledged that they hadn't given a moment's consideration to Ruby Bates's retraction.

Two months later Judge Horton took the occasion of a hearing on a defense motion for a new trial to deliver a long and closely reasoned analysis of the trial testimony. His conclusion was that the verdict was not justified by the evidence. He set the judgment of the jury aside and ordered a new trial.

It was his hope that by devastating the prosecution's case he would discourage Tom Knight from pursuing it. No such luck. The attorney general, white with anger, vowed to go after Haywood Patterson again as soon as it could be arranged.

The judge's fairness and calm common sense was applauded by some in the South. Most were not swayed by his logic. The following year Judge Horton was defeated decisively for reelection. His house in nearby Athens was stoned. When his wife came down with polio, someone painted "This is God's will" on the Horton front gate. The judge had means, a successful law practice, and a family plantation to supervise. He remained in the community, perhaps hoping that in time his neighbors' views might stretch to meet his own. I later came to know him and found no reason to change my original estimation of him: "courteous, generous, and scrupulous." His act took courage and decency rare for that place and that time.

Judge William Washington Callahan, assigned by the State to conduct the third trial, in November, was in every way Horton's opposite. He was a stocky, stubborn, self-important man of seventy, with thinning silver hair, freckles, silver-rimmed spectacles, and a fierce determination to try cases speedily and with a tight rein on the defense. For the duration of the trial I lived at a boardinghouse in Decatur run by two splendid old women who nearly refused to rent me a room when they learned I was from the North and a reporter to boot.

Counselor Leibowitz managed to get the Jackson County jury rolls entered as evidence to show that Negroes had been systematically excluded at the time of the original trial, a violation of "due process." And there was a sensation when it appeared that the names of some few Negroes had been entered at the tops and bottoms of ledger pages. An expert pronounced these forgeries, recently written in, but Judge Callahan, impatient with such niceties, refused to rule on the issue.

This set the tone. "From that time on," I wrote, "the defense suffered staggering blows from the jurist's rulings. In fact, Judge Callahan was often a more able prosecutor than the Attorney General. Vital testimony which Judge Horton had admitted was barred by Callahan as 'immaterial.'. . .

"Callahan heckled, interrupted, and glowered at Leibowitz throughout the trial, to the delight of the spectators. 'Now we got a *real* judge,' one of my neighbors whispered to me the first day."

For me the most dramatic moment of the trial came during Tom Knight's summation. Again quoting myself: ". . . while Knight was telling the jury that a conviction with the death penalty would mean staying the stand of future rapists, Leibowitz stood up with an objection. 'Your Honor, this is an appeal to passion and prejudice.' Tom Knight whirled around, still excited. 'It certainly is. . . .' He attempted to correct the blunder, but too late."

Judge Callahan charged the jury without explaining how to return a verdict of not guilty, an oversight terrible in its implications, which Leibowitz rushed to inform the bench. As in the original trials, a new case got underway as soon as the jury for the preceding one retired. But after the convictions of Patterson (for the third time) and Norris (for the second), the judge, appalled by the $1,200-per-day costs of the proceedings, agreed with Leibowitz to postpone further trials until appeals could be adjudicated.

As before, the cases were heard by the Supreme Court, and as before the lower court was reversed. Haywood Patterson went on trial for the fourth time, before Judge Callahan, with Tom Knight prosecuting, and dogged Sam Leibowitz defending.

Most of us who had been in attendance—most of America, for that matter—were dropping away now, moving on to other things. Yet the case went on, the boys languishing in jail, the years passing by, the legal contortions continuing. From constant retelling the prosecution's story fell apart, like cheap shoes, but the South never faltered in its determination to kill the Scottsboro boys. As for Sam Leibowitz, I found him an anomaly. Although I admired his efforts and the truly prodigious preparations he had made for the trial, I resented what seemed to me his cynicism about the case. Yet the fact remains that he stayed with it for three years, and his clients were not executed.

In 1937 Tom Knight died and a major obstacle to a resolution of the case was removed. Shortly thereafter four of the boys were released: Montgomery, Roberson, Roy Wright, and Williams. There were commutations, paroles, releases.

And new troubles. These were boys—men, now—with not much of a hold on life. Haywood Patterson died of cancer in prison in 1952. Roy Wright, on the outside, committed suicide in 1959. One by one lives ended. Only Clarence Norris is still known to be alive. In 1976 Governor George C. Wallace of Alabama gave him an official pardon which acknowledged his innocence of the charges to which he had been subjected. High time.

Even the NAACP came out of it looking pretty good. Together with the tenacious ILD, the American Civil Liberties Union, and several other organizations, it formed the Scottsboro Defense Committee in 1936 to carry on the struggle. And I had long since joined its board.

There was a surprising personal postscript to the case. Following my coverage of the second trial I visited Tuskegee University. White visitors usually were assigned a special house on campus, but I stayed with Max Bond, a professor of economics and uncle of civil-rights leader Julian Bond. Professor Bond told me that by order of the trustees no mention of the Scottsboro case was permitted at the university.

"That's ridiculous," I told him. "A first cousin of mine is chairman of your board."

"Not only can no one speak of it," Max went on, "but if he does he will be fired."

One night soon afterward I was at Dellwood for dinner. It was a large party which included my mother's first cousin, Louise Shepherd, and her husband, Dr. William Jay Schieffelin, the Tuskegee board chairman. Cousin Willie sat on my mother's left at one end of the long table, while Louise sat on my father's left at the opposite end. I arrived with a rather large chip on my shoulder, but I had to await my chance and speak loudly to be heard.

"The most important trial probably in this country is still going on," I fairly shouted, "and it can't even be discussed at Tuskegee!"

"That's very simple," Cousin Willie answered. "Those men are guilty."

At that point my father exploded. He told Cousin Willie he didn't know what he was talking about. Later he took him aside for a private chat. He must have been convincing, for in three months Dr. William Jay Schieffelin took over the chairmanship of the Scottsboro Defense Committee. It completely changed his life. Once head of the YMCA and of the New York Society for the Suppression of Vice (in whose interest he used to raid the Gotham Book Mart, the town's most distinguished avant-garde bookstore, and similarly ill-chosen targets), he now tilted spectacularly leftward. In 1935 he joined Sidney Hillman in founding the American Labor Party and came to know every radical extant. His fiat restricting discussion at Tuskegee reflected his paternalism toward blacks, rather than his understanding of them. His attitude was an old-fashioned one, and because Tuskegee received some support from the State of Alabama he had thought it best not to make waves. That changed, too.

And all because at dinner one night in Mount Kisco my father had once again defended me. He had kept an open mind. He knew the facts. Cousin Willie did not. Mother and I were not the only reformers in the family.

X

In the spring of 1933 I returned to England aboard the *Homeric* with a famous fellow passenger, Louis Armstrong. Louis was married then to his third wife, Alfa, a very attractive girl from Sebastian's Cotton Club chorus in Los Angeles. With Louis was his manager, Johnny Collins, a man I disliked. One night he got very drunk in Louis' stateroom while I was upbraiding him for using the word "nigger" and for his shabby treatment of Armstrong, who was, after all, Collins' bread and butter. The manager became so furious he took a swing at me. Somehow, for I am certainly no fighter, I managed to counter his punch and knock him on his behind. I think Louis never forgot that fight. It was probably the first time a white man had thought enough of him to fight someone who abused him.

Louis stayed with Collins, however, for another year at least. He was a man used to taking orders, letting someone else make his business decisions, and he continued to do so for the rest of his life. But after Joe Glaser took over his career at Associated Booking Corporation there was considerable improvement in Armstrong's management.

In those days Louis swore by two cures for all that ailed him. One was marijuana, the other Abilene Water, which was a violent purgative. He believed that by keeping his system clean he would remain in good health. He considered alcohol evil and marijuana virtuous, and he smoked it constantly, to my horror. It never led him to try anything stronger, however, but in my opinion it did hurt him, for it enabled him to become the exhibitionist he became to the detriment of his genius. "It makes you feel good, man. It relaxes you, makes you forget all the bad things that happen to a Negro. It makes you feel wanted, and when you're with another tea smoker it makes you feel a special kinship." That was his explanation. If I didn't buy it for myself, it may still have been reasonable enough for him.

Armstrong had been introduced to marijuana by the white clarinetist Mezz Mezzrow, and he used to call marijuana cigarettes "mezzes," as most musicians did. I thought it nothing more than dope and hated to see anyone dull his inspiration, either by drinking too much or by any other over-indulgence. I felt that any artificial stimulus was a denial of the music I loved, that playing that music under the right conditions and with other talented people was more inspiring than anything that could be found in alcohol and drugs. I used to argue with Louis about it, neither convincing him nor endearing myself to him for my efforts. I was, after all, my mother's son, not quite free of her proselytizing impulse or the certainty of knowing what was good for other people. This is not to say that I have remained a teetotaler. I enjoy a martini before dinner, appreciate wine, and have long since abandoned my efforts to persuade others to change their habits, although I still believe that alcohol and drugs produce inferior musical performances.

Louis Armstrong made his greatest records, the Hot Fives and Hot Sevens, in the mid-twenties, before I knew him. I think the first time we met was in New York in 1929, when he was featured with Leroy Smith's band in Connie's *Hot Chocolates* revue at the Hudson Theater. I still consider Armstrong a great musician. To me his deterioration began when he chose to think of himself as a soloist, as a performer, rather than as an ensemble musician. He began as second cornet in Joe "King" Oliver's band, then moved on to a succession of groups, including Fletcher Henderson, Lil Hardin, the piano on many of the Hot Fives who became his second wife, and Luis Russell. He always listened to what other musicians were playing, and while he was with Carroll Dickerson he listened closely to what the band's pianist was playing. This was Earl Hines at his superb early peak, and the music he and Louis recorded together was unique in all jazz. In those days Louis considered himself a musician among equals and played with them as equals. In Fletcher's band he played with the vastly underrated Joe Smith. To my mind, Joe was a greater trumpet player than Louis. He was a black Bix Beiderbecke, and like Bix died young—at thirty-five. His tone was ravishing, his emotionalism almost unparalleled, his improvisations unbelievable. I would say he was as original as Lester Young. Joe had great sensitivity to singers and recorded with the best—Bessie Smith, Ma Rainey, Ethel Waters. He listened to what they were doing and supported them warmly. Bessie said that given a choice between Joe Smith and Louis, she'd take Joe every time. Joe could make an audience cry. Louis could rouse them, excite them, but he could not make them cry.

What happened to Louis Armstrong was the public's discovery in "Hotter Than That" (1926) that he was an unsurpassed scat singer. He became a vocalist, a showman, a soloist. He did return briefly to groups with Hines and Jack Teagarden, where once again he was among musicians as great as he was, but unfortunately not for long.

I arrived in England something of a celebrity. Once again my mentor was Spike Hughes, whose friends included most of the important people in music, among them Constant Lambert and Freddy Ashton, the choreographer, and Spike's closest friend, Hyman "Bumps" Greenbaum, who was a fine musician and the recording director for the recently activated Decca Records. Spike himself was then record editor for *Melody Maker* and a producer for English Decca. Spike had visited the States earlier in 1933, at which time I got together a superlative group of musicians from the Benny Carter, Elmer Snowden, and Fletcher Henderson orchestras, including Coleman Hawkins, Chu Berry, Red Allen, Dickie Wells, Sid Catlett, and Wayman Carver. We did about sixteen sides, including "Donegal Cradle Song." Spike's problem was that he could not write music that swung. His arrangements of ballads were beautiful, but with the musicians I had gathered for him ballads were not enough to show off their talents.

Edgar Jackson of *Gramophone* also welcomed me and introduced me to Sir Louis Sterling, then the president of the Columbia Graphophone Company of England, which included the Columbia, Parlophone, and Regal labels. Sir Louis decided that with American Columbia in bankruptcy it was important for him to have an American who could record jazz for the English market. Through him I made a deal with English Columbia and Parlophone for a number of record sides for the English market, enough for a year's supply.

For Columbia, I promised to deliver eight sides by the large Fletcher Henderson orchestra, eight by Benny Carter's large band, four sides by a Benny Goodman group, and four sides by a Joe Venuti sextet. For Parlophone I would include Fletcher Henderson's band, but under the direction of his brother Horace, a small band called the Chocolate Dandies led by Benny Carter, and some sides by Coleman Hawkins and a group out of the Henderson orchestra. I would also include a couple of sides with Hawkins and pianist Buck Washington of the Buck and Bubbles team.

We signed the contracts in England, and in my enthusiasm I agreed to take little more than my expenses for my contribution. A more serious problem was that I signed on behalf of these artists without their being aware of the deal, and, in the case of Benny Goodman and Joe Venuti, without even knowing them. I wasn't worried. Record contracts were rare. I was sure everyone would grab the opportunity. Almost no jazz was being recorded in America and musicians were paid less than minimum scale for what little there was.

I returned to New York very excited about my recording contract and headed straight for Benny Goodman. I knew he often hung out in a 52nd Street speakeasy called the Onyx Club, so I went there first. Sure enough, about ten-thirty he arrived. I felt a little shy about reintroducing myself, but it had to be done. "Hi, Benny," I said, "I'm John Hammond and I want you to know that I've got a Columbia recording contract for you."

"You're a goddam liar," said Goodman, "and the reason I know you're a liar is that I was down at Columbia last week and Ben Selvin told me the company is bankrupt. They can't record and there's no way I can get a contract."

"But this isn't American Columbia," I explained. "This is with English Columbia, which has money. English Columbia will own the masters, but will allow American Columbia to release them if the royalties are paid." Pressing, to keep him from interrupting and turning me down, I said: "This is a good deal for you, Benny, because they'll be released here and in England."

Goodman was still skeptical, but as he was playing only one radio show a week for about $50, it might just be worth it, if I knew what I was talking about. "What kind of band should we have?" he asked.

"I don't want any arrangements at all," I told him. "I just want the greatest musicians we can get. I think we should use Coleman Hawkins and Benny Carter, Joe Sullivan, Gene Krupa, Artie Bernstein, and Dick McDonough [a fine guitar]." I wanted a mixed band under Benny's direction.

Again Goodman thought I was crazy. "Well, I don't know, John. I tell you what. I'm rehearsing a band now for a radio show. I'd like you to hear it and tell me what you think, because I think it's just what you're going to like."

"Fine," I agreed. "If you have some musicians better than the ones I suggested, we'll use them."

"You come down," Benny said. "I've got a great drummer called Happy; he plays with Meyer Davis. And I've got all the best studio men in New York."

The next day I went to the rehearsal at the Gotham Studios in the Grand Central Palace building. When I heard the band I started to laugh. These guys were worse than the Russ Columbo Orchestra. It was the dreariest group of musicians I had ever listened to, so I said, "Benny, this band is out. If you insist on using this bunch, we'll have to call the whole thing off, because I won't be associated with any group like this, and the English public will laugh us both off the turntable."

I don't think Benny had expected me to be so adamant. He knew jazz was not selling, that commercial music was where the money was. He also knew as well as I did that his band was no jazz group. Again I listed the kind of people we should get. Hawkins was out as far as Benny was concerned. "If it gets around that I recorded with colored guys I won't get another job in this town," he said.

"It can't be that bad," I protested.

"John, you don't know. It's that bad."

And, of course, he was right.

Benny also said that jamming was out, that we must have written arrangements. And he insisted that Arthur Schutt write them. That did not upset me because Schutt had been an idol since my trip to London in 1923, and had played creditably for Red Nichols and Miff Mole since.

For Benny I expected him to write as creatively as he played. Little did I know. Goodman insisted on Manny Klein as a trumpet player because Manny was the leading contractor in New York and Benny needed all the jobs he could get. Teagarden and Krupa would be a problem because both were with Mal Hallett's orchestra in Boston, but I agreed to pay their fares to come to New York.

Benny went to some music publishers to find the tunes. One was "Ain'tcha Glad." Another was a new Harold

Arlen song written for the *Cotton Club Review* called "I Gotta Right to Sing the Blues," and because the publisher was Irving Mills, Benny could get him to pay for the arrangement. I wanted one blues and one original tune. The original we found was "Dr. Heckle and Mr. Jibe," written by Dick McDonough. The blues was "Texas Tea Party," which was built around Jack Teagarden.

Meanwhile, I went to Boston to persuade Krupa and Teagarden to make the date. Krupa balked. "I'll never work for that son of a bitch again," he told me. "When he hired me for the Columbo band he would only let me play with brushes."

I assured Gene that there would be no such problem with this band. Reluctantly, with misgivings, he agreed. Teagarden loved to make records and any excuse to get away from the Hallett band for a day suited him fine. They both would come to New York by train.

The recording date was set for the morning. The band included Manny Klein and Charlie Teagarden on trumpets, because Jack insisted that his brother play any date he played. Benny insisted on using Artie Karle, a member of Ruby Newman's orchestra on tenor saxophone, but Karle turned out to be pretty good. I was allowed to use Artie Bernstein, Dick McDonough, and Joe Sullivan, so the rhythm section with Krupa was good. The problem, however, was immediately obvious. Arthur Schutt's arrangements were filled with commercial introductions and pat transitions. I knew they would not work and said so to Benny. We struggled with the arrangements of "Ain'tcha Glad" and "I Gotta Right to Sing the Blues," tearing them apart and chopping them up, for so long that we could only record those two sides in the three-hour session.

As a result, the band had to return the following week. Joe Sullivan was not available and the best pianist we could find to replace him was Frankie Froeba. I managed to persuade Columbia to pay the transportation for Krupa and Teagarden for the return trip from Boston, although we were over budget by needing two sessions to make four sides. The guys in the band were happy just to be paid recording scale, which was $20 per man for three hours. The results were not what I had hoped for, but not bad, either. I succeeded in having Jack Teagarden sing on the first two sides, and the final two, "Dr. Heckle and Mr. Jibe" and "Texas Tea Party," were improvisations. "Ain'tcha Glad" caught Ben Selvin's fancy at Columbia, so he decided to release it in America, but he didn't think "I Gotta Right to Sing the Blues" was strong enough for the reverse side. He had a record he thought would be just right: Clyde McCoy's mucilaginous "Sugar Blues."

Well, I screamed so loud at this suggestion that the argument was heard by E. F. Stevens, the sales manager, and Harry Kruse, the promotion manager. I enlisted them in my cause and told Ben Selvin, "You can't humiliate a musician like Benny Goodman by backing his record with that piece of corn." I won. The first record by Benny Goodman and His Orchestra came out and sold 5,000 copies, which, for 1933, was a hit.

I remember that Benny was going with a very attractive girl named Thelma, who was an avid dancer, as was Benny, and had very high social ambitions. Benny was neither high in social circles nor well off financially, but Thelma was crazy about him, as were many other beautiful girls during his bachelor days. One evening I was driving Benny and Thelma through Central Park, and I was razzing Thelma about her musical tastes. She thought the greatest piano player in the world was Eddy Duchin, who was playing with Leo Reisman's orchestra at the Central Park Casino. I told Thelma I though Duchin was the most florid piano player I had ever heard. "How can you make Benny, who is a great jazz musician, listen to Duchin?" I asked her.

Thelma became so upset with me she asked me to stop the car. She got out in the middle of the Park—you could do that in those days—and left us. I apologized to Benny for upsetting his girl. "It doesn't matter, John," he said. "It's good for her."

I also did all the other recording I had promised to English Columbia. I still consider the Fletcher and Horace Henderson sides among the best. The Joe Venutis were pretty good, but Eddie Lang, the fabulous guitar with whom Joe had such a symbiotic musical relationship, had died earlier in the year, and Dick McDonough, while good, just couldn't take up the slack. Further, Joe decided to use Adrian Rollini and his bass sax instead of Artie Bernstein, so the bass line left something to be desired.

The Hawkins sides were the only ones I did with him, and I caught him at his best. He was at the very top of his creative form. He was a small, reserved, not very impressive man, but he played like a giant. He had that fat, luscious tone and complete command of his instrument. The rhapsodic excesses which later blunted his cutting edge had not yet emerged. He was generally agreed to be "the inventor of tenor sax," even as Louis had shown everyone the way on trumpet. He was the first exponent of what later came to be known as "the Texas sound" that identified Ben Webster, Chu Berry, Herschel Evans, Buddy Tate, Lucky Thompson, and others. He was a tremendous influence on white musicians, as well.

What I liked about him was that he was a splendid ensemble musician and a good leader. The sides I did with him were his first as leader and he allowed plenty of room for others' improvisations. I did two sides with Hawkins and Buck Washington, and two with Hawkins, Red Allen, and the Henderson rhythm section—John Kirby, Walter Johnson (drums), Horace Henderson (piano). (Horace was a much better piano player than Fletcher and I used him whenever I could.)

The Benny Carter sides had a special attraction: They introduced Teddy Wilson to the world.

One night I was listening to a broadcast from the Grand Terrace in Chicago, where Earl Hines was playing. That night Father was off. His substitute, I suddenly realized, was absolutely unique, with a cleaner and more elegant sound than Hines', never flashy, but swinging and with an excellent left hand. I called the station—WMAQ—and asked who he was. Teddy Wilson, they said. I called Benny Carter, who was searching desperately for a pianist. "Have you ever heard of Teddy Wilson?" "Sure," he said. "I know him. He worked with Art Tatum as a piano team in Toledo, and he's probably the best there is."

"Well," I said. "He sounds to me like just what you're looking for. Why don't you run out there and see if he's available?" I gave Benny $150 to go to Chicago. His mission was successful. Teddy showed up at the Columbia studios at 55 Fifth Avenue while we were recording the Carter band as the Chocolate Dandies. He sat in, and a great and continuing career was launched.

(In the summer of 1961 I received a letter from Carter, who was writing for motion pictures and for various Hollywood recording orchestras.

(Dear John [it said]
(You have probably forgotten all this, but in 1933 you
(gave me $150.00 to bring Teddy Wilson to New York. It's
(still on my conscience. I'm only sorry I can't afford
(compound interest, but here's my check for the original loan.
Benny)

Most of the jazz players who interested me during those Depression years were given an occasional boost with some of my own money. This was in part to bring national recognition to great Negro players I thought needed help at a time when both the economic conditions in the country and the rigid segregation which prevailed, even in the jazz world, made such recognition very difficult. It was also based on my desire to hear these players, to bring together musicians who had never played together before. For instance, I brought together Red Norvo and Teddy Wilson, Norvo and Chu Berry, Teddy and Artie Bernstein.

Often my help and sponsorship were suspect. I have been accused of playing Pygmalion, of interfering in other lives, even of profiting at others' expense. Not so. I never made an investment for monetary gain. As to any resem-

Stars of 1933 Hammond
recordings: Gene Krupa
(drums) and Jack Teagarden
(trombone), among the first
to play with Benny
Goodman. And Coleman
Hawkins at the peak of his
powers.

blance to that famous reformer Pygmalion, I cannot plead total innocence. After all, my mother passed on to me the urge to change the world I thought needed changing. Sometimes that even included jazz.

Fletcher Henderson was one of my earliest enthusiasms, but Fletcher had a lassitude born of years of exploitation, so that when opportunities came to help himself he was unprepared to take advantage of them. I tried and sometimes succeeded in pushing Fletcher to realize his potential. Benny Carter's problems stemmed from opposite causes. He tried to do too many things at the same time. Not content to be a great alto saxophonist, he also had to be an arranger—and, of course, he was a top arranger—and a trumpet player. He was not a top trumpet player. He was more interested in those years in exhibiting his versatility than in making great music, and I believe this is one reason Benny never became a great bandleader. I invested a deal of money in Benny's career, but money was not enough.

Teddy Wilson was perhaps the first man I met in jazz whom I thought I could really help. Teddy's mother taught English and was the librarian at Tuskegee; his father had been the head of the history department. Teddy rejected a good part of this academic background. He left Tuskegee and later Talladega to play jazz in Chicago. Still, he had the bearing, demeanor, and attitude toward life which would enable him to survive in a white society. I have always considered him a man of destiny, and I suppose that my role in his later career reflects this confidence that he not only had the talent to make it in any surroundings, but the mental and emotional equipment to do so.

The success of Benny's "Ain'tcha Glad" and "I Gotta Right to Sing the Blues" on the American Columbia label provided me an opportunity to play two of my favorite roles, producer and catalyst, with two of my greatest enthusiasms at that hectic time. Now that Goodman and I were friends, as well as business associates in recording, I made sure he heard Billie Holiday. I took him repeatedly to Harlem to hear Billie sing, and

Benny heard what I had heard earlier in the year—the greatest jazz singer ever.

Billie was singing at Pod's and Jerry's Log Cabin, a club on 133rd Street, near Monette Moore's old place, and the one spot in Harlem known to many white musicians. It stayed open until dawn and was presided over by one of the original characters of jazz, Willie "The Lion" Smith, who conversed flamboyantly while playing fine stride piano. It also often featured a blues singer named Mattie Hite, who had made a couple of Columbia records in the twenties with Cliff Jackson on piano, records that were among my favorites. At that time I believe Billie was accompanied by Garnett Clark, who was good though not in the Bobby Henderson class.

My interest in Henderson continued, and I soon discovered that he had another family in Albany, New York, where he played under the name of Jody Bolden. I made several attempts to get Bobby into the New York City Local 802 of the American Federation of Musicians, but he failed repeatedly to show up for the pro-forma test of music-reading ability. I also tried to persuade Columbia to record him, as well as Billie, but again he would never show up for recording dates. His excuse was that he had been arrested for spitting in the subway! Henderson's career never materialized because of this strange self-destructiveness which prevented him from taking advantage of the opportunities his talent attracted.

Speakeasies in Harlem in those days were all located in brownstones, with tenants living above the ground-floor night clubs, and an inordinate amount of noise from brass instruments or drums was not permitted. In such places Billie could sing only with piano accompaniment, a particularly unfortunate limitation because, as her later records demonstrated, she thrived on the competition of top horn players. Even on-the-spot recordings of such superb artists as Art Tatum had to observe this restriction, and, if drums were included, the rhythm was produced by brushes beating on a chair seat.

Among the people I took to hear Billie was Charles

Benny Carter (alto) desperately needed a piano for his Chocolate Dandies. John thought Teddy Wilson, whom he'd heard on radio, would do. He did.

Laughton, who was appearing in his first Broadway play, *Payment Deferred*. Night after night Charles and his wife, Elsa Lanchester, went to Harlem to listen to Billie. Billie's appeal to theatrical people, the gay crowd, and others outside the social norm was tremendous. Her message to them entirely escaped me, but it was strongly felt by others. Her appeal to jazz musicians also was immediate, and Benny Goodman wanted to record with her.

American Columbia, although still in financial difficulties, wanted to follow Goodman's initial success with another record which it would pay for. The fall of 1933 was perfect timing. Goodman wanted to record, using Billie Holiday. Columbia wanted to record Goodman. My chance had come at last to put her on records.

Benny signed his first contract with American Columbia and dates were set for November. It was an event in many ways. The titles we recorded were "Riffin' the Scotch" and "Your Mother's Son-in-Law." This was not only Billie's first recording session, but the first time Benny had recorded with a Negro musician—Shirley Clay, one of Don Redman's trumpets—in his band. Jack Teagarden also sang on the date, and the records are now collectors' classics. Goodman and Holiday each had taken a giant step forward.

XI

When I decided to record Bessie Smith, I faced the realities of the record business at its lowest point. Not only were the American record companies bankrupt or close to it in 1933, but the Negro record buyer was in worse shape. Blues records, even by an artist of Bessie's stature, were at the bottom of any list of record sales, and what records were being made for the almost nonexistent Negro market were washboard bands whose performers were not considered to be legitimate musicians by the union and therefore did not have to be paid scale. Worse still, from my own standpoint, blues did not sell in England as jazz did, so Bessie was not wanted abroad and could not be recorded under my English contract.

Still, Bessie Smith was a star. She had to be paid, even though she had made no records since 1931. I persuaded Columbia to let me record Bessie for Okeh. I knew it was reluctant, but I was persistent. Her records had been a treasured part of my collection since my Hotchkiss days, and I had not forgotten that night after my violin lesson when I first heard her in person. She simply could not be silenced by a Depression and jittery record executives.

Bessie was working as a hostess in a speakeasy on Ridge Avenue in Philadelphia. She was singing with a bad piano player and she was depressed. I went to see her, introduced myself, and said, "Miss Smith, I'd love to get you back in our recording studios. It's been two years since you've recorded, and I'll hire the greatest possible musicians for you."

"What would it pay?" she asked.

I told her that the records would have to come out on Columbia's thirty-five-cent label. I couldn't tell her that English Columbia would not even release them. I offered to pay her way to New York. I could offer no more. Bessie was drunk when we talked. I didn't realize that her current boy friend was Richard Morgan, an uncle of Lionel Hampton's and a bootlegger in Philadelphia.

Bessie agreed, but she said, "Nobody wants to hear blues no more. Times is hard. They want to hear novelty songs."

She wanted to ask Coot and "Socks" to write four tunes for her. Coot Grant and "Socks" Wilson were husband and wife, Coot a fine blues singer in her own right, and "Socks" was a singer and the writer of one of the splendid pornographic blues of all time, "Big Trunk Blues." They had also recorded with Louis Armstrong on Paramount Records, and I felt that if they wrote for Bessie the tunes would not be too far from the blues. Their songs were "Do Your Duty," "Give Me A Pigfoot and A Bottle of Beer," "Take Me for A Buggy Ride," and "I'm Down in the Dumps."

Bessie arrived in New York with Morgan the day before the recording session. I went to see her at 127th Street in a railroad flat with lots of rooms off one long corridor and obviously lots of activity going on. Bessie, "Socks," and I finally reached a sort of parlor, and although "Socks" was not the greatest pianist in the world I gathered that the tunes were pretty good. For the date I had Jack Teagarden, Chu Berry, Frankie Newton, and a wonderful bass player, Billy Taylor, Sr. (Not the father of the pianist, but of another bass player.) I had also hired Sid Catlett to play drums. When Bessie heard that she said, "I don't want nobody settin' time for me. I only used a drummer once and it was no good." So there would be no drummer. I was embarrassed to un-hire Big Sid, but he was amused and laughed it off.

I got Buck Washington to play piano. I thought of him as a vaudeville pianist—he had made a record of "Dear Old Southland" with Louis Armstrong—and because Bessie was basically a vaudeville singer I believed the combination might work. I purposely went out of jazz when I hired Buck, who also couldn't read a note, hoping the fact that none of the other musicians had played with him might be an asset. One strange player in a jazz group often injects an element of surprise that creates a more exciting performance.

And there was Benny Goodman. I knew Benny was due in the next studio at eleven o'clock to record a commercial song with Ethel Waters and an accompanying band led by Ben Selvin. His name would certainly mean something on the label and we might get at least one tune recorded before he had to leave. As it turned out, we did. You can hear a couple of notes by Benny in Bessie's "Gimme A Pigfoot," recorded between ten-thirty and eleven that morning.

The rest of the band was impressed to be playing with Bessie. Jack Teagarden was flying. He had dreamed of recording with her and thought he never would.

The records came out and, true to Columbia's prediction, nothing happened, except that "Gimme A Pigfoot" later kept appearing on juke boxes and became a standard in the Okeh, and later the Columbia, catalog. Of course, the records have been reissued many times since for a couple of new generations of Bessie Smith fans.

The Bessie Smith records gave me a wonderful feeling of accomplishment and they established a warm relationship with her which lasted to the end of her life. She came back to New York several times after 1933, when she appeared at the Apollo Theater and the Newark Opera House and, of all places, Connie's Inn, where she lasted three nights. This was when Connie's Inn was in midtown Manhattan, where the Latin Quarter later located, and Bessie just could not sing comfortably for white audiences.

I think it was in 1936 that Milt Gabler, who owned the famous Commodore Music Shop on East 42nd Street and recorded a great deal of jazz on his Commodore label, started the United Hot Clubs of America. We had a Bessie Smith concert at the Onyx Club, a white audience, and a fine occasion for her. Archer Winsten, the movie critic for the New York *Post*, accompanied me to that concert and reminded me that Teddy Wilson played for Bessie, a very unlikely accompanist for her. Bessie's record audience was also black, except for either a slightly dirty song like "Empty Bed Blues," which was banned in Boston and therefore brought to the attention of white audiences, and a few pop tunes she recorded in 1927.

I finally persuaded Dick Altschuler, president of Columbia Records, to allow me to sign Bessie to a proper contract, one which would pay her royalties on Brunswick, then the Columbia popular label. But I never knew where to find her. She finally let me know that she was going to join Silas Green, a tent show in the South, where she could still make money. It was while en route to join that show that she was killed.

There are various theories about how she died. In 1937, during one of my trips to Huntsville, I heard what I thought was the true story. This was about five weeks after Bessie's death. I talked to the owner of the Green show, who told me how the old Packard in which Bessie was riding had been forced off the road and her arm nearly severed. He said that two ambulances had passed her by because she was black. It was a long and convincing story from a man who was in a position to know the truth, and there were two other people there nodding agreement as he told it to me.

When I told him I wrote for several magazines and was interested, as my readers would be, in what had really happened, he said, "Don't quote me." His tent shows played every tank town in the South; in Huntsville the show was a big event and I went to see it whenever I was there. They had separate shows for blacks and whites, but I was given the privilege of going to the midnight show and standing backstage when they played for blacks.

That was as much as I could find out about how Bessie Smith died. She was unique for her time, an urban blues singer, and had she lived even a few years longer she would have become a star again. Lil Green, who came soon afterward, was a major recording star, and there are people who believe Ma Rainey was better than Bessie, but I am not one of them.

XII

It would be difficult to imagine a more unlikely boss for me than Irving Mills. He was a minor colossus in the music business of the mid-thirties, a manager of talent, a supersalesman whose product happened to be the songs and the performances of many stars of the day. It is also no more than fair to say that his offer to hire me could not come at a more opportune time.

Irving and his elder brother Jack were song pluggers, members of a vanishing fraternity whose job was to turn newly published songs into profitable hits. The best way to accomplish this was to convince bandleaders and singers to record their songs, to perform them in clubs, and to broadcast them by radio. Such first performances not only produced income from record royalties and fees paid through music-performance societies, such as ASCAP, and later Broadcast Music, Incorporated (BMI), but by exposing the song to the public encouraged profitable sales of sheet music. Wherever professional musicians performed, song pluggers appeared with their latest wares. Of course, bandleaders and their singers constantly needed new songs with which they could become identified, so the song salesmen were welcome, although as in any marketplace, there were more new songs than customers, more bad tunes than good, and preferred customers got first choice.

Irving Mills was a song plugger—and more. He was a conglomerate. He was vice president of Mills Music, a major publisher of which brother Jack was president. In addition, he was the manager of such attractions as the orchestras of Duke Ellington, Cab Calloway, the Mills Blues Rhythm Band, the Will Hudson-Eddy DeLange band, Ina Ray Hutton, and other Negro and white performers. He was an entrepreneur and a shrewd promoter of talent. In the 1920's Jack Mills had bought the Watterson, Berlin, and Snyder music catalog from Irving Berlin, though without title to Berlin's own songs, to form the basis of Mills Music. While Irving continued as vice president and co-owner of the new Mills company, Jack promoted black talent in his own offices. Mills was no real talent himself (although he had started as a singer in the Hotsy Totsy Gang), but he was able to add his name as lyricist to many of the songs published by Mills Music, thus participating in the composers' royalties, as well as in the publisher's percentage of the songs' earnings. Whether he actually contributed to the writing of the words, for instance, to many of Duke Ellington's hits, or whether his control of the songs and of Ellington's career made it possible to simply add his name was never clear to me.

When Mills offered me a job, he owned several publishing firms apart from Mills Music: Lawrence Music, Exclusive, the American Academy of Music. He wanted to establish ASCAP ratings for his new firms, although he was already receiving considerable ASCAP earnings as a lyricist and a Mills vice president. To accomplish this he had to record as much material published by these fledgling music companies as he could. He was aware that the recording industry was practically bankrupt, that without subsidy his bands could not record. He was willing to pay the meager recording costs in order to collect the statutory payments made by record companies to music publishers, a fee that is divided equally between the publisher and the writers. Mills participated both ways. The recording of Publisher-Lyricist Mills' songs also promoted sales of sheet music. Finally, by having his songs recorded by artists whom he managed, he profited from their enhanced reputations. It was an unbeatable arrangement for Irving, but to give him his due he made much recording possible which might not otherwise have been, and he certainly contributed to the success of Ellington, Cab Calloway, and many others.

In 1934 Irving Mills could underwrite the costs of a recording session for a very modest amount of money: $50 to $75 for an arrangement, union scale for each musician and singer, and a fee for studio use and equipment. The cost of pressing the records and selling them was borne by the record company, and with the sale of a few thousand records everyone did nicely.

Mills had offices on the fourth floor of a building at 799 Seventh Avenue, at 52nd Street, an ideal location—later acquired by Columbia Records—near several jazz clubs, rehearsal studios, and Broadway theaters and restaurants. Mills, having heard of me from friends at Columbia, from Duke Ellington and other musicians, phoned to offer me a job as associate editor of *Melody News*. This was a Mills house organ, but at a time when, aside from *Metronome*, which concerned itself primarily with white commercial bands, there was no American magazine devoted to popular and jazz music, it represented an opportunity. (*Down Beat* wasn't yet in existence.)

"How much do you want to work for me, John?" Mills asked.

Without batting an eye, I answered, "One hundred dollars a week."

"I'll hire you half time for fifty dollars a week," he said.

I accepted. I was twenty-three years old. The job included supervising record sessions underwritten by Mills, an opportunity I could not have found elsewhere. I had fulfilled my English Columbia contract, as well as producing several records for American Columbia. There was no chance to continue recording without the sort of setup Mills was offering. I knew recording for him meant that he would publish original material and that most of the popular songs I would make would be Mills songs. Still, Mills songs were usually better than most.

My responsibilities as associate editor of *Melody News* would create problems, although the editor, Ned Williams, also Mills' press agent, was a man I liked and could get along with. Ned was to become editor of *Down Beat*, America's first music magazine which would give coverage to jazz, particularly Negro jazz, and our association at Mills led to my becoming *Down Beat*'s first columnist. As usual, I intended to write what I felt, regardless of Mills' authority, and for a while I got away with it.

My first meeting with Irving Mills was when I went to his office to accept my new assignment. On his walls I noticed large blank spaces. "You know what we're going to put there?" he asked, waving his cigar. "Muriels," he said. And indeed murals finally appeared, terrible depictions of Harlem scenes.

Like most music publishers in those days, Mills often took advantage of young talent. One young composer who worked for him was George Bassman, who became a friend of mine. One night at the East 91st Street house George kept Artie Bernstein and me awake while he worked on a melody at the piano. As he played, repeating again and again a phrase which reminded me of one of my pet abominations, *Trees*, Artie and I suffered. But by morning George had his melody. It was "I'm Getting Sentimental Over You," which he sold to Irving Mills for $25. With Ned Washington's lyrics the song became a hit and Tommy Dorsey's theme song. It was not until twenty-eight years later, when copyright was renewed, that Bassman began to receive royalties. It seems unfair, but George was a staff writer for Mills Music, and Irving took no more advantage of him than other publishers would have in similar circumstances.

While most of my time and enthusiasm were devoted to artists who would become major economic and musical successes, some of my cherished memories and greatest jazz experiences had to do with people who never impressed the record-buying public as they should have. One of these was Kenneth Norville, better known as Red Norvo, a sensitive and creative man, a trainer of young players, and a superb jazz improvisor. I recorded Red while working for Irving Mills, but I had first heard him when he was playing with Paul Whiteman's unspeakable orchestra at the Palace Theater. Despite the commercial swamp of the Whiteman band, Norvo was always a jazz player.

In 1933 Red made an exquisite record on Brunswick called "Dance of the Octopus," and although he was a xylophone player, here he played the marimba flawlessly. Artie Bernstein was in the group and Benny Goodman played bass clarinet. It was real chamber jazz, unlike anything I had ever heard, sensitively written and beautifully played. Red was playing at the Hickory House, around the corner from the Mills offices, and I was able to arrange two small-band dates in the Columbia studios at Irving's expense.

The first session was a septet which included Artie Shaw, Jack Jenney, who played the kind of trombone Tommy Dorsey always wished he could play, Charlie Barnet, whom I had used in my WEVD jam sessions, and Teddy Wilson. The hit of the first Norvo date was "I Surrender, Dear," a good tune with an improvised solo which has become a classic Red still plays. On the second session Bunny Berigan was unbelievably impressive, particularly on "Blues in E-Flat," and Chu Berry, even better than Barnet, was the tenor saxophone. Shaw and Teddy Wilson were again superb.

Other Norvo dates were among the most pleasurable I have ever produced. Irving Mills published the original tunes, of course, and the $50 a week he was paying me covered my salary as producer. Benny Goodman also recorded for Mills on the Columbia royal blue label (the record itself was of blue material, and Columbia records were sturdier than others because in cross-section they consisted of five layers: shellac, paper, a core of ground-up record fragments, then more paper and shellac), although Irving always wanted the lyrics of his songs included. No one could do this better than Mildred Bailey, who became Norvo's wife. She and Benny made many beautiful records, among them "Old Pappy," which was one of my favorites. Mildred was quite a girl: hard-swearing, sensitive, insecure, domineering, and very vain. She was always fat; she preferred that you notice her long Indian-black hair and slim ankles. Mildred was proud of both and to admire either was to become her friend. She was a mass of contradictions, and above all an original.

I had heard Mildred since her early days with Whiteman and came to know her well during my term with Mills. I recorded her with Goodman, visited her and Red, and succeeded in the difficult task of being her friend. I never considered Billie Holiday a friend despite all I tried to do to help her career, and I think she felt the same way. But Mildred was jealous. During the time I was always touting Billie, I took Mildred to hear her in Harlem and, although she hated to admit it, she was impressed. Mildred had her own way of putting Billie down. She employed Billie's mother Sadie as a housekeeper. Sadie was short and dumpy, not beautiful like Billie, deeply religious and messy. Mildred complained constantly about Sadie's work, and now and then—to Mildred's satisfaction, I'm sure—Billie appeared at Mildred's house to help Sadie in the kitchen.

Mildred had Indian blood and was proud of it. She had no racial prejudices, admired and respected Negro jazz players, and was glad to record with them. But she would not appear in public with Negro musicians until it was socially acceptable to do so. She would not risk money or reputation at a time when mixed bands were banned in public places. Nor did she like competition. The best place for Billie Holiday was in Mildred's kitchen, helping out.

Mildred loved food. She introduced me to the greatest steak house in New York, Frankie and Johnny's, on the second floor at the northeast corner of 45th Street and Eighth Avenue, a restaurant with sawdust on the floor and unbeat-

Mr. and Mrs. Swing: The subtle and creative Red Norvo and his wife Mildred Bailey, a fat girl who sang slender—"the finest white jazz singer I've ever known."

able food, one I still choose whenever I go to the theater. She also loved to cook for her friends, specializing in Italian food and Southern-fried chicken. It was on one of these occasions at Mildred's place in Forest Hills that Benny Goodman and Teddy Wilson first played together with Mildred's cousin, Carl Bellinger, whisking brushes on a suitcase. It was a historic meeting. I had always considered Teddy Wilson the only pianist capable of matching Benny's technique and I had hoped to bring them together. It happened first at Mildred's house. I was there and I'll never forget it.

My association with Mildred and Red continued on and off long after I left Irving Mills. Red formed a large band which played arrangements by Eddie Sauter; he and Mildred were billed as Mr. and Mrs. Swing. I recorded Mildred again early in 1936 with Teddy Wilson, whom she loved, and a small group which included Bunny Berigan, Johnny Hodges, and a fine bass player, Grachan Moncur, Sr., whom I had heard on my car radio from a roadhouse in New Jersey. I decided for that session to take a leaf out of Bessie Smith's book and omit a drummer. Mildred thought I was crazy, but she went along with it, and we recorded "Willow Tree," a tune by James P. Johnson and Fats Waller from the 1927 show, *Keep Shufflin'*. We also made "Down Hearted Blues," one of the first blues Bessie ever sang, and "Honeysuckle Rose," another Fats Waller song.

There was also an element of surprise in the fact that the combo was new to each other. Berigan had never played with Hodges. Hodges had never played with Moncur or with Mildred. Everyone had played at one time or another with Teddy. In this case, the blend worked well. Berigan and Hodges were finally exchanging fours (four-bar phrases), Bunny establishing an idea and Johnny carrying it in exciting new directions.

They were among the most beautiful records I ever made. Although Mildred was paid only $37.50 per tune (the same amount Bessie Smith had been paid in 1933) and complained bitterly, these records turned her into a jazz singer. She continued to sing these songs for the rest of her career.

In 1939 I recorded Mildred with a small band she called her Oxford Greys. It was an all-Negro group with Mary Lou Williams on piano and Floyd Smith from Andy Kirk's band on guitar. That was the session during which Mary Lou told me about a young electric-guitar player in Oklahoma City named Charlie Christian. But that's another story. I suppose Mildred chose Oxford Greys because of the band's color; they certainly weren't from Oxford. Again that year I recorded her with Benny Goodman's band just after I had persuaded Benny to leave Victor for Columbia. It was in one of those Goodman sessions that Mildred sang one of the great songs of the decade, "Darn That Dream," written by Jimmy Van Heusen. The song came from a theatrical fiasco which should have been a great hit, *Swinging A Dream*, based upon *Midsummer Night's Dream* and featuring an all-black cast, except for the Benny Goodman Quintet.

I always believed Mildred sounded better with Benny than she did with Red's band, perhaps because Benny was more disciplined and gave her rock-solid support. She loved singing with him and they made several marvelous records together. Then, in the 1940's, her health began to fail. She continued to sing, dauntlessly. Sadly, she seldom sang well and our friendship deteriorated for reasons I was never sure of. Her marriage to Red broke up, and the fact that Red's second marriage was a very happy one did nothing to improve Mildred's spirits. She hated people who tried to help her, yet she needed and asked for help. She complained constantly about being forsaken by her friends and those she had helped—Bing Crosby, for instance. She always said Bing owed his start in show business to her. She persuaded Paul Whiteman to hire The Rhythm Boys, two of whom were Mildred's brother, Al Rinker, and young Harry Crosby. It was, in fact, a measure of Mildred's distress that she should flail about so inaccurately and unfairly. Actually, Bing was one of many old friends who weighed in with tangible help in those hard days.

I believe Mildred was the best white singer I ever worked with. She could convey the very heart of a lyric, and she became a brilliant jazz musician. My final tribute to her was a memorial album I assembled for Columbia in the late 1950's in which I was able to include her finest performance on a variety of defunct labels. I am sad to say that as of this writing the album is out of stock, an inexcusable omission by Columbia, for there is a new generation which has never heard Mildred Bailey sing.

The perhaps inevitable Hammond-Mills clash came over reviews I wrote for *Melody News*. I insisted on writing about groups Irving did not control, and when a Mills record was bad I said so. Ned Williams used to say, "John, nobody does this to Irving."

"If I lose this job, I'll still live," I told Ned, and for four months I survived in the Mills machine. I produced some of my favorite records and made many new friends in jazz. And I was not to leave Mills without another invaluable experience. The Duke Ellington-Irving Mills relationship was unique, and, as a recording director for Mills, I was able to understand its workings as well as anyone could. I was as close to Duke as I would ever be.

I still have affection for Irving, and I think he does for me. He was a man who saved black talent in the 1930's, when there was no one else who cared whether it worked or not. If he was nowhere near perfect, he was far better than most of his competitors on Broadway.

It's impossible to like jazz without liking Duke Ellington. Yet I know I have puzzled or annoyed Duke's many admirers by my criticisms of his bands and his music. The reasons for my reservations about Duke should be discussed, even if they are more revealing of me than of him.

I was first attracted to Duke about 1925, when the band was called Duke Ellington and His Washingtonians and recorded for the Gennett label. The first Ellington record I had was "Black and Tan Fantasy," although it was cut under one of his many pseudonyms: Sonny Greer and His Orchestra, The Washingtonians, The Ten Blackberries, and many more; there was one for each label.

The first year I saw anything of Duke was 1932, by which time he was not only a veteran bandleader but that rare exception among black musicians: a successful bandleader and celebrated composer.

I was present at his recording sessions for Mills and Columbia, although I was in no sense his producer. In matters musical Duke was the boss and no one ever told him how the Ellington band should sound. It was my feeling that the band was a perfect expression of Duke's musical personality, which most Ellington students would agree with. My further opinion that it was not all that a jazz band should be, particularly rhythmically, is not so generally shared. I thought Sonny Greer a melodic drummer, meaning that he played the top of the tune rather than with the drive the band needed. And until the short-lived Jimmy Blanton came along I thought Duke was not well served by his bass players. My favorite Ellington record was "Rockin' in Rhythm," one of the better examples of the band when it really swung.

I did not consider Ellington a first-rate jazz pianist. I considered him a supreme jazz arranger and a great although limited composer. I thought his "Black, Brown and Beige" suite pretentious and not an accurate reflection of his true genius as a composer; I said this in a review of an Ellington concert many years ago and lit a fire among Duke's fans that hasn't quite burned out yet.

My biggest argument with him concerned his failure, certainly his inability, to get people up on a floor to dance. One of the reasons Benny Goodman set such perfect dance tempos was that he could dance so well himself. Since Duke could, too, I wondered why he did not seem to feel that his group was obligated to play well for dancing, aside from simply playing well. Of course, Duke always was a personality, a tremendous stage presence—"superleviathanic," to appropriate a word from his own hyperbolic and amusing vocabulary—and his orchestra performances were an event. While

A young and beautiful Duke Ellington, 1920s. Some of the famous sidemen: Top—Johnny Hodges (alto), Otto Hardwicke (baritone), Barney Bigard and Harry Carney (tenors), c. 1932. Bottom: Duke with trumpeters Artie Whetsol, Cootie Williams, Rex Stewart, c. 1934.

the days of jazz concerts performed for a seated audience had not yet arrived, his writing and playing anticipated those conditions.

In the late 1920's and early 1930's Duke·played almost exclusively for white people at such places as the Kentucky Club on 49th Street, which barred Negro patrons. From there he went to the Cotton Club (142nd Street and Lenox Avenue), and although this was Harlem and the show entirely black, Negro patrons were not welcome here, either. Ellington's was the first large Negro band to make motion pictures and to play as a vaudeville attraction on the Balaban and Katz, RKO, and Loew's circuits. One movie I remember which included Duke was *Check and Double Check*, starring Amos 'n' Andy. Among other things, it introduced "Three Little Words."

Duke had, I felt, an old-line point of view of the Negro's ability to survive in a white commercial world. Understandably, he wanted to safeguard the position he had won for himself in that world at the expense, perhaps, of racial solidarity. Mine was an idealistic point of view, I realize, but because of it I felt more warmly toward some bandleaders than I did toward Ellington. I also knew that the real enemy was not the leaders like Ellington and Noble Sissle, who compromised in order to crack the racial barriers which prevailed. It was rather the segregated society which created all-black and all-white bands in an art form where color should never have been a criterion at all.

I can remember arguing with Duke about my efforts to create mixed bands. His point was: Why help the white bands by filling them with black players, thereby threatening the survival of the Negro bands? I know that Ellington felt that white bandleaders were trying to steal the Negro's music, as well he might have, for not only were his musicians stolen, but also his tunes and even the sound of his band, to the extent that was possible. I disagreed with this. I am aware that there is a school of critics which believes that jazz has exclusively Negro origins. I have never gone along with this. I agree that its Negro origins are probably the most important ingredient in the evolution of jazz, but they are not the only ingredient, and I feel that jazz always has had a duty to promote racial understanding and interracial cooperation.

When I joined Columbia in 1939, Duke's was the only Negro band on the label. I later persuaded Basie to switch from Decca to Columbia, but because of Ellington's understanding with Columbia, Basie's records had to be released on Okeh. When Basie finally moved to Columbia, Ellington left and went to Victor. I never understood the jealousy and resentment Duke seemed to feel toward other black bandleaders. His place was secure, his genius recognized, yet he seemed to feel threatened. I do know that Basie worshipped him.

None of this is to suggest that Duke was not proud of his own people. In his way he fought the battle for equal rights as effectively as any other Negro leader. Duke loved the highest of societies, white or black. He sought the best locations, both because he enjoyed mingling with the cream of any social circle and because the money was better. Ellington and his players were better paid, if not always better treated, than any black orchestra traveling the country in those years.

I felt, however, that he lost contact with his origins, although I certainly understood his desire to succeed in an alien world. As he grew more successful, I missed the beat, the intensity his music had had in the early days. When Lawrence Brown, a most sophisticated trombonist, joined the band and I heard Duke record "Sophisticated Lady" for Victor, I remember thinking that the orchestra was never going to be the same again. But it was part of Duke's personal expression of his music to choose instrumentalists who suited his concept of the song. A sophisticated trombonist playing the solo on "Sophisticated Lady" made sense to him.

My enthusiasm for the Ellington band was always tempered by my love for the soloists in Fletcher Henderson's band. I felt that as far as pure jazz was concerned Fletcher was much closer to the mark than Duke. Duke dominated his people to such a degree that they were not so free and uninhibited as Fletcher's sidemen were. Fletcher was often too phlegmatic for his own good, except that in taking the path of least resistance he let many a fine player be himself. Duke's sidemen played Duke's music most of the time, whereas Fletcher considered himself an arranger rather than a composer of jazz. Ellington's band was built as an expression of the Duke. He had no qualms, for instance, about using two clarinets playing two styles at once: one tootling New Orleans on a B-flat instrument, the other the more common, Goodman-type A, which has both different fingering and a different sound. Duke liked both, so he had both. He sought the *sound* he wanted, not simply a superb jazz player with his own individual style. I suppose I am suspicious of guiding geniuses, although I have been accused of trying to be one myself. Any group of musicians must have discipline; still, I believe the discipline should be self-imposed. Under leadership such as Count Basie's, for instance, the members of the band are led without being aware of it.

I never felt close to Duke as a person, and, indeed, there were few who did. For all the up-front gregariousness—"We love you madly!"—he was a very private person. He also demanded of his friends almost total acceptance of his performance as a leader, pianist, and composer. He was uneasy around critics, even those he knew admired him, and rarely read their comments. As much as possible he avoided anything upsetting.

And part of me says, "Well, why not?" If his success was greater than that of most blacks, his path was no less thorny. As far as my relationship with him was concerned, I can see that there was little, if anything, I could do for him. He didn't need my advice. He didn't want me to find him a better drummer than Sonny Greer. The one time I tried to give him something—a portable phonograph so he could listen to his records aboard ship while en route to Europe—I had the feeling he may have thought the gesture patronizing, though it was made sincerely. So, ultimately, for both of us it was an arm's-length relationship. I like to believe, however, that my criticisms of his band and his music were honest and firmly based.

Duke had a great feeling of loyalty to Irving Mills, who made him into a national figure in music and whose publishing company made him the best-paid ASCAP Negro composer in America. I think Ellington felt it was his business and nobody else's, that he would go along with whatever it took to repay Mills. He also felt that if he were ever in trouble he could always go to Irving Mills and to no one else. It was not until Bill Morris of the William Morris Agency came along to give Duke Ellington a new sense of personal dignity and to back up his advice with superior bookings that Ellington left Mills. I give Bill Morris enormous credit for much of the later growth and success Duke enjoyed.

My opinion of Ellington's place in jazz has not changed. I liked his band better in its early days. I was sorry to see the critics, particularly in England, hailing him as a new Delius and a significant composer of serious music when, in fact, he was a jazz composer, a tribute he certainly should not have been ashamed of. That was my basic difference with Duke Ellington in the early 1930's, and it still is.

I celebrate his accomplishments and especially the recognition he received late in his life. All jazz musicians share in the glory Duke won for his and their music. In his own way, Duke did more than anyone to give jazz and its players the dignity and the serious consideration they deserved. If he was basically suspicious of whites in the white world he lived in most of his life, perhaps he had good reason. Certainly, his accomplishments raised the aspirations and contributed enormously to the self-esteem of his people.

XIV

"You know, John," Benny Goodman said to me one day in early 1934, "there's no future for me as a sideman. I'm going to have to get my own band."

Benny had moved his family from Chicago to New York, where there was work for musicians of his caliber. He played in the saxophone section of Al Goodman's radio band and also found work with Harry Reser's Clicquot Club Eskimos on another radio show. He worked club dates, recording dates, and whatever else there was, but as the Depression deepened work for even the best musicians, meaning those well enough trained to be able to play any music put before them, was drying up. Even Goodman could no longer depend on weekly income sufficient to support himself and to help out his family.

"Fine," I told Benny. "I'll do everything I can to help you find the musicians. I'm at your service. I'll listen to everybody. I'll even go around to Chinese restaurants, anywhere anyone is playing." And one of the first men I found was a wonderful bass player named Hank Wayland in a Chinese restaurant on 58th Street.

Although there was no money, not even the likelihood of steady work, the band began to come together. Benny got Claude Thornhill as his pianist. We both found a good trombone named Jack Lacey. Goodman picked up a trumpet, Sammy Shapiro, who as Sammy Spears later became Jackie Gleason's conductor. The drummer, Sammy Weiss, was stiff but adequate. George Van Eps was the guitar.

As the Goodman band materialized, Prohibition had been repealed, although in New York nothing stronger than 3.2 beer could be bought in restaurants. One New York beer mob had just bought the old Hammerstein theater at Broadway and 53rd Street and renamed it the Billy Rose Music Hall. Around the corner another mob opened another night-club restaurant with two bands, Ben Pollack and Don Redman, plus a naked girl in a fish bowl and better food than Billy Rose served. Benny was going around with Hannah Williams, one of two beautiful singing-dancing showgirl sisters (she later married Jack Dempsey), and because of her and the fact that Benny had worked for Billy in one of his shows, he and Rose were friends. Billy was already famous as a lavish Broadway producer, a dynamic showman whose name was as well-known to the public as Ziegfeld's. A night-club restaurant bearing his name would attract the public. How much backing he received from the beer people I have no idea, but once he became proprietor of his Music Hall he went to Benny. The opportunity was made to order for Goodman. Rose hired songwriter Harold Arlen's brother Jerry to lead a second band to play the show, leaving Benny's band to play for dancing. The job also offered local radio broadcasts over WMCA, as well as a twice-weekly network wire. For a new band the job was ideal.

Unfortunately, the competition around the corner was fierce and Rose decided he could afford to keep only one band, not Goodman. Benny got his notice after about six weeks, but his luck was about to change. Now Willard Alexander entered his life. Although Willard and I were to become lifelong friends, I had nothing to do with his meeting Benny. They found each other.

Willard was a booker for the Music Corporation of America, the largest agent for bands in the country. He had been a bandleader himself at the University of Pennsylvania and had been hired by Billy Goodhart, the New York representative of MCA's big boss in Chicago, Jules C. Stein. From my observation of the business, I could not conceive of a band agent as anything but musically ignorant, out to exploit all musicians, and without the slightest concern for, or ability to guide, their careers. Willard Alexander was and remains the exception to this stereotype, and he became as important in Benny Goodman's early career as anyone.

Willard and another MCA agent, David "Sonny" Werblin, who has since become an important figure in the sports world, first with the New York Jets and then with the New Jersey Meadowlands, had a swinging apartment at the Alrae Hotel on East 64th Street. The MCA band department was the biggest and most effective one around. Werblin handled Eddy Duchin and Guy Lombardo. The Chicago office handled most of the important Midwest bands. For Willard to take on anyone like Benny Goodman was a new experience. Benny's band was certainly not the commercial success MCA usually represented.

At this point, the National Biscuit Company agreed to

sponsor one of the more unusual network radio programs ever broadcast: Let's Dance, a three-hour dance party every Saturday night. Actually, it was a five-hour show, of which three hours were heard, progressively, in each time zone. New York heard the earliest three hours, the West Coast the last three. There were to be three bands: Xavier Cugat for Latin music, Kel Murray for popular dance numbers, and Benny, the last band on the program, for jazz.

Not only was Benny hired for the sponsored network show, he was given a weekly allowance for eight new arrangements at $75 each. He hired Fletcher Henderson, Jimmy Mundy, Edgar Sampson. Some of Fletcher's great numbers, like "Big John Special," he had already recorded. But that would make no difference to the new national audience the band would reach.

The most important result of Benny's being able to hire top arrangers was that for the first time the stranglehold music publishers had on the performance of popular songs was broken. Because publishers were interested only in selling the melody and the lyric of their songs, no band arrangement could take liberties with the melody, as Benny's band did. Fletcher wrote arrangements for Goodman's band which included a first chorus emphasizing the tune, but after that allowed the band to take off with backgrounds for jazz soloists and last choruses in which the Goodman style, rather than the tune, prevailed. Early Goodman masterpieces like "It's Been So Long" and "Sometimes I'm Happy" were made possible by this freedom to play the songs Fletcher's and Benny's way.

Until then Benny had not had a singer of any consequence. At Billy Rose's Music Hall he hired a beautiful girl who was certainly decorative and may have been a friend, but she never sang when the band was on the air. The popular songs he recorded for Irving Mills often included Buddy Clark, a good commercial singer, to sell Mills' lyrics, though not one who fitted the Goodman style. Only when he hired Helen Ward did he have the singer the band's sound required. Helen was largely responsible for the popularity of some of the early Goodman hits.

The liberties Goodman was allowed on Let's Dance were made possible because Cugat and Kel Murray were playing in straight, commercial fashion. By the time Benny came on the air he could play his own way. The Let's Dance series was renewed for a second thirteen weeks, and although Goodman's allowance for arrangements was cut to four a week, it still enabled him to add new charts to his growing library. By the end of the second thirteen Benny had a book no other new band struggling for recognition could have afforded.

The only trouble with Benny's band at the beginning of the Let's Dance broadcasts was that it did not swing. Frankie Froeba, the pianist, was a good technician, but he rushed— that is, his tempos tended to speed up. An even greater problem was the drummer, Sam Weiss. I decided to go to Chicago once again to persuade Gene Krupa to join Benny. Krupa was playing with Buddy Rogers' orchestra, a large, commercial band. I waited for an intermission, then said to Gene, "Listen, Benny's got a band that's really swinging except it needs a drummer. Won't you come to New York?"

"Again, John?" Krupa snapped. "You must be kidding."

"Come on, Gene," I persisted. "He's a marvelous clarinet player, and he's changed. He's not so commercial. Bunny Berigan is in the band. We've got Fletcher Henderson arrangements, and we'll see that you're featured."

At that point Gene had to play for the floor show, during which Buddy Rogers went through his usual act, playing a variety of instruments, each worse than the last. At the next break Gene returned to my table and said, "All right, John. I'll come."

So he did. I had another mission in Chicago. That summer I had heard a record on Columbia's Okeh label by Paul Mares' orchestra, supervised by Helen Oakley. I called Helen to ask who the piano player was.

"He's a guy from Chicago," Helen told me. "He's very strange, very quiet, and his name is Jess Stacy."

I found Jess in a place called The Subway, famous for having the longest bar in Chicago. He was playing the same tasteful jazz I had heard on the Mares record. He was not a flashy soloist, but an excellent rhythm pianist with a steady beat, supportive at all times. I persuaded him to come to New York to replace Froeba. George Van Eps remained on guitar and Harry Goodman, Benny's brother, was the bass player.

Benny had hired Toots Mondello to play first alto saxophone and Hymie Shertzer on third alto. The tenor saxophones were Dick Clark and Arthur Rollini. The trumpet section was Berigan (later replaced by Pee Wee Erwin), Ralph Muzzillo, and Jerry Neary. Joe Harris, who had a fine, Teagarden-like tone, and Red Ballard were the trombones. This was the band that played the early Goodman classics.

Benny continued to record for Irving Mills on the Columbia label until the end of 1934. Irving would pay to have his music played and recorded, and for Benny, staggering under a big payroll, these fees were a way for him to hold the band together. Thereafter, Ted Wallerstein, president of Victor and a Goodman fan, instructed his recording director, Eli Oberstein, to sign him. Meanwhile, I continued to record him when ever I could. While I was still working for Mills I managed to get Benny and Teddy Wilson together in a studio with a small group. The stage was set for the first Victor records by one of the most notable of all chamber-jazz groups, the Benny Goodman Trio.

Finally, for the Let's Dance programs Benny hired George Bassman, the young composer who had written "I'm Getting Sentimental Over You," to arrange Weber's "Invitation to the Dance" as the Goodman theme.

It is difficult some forty years later to remember in detail my role with the first Goodman band, and, of course, much easier to remember the successful contributions than those which did not work out. But the result of my efforts to help Benny form his first band created a bond of friendship and professional trust in each other's judgment. There would never be another year when Benny and I were not important to each other.

Although the summer and fall of 1934 stand out in my memory as a time of great musical accomplishment, the establishment of Benny Goodman's band and its early success, a year in which at least in recording studios the color of the players no longer mattered, and some of the records I am most proud of were produced, I was still never so involved in any one project that another could not tempt me. Joe Losey, my production partner in Henry Hammond, Inc., kept spurring me on to join him again in a Broadway theatrical production. Joe's life was the theater. Part of mine was, too, so when we found a script, it required little persuasion to reactivate our production company and try again.

The script we chose came from an unlikely team of playwrights: Lloyd Lewis, the drama critic of the Chicago *Daily News* and a Civil War historian of renown, and the novelist, Sinclair Lewis. Critic Lewis had written *Myths After Lincoln* and a biography of General William Tecumseh Sherman, but he had never written for the theater. Novelist Lewis was at the peak of a distinguished career. Together they had hit upon the story of a scheming, unscrupulous Civil War politician named Asa Burdette, otherwise known as "Ace" and "Jayhawker." Billed as "a story of American politics," the play was about a repentant sinner, a rascal and a hypocrite, a Senator profiting from bloodshed who is finally overcome by the tragedy of war, who tries unsuccessfully to mend his and his country's ways with the camp-meeting tactics and oratory he used so successfully in seamier days.

Unfortunately, "Jayhawker" Burdette was much more entertaining as a sinner than as a savior and this became the play's undoing. There were also other problems. Although Sinclair Lewis had tried his hand at dramatizing his own books, he had never before written an original play for the theater. Lloyd Lewis, although a very reliable source for material and authenticity, had no experience as a dramatist. Joe Losey, who directed, and I could do little to improve the sagging third act. I used to go to Bronxville, on the fashionable suburban fringe of New York City, to visit Red Lewis, who was then married to the prominent political columnist,

Dorothy Thompson, but to no avail. Lewis was drinking heavily. We could not persuade him to fix his script.

Jayhawker opened at the Cort Theater with Fred Stone in the title role; he was marvelous and universally praised by the critics. The cast also included Walter Kelly and Carol Stone, Fred's youngest daughter. A review in *The Nation* concluded: "If the drama were played backward like *Merrily We Roll Along* it would work up to a smashing climax instead of petering out as it undoubtedly does. *Jayhawker* remains very distinctly a play to see. Its lesson gets across better than most dramatic lessons do."

Jayhawker lasted six weeks. Fortunately I had no investment in it. With its closing the production company of Henry Hammond, Inc., dissolved. Joe Losey went on to become a successful producer of B pictures in Hollywood from about 1937 to the early 1940's. During the infamous blacklisting period he refused to hide behind the Fifth Amendment, nor would he risk being sentenced to jail. Instead, he went to England and began a completely new life.

Although *Little Ol' Boy* and *Jayhawker* were disappointing experiences, especially because each was critically praised, the stage and live performance remained irresistible to me. I was not officially involved with the Goodman band nor fully occupied with recording. I was still moving, still searching for every opportunity which interested me, and two stage failures did not discourage me. I still read *Variety*, saw every show I could, and was as restless as ever.

With Goodman at Victor and Columbia unable to provide funds for recording much of the time, even as interest in jazz grew ever stronger, it was time to search farther afield. I decided to return to Europe.

XV

I returned to England in June of 1935 with some of the best jazz records ever made, my credentials for a new contract with English Columbia for more American recording. My collection included the first four sides by the new Benny Goodman Trio, recorded by Victor and the first jazz chamber music to become popular. The Victor experiment of recording Benny with Teddy Wilson and Gene Krupa was an immediate success, and Victor was to profit not only from the sales of the Goodman band, but from the unexpected popularity of the Trio. It was like having three hit artists in one. Spike Hughes and the English Columbia people, as well as the English jazz critics, were delighted with Benny's Trio records, and there was more to play for them.

I also brought the first Brunswick test pressings of four sides I had recorded with Teddy Wilson and Billie Holiday. When Benny recorded with Wilson on Victor, Teddy was under contract to Brunswick, a situation which always creates a delicate contractual negotiation between record companies. I had no difficulty persuading American Brunswick to allow Teddy to record with Benny for Victor, because the association with Goodman, who was now beginning to sell, could only enhance Teddy's own reputation and sales on Columbia's Brunswick label. But I also wanted the favor returned. I wanted Goodman in the Wilson group for the Billie Holiday recordings, and I also managed that. Such trades are standard procedure in the industry and Benny recorded as a sideman several times during his years with Victor. He often used the pseudonym Shoeless Joe Jackson, although there never was any doubt about who was playing, and his contribution to the Wilson-Holiday sides was enormous.

Billie had made no records since the sides she cut with Benny nearly two years earlier, despite my continuing to write about her as the best singer I had ever heard. The four sides we made just before I left for England are still among her best, in large part because of the brilliance of Teddy's band. Roy Eldridge was on trumpet, Ben Webster on tenor, and John Truehart, who was with Chick Webb, on guitar. John Kirby was on bass and Cozy Cole on drums. Plus, of course, Benny. They played sensationally well and the tunes were right for Billie: "Miss Brown to You," "What A Little Moonlight Can Do," "I Wished on the Moon," and "Sunbonnet Sue" (without Goodman).

It astonishes me, as I look back, at how casually we were able to assemble such all-star groups. It wasn't that we didn't know how great they were. We did. It simply was a Golden Age; America was overflowing with a dozen truly superlative performers on every instrument. And yet business wasn't that good. Compared to the kind of money that's around today, they all came for scale.

By now Benny and Teddy knew each other well and complemented each other's talent marvelously, although they never really got along. Wilson was suspicious of everybody, particularly whites, even though, as I believed when I first met him, he was uniquely qualified to handle the delicate challenge of working with white musicians in public. In 1936 he was the first black man to join an all-white jazz organization. That he handled the role successfully there is no doubt, yet he and Benny were never at ease with each other. At the Chicago telecast of *The World of John Hammond*, filmed in the summer of 1975, Esmé and I were sitting with Teddy waiting for Benny Goodman to arrive. "They're really rolling out the red carpet for Benny," Esmé observed to Teddy. "Yes," he said, "and it ought to be live coals."

I arrived in England also as an active newspaper man. Immediately after leaving Irving Mills' *Melody News* I began writing for *Down Beat*, the first music publication in America to give jazz and Negro musicians full coverage. But even at *Down Beat* I was blue-penciled in areas important to me. I could write about Negro musicians, but not as people who could not get a break because of their race. Nor could I write about the many malpractices I had discovered in the band business while working for Mills. This was a shock. In the old days I could write about abuses without really knowing what they were. Now that I had witnessed at first hand the sort of exploitation musicians had to put up with, I was well equipped to protest yet unable to do so, at least in the pages of *Down Beat*.

But I could and did speak my mind on matters musical. I hailed the breakup of the Dorsey Brothers' band when Tommy announced that he would start his own. "Despite the presence of the magnificent Ray McKinley on drums," I wrote, "the rhythm section has been woefully weak, the arrangements flashy and pretentious, lacking even the rudiments of swing, and the commercialism nothing more than infantile." Of Ray Noble's new American band I wrote: "One of the great disappointments of the winter [1935-36] has been the musical fizzle of the Ray Noble orchestra. Very few of the arrangements, whether they be by the leader, Glenn Miller, or Fred Van Eps, have the slightest distinction, and the general effect of the band is pretty soggy." Of the new Benny Goodman band I reported: "It is a sad commentary on the business that Benny should be able to make his band unrivaled in the short space of six months. The fact of the matter is that Benny's orchestra is the only one daring and astute enough to realize the commercial value of simplicity in music with the result that the group is fast climbing to prominence." In *Down Beat*'s June issue I called the jazz world's attention to Teddy Wilson, prophesying both that he would have a brilliant future and that he might "wind up in some lousy outfit like Cab Calloway's." I said of the latest Ellington records on Brunswick that they had hardly any of the old-time Ellington sincerity and originality. "Even so," I confessed, "I'll buy them all."

In addition to reporting the New York jazz scene for the Chicago-based *Down Beat*, I became a music critic for the Brooklyn *Eagle*, where my friend from WEVD, Bernard Haggin, was my boss. On weekdays I reviewed serious music, mostly chamber music, for the paper. I was a second- or third-string critic, and after attending a concert in Manhattan I typed my review and sent it in from the Western Union office at 1440 Broadway, so I did not have to drive to Brooklyn every night. The *Eagle* was a morning paper and could take my copy until two in the morning. I also wrote a Sunday column in which I could comment on anything new in jazz, a new restaurant I liked, records and musicians I had found, all of this without pay.

The American Newspaper Guild was being formed while I was writing for the *Eagle* and in the spring of 1935 the first Guild convention took place in Atlantic City. A newspaper friend, Sam Shaw, who later became a Hollywood producer, was a delegate and included me as an alternate, so I could be there. I attended illegally because I was not on the *Eagle* payroll, but that didn't stop me. I was a unionist at heart, with or without salary, and I still treasure my Guild card.

Working for the *Eagle* was satisfying in another way. My interest in chamber music continued and I was able to hear every concert in the city. My friendship with Bernard Haggin was renewed, and the day would come when my familiarity with the world of classical music would allow me to bring its artists to the recording studio.

At the conclusion of the Let's Dance broadcasts Benny Goodman and His Orchestra were nationally known. Their first records had been released by Victor and were selling well, but the band was out of work. Sonny Werblin came up with the idea of booking Benny into the Roosevelt Hotel. For the first time in years Guy Lombardo was about to embark on a tour of one-night stands, and as Lombardo's booker Werblin would have a voice in hiring the replacement.

I was in the Roosevelt Grill on opening night. Customers were sitting at their tables in shock. Waiters were moving through the room with their fingers in their ears, even though Benny's brass section was muted and the band was doing its best to provide the brand of dinner music the Roosevelt clientele was used to. Benny's engagement at the Roosevelt ended after two weeks, a disaster which forced Willard Alexander to put together a tour for him. There was no other place in New York where the band could play.

The tour began in Boston with a week at one of Charlie Shribman's dance halls and a few one-nighters in the area. I drove up to see how things were going, and business was not all that bad. But as the band moved into the Middle West business fell off and things became much tougher. I left the band about this time to go to England, so I missed what must have been the low point in the Goodman band's history. When I arrived in England a long, handwritten letter from Benny awaited. He described the band's appearance at Elitch's Gardens in Denver, where they were made to wear funny hats and Benny was forced to do his imitation of Ted Lewis, a vaudeville act he had performed as a boy in Chicago. The engagement was a flop.

Benny's letter went on to describe the night the band reached Los Angeles to play the Palomar Ballroom. Nobody was dancing, he wrote, and a crowd was clustered around the bandstand. Goodman didn't know what to make of it, so he was very careful, waiting to see whether the mob would attack or applaud. Soon there were shouts for "King Porter Stomp," "Down South Camp Meetin' " and all the great arrangements in the Goodman book. So Benny gave them the Henderson arrangements, all the great swinging classics, and suddenly he and the band were a hit. The explanation was clear. This crowd had heard the late hours of the Let's Dance broadcasts, so Benny had fans ready and waiting.

The story of Benny's first triumph on the West Coast has been told many times, but it was as simple as the three-hour difference between New York and Los Angeles. Unfortunately, it was one of the few important nights in Benny's career I missed.

In England my contract with English Columbia was renewed on the strength of the Wilson-Holiday records. I could return to record more American jazz, records by Jimmie Noone, an old-time clarinet whose style influenced Goodman, Meade Lux Lewis, the Gene Krupa Chicagoans, and many other jazz players who deserved to be heard. My friendship with Spike Hughes was renewed, and I visited my sister Alice, still happily married to Arthur Duckworth. I had last seen Alice on her trip to New York the summer before, when we went to hear Benny Goodman at Billy Rose's Music Hall. That was the first time Alice met Benny. In London she continued to entertain friends of mine and to be interested in my various enterprises.

One American visitor Alice entertained was Irving Jacoby, my production partner in *Little Ol' Boy*. Irving was an Orthodox Jew who insisted on going to kosher restaurants and delicatessens when we ate together. Nothing else would do. When Irving visited Alice in London, she made probably the first trip of her life to a kosher butcher to buy chicken to serve Irving for lunch. She served him *creamed* kosher chicken, but Irving politely ate it. He told me later that Alice's creamed chicken changed his life. He never ate kosher again. Even when we don't intend to be, we Hammonds seem to be reformers.

One of the first things I did when I reached England was to apply for a visa to visit the USSR. I put on my application that I was a member of the American Newspaper Guild, hoping that its left-wing reputation would make me pleasing to the Soviets. I was, of course, no more than an illegal delegate to the Guild convention; perhaps the Russians knew. In any event, I was turned down.

My mother and father were also in England at that time, but there was nothing they could do, nor did my knowing such notable correspondents as John Gunther and Walter Duranty help. Weeks went by. I waited. Then I remembered hearing that William L. Patterson, my old friend from the Scottsboro trial days, had gone to Russia to recover from tuberculosis.

I managed to get an address and sent him a wire. The following day I received my visa. Pat was a friend of Paul Robeson's and was considered a friend of the Soviets. Although we did not meet when I got to Russia, he later told me he had assured the Soviet authorities I was to be trusted, that I had helped in the Scottsboro defense, and should be allowed to visit their country.

I traveled by train to Berlin and through Poland to the Soviet border, then flew to Moscow. Air travel, as I was to discover, was primitive. I remember my embarrassment at the border when a female customs-inspector comrade found a pair of silk shorts in my suitcase. She held them up for all to see, laughing and waving them in the air. "They're comfortable" was the best I could manage as an explanation. In Moscow I stayed at the Savoy, about the fourth best hotel in the city, and roomed with a man named Sir Orme Wilson, another visitor, who later became prominent in the British government. The hotel was old-fashioned, the food mediocre, but the caviar was superb, and I love caviar. Of course, I was afflicted by *turista* almost immediately and not particularly comfortable with my accommodations. I found I had a friend in town, however. His name was Jay Leyda, now the curator of film for the Museum of Modern Art. He had heard from Sergei Eisenstein of our evening together when Eisenstein came to the opening of the Public Theater. Jay had been among the American artists invited to Russia to make the film about American Negroes which never got made; he had remained in Moscow and married a girl named Sylvia Chen, whose father was one of the leaders of the Chinese Communist revolutionaries.

Leyda invited me to stay with him. He and his wife were living in a workers' apartment with a communal kitchen on each floor and a couple of communal bathrooms. They had an extra bed, so I did stay with them for a few days, all the while subjected to a torrent of political discussion. But I was not in Moscow to talk politics. I was there to visit the Russian theater and, especially, to see Eisenstein, who was making a movie outside the city. Leyda arranged for me to visit the set every day.

Soviet Russia was in Stalin's grip and a year away from the sensational Moscow treason trials. While pretending to grant various Soviet ethnic groups self-determination, the regime was in fact insisting that Jews and minorities from the Asiatic regions conform to the majority mores of the country, so it was really not self-determination at all. The Soviet Theater Festival, however, was open to tourists and American visitors were being welcomed.

Eisenstein was making a movie of a Turgenev story attacking the Russian kulak, the relatively rich peasant farmer who, by the 1930's, was opposing the Soviet program for collectivizing the land. Turgenev's kulaks were a convenient allegory. The movie set was constructed inside a studio thirty miles from Moscow where a beautiful wheat field, farm implements, and the rural atmosphere of a real farm had been reproduced. While elaborate sets were nothing new for the movies, this was still a very advanced indoor setup for 1935. Eisenstein and his superb cameraman, Eduard Tisse, had already shot a couple of hundred thousand feet of film. Before I left, the government policy toward kulaks was relaxed and every foot of film was ordered scrapped—the old story of art at the mercy of politics.

Our first night together Eisenstein took me to dinner. He chose a Georgian restaurant where the music was played very loud—loud enough, he explained, so that no one could overhear our conversation. We arrived at the restaurant about eight o'clock and left at five the next morning, time enough for him to tell me what it was like for an artist in the Soviet Union. In New York in 1932, Eisenstein had been a Trotskyite; by 1935 he had changed his mind. Although he hated Stalin, he believed that Trotsky's ideas would have resulted in defeat for the Soviets. He was depressed by the state of the arts in Russia, repeating that it would be at least two generations before any real culture would emerge in his country. Architecturally, he felt Russians had been deprived for so long that all they wanted was gingerbread. (Eisenstein spoke some fourteen languages, and he used the English word "gingerbread.") As for music, they did not want experimentation. He was planning to work with Prokofiev on the scores of *Ivan the Terrible* and *Alexander Nevsky,* and it seemed to me that Prokofiev music would overwhelm the dialogue. "Look,

John," he said, "I could think that way, except that I like Prokofiev and I won't keep his music in the background."

While I was in Russia I tried to make a deal for the American Record Company to import Russian records. I went to see the heads of the Gramophone trust, who turned out to be the biggest squares I ever met. They disapproved completely of contemporary Soviet music, and not one piece of Prokofiev, Shostakovich, or even Khachaturian had been recorded in Russia. All they recorded were Rachmaninoff, Tchaikovsky, folk music and songs by the Red Army Chorus. They had no interest in American popular music, and while they expressed some interest in American classical records they had no way to pay for them. Their recording equipment was rudimentary. They were just experimenting with electric recording, a ten-year-old art in the rest of the world by 1935.

The Russians did have an extraordinary experimental theater, however, and were doing Shakespeare in modern dress. Irwin Piscator, one of the truly innovative directors, was active. Stanislavsky, although not very innovative, was represented, and the Russian theater was one branch of the arts up to the standards of the rest of the world.

A car was sent each morning to transport me to Eisenstein's set, and all went well until the day before I was to leave Russia. Eisenstein was ill and filming was suspended. Jay Leyda called to tell me Eisenstein wanted to say good-by, "but he can't get out of bed." Of course, I agreed to go to him. Eisenstein, a bachelor, had a wonderful old live-in nurse to care for him. I felt his brow, which was burning. No diagnosis had been made, but he was obviously very sick. We said good-by for what was to be the last time. Eisenstein died in 1948, still a comparatively young man of fifty.

I decided to leave Russia by plane, not realizing that aviation, like much else in the Soviet Union, was years behind our own. I arrived at what purported to be the Moscow airport at about eight o'clock in the morning, feeling miserable. The terminal was unheated and I was without warm clothes. There was no tea or coffee. A thick fog hung over the airport, almost obliterating an old Curtiss JN-4D Jenny waiting to take us out of Russia. Two other passengers boarded the plane, which had no ventilation, and with the pilot, navigator, and what passed for a stewardess we flew out of Russia with several stops and long delays. The pilot spoke Russian and German, and a Nazi soldier aboard spoke only German. I spoke English and French, so there was no communication of any kind during the worst flight I have ever made. We landed finally in Poland, whence I managed to get to England.

There I boarded the *Homeric*, a ship of the United States Lines of which my brother-in-law, Jack Franklin, was now president. Even so, I traveled in third class, making the voyage with three other passengers in my cabin. Two days out of England I felt sick and went to the ship's doctor who diagnosed my illness as chicken pox. He warned me that unless I avoided the other passengers the entire third class would have to be quarantined. Furthermore, I would have to cover my rash with powder when we arrived at United States Customs and say nothing about my disease. I followed his instructions and no one aboard knew how sick I was.

When the *Homeric* docked in New York, the family chauffeur was waiting to take me home. I was terribly discomfited by such attention and could not understand why anyone would have sent a car to pick me up. When I reached my family's house, however, I found that Leyda had cabled to tell my family that Eisenstein had been found to have a severe case of small pox, and that I had probably been exposed during that good-by visit. I had not been vaccinated for smallpox since I was at Hotchkiss, but apparently the old vaccination helped, because I had a light case and recovered without any scars.

XVI

By 1935 I was ready to join the NAACP board of directors. The organization was changing. It was losing some of its middle-class, middle-of-the-road caution. It was no longer content with small victories and slow progress. It was becoming more aggressive and a champion of all blacks.

I was particularly impressed by the chairman, Louis T. Wright, a neighbor of Fletcher Henderson's on 139th Street, a first fellow of the American College of Surgeons, and, unlike most of the professionals formerly influential in the NAACP, an extremely militant leader. Louis Wright had no worries about labels. He didn't care who called him a Red or a leftist. All he cared about was that there should be real progress in race relations. Needless to say, I found him stimulating and completely compatible with my own understanding of the NAACP's role.

We had a healthy minority on the board which felt as Louis Wright did, a minority which, while applauding the improvements already made, was eager to push for even more rapid and fundamental change. At board meetings I found myself sitting next to Adam Clayton Powell, Sr., the father of the Congressman, Eleanor Roosevelt, who was very active, Herbert Lehman, the ex-governor of New York, and Earl Dickerson, the head of one of the large Negro insurance companies, the richest and most radical member of the board.

The concern of some board members that Communists were infiltrating the organization was not a concern of mine. I felt there was so much work to be done for the betterment of blacks in America that I hated to divert energies to keeping people out of the NAACP because of suspicion that they might be Communists. I was certain that the NAACP position was so much sounder and more convincing to American Negroes than the Communist line that even if Communists were to try to disrupt its work, they—not the NAACP—would lose out. And that is just what happened.

The Communists in the mid-1930's were preaching self-determination, a line which encouraged segregation, rather than the integration of Negroes into American society. They even had a region in the South laid out where there would be a black majority and where a sort of black forty-ninth state would be established. It was a separatist line, one I have always opposed, and a reactionary rather than a progressive solution. It would also keep Negroes in a super-minority status. It seemed a crazy solution to me, but it was the Communist position for many years.

One of the major changes I contributed to was the establishment and distribution of the *NAACP Bulletin,* a monthly tabloid which was the first regular contact the organization had ever had with its national, dollar-a-year membership.

Joining the NAACP board was the beginning of a thirty-year association in which I served actively and proudly, the largest and most influential effort to achieve integration in America. Next to jazz, the NAACP became the means to fight for the social change I sought.

XVII

Although I missed the sudden turn in Benny Goodman's fortunes at the Palomar Ballroom, I was on the scene—recording for English Columbia—when the band opened at Chicago's Congress Hotel in October. The Congress was a good hotel whose reputation had been ruined during the World's Fair of 1933, when a number of guests came down with amoebic dysentery, evidently from faulty plumbing. It was in receivership, though operating under the direction of a charming fellow named Harry Kaufman. The major bands usually played the Trianon and the other ballrooms; Harry decided to try shaking the curse on the Congress by booking Goodman. It was a risk, for neither the band nor the hotel had much standing.

I was curious to see the response to the band after its California success, so I made sure to be at the Congress for the opening. Benny was sensational and there wasn't room enough to hold all the Chicagoans who wanted to hear him. His personnel had changed, for the better. He had a young trumpet, Nate Kazebier, who was marvelous. Allan Reuss had replaced George Van Eps on guitar, and the reed section was much improved.

I stayed at the Congress, recording for Parlophone

days and hearing music nights: Benny, of course, but also Albert Ammons, whose boogie-woogie piano could be heard at the Club DeLisa with a phenomenal sixteen-year-old bass named Israel Crosby, Fletcher Henderson at the Grand Terrace, and anyone else I could find at the big South Side clubs or the little Negro joints, some of which were still flourishing with the first-generation jazzmen who had come to Chicago a decade earlier from all parts of the South.

The Goodman band not only overcame all fears of dysentery at the Congress, it returned the next winter in triumph to open a new room for Harry Kaufman with twice the capacity of the old one.

It was during this second stand that Edwin M. "Squirrel" Ashcraft III, an aficionado, booked the new room for a Sunday afternoon concert sponsored by the Chicago Hot Club. He was so impressed by the Goodman Trio records that he insisted on Teddy's appearance at the Hot Club concert with Benny and Krupa. It was the first public performance of the Trio, an historic occasion, for after that Teddy became a regular member of the Goodman organization.

The credit really goes to Harry Kaufman, who came to Benny after the Trio's special appearance that Sunday afternoon and said, "You've got to keep the Trio in your act as long as you're here." Of course, Benny did, and Teddy Wilson became the first Negro musician to join an all-white band.

Late in 1935 Mother and I decided to combine forces, as we had in the past, to present a recital for our friends in the ballroom of the East 91st Street house. She would invite her friends, I would invite mine, and we would entertain them, although not quite as we once had with piano and violin sonatas. This time there would be an extra added attraction. To the string quartet I added Benny Goodman to play the Mozart Clarinet Quintet, the first time he had played a serious piece before an audience.

The recital took place in the second-floor ballroom, which could seat about two hundred and fifty people. It had an eighteen-foot ceiling with two ornate chandeliers, and there was an adjoining library whose paneled doors could be opened to seat about a hundred additional guests. Mother thought it would be appropriate to open the program with a Handel sonata for viola, featuring her and her son. The string quartet was Artie Bernstein (cello), John Dembeck, an excellent violinist who became the concertmaster of the Toronto Symphony, Ronald Murat (second violin), and I. Benny would join us for the Mozart.

By this time Mother accepted her son's political and social eccentricities with equanimity. She made no attempt to understand them, but she was tolerant and she trusted me to do what I believed was right. She was proud of my accomplishments and charming to my friends. I had no concern about inviting them to the concert. I knew they would be welcome. My own guest list included Fletcher Henderson and his wife Leora, Walter and Gladys White, Charlie Buchanan, the manager of the Savoy Ballroom in Harlem, and his wife Bessie, Mildred Bailey and Red Norvo, and Charlie Barnet. Mother's guests included Mrs. Andrew Carnegie, Miss Alice Van Rensselaer, Aunt Edith Robbins, Cousin Gertrude Whitney, and other members of her circle. Father invited his present and former partners. Benny invited most of the music publishers he knew.

It had been my idea to expand Benny's career to include performances of classical music, and I believe now it was one of the worst ideas I ever had. I had visions of bridging the gulf between classical music and jazz, which I thought could be important to jazz. The combination of Goodman and Mozart seemed a fine idea. Benny was nervous—as was I— but the first movement of the Mozart went quite well, even if we were an amateur quartet and Benny was still using the jazz-clarinet tone he later discarded when he played classical repertoire.

Some of the audience sat on spindly gilt Hammond chairs, the rest on rented folding chairs. At the conclusion of the first movement, Charlie Barnet, a tall man who was feeling a bit cramped, stretched, pushing his feet against the chair in front of him. There was a resounding crash as it collapsed and Mrs. Murray Crane, the head of the newly opened Museum of Modern Art, and a woman of generous proportions, went sprawling to the floor. Mildred Bailey, sitting in the front row next to Leora Henderson, observed the downfall of Mrs. Crane, considered the fragile support under her own couple of hundred pounds, and asked aloud, "How'm I doin'?"

After the concert the audience was invited to a reception on the fifth floor. The front elevator of the house held only half a dozen passengers; I rode up with Fletcher, Benny, and three other guests. Benny, relieved to have the performance over, appointed Fletcher the elevator operator, a common occupation for Negroes in New York department stores in those days. As Fletcher opened the elevator doors at each floor, Goodman would announce, "Fourth floor, men's and boy's clothes. Fifth floor, women's ready-to-wear."

Several years later, when I was profiled in *The New Yorker* by E. J. Kahn, Jr., the 91st Street concert evidently came up in our talks, but like all subjects of Profiles I was not shown Jack's piece until it was published. The story of Mrs. Murray Crane's collapse was included and to my embarrassment she called and was furious. Her dignity, at least, had been bruised.

Certainly, the Mozart performance at our house was a first in many ways. An integrated audience filled the room and it did emphasize the respectability of jazz when Benny Goodman, by then well known even to Mother's guests, played music they considered proper. I believed then, as I still do, that jazz is just as valid an expression as any other, and that American jazz deserved recognition as our greatest cultural contribution. I have come to the conclusion since that, while it is fine for jazz musicians to play classical music and vice versa, it is unwise to make public appearances until each is ready to do so. In 1936 Benny recorded with the Pro Arte String Quartet for Victor, records which did not turn out well. The string players did not treat Benny with the respect he deserved, and in the uncomfortable atmosphere he froze. Later he recorded the Mozart with the Budapest String Quartet, a far better group, but again the performance was not particularly good.

I cannot, however, take all the credit or all the blame for bringing Benny to classical music. He has always had an urge to do more than improvise jazz. I believed he could handle two musical lives independently of each other, but in looking back I think I was unfair to him. It is almost impossible for anybody, much less the most successful bandleader in the country, to handle successfully two completely different approaches to music.

The performance of classical repertoire for the clarinet usually requires the use of the A, rather than the B-flat instrument, not a difficult change since both of them use the Boehm system of fingering, as opposed to the Albert system used by most New Orleans clarinetists. The A clarinet is simply a slightly longer instrument pitched a half-tone lower. But the embouchure of clarinetists who play classical literature is quite different. When Benny became seriously involved with a classical career he began studies with the formidable Reginald Kell and switched to the double embouchure Kell used, although against Kell's advice. This method of holding the clarinet differs from the single embouchure Benny was taught, requiring the mouthpiece to be held between both lips, instead of the upper lip and lower teeth. The change produces a purer sound, without a jazz vibrato, one all symphony players produce. But many believe, as I do, that when Benny adopted the double embouchure his playing suffered. It lacked the attack, the drive, and the wide range of gut sounds which made his original style so exciting.

As a youngster Benny had studied with a very good teacher at Hull House in Chicago, Franz Schepp. He stopped when he was fourteen and had had no time to study in any consistent, academic fashion since. My later doubts about the wisdom of urging him to tackle two careers, not only for his own social and musical satisfaction, but to gain for jazz the respect it deserved and sadly lacked in the 1930's, have been reinforced for opposite reasons more recently. Many contemporary black musicians well trained at Juilliard, the Manhattan School of Music, the Curtis Institute, and such places, have turned to jazz either because it is more lucrative or more glamorous than life as a sideman in a symphony orchestra. But the crossover from jazz to classical or from classical to jazz is rarely successful. I believe it is often from these classically trained musicians who choose to play jazz that the most congenial wedding of the two has come.

There has been a conscious attempt in recent years to eliminate what Duke Ellington used to call the pigeonholing of music. The lessening of differences between country and popular music, between folk, rock, jazz, gospel, and other categories has been welcome, not only because it produces a wider general audience for all music, but because, in the case of Negro jazz players, it has eliminated one form of what they considered segregation. Ellington hated to hear his music called jazz because he believed it labeled him unfairly. But the intellectualizing of jazz in recent years, I think, has hurt it even more. As it has become overly technical, as it has entered the curricula of music schools and been taken very seriously, it has lost much of its freedom, its humor, and its simplicity. Jazz is jazz these days if its composers and players call it jazz, but to compare the playing of, say, Lennie Tristano with Fats Waller, or to enjoy Gunther Schuller's performances as I have enjoyed those of the Basie band raises doubts about how seriously jazz should be taken. A swinging performance is still, for me, the criterion above all others by which jazz should be judged. And no player can be taught to swing.

If the recital at 91st Street was an event whose consequences were not so mutually beneficial to Benny and to jazz as I had hoped, it was still an evening unique for its time, and for the first time, Mrs. Vanderbilt, Mrs. Carnegie, and Mrs. Hammond heard Benny Goodman live.

Benny's return to the Congress took place in the winter of 1935-36. Again I drove to Chicago to hear the band and to continue my recording for the Parlophone label. As things turned out, it was one of the more fruitful trips I ever made anywhere.

Ever since 1928, when I first heard Clarence "Pinetop" Smith's original boogie-woogie piano, I had been fascinated by this eight-to-the-bar left-hand blues style, which had never been recognized by white audiences. And when I heard a record of "Honky Tonk Train Blues" in 1931 I knew I had found the ultimate practitioner in Meade Lux Lewis. But no matter where I looked, or whom I asked, I couldn't find him.

Now, years later in Chicago, I raised the question again while chewing the fat with Albert Ammons. "Meade Lux?" said Albert. "Why, sure. He's working in a car wash around the corner." And so he was! That fall I brought him to New York for a concert and an engagement at Nick's, a Dixieland spot in the Village. Unfortunately, he made only a slight impression and went back to Chicago thinking himself a failure.

Two years after *that*, however, I had the inspiration to bring three fabulous boogie-woogie pianists together for the *From Spirituals to Swing* concert: Meade Lux, Albert Ammons, who proved to be his equal, and Pete Johnson, who played at the Sunset Club in Kansas City, where the marvelous Joe Turner was both bartender and singer, and who proved to be as good as the other two. Their performance at Carnegie Hall created a whole new trend in music culminating in the dreadful song, "Beat Me, Daddy, Eight to the Bar," which made a national fad out of boogie-woogie.

While in Chicago I did a session with Albert Ammons' little six-piece group for American Decca, plus three lovely sessions for Parlophone. One was with Gene Krupa's Chicagoans, which meant Benny, Stacy, Kazebier, Joe Harris on trombone, and young Israel Crosby on bass. The most spectacular side was "Blues of Israel," which began and ended with perfect, economical bass solos by the brilliant Crosby. A second was my only recording with Jimmie Noone, the early New Orleans clarinetist whose style influenced Benny, among others. Finally, I did two sessions with Meade Lux, one for Parlophone and one for RCA Victor.

But my happiest discovery occurred one night about two weeks before the famous Hot Club concert at which the Goodman Trio was introduced. Having heard enough of Benny's music for the evening, I went out to my car, parked across the street from the Congress, not quite decided where to go next. It was cold as only Chicago in January can be, and I turned on the car radio. I had a twelve-tube Motorola with a large speaker, unlike any other car radio in those day. I spent so much time on the road that I wanted a superior instrument to keep me in touch with music around the country. It was one o'clock in the morning. The local stations had gone off the air and the only music I could find was at the top of the dial, 1550 kilocycles, where I picked up W9XBY, an experimental station in Kansas City. The nightly broadcast by the Count Basie band from the Reno Club was just beginning. I couldn't believe my ears.

Two years before, when Coleman Hawkins had left Fletcher Henderson for his celebrated expatriate sojourn in Europe, Smack discussed with me the possibility of bringing in Lester Young as a replacement. He was playing out in the sticks with a small band headed by Bill Basie and probably would welcome a shot at the big time.

I remembered Basie, of course, from that night at Covan's, behind the Lafayette Theater in Harlem, when he was Benny Moten's second pianist. He was a little guy then, weighing about one hundred and twenty pounds, and playing up a storm (as he also did on his first important record as featured soloist, "Prince of Wails"). I had heard Young with King Oliver in 1933, although not enough to form an opinion one way or the other. If Fletcher wanted him that was enough for me.

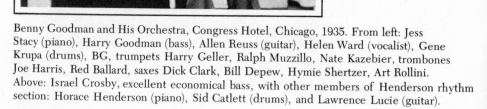

Benny Goodman and His Orchestra, Congress Hotel, Chicago, 1935. From left: Jess
Stacy (piano), Harry Goodman (bass), Allen Reuss (guitar), Helen Ward (vocalist), Gene
Krupa (drums), BG, trumpets Harry Geller, Ralph Muzzillo, Nate Kazebier, trombones
Joe Harris, Red Ballard, saxes Dick Clark, Bill Depew, Hymie Shertzer, Art Rollini.
Above: Israel Crosby, excellent economical bass, with other members of Henderson rhythm
section: Horace Henderson (piano), Sid Catlett (drums), and Lawrence Lucie (guitar).

His band, interestingly enough, didn't agree. They wanted Chu Berry because he had Bean's full-bodied tone, which Lester certainly did not. John Kirby, Buster Bailey, that fine clarinet, and Russell Procope, the tasteful alto who later settled in for a long term with the Duke, they were all groaning about Lester. Fletcher took him on anyway, although it wasn't a happy experience. For one thing, until he found digs of his own Lester stayed with the Hendersons, and Leora made him miserable by constantly playing Hawkins records, evidently hoping that Bean's booming solos would influence Lester's style of playing!

It was not long before Lester returned to Basie.

So, I had known of the Basie band without ever having heard it play. And what I picked up from Kansas City was amazing. Basie had developed an extraordinary economy of style. With fewer notes he was saying all that Waller and Hines could say pianistically, using perfectly timed punctuation—a chord, even a single note—which could inspire a horn player to heights he had never reached before. This inspired economy, the right note at the right place, has always been one of my criteria for fine performance, whether jazz or classical. It accounts for my early interest in Bartok quartets, for my becoming a Stravinsky fanatic, as well as a jazz buff, and perhaps it explains why I have always found excitement in both kinds of music. Somewhere between 1932 and 1936 Basie had discovered how effective simplicity can be.

After that I went to my car every night to listen to Basie. Once I dragged Benny out to listen with me in that cold, cold car. He was less impressed than I'd hoped ("So what's the big deal?"); when I am enthusiastic I often expect my companions to feel what I feel. Just as I could hardly expect Mildred Bailey to pronounce Billie Holiday the greatest jazz singer she had ever heard, I suppose I was asking too much of Benny. There I was in the parking lot of the Congress, telling him that a nine-piece group in Kansas City was the best I had ever heard, while across the street he was enjoying a triumph with one of the smash bands of the country. He made no comment.

I immediately began writing about Basie in *Down Beat*. I talked about the band wherever I went and as soon as possible I went to Kansas City to see for myself. After checking in at the Muehlebach Hotel I walked down to 12th Street to a dingy building with a second floor which must have been a whorehouse, because there were girls lounging on the stairway. On the street level was the Reno Club with signs advertising domestic Scotch for 10¢, imported Scotch for 15¢, and beer 5¢. Hot dogs were 10¢, hamburgers were 15¢, and drinks served at tables were 25¢. There was no cover, no minimum, and there was a show which included chorus girls and the Basie band with Jimmy Rushing and Hattie Noel as vocalists. It was quite a bargain.

The first thing I saw was the high bandstand, at the top of which sat Jo Jones surrounded by his drums. Basie sat at the left with Walter Page and his bass crowded as close to the piano as he could get. In the front line were Lester Young, Buster Smith on alto, and Jack Washington on baritone. Behind them were two trumpets, Oran "Lips" Page and Joe Keys, and the trombone, Dan Minor. Jimmy Rushing, the famous Mr. Five-by-Five, sang the blues, and Hattie Noel, as big as Rushing and dressed in a ridiculous pinafore, was the comedienne and a fairly good singer.

The band played long sets, working almost constantly, and on Saturday nights it played a so-called "spook dance" which lasted from eight in the evening to eight the following morning. I noticed an open window behind the bandstand at which occasional transactions took place; I assumed that "tea" was being passed. And no wonder. Liquor, even at those prices, was too expensive for musicians who were making $15 a week. Basie was paid $18, but he had a day job playing the organ at Station WHB, so he paid Lester, Jo Jones, and Walter Page a little extra each week. It was the announcer at WHB who dubbed Basie "Count" because, as he pointed out, there was an Earl Hines, a King Oliver, a Duke Ellington, and Bill Basie deserved to join the royalty of jazz.

But the band! Jo Jones has always been my favorite drummer. His subtle playing with brushes or sticks, and the effects he got with cymbals, particularly the high-hat, were beautiful. There was extraordinary wit in his playing. His foot on the bass drum never pounded, yet the accents were where they needed to be. And the wide smile he wore showed clearly that he felt the lift he gave the band and enjoyed it thoroughly. (Born Jonathan, I shortened him to Jo—not Joe—so there would be distinction in his name, as well as in his drumming.)

Buster Smith was the best lead alto Basie ever had. It was Buster who taught Charlie Parker, and who led Basie's reed section as no one has since. But Buster was a strange man. He would not leave Kansas City with the band because he was sure it would never make it in the big time! Instead, he remained behind, working in the Midwest and Texas. Even when Basie celebrated his twenty-fifth anniversary as a bandleader, no one could persuade Buster to get on an airplane and lend his alto to the occasion.

Lester Young—not yet known as Prez—and Lips Page were the soloists. Enough has been heard of them since their stand at the Reno Club to need little amplification here. I might say, though, that Lester was already at his absolute zenith. He already had that contained, unemphatic tone and legato phrasing; he was phenomenal. Walter Page, half-brother to Lips, was a seasoned and superb bass. Basie, Rushing, and Young had all been with his Blue Devils several years before. Now he was the man on whom Basie depended most. He wanted Walter as close to the piano as he could place him, well aware that the economical Basie style demanded the support and rhythmic line of a great bass player.

Later that night we ended up on 18th Street, where Lester Young sat in with Clarence Johnson, a fabulous boogie-woogie pianist. This was the era of the Pendergast machine in Kansas City, and the town was wide open and filled with jazz. Rachel Maddox, the short-story writer, lived in Kansas City, and one night while I was there I took her to hear Basie. Rachel wanted to return the favor, so she took me to a club called the Orange Blossom in Kansas City, Kansas, where, she said, there was a wonderful girl pianist, Vassie Mae Mc-

Ghee. Vassie was indeed great, and it was only after we listened for two and a half hours that I realized that Vassie Mae was a female impersonator. Later I asked Pete Johnson about her. "You mean Joe McGhee?" Pete asked. "He's a hell of a piano player." I never could bring myself to look up Vassie Mae again. What would I have done in the mid-thirties with a jazz pianist in drag? But thanks to Rachel Maddox at least I heard one.

What I heard in that first nine-piece Basie band was the sort of free, swinging jazz I have always preferred. Fletcher's band had the same elements; so did Benny Moten's, back in 1932, when Basie played with him. To me this sort of unbuttoned, never-too-disciplined band is the foundation from which inspired jazz solos spring. Not everyone agrees. Even in those days many people were more impressed by the disciplined ranks of Ellington's show band, the vaudevillian backdrop which Cab Calloway's band provided, and the parade-ground precision of Jimmie Lunceford. I first heard Lunceford a week after the Basie appearance with Moten. He was tall, immaculately dressed, waved a long baton, and wowed the Harlem squares. The "Harlem Express," they called him. And, in fairness, he always had excellent players in the band—Sy Oliver, Willie Smith, tenor-playing Joe Thomas—and his music was danceable. ("For Dancers Only" was one of his successful records.) But I thought the rhythm section stiff, the squealing trumpet of "Steve" Stevenson flamboyant, and the band as a whole over-conducted. I had one recording session with Jimmie for Majestic shortly before he died in 1947.

But for me there has never been anything like the early Basie band. It had shortcomings. Its sound was occasionally raw and raucous, but you expected it to erupt and sooner or later it did.

I spread the news of Basie's band to everyone interested in jazz, and I went to Dick Altschuler at the American Record Company to urge him to sign Basie for the Brunswick label. Dick agreed, so back I went to Kansas City to sign the band to its first recording contract. Basie said, "A friend of yours was here to see me, John."

"Who?" I asked. "I didn't send anyone to see you."

"Dave Kapp."

Dave, the brother of Jack Kapp, the head of Decca Records, was no emissary of mine, but I knew why he had come to see Basie. "Let me see what you signed," I said, fearing the worst.

Basie showed me the contract. It called for twenty-four sides a year for three years for $750 each year. To Basie it seemed like a lot of money. To me it was devastating—for both of us. There was no provision for royalties, so that for the period when Basie recorded "One O'Clock Jump," "Jumping at the Woodside," and the rest of those classic hits, he earned nothing from record sales. It was also below the legal minimum scale demanded by the American Federation of Musicians for recording.

Back in New York I called Local 802 to protest these outrageous terms, and did manage to raise the per-side payment to scale, but there was nothing the union would do to break the contract. The loss of Basie to Decca was partially my own fault. I had praised the band in *Down Beat* for months. I had talked about Basie to everybody I knew, and in the music business there are no secrets. Every record executive knew about Basie by the time I went out to sign him. Even Joe Glaser, the head of Associated Booking Corporation, had hurried to Kansas City before me, except that he thought Lips Page was the star and that Basie was no leader; so he signed Page and not Basie.

Glaser's mistake turned out well for Basie. We replaced Lips with Buck Clayton, one of the best—as well as one of the handsomest—trumpet players in jazz. Buck had been playing for Lionel Hampton in Los Angeles, and by accident had burst into a wrong room to the embarrassment of Hampton's wife, Gladys, the real boss of that band. She had fired him. Buck joined Basie and you'll just have to believe me when I say Lips was never missed.

While my enthusiasm for the Basie band did result in the miserable Decca contract, it helped Basie in other ways. One of these was Willard Alexander's immediate interest in the band and his signing Basie to MCA. In fact, Willard deserves as much credit as I for the band's escape from Kansas City to national prominence. Willard accomplished an almost impossible task when he persuaded MCA to represent Basie. Never before had the giant agency taken on such a rough-hewn, still-to-be developed group, or used its prestige with club and theater owners to book an untried band into prime locations. Of course, Willard's persuasive power at MCA had been considerably enhanced by Benny Goodman's success. Now a major attraction, Goodman's earnings were growing, and MCA was getting ten per cent of the gross from location bookings and fifteen per cent from one-nighters. It could afford to take a chance with Basie.

After playing a final Kansas City date, the Basie band boarded a bus for Chicago and the future. It opened first at the Grand Terrace, the home of Earl Hines and Fletcher Henderson, a night club with an elaborate floor show that was a challenge to any band. Although Basie had by then enlarged to the usual dance band complement—four saxophones, five brass, and four rhythm—he had few arrangements. Worse, only about half the band could read music well. Remembering those first nights at the Grand Terrace, I am astonished they were not fired. They struggled through Ed Fox's show arrangements, but the chorus girls loved the band because it was so easy to dance to. Jo Jones, a dancer himself, knew how to play for dancers. Fletcher came to the rescue, allowing Basie to use half his own library of arrangements, one of the generous gestures which endeared Fletcher to so many jazz musicians.

The Grand Terrace engagement lasted long enough for the band to get used to each other and to prepare for the crucial test ahead in New York. After Chicago they played one-nighters, heading east until they reached New London, Connecticut, where they played on the night of a terrible New England storm. Edgar Siskin drove with me to hear the band in a ballroom which normally held about sixteen hundred people. That night there were no more than four hundred.

The band now included Couchy Roberts, a bald, dour man who replaced Buster on first alto, Lester Young and Jack Washington, and an extraordinary tenor saxophone from Texas, Herschel Evans. The trumpets were Carl "Tatti" Smith, Buck Clayton, and Joe Keys. The trombonists were Dan Minor and Rabbit Hunt. Walter, of course, was the bass player, Jo the drummer, and Claude Williams, who played wonderful guitar and an excruciating violin. Claude loved to play his violin, in those days still a rare instrument in jazz played well only by Joe Venuti and Stuff Smith. Basie loved Claude Williams and willingly, if ill-advisedly, put up with his violin.

Storm or not, that night in New London was one to remember. Lester and Herschel, two completely opposite kinds of jazz players, became involved in a battle of saxes. Herschel had the big "Texas sound." Lester's sound was unusually light for the instrument—something like the Frankie Trumbauer, C-melody sax sound. But his inspiration never flagged. He could play sixty choruses, each different from the last, each building from the preceding one. Actually, no one could win a contest against Lester; he could cut anyone in the world. But their contrasting sounds, their alternating choruses, inspired them to play better than either would have without the other. They were totally different personalities, too. Herschel was the banker of the band. He saved his money, and when he made loans to the other players he charged interest. Lester lived in a world of his own, communicating very little with anybody, speaking his own language. He chose to be different and he was. Both men joined Basie in 1936. Herschel died in 1939. Lester left the band in 1940 and died in 1959, a mere fifty years of age.

The New York debut was at the Roseland Ballroom in November. A crowd was on hand, including many jazz critics, to hear what I had been raving about for so many months. One critic, George Simon, whose books on the big-band era are now widely read, could not stand the band. He said it was the most out-of-tune bunch he had ever heard and that Jo

Lionel Hampton in 1937. Benny
Goodman Trio became a Quartet with the
addition of his lively vibraharp.

Jones rushed the tempos. Well! George soon acknowledged this sacrilegious first impression as one of the all-time critical goofs and, of course, has been a Basie fan for years. The band was far from perfect that first night, but it was the swingingest band ever to play for dancers and it could only get better.

While Basie was playing at Roseland, Benny Goodman was playing in the Madhattan Room of the Hotel Pennsylvania, so these two splendid instruments were within a mile of each other.

Benny's band now had a Quartet, as well as a Trio, by the addition of Lionel Hampton and his "vibes"—vibraharp, that is, not vibrations, although he had those, too. I had found Lionel leading an eight-piece group at the Paradise Cafe, on Main Street, a crummy section of downtown Los Angeles. I don't think there was another jazzman in the country at that time playing those metal-keyed, resonating vibes. A few, most notably Red Norvo, used the xylophone; Red didn't switch to vibes for some years. Lionel had gotten his instrument as a present from his wealthy bootlegger uncle, Richard Morgan, Bessie Smith's friend. I took Benny to hear him and he was delighted and signed Lionel on. Since Hamp was also an accomplished drummer, he got an exhilarating splash of sounds on up-tempo numbers. That plus his engaging grin and nervous, almost involuntary "yeah, yeah, ye-ahhhhhs" as he bent over his vibes, cutting in and out of complex rhythmic patterns, made him an exciting performer and a tremendous stimulus to Benny.

That Quartet was a beautiful sight: Teddy, cool, correct, the impeccable piano; Gene, with the chomping jaw, shaking head, and falling lock of hair, crouched over his powerful drums—he had a heavy foot, did Gene, but an urgent, pulsating drive; Benny, with clarinet an inch or two from his mouth so he could smile beatifically at some little four-mallet riff of Lionel's, then answering with one of those perfectly controlled, razor-edged, scintillating Goodman runs. I tell you, those were lovely times!

My own favorite hangout was a small club called the Black Cat, a mob-owned joint on West Broadway, between

3rd and Bleecker Streets. The manager, Sonny, had become a friend of mine, and he served either Chinese or American food for 99¢ with a free daiquiri or martini included. There was a six-piece band at the Black Cat led by Skeets Tolbert and a show which included at least one naked girl, always a welcome added attraction for me. It was the biggest bargain for food, jazz, and entertainment in the city.

The band at the Black Cat included two cousins, the drummer Kenny Clarke and the bass player Frank Clarke, but it was the guitar who interested me most. His name was Freddie Green and I thought he was the greatest I had ever heard. He had unusually long fingers, a steady stroke, and unobtrusively he held the whole rhythm section together. He was the antithesis of the sort of guitar Benny Goodman liked, the stiff, chugging rhythm guitar exemplified by George Van Eps and Allan Reuss. Freddie was closer to the incomparable Eddie Lang than any guitar player I'd ever heard. He was perhaps not the soloist that Lang was, but he had a beat. He was the ultimate ensemble player I had always looked for.

About a week after the Roseland opening I arranged to take Basie, Lester, Walter, Jo, and Buck down to the Black Cat. And because Benny also closed at one o'clock I persuaded him to join us. I wanted Bill's rhythm section to hear Freddie and—always thinking, always thinking—I wanted Benny to hear Lester sitting in and blowing freely in the intimate sort of musical surroundings a small jazz group always offers. I was sitting with Benny as Lester's first notes floated our way. He turned to me and said, "My God, John, that's the most wonderful tone I've ever heard. That's just the way I play tenor"—meaning the sound he'd tried to achieve in the days he played tenor as a sideman with Al Goodman and other studio bands.

It was quite a night. Benny had brought his clarinet, so he sat in. Basie took over at the piano and Jo on drums, but Frank Clarke remained on bass and, of course, Freddie Green continued to play guitar. Goodman played so beautifully that everyone in the room was overwhelmed. Lester had brought along a metal clarinet, an instrument much less expensive and not so tonally rich as the wooden clarinet most players use. Lester did not have much clarinet technique, but he did have the same intimate sound and sense of phrasing he had on the saxophone. After Lester played a while Benny handed Lester his clarinet. "Here," he said, "take mine"— meaning, keep it. Goodman could get as many clarinets as he wanted; still, it was an extraordinary gesture, a tribute to Lester's playing, an indication that if Benny cared he could be very generous.

In the Skeets Tolbert band there was also a spectacular trumpet named Bobby Moore, the kind of player Basie badly needed to compete with such exciting players as Ellington's Rex Stewart. The result of our visit was that Basie hired Moore to replace Tatti Smith and—my prime objective—he hired Freddie Green to replace Claude Williams. Dropping Claude nearly broke Basie's heart, but Green was too great to pass up. Both men joined the Basie band at the end of the Roseland engagement. Bobby Moore lasted for about a year, then blew his top and was hospitalized. Only recently did I learn that he is still playing with a band at the hospital. Harry "Sweets" Edison, one of Basie's finest trumpets, replaced Bobby and, of course, Freddie Green is still with Basie.

Basie's stand at Roseland was a successful and enjoyable one for me. The manager was a tough man named Joe Belford, whose cousin happened to be our family gardener in Mount Kisco. As soon as Joe found that out I was always a welcome guest. I always felt uncomfortable at Roseland because, like every other customer, I was expected to buy a roll of ten-cent tickets and dance with the hostesses. I didn't dance and was never very popular with the girls, whose income depended on the number of tickets they collected. With Joe Belford's blessing I was passed up the back stairs and never bought a dance ticket again. Roseland was also fairly generous with time, allowing something more than the usual dance hall's ninety seconds before a rim shot from the drummer signaled the next dance. Although Basie could not stretch out the way he wanted to, he could at least play a complete arrangement.

Basie shared my feelings about Roseland. It was then a segregated dance hall. No black patrons were admitted. Even Puerto Ricans were discouraged. But it was Basie's first successful booking and he was allowed to play late dances at the Savoy Ballroom in Harlem, so that Negroes danced to Basie in New York as soon as whites did.

From the Roseland Basie went to the Apollo, a crucial test because untried bands were made or broken by Apollo audiences. For a Negro band making it at the Apollo guaranteed acceptance by blacks everywhere. The Apollo was also important to me. It was owned by Leo Brecher, who also owned the Lafayette, Olympia, Plaza, and Little Carnegie theaters, and whose daughter Vivian was my favorite girl, one of the nicest I've ever met. Lena Horne's uncle was the assistant manager, and the man who handled the lights had been our chief electrician at the Public Theater in 1932. The Apollo was family territory to me and I had enough influence to get a place in the stage show for any act that particularly interested me.

Although Basie was no big name when he opened at the Apollo, Willard Alexander insisted on and got good money for him. Willard also persuaded the Apollo to spend extra money to promote Basie's debut. Nobody in Harlem will ever forget the opening. Basie passed the test. He was on his way. Nothing could stop him—or so we thought.

Bill had come into my life in the parking lot opposite the Congress Hotel in Chicago just a year before his New York triumphs. He'd traveled a far piece since then. I was thinking of Benny's less-than-enthusiastic response to the band when I visited him and his current girl friend, Phoebe Terbell, in her apartment in Westwood, California, a year later. I had brought the new Decca record of Basie's "One O'Clock Jump" to play for Benny.

Phoebe had an early Capehart, a very expensive phonograph which played both sides of a record automatically, often breaking it in the process of turning it over. I put the Basie on the Capehart, adjusting the machine so that it would repeat the side rather than turn it over. Benny listened. And

Superb Basie band in 1940.
Trumpets (l to r): Buck
Clayton, Ed Lewis (hidden), Al
Killian, Harry "Sweets"
Edison. Trombones: Vic
Dickenson, Dickie Wells, Dan
Minor. Saxes: Buddy Tate, Tab
Smith, Jack Washington,
Lester Young. Rhythm: Walter
Page, Jo Jones, Freddie Green
(behind Tate). Left: Prettified
publicity shot of Basie, 1944.

listened. He let the record play over and over, absolutely knocked out by "One O'Clock Jump." He was finally persuaded that Basie was a big deal, indeed.

XIX

With the combination of courage, inspiration, and effrontery only an agent can muster when he believes in a band, Willard booked Basie into the William Penn Hotel in Pittsburgh. The William Penn was a landmark, a sedate establishment known for its old-fashioned luxury. It had never had a Negro patron or a Negro band in residence. It did, however, have a network-radio wire, which made it a very important location for orchestras, particularly for one like Basie's which needed both the national exposure network broadcasts provided and the distinction of appearing at the best hotel in Pittsburgh.

I went to Basie's opening to see what would happen. Bill did his best to accommodate the William Penn customers, muting the brass, keeping the guys on their best behavior, but the band couldn't help swinging. It was a replay of Benny's opening at the Roosevelt—a disaster. I was sitting with Harold Cohen, the correspondent for *Variety* and a fine theater critic. He just shook his head. "John, this is never going to go in Pittsburgh."

The band managed to survive the first week, however, without either winning the approval of the William Penn patrons or being fired. Couchy Roberts, the grumpy alto, was replaced by a handsome young man named Earl Warren, from Springfield, Ohio, another of Willard's missionary accomplishments, and it began to look as if the band might complete its two-week stand without incident. I returned to New York, where I had just accepted a job with the William Esty Advertising Agency as music consultant for Benny Goodman's new radio show, The Camel Caravan. Then the roof fell in. One night, after finishing the stint at the William Penn, a key member of the band had created a violent scene in a night club. The police had been called. The musician had been arrested and on the way to the station he evidently had knocked out two policemen. He was being held in a strait jacket at the Mayview Asylum for the Criminally Insane. No one could even speak to him. All this I learned four days after the event.

I took an immediate leave of absence from the Esty Agency to drive to Pittsburgh. If our fellow remained in Mayview he would be lost to music forever. Moreover, the publicity could hurt the Basie band's chances to make it in other William Penns, the kind of location a band must play if it is to receive the top money Basie deserved. Fortunately, I had a friend, a psychiatrist named Dr. Arthur Clinco, on the staff of the Neurological Institute of New York. Clinco was a musician himself and would be well acquainted with the kind of stress musicians were subject to. Before leaving for Pittsburgh I asked him if it would be possible for the Institute to admit our man to one of its semiprivate floors, where the rate would not be too exorbitant and where he would receive the treatment and observation he needed.

Negro patients had never been admitted to Neurological, but Clinco discussed the problem with his superior, Dr. Earl Cheshire, and they decided that it was as good a time as any to begin. They told me that if I could get him out of Mayview I could move him to the Institute immediately.

In Pittsburgh I checked first with the members of the band. The idea that their friend might be insane had frightened them all so much that they would not even discuss the situation with me. I was also told that it would be impossible for me to see him. He had been in a violent ward for a week. The news was alarming, but I had resolved to do something and I was not to be put off, no matter how hopeless things seemed.

I found that a social worker had been put in charge of the case and made an appointment to see her. I was certain she would already have pegged the patient as some kind of degenerate and me as a typical Broadway agent who understood none of her problems. I went to her office carrying a copy of the *Survey Graphic*, a magazine I knew to be the social worker's bible, and the latest issue of the *New Republic*, an indication, I hoped, that I was not just another show-business type.

Actually, I found on meeting her that she was a nice woman, reasonable and sympathetic. I decided to try a frontal attack. "I suppose you think that because X is a musician he's syphilitic and a drug addict," I began.

She drew herself up, frigid and defensive. "I want you to know, Mr. Hammond, that I am on the board of the Urban League of Pittsburgh. Many of my closest friends are Negroes. I have none of the prejudices about black musicians you might expect to find here."

I seemed to have come to the right person. She got out the case record and we read it together. X had indeed knocked out two attendants in the patrol wagon. He is not a large man, but he is powerful. I could imagine what he must have been like that night. The hospital records indicated that he did, indeed, have syphilis and that he was in a very disturbed state of mind. Because he was not a native Pennsylvanian, the chief psychiatrist at Mayview had called his mother and his wife, so he could be transferred to an asylum in his home state. Mother and wife had hurried to Pittsburgh, something even the band members did not know, and from the social worker I learned the hotel where they were staying. I also asked if it would be possible for me to visit X.

"That's completely against regulations," she told me. "For what purpose?"

I explained that I had made a reservation for him at the Neurological Institute in New York.

She was flabbergasted. "They don't take Negroes."

"Yes, they do," I assured her, showing her the written slip from Dr. Clinco authorizing me to present his acceptance to the Mayview psychiatrist and saying that there was a room ready for X at the Institute.

"In that case, of course," the social worker said. "I'll let you go, but you're going to have a hard time making those doctors believe you."

Next I went to see the wife and mother. His mother was almost hysterical. What had her erring son done to cause

God to wreak such vengeance, to put him in an insane asylum? The wife was calm though puzzled by what she had heard. She was six months pregnant and frightened. We had a long talk and decided to go together to Mayview. We would not take his mother with us because she was too distraught to help the situation. We drove some thirty miles outside Pittsburgh to the asylum and went in search of the doctor in charge.

The doctor, whose name I have forgotten, brought out his charts, confirming that X had a secondary stage of syphilis, that he had been smoking marijuana when he was arrested, and that he was indeed in a strait jacket in the violent ward. I could visit him, the doctor said, at my own risk. I told the doctor X was going to the Neurological Institute. He just could not believe it. "You go see him first," he said. "Then decide whether you want to take him there. You might as well face it, Mr. Hammond, this man is hopeless. There's nothing that can be done for him."

I explained that there was a psychiatrist at Neurological who was a musician. "He understands musicians' neuroses," I said, "and with that kind of help maybe our friend can return to music." I had an awful lot of faith, perhaps from my Christian Science days. I just knew X would be all right.

The doctor wrote out a slip to allow us to visit the ward. The wife was waiting for me. She had not seen her husband either, and I realized that it would be very important when we did see him that the meeting be casual, as if nothing had happened. She agreed. We waited together until he strolled in wearing pajamas, apparently as normal as any man. We discussed what had happened. He told us some of his experiences at Mayview, adding that he didn't think anyone was ever going to come. I tried to reassure both of them that arrangements had been made to take him to New York, that he would be treated, that everything would be fine. Neither of them believed me.

I went back to the doctor in charge to tell him X seemed normal to me. I wanted to take him with me to New York that evening or the next day.

"I can't let you drive him back alone," he said. "If you go over a bridge he might try to grab the wheel. Your life wouldn't be safe. I'll have to insist that a third person go along. If you can find someone responsible, a resident of Pittsburgh, to drive with you, I'll permit it." Even so, he reminded me, it was a most irregular procedure.

I went to the secretary of the Negro musicians' union in Pittsburgh, a powerful man willing to go along with me to New York if I paid his fare back. The next morning the three of us began the eight-hour trip. It was March and the roads were icy. There was no Pennsylvania Turnpike in those days, but we had a delightful journey. Before going to Neurological, we stopped at my apartment on Sullivan Street, where X played the piano, the first I knew he could play the piano at all. He played the blues, the simplest way to express his feelings.

We arrived at the Institute about eight o'clock that night. A room was ready and the doctors were waiting. For the next two weeks he underwent therapy. By the third week he was back playing with the Basie band on the stage at the Apollo Theater. During his recovery I had many long talks with Dr. Clinco to find out the psychological reasons for his aberration. He told me that in his opinion marijuana by itself was not a dangerous drug. "However," he said, "marijuana in conjunction with venereal disease is an absolutely shattering blow to the nervous system. The use of any stimulant at such a time can cause immediate and sometimes irreparable damage."

Dr. Clinco did not consider X an addict; when he reached New York for the opening at Roseland he had an occupational rash musicians often get from sitting for hours. He was convinced he had syphilis and moreover, that he had given it to his wife during her pregnancy. He had terrible feelings of guilt, heightened because the rash grew steadily worse while the band was in New York. Clinco told me that as far as he could find out, X had not had intercourse in New York, but that after he reached Pittsburgh he was so worried he began smoking marijuana and tearing up the town. The record, Clinco found, did indicate that X had had syphilis long ago and that it had only partially been cured. That was long before penicillin, of course, and the still-virulent disease had had such an effect on his nervous system that his whole mental process was deranged.

Dr. Clinco recommended that a close watch be kept for a while, and that the entire band have physical examinations immediately and at regular intervals for the next two or three years to prevent any recurrence of such a crisis. He impressed me with what was not generally recognized in the medical profession at that time: that although marijuana is not the addictive drug others are, it can be equally dangerous at such times; that venereal disease in combination with any narcotic is very dangerous; that alcohol is not nearly so damaging under similar conditions.

Clinco gathered that other members of the band were infected, and, as it turned out, three of them were. All were cured. We even found one or two members of the band with hernias that needed treatment, and we all learned a valuable lesson from this experience.

XX

By the winter of 1936-37 Benny Goodman had become so popular that he was offered his own radio network show sponsored by Camel cigarettes. The William Esty advertising agency had the Camel account, and its target was the college market, the most enthusiastic Goodman fans. The Camel Caravan was created as a weekly half-hour show and through Benny I was hired as a writer and consultant at the Esty Agency. Although I was not particularly fond of Bill Esty and his accommodation to the North Carolina prejudices of his sponsor, I accepted the job because it would help assure Benny a better show. It would in any case be a temporary assignment, lasting only for the duration of the twenty-six-week contract, and it did not require all my time.

As a device for promoting Camels on campus, Esty

sponsored a talent hunt for promising musicians or singers, the winners to appear with the Goodman band on the show. It became part of my job to travel to various colleges to look for young talent, preferably in the popular field, and to offer a network appearance to the best of those I found.

One of my worst experiences happened at Wesleyan College in Middletown, Connecticut. Here the most likely possibility was a protégé of Joseph Daltry, a leading expert on seventeenth-century music. I spent an evening with the Daltrys and their young singer to find out more about him, for he had a fine voice with an unusual range. Along the way I asked where he had gone to school. "Don't tell him," Mrs. Daltry said. I kept at him until he finally told me he had gone to Lincoln University, in Pennsylvania. "My father is a minister in Oxford, Pennsylvania," he told me.

Now I knew why Mrs. Daltry had tried to keep his secret. Lincoln was an all-black university and this young man was white. "That's fascinating," I told him. "I know the Lincoln campus well. Did they allow you to sing in their choir?"

"Of course not," he answered. "My white voice would have loused up the choir's sound."

I brought the young singer to New York to be the guest on the Goodman program. For his first number he chose an innocuous semiclassical song, but then he wanted to do a Schumann piece with his own piano accompanist. The Esty agency objected strongly. It tried to cut the Schumann to fifty-eight seconds. I would accept only a full performance. That incident paved the way for my parting with the Esty Agency. Perhaps, as I told Ned Williams when I would not compromise with Irving Mills, the fact that I could get along without any of these jobs made standing up for principle easier than it would have been for others in that time of economic distress. Financial independence does bolster one's integrity. There were times in my career when I *did* need my employer's money and was compelled to record artists whose music I could not stand, or otherwise make the small compromises most of us must. But I was born with my mother's will to obey one's conscience, and I don't believe either of us ever sold out our principles. I could not change the Esty Agency. I would not change myself.

My writing on jazz continued in *Down Beat* and occasionally in other publications. Yet as I learned more about everyday abuses and the shocking exploitation of recording artists, I became increasingly frustrated at being prevented from writing about these aspects of the music business. The experience with the Basie Decca contract was one example of what I knew to be happening at the three major record companies, but no music magazine wanted to expose the facts as I knew them. In the spring of 1937 Eric Bernay of *New Masses* offered me the opportunity. "We can't pay you, John," he said, "but you can say whatever you want." This proved to be not quite true, but true enough to give me the medium for a series of articles I wanted to write. I accepted and began my series with Decca.

Under the pseudonym of Henry Johnson I wrote a piece on the business practices of the Decca executives. I disclosed the underscale contract Basie had signed. I told how Jack Kapp, president of the American Decca company, then wholly owned by English Decca, had a company called State Street Publishing which bought up copyrights for a flat rate. I revealed how Kapp had acquired "Pinetop's Boogie Woogie" and copyrighted the words "boogie-woogie" so that any song title using them would have to pay a royalty.

When the article appeared, Jack Kapp was furious. In the presence of Milton Diamond, his attorney, he said that Decca was going to sue me for $100,000 for defamation of character and other charges. But I had come prepared. I had a copy of the Basie contract. I had documentary evidence from Columbia's licensing agreements with State Street Publishing. I said, "Jack, you have a lot to answer for, and your suit will never stand up in court."

As it happened, E. R. Lewis, the head of English Decca, was next door and heard the rumpus. He came in to ask what the trouble was about. I explained to Ted Lewis my charges and Kapp's threat. Lewis turned to Kapp, "Jack, if you want to sue on your own, it's perfectly all right with me, but I will not permit Decca Records to be a party to the action."

That was the end of that.

I then discussed the practices of RCA Victor, and finally those of American Record, parent company of the Columbia label.

While I intended to be fair, to spare none of the three major companies (and in the 1930's RCA Victor, Columbia, and Decca were the only record companies of any significance), my principal target was American and I was especially prepared for what I had to say about it.

I had been serving as chairman of the Trade Union Service, a position in which I met many unionists. In early 1937 the United Electrical and Radio Workers' Union was attempting to organize the Columbia factory, along with the General Electric and Singer plants, at Bridgeport, Connecticut. Through TUS, I came to know Julius Emspak and James Mattles, who were the president and secretary of the UE. They told me the conditions which prevailed in American Record's factory. The average worker was being paid $16 a week and there had been fourteen violations of the State sanitary code reported within the past month. The TUS operated the People's Press, publishers of a number of trade-union papers, among them the *U. E. News*, the official publication of the union. I had access, of course, to the information in this publication, as well as to the union leaders who had accumulated it.

I also had many friends at the American Record Company. From Herb Allen, the company secretary, I learned horrifying stories of factory conditions in Bridgeport. My old friend Herb Goldfarb gave me information on the state of manufacturing there, and I knew at first hand that something was wrong. Many of the records I had produced for the company were of very poor quality technically, a frustrating discovery for any record man who knows how the music sounded in the studio.

The president of American Record was Herbert Yates.

The company was a subsidiary of Consolidated Film Industries, of Hollywood, a holding company which also owned Republic Pictures. Yates hated unions, so much so that when the AFL attempted to organize the Scranton factory he was using to press records he closed it. With the assurance of Jasper McLevy, the socialist mayor of Bridgeport, that the Columbia factory would never be unionized, Yates bought Columbia. His fear of unions was so intense that when "that man" Roosevelt was re-elected as a pro-labor president in 1936, Yates was said to have locked himself in his office for an entire day.

The Columbia factory was the hottest and dirtiest place I had ever seen, although from the outside it looked impressive. On a tour of the plant I found the pressing room unequipped with air conditioning, which other plants of its size were then installing, and so hot it was barely possible to breathe. The mill where the compound was mixed for the laminated records was antiquated. There were about fifty ten-inch presses and ten twelve-inch presses in the plant, and the mess was unbelievable. Soot covered the floor. It was obvious that the plating facilities were outdated, and equally obvious why the pressed records sounded so much worse than the masters made in the studios.

My article on these conditions brought an immediate response. Dick Altschuler, president of the Brunswick-Columbia division called. "Are you writing under the name of Henry Johnson?"

I confessed that I was, although by that time I was not proud of having used a pseudonym.

"Somebody just showed me the piece you wrote in the *New Masses*," Dick said, "and it's a pack of lies."

"No, it isn't, Dick. I know what I'm talking about."

"John," Altschuler said, "I'm going to offer you a sporting proposition. Are you free tomorrow?"

I said I was.

"Meet me at Grand Central," he said. "We'll take the club car to Bridgeport. I want to take you through the factory myself."

I agreed. I welcomed the guided tour.

"I want to warn you," Altschuler added, "you're going to meet Roy Marquard. He used to run the Scranton factory before Yates leased it, and he's an honest man. You can bring up all your points and we'll ask Roy what's true and what's not. And if any of your accusations are untrue, I'm sure you'll retract them."

I promised I would, so Dick and I met and rode the New Haven railroad club car to Bridgeport. I discovered that he was only three years older than I, and I liked him very much. I was also beginning to feel uneasy about my article. My facts had come from reliable sources, including the UE shop steward. Still, I might have been carried away. Columbia had always been my favorite record company. I expected more from it than I did from the others and might have been unfairly critical. But when we met Roy Marquard at the plant, nine of the ten points I had made were completely correct. As for the tenth: There had been fifteen violations of the sanitary code, not fourteen. My information on salaries was true.

"How did you get all this information?" Marquard asked me.

"That's my secret," I told him.

As a result of the article, our visit, and the integrity of Altschuler and Marquard, the plant was cleaned up, and the American Record Company recognized the UE by signing the first CIO closed-shop contract in the state of Connecticut. The power of protest in the press had not diminished.

Soon after our factory visit Dick Altschuler and I got to talking about music. "You seem to know a lot about classical music," he said. "Are you a musician?"

Yes, but an amateur.

"I want to develop the Columbia classical catalog," Dick went on, "but we're not in any stores. We only have two or three per cent of the business."

How well I knew. The American Record Company's English affiliate was Electrical Music Industries, a prime source of excellent classical material but none of it could be found in American record shops. "You're not even in Macy's or Liberty's," I said, "the two largest classical record dealers in New York."

The classical department was then being run by a man who was little more than an office boy, and salesmen were making no effort to compete with RCA Victor for classical-record sales. "I'm going to make you an offer," Dick said. "How would you like the job of sales manager of our classical department?"

I was overwhelmed. "You're putting a lot of faith in me," I said. "I've never been a salesman before. But if you mean it, I accept."

I bought myself a sample case, filled it with the best of the Columbia line, and tackled my first account, Macy's. I called on the record buyer, Bob Jordan, and in my usual way of making friends, discovered that he was married to the daughter of the much-admired Judge Learned Hand. We hit it off immediately. Macy's put in an order for the entire Columbia classical catalog. I then went to the Liberty Music Shop, where the buyer said, "Sure, we'll put in Columbia Masterworks. Nobody's ever been around to ask before." Flushed with such successes, I traveled next to Woodward and Lothrop in Washington, D.C., and to H. Royer Smith in Philadelphia, stores where I had bought records myself. I returned to New York with a fistful of orders. Also, taking advantage of my new job and Altschuler's faith in me, I recorded Joseph Szigeti playing a newly discovered Mozart Divertimento, all this in the space of three weeks.

I arrived back at the office I shared with the fellow who had been handling the catalog to find him reading a letter I had left in my typewriter. That infuriated me. Next, my secretary, Rose Rivkin, burst into the office in tears. "I've been fired," she cried.

"Why? What for?"

"The salaries are so low around here," she told me between sobs, "that I was trying to organize a chapter of the United Office and Professional Workers, so they fired me."

"They can't do that," I said. "I'm your boss. They have to come to me."

I went to Dick Altschuler to protest. "John," he said, "you can't fight it and neither can I. Yates is not going to allow this office to be unionized."

That ended my brief tenure as sales manager of Columbia Masterworks. I could not last under that sort of management. I was and am a union man, and Herbert Yates was not. Unfortunately, he ran the company. The only thing I got out of my three weeks as a full-time employee was a Social Security card.

XXI

By 1937 the phenomenal success of the Benny Goodman band, both financially and artistically, was the talk of the music industry. The new Basie band was not far behind and steadily increasing in popularity, a fact perhaps even more satisfying to me. Nothing I had accomplished in jazz meant more than the success of these two bands. Now, however, there seemed little more I could do for either one. My devotion puzzled even Benny and Basie, I suppose, and was certainly a cause of misunderstanding and, occasionally, unwarranted suspicion among music professionals. Most believed I had a financial stake in either Benny's or Basie's success, and they simply wrote me off as a rich dilettante, an amateur indulging his enthusiasm, protected from the responsibilities and the necessary compromises full-time employment in the music business imposes on its professionals. The charge was understandable, but not true. I wanted very much to make my career in records and was determined, as far as possible, to achieve my goal through music I liked. If, as was the case with Goodman and Basie, that music also made money for the company the satisfaction was even greater. But the freedom to search for new talent, to participate in bringing it deserved recognition, to help erase discrimination in the increasing financial rewards for great artists in jazz, were essential to any professional position I might be qualified to accept. In 1937 such an opportunity simply did not exist in the three major

Goodman band—in Hollywood for a film appearance—at height of
1936-37 popularity. Rear (from l): Harry, Stacy, Krupa, Benny, Pee
Wee Erwin, Reuss. Middle: Irv Goodman (trumpet), Murray
McEachern (trombone), Ballard, Chris Griffin (trumpet).
Front: Clark, Shertzer, Depew, Rollini. Bunny Berigan had come
and gone. Ziggy Elman and Harry James were about to arrive.

record companies. I could afford to wait, and fortunately both Goodman and Basie still welcomed my help.

The Basie band, after it left the William Penn, had set off on a tour of one-night stands, each date more successful than the last as word spread and the band became better known. Only one small incident occurred to diminish the welcome it got wherever it played. When the band arrived in either Hopkinsville or Owensboro, Kentucky—can't remember which—members of the band noticed that Earl Warren, the handsome new lead alto, was jittery. The reason soon became clear when a deputy sheriff arrived at the dance hall to order him out of town for sitting in with a "nigger band." It seems that light-skinned Earl had led an all-white group there four months earlier and was assumed to be white himself!

Basie's Decca records were being released, and "Jumping at the Woodside" was an early hit across the country. Another was "Pennies from Heaven" with an unlikely vocal by Jimmy Rushing, who was more at home shouting blues. Basie needed a girl singer, however, and for his summer tour he signed on Billie Holiday, by then a recording star in her own right. It was during Billie's stint that Basie played the Ritz-Carlton in Boston, one of Willard Alexander's notable bookings. Willard and Benny Goodman persuaded the Ritz-Carlton's owner, Ed Winer, that the Basie band would be a success, as indeed it was.

I drove to Boston for the occasion. Even in summer students from Harvard and Boston University were flocking to hear the band. Both Basie and Billie had rooms at the hotel, and all in all it was a triumph. But Billie was unhappy. When I joined her at a place called Mother's Lunch she was complaining bitterly. She said she was making $75 a week; I think it probably was a bit more. Still, touring Southern towns in buses without air conditioning, relegated to the poor hotels that would take blacks, and leading the generally rough life of a band on the road were too much for her. She left after the Boston stand to join Artie Shaw, with whom, unfortunately, she encountered racial discrimination even more insulting. Artie personally had nothing but contempt for the pious cruelties of segregation and fought them where he could. But he led a white band that played for whites in white playgrounds and he couldn't call the shots. Billie was not even allowed to sit on the bandstand (although, of course, Helen Forrest, the white singer, could). She had to make her entrances from the wings. And when Shaw appeared at the inappropriately named Lincoln Hotel in New York, Billie was obliged to use the freight elevator.

Meanwhile, Basie was again without a female vocalist. Little Jimmy Rushing, a proud man whom Basie loved, saw no reason to share the bandstand with another singer and removed himself from the situation. Basie was most uncomfortable. To succeed as a commercial attraction he had to have a girl singing the ballads that just weren't Jimmy's forte.

I thought I could help. I had heard a girl singing with Vernon Andreade's band at the Renaissance Ballroom in Harlem who was one of the best I'd heard in years. I also had "Do What You Did Last Night," an old Okeh she had recorded at age fifteen—hardly more than a child but already a fine jazz singer. She would be perfect for Basie. How to get her into the band without offending Jimmy Rushing was the problem. I thought I saw a way to work it.

The Apollo sponsored an amateur contest for young singers as a regular part of its stage show. The winner was awarded a week's engagement with whatever band was playing. Because of my own friendship with the Apollo's owner—Vivian was still my girl—I arranged for Helen Humes to enter the amateur contest held while Basie was appearing at the theater. I had no doubt that Helen would win, and winning would bring her to the band without Basie's having to hire her. It seemed a perfect solution to me and Basie agreed.

The record hit of the country that summer was "A-Tisket, A-Tasket," sung by Ella Fitzgerald with Chick Webb's band. From coast to coast young girls were copying Ella, sometimes note for note. As luck would have it, one of these Fitzgerald copycats entered the contest with Helen and won. Helen came in second. By the second week the time for artifice had passed. Helen joined the band with Jimmy Rushing's blessing and stayed for the next five years. She was the perfect complement to Rushing, and she and Jimmy became lifelong friends.

Helen Humes made few records with Basie while he recorded for Decca. In 1939, however, when I brought him to Columbia, I saw to it that she sang at every Basie session. I even began recording her *before* she joined Basie—in 1936, when I gathered a band for Harry James. James, then playing with Benny Goodman, of course, already had dreams of leading his own band. It was also perfectly legal for him to record for Brunswick under his own name while he was with Benny.

The studio band I put together for him included Basie's rhythm section (Jo, Walter, and Freddie) with Jess Stacy on piano. Harry did not like Lester Young—crazy man—but he thought Herschel Evans was fine. We also used Buck Clayton and Jack Washington, with Dave Mathews as the other saxophonist. Helen recorded "Song of the Wanderer," a masterpiece. However, Harry soon found a young singer in Hoboken he preferred. His name was Frank Sinatra. I couldn't stand him. I said so in *Down Beat* and have never exchanged a civil word with him since. When I guess wrong, I do it in a big way. Nonetheless, I still don't like Sinatra.

During the summer, after my short-lived job as Columbia Masterworks sales manager, I drove to California to join Benny in Hollywood, where he was appearing in Warner Brothers' *Hollywood Hotel*. Goodman had a new sponsor for his fall radio show, and once again I was asked to serve as a music consultant, this time to J. Walter Thompson, the agency representing the sponsor, Old Gold cigarettes. It was neither a demanding nor a full-time job, and it was a way to help assure Benny the best possible musical supervision for his weekly show.

I had many friends on the Coast; one in particular was Cecilia Ager, whom I had met through Bill Morris, Jr. She was on the staff of *Variety* and had vast knowledge of show business and everyone in it. She also was the wife of Milton

Ager, the composer of such hits as "Happy Days Are Here Again," "Five Foot Two, Eyes of Blue," and "Ain't She Sweet?" (which was written in honor of their daughter Shana, now journalist-writer-editor Shana Alexander). If she had not been married and the mother of two small children, I might well have tried to be more than a friend to Cecilia. Although marriage was the furthest thing from my mind in the mid-thirties, I found Cecilia fascinating and saw her often in New York and in Hollywood.

I called her the moment I arrived in California on the trip to see Benny, and was told I could reach her at a home she was visiting that evening, next door to Marion Davies' mansion at Malibu. Cecilia, in turn, told me to come to Malibu as quickly as possible. She was with interesting people I should meet.

Waiting to greet me that night were all my Wolfe relatives! I had told Cecilia most of my family history, and on one occasion, when we drove to the White Tower, in Pleasantville, New York, to hear a wonderful band which was to become the famous Savoy Sultans, I had told her about the Wolfes, my suspicion that there might be Jewish blood on my father's side of the family, and my unsuccessful attempts to find out about Uncle Louis Wolfe. She thought these must be the Wolfes she knew in Hollywood, but kept her counsel until she could be sure. Now, a year later, she had arranged a meeting and reconciliation.

Uncle Louis was in a wheelchair, a charming man whom Cecilia knew well. Aunt Georgia, still involved with Actors' Equity, turned out to be as Irish as they come and completely delightful. There were also three Wolfe daughters: Mary, married to Herbert Stothart, the musical director at MGM and a film composer in his own right; Alma, married to Eduardo Ciannelli; and Constance, the youngest, a most attractive girl.

At last I heard the story of Louis Wolfe, the black sheep of my father's family, banished long ago and never mentioned by my father. To my chagrin, I learned that Louis and Georgia had lived on West 91st Street while I was grow-

Little Jimmy Rushing
(below) thought he was all
the singer Basie band
needed, but changed his
mind after hearing Helen
Humes. Artie Shaw in 1935.

ing up in the East 91st Street mansion, and that when they passed the house of their rich relatives the girls used to spit at it! I tried to explain to Uncle Louis the terrible misunderstanding which had separated us for so long, but I could not tell him of my father's efforts to keep all the young Hammonds from meeting our Wolfe cousins.

"I just want you to know, John," Uncle Louis said, "that if it had not been for your father we would have starved. I never really made it as an actor, and if your Aunt Georgia had not worked we could not have gotten along. Your father's monthly check saved us and I'm very grateful to him."

I owe that memorable evening to Cecilia, and because both Uncle Louis and Aunt Georgia Wolfe died only a few years later, I might never have known them if we had not all met that summer in California. Of course, I continued to see my Wolfe cousins thereafter. Whether or not Louis Wolfe was Jewish remains a mystery I never solved. In St. Paul, where he and my father grew up, there were those who believed the Wolfes were Jewish. If any member of the Hammond family knew anything for a fact, he or she never enlightened me. My effort to confirm a drop or two of Jewish blood in my veins failed, but at least my Wolfe relatives no longer remained hidden from me.

For several years I had wanted to present a concert in New York which would bring together for the first time, before a musically sophisticated audience, Negro music from its raw beginnings to the latest jazz. The concert should include, I thought, both primitive and sophisticated performers, as well as all of the music of the blacks in which jazz is rooted. I wanted to include gospel music, which I listened to in various store-front churches wherever I traveled, as well as country blues singers and shouters, and ultimately the kind of jazz played by the Basie band.

I needed a sponsor to underwrite the considerable

costs of putting together such a production, but could not find anyone interested. The NAACP turned me down. Jazz and, particularly, primitive black music were too unfamiliar to the middle-class leaders of the NAACP to be anything they could take pride in. I approached the International Ladies Garment Workers Union, the ILGWU, which had produced the successful revue, *Pins and Needles*. Another turn-down. Their most recent venture, an opera by James P. Johnson and Langston Hughes called *De Organizer*, and closed after a short run. Backing another show seemed a poor idea.

Early in 1938 I finally found my angel: Eric Bernay of *New Masses*. He agreed to underwrite the talent search and the Carnegie Hall production of what I had decided to call *From Spirituals to Swing*. I was not completely comfortable about Bernay's backing. *New Masses* was, of course, a Marxist publication. Eric promised he would not make political capital of our association, however, and he was true to his word. He saw the concert as a landmark event, the first major concert to be produced in New York for an integrated audience and one which would bring both profit and prestige to its sponsor. I insisted that there be no obvious involvement with *New Masses*, that the concert be advertised and presented simply as the musical event it became. The tremendously successful Benny Goodman concert at Carnegie Hall had already taken place (an idea originating with Wynn Nathanson of the Sol Hurok office). I had participated only to the extent of helping Benny to get musicians from the Basie and Ellington bands to complete the cast, which, of course, starred the Goodman band, Trio, and Quartet. My own idea for *From Spirituals to Swing* was to present artists not widely known to jazz fans, artists whose music had never been heard by most of the New York public. With Carnegie Hall booked for the night of December 23, and the costs of a talent search assured by early summer, I could begin to find the show.

I went first to the American Record Company on whose Vocalion label several comparatively successful primitive blues singers were being released. One who interested me was Blind Boy Fuller, discovered in Durham, North Carolina, by the company's talent scout, a man named Jimmy Long. I got Long's telephone number and called him at Elon College, a small town named for the local college. Long turned out to be the manager of a five-and-ten-cent store, as well as a talent scout. He knew where to find Blind Boy Fuller and Mitchell's Christian Singers, a gospel group I also wanted on the show. He would do all he could to help.

Through Alec Wilder, the composer whose Octet was just beginning to be known, I had recently met Goddard Lieberson, a fellow student of Wilder's at Eastman School of Music in Rochester. I found Lieberson delightful, and because he was not working and I wanted a companion on the trip south I asked him to go along. We set off in my Terraplane convertible to search the backwoods of the South for performers.

I came to know Goddard pretty well on that trip and decided he was the wittiest man I had ever met. Not particularly a jazz fan, he was nevertheless curious about all music and ready for whatever might happen. Jimmy Long and his wife, we found, were big shots in Elon and very cordial. Long was anxious to introduce us to Blind Boy Fuller. I didn't particularly like his records because he whined when he sang, but of course we agreed to meet him. Durham was about forty-five miles away. We arrived to find Blind Boy in jail, charged with shooting at his wife. Goddard was fascinated by the problems inherent in this accomplishment and discovered that Blind Boy had managed by standing in the center of a room, rotating slowly, and firing intermittently—fortunately missing.

Next door lived a blind harmonica player named Sonny Terry, and as soon as we heard him play and shout his unique songs we decided he was a far superior performer. He definitely should be brought to New York for the concert. We then drove to Kinston to hear Mitchell's Christian Singers, four laborers who got together on Sundays to sing without accompaniment. Goddard and I found them in a backwoods shack with no running water and no electricity, and I'm sure we were the first white people who ever entered their house. Jimmy Long, a paternalistic Southerner, could not understand how we could visit black people in their homes; Goddard and I agreed there could not be a concert without the Mitchell Christian Singers.

Above all, I wanted Robert Johnson as our male blues singer. Although he was virtually unknown to the general public, I considered him the best there was, We discovered, however, that earlier in the year he had been killed by his girl friend. Years later, when his records were reissued, he influenced artists as widely divergent as The Beatles, Bob Dylan, and the Rolling Stones. Ironically, his death occurred just as the blues he sang were becoming popular with jazz fans. Instead, we signed Big Bill Broonzy, another primitive blues singer whose records I loved.

The *New Masses* did a magnificent job of promoting the concert with large advertisements in the *Times* and *Herald Tribune*, always honoring its pledge not to push any self-serving political message. Tickets sold so well that we had to put chairs on stage for an additional four hundred people. Only one problem developed. Our master of ceremonies wired at the last moment to say he was stuck in Mexico and could not make it to New York in time. That left me as the reluctant replacement, not a role I relished at all. Goddard was stage manager, seeing that all our performers appeared on cue.

I had decided that an appropriate way to begin the program was to play music recorded in West Africa. I thought it would be an effective way to show how American Negro music had evolved from African roots. I began to speak. My voice evidently was pitched at the wrong level. The audience shouted, "Louder!" I gave them a signal backstage to boost the volume for my microphone. Instead, they put on the African records, drowning me out in a rataplan of native drums. As I stood there, shriveling in embarrassment, noting the expectant faces of my family, of Carl Van Vechten, Vivian Brecher and her family, of everyone I knew and wanted to impress, the audience broke up. Goddard finally managed to get the African records under control and I completed my lame, and by now limping, introduction.

Of course, the concert picked up where I left off and from then on we were sailing. It started on a high level of musical excitement and stayed there.

As the stage lights came up the audience saw an old upright piano at stage center. It was a Wing & Son, a duplicate of the piano on which Mother had played Chopin in that boardinghouse at Kanab, Utah. I had located Mr. Wing at Ninth Avenue and 14th Street and learned that he still had four left in a warehouse. For $10 plus cartage I got a genuine boardinghouse piano for Albert Ammons. We rolled on a Steinway for Meade Lux Lewis and Pete Johnson to play, and together these three great boogie-woogie pianists opened the show. Lewis and Ammons then left and Pete introduced his longtime Kansas City sidekick, Big Joe Turner. Joe shoved the mike out of his way, as though flicking lint from a lapel, picked up the beat, and started shouting blues in an open-throated tone that carried to the far reaches of the hall. Joe Turner was among us and feeling well.

Then came Sister Rosetta Tharpe, a gospel singer and forerunner of Mahalia Jackson. Except for one fleeting appearance at the Cotton Club, she had never sung anywhere except in Negro churches. She was a surprise smash; knocked the people out. Her singing showed an affinity between gospel and jazz that all fans could recognize and appreciate, helped on by Ammons, Jo Jones, and Walter Page.

Ruby Smith followed, singing lovely blues with the splendid James P. Johnson. Ruby was popularly believed to be Bessie's niece, but actually they were not related. Mitchell's Christian Singers were next, then Sonny Terry, playing and shouting his incredible "Fox Chase."

After that came a special treat. To build toward the Basie brand of music, I put together the epitome of New Orleans "jass" bands: James P. on piano, Tommy Ladnier on trumpet, the legendary Sidney Bechet on soprano sax, and Dan Minor, from the Basie band, on trombone. To give them a driving beat I added Jo Jones and Walter Page. Jo and Walter hadn't played Dixie for years, but professionals that they were, they melded right in and gave the boys tremendous support. Lad-

From Spirituals to Swing. Hit performers at landmark 1938 concert included boogie-woogie pianists Albert Ammons (l) and Meade Lux Lewis, blues-shouter Big Bill Broonzy, elegant James P. Johnson (piano), and the ancestral Sidney Bechet (clarinet & soprano sax). (Bechet picture is many years after the event.)

nier was marvelous. I don't think he'd ever played in a group this good. And it was, incidentally, his last appearance before his death the next year at thirty-nine.

After them came another free-wheeling but fine-tuned combo: the Kansas City Six—Buck Clayton, Lester Young, Dan Minor, Jo, Walter, and Leonard Ware on electric guitar, not yet the instrument it has since become.

Big Bill Broonzy sang with backing by Ammons, Jones, and Page. Backstage, Big Bill mentioned to Goddard that he'd always disliked Chicago. "But you're not in Chicago," Goddard explained, soothingly. "This is New York." Bill, who farmed in Arkansas with a pair of mules, shuffled out and sang about a dream he'd had in which he sat in President Roosevelt's chair in the White House. The audience screamed. It had never heard anything like this.

The second half was devoted to the Basie band with Jimmy Rushing and Helen Humes, plus a jam session in which James P. and Sidney Bechet took part. One of the highlights certainly was the reunion of Lips Page with the Basie band (courtesy of Joe Glaser). It was a highly emotional moment. I think you could go a long way and wait a long time before you heard anything better than "Blues for Lips."

The concert was a hit. Reviews in the *Times* and *Trib* hailed it as unlike anything ever presented in New York before. There was no criticism of the *New Masses* sponsorship, and stars were born that night as sophisticated jazz fans heard at last the sources of their music.

A seemingly unrelated opportunity came my way during the late-fall rehearsals for *From Spirituals to Swing* and from an unexpected source. As things turned out, the concert at Carnegie Hall and the opening of one of the most successful and controversial night clubs in New York took place on the same night and were very much related. A former colleague of mine on the Brooklyn *Eagle*, Sam Shaw, called me late in the summer of 1938. "John," he said, "I have a friend named Barney Josephson who is opening a club on Sheridan Square in the Village. He already has persuaded some remarkable artists—Stuart Davis, Sid Hoff, Hugo Gellert—to contribute satirical murals, but Barney knows nothing about music. He used to own a shoe store in Trenton, New Jersey, and he's a very nice guy. I just thought you might be the right man to set Barney straight on the music for his club."

Barney and I hit it off immediately. He wanted what I had always wanted: an integrated night club with mixed entertainment and mixed audiences. The only problem was that Barney had a rather notorious brother, Leon, whom I knew to be connected with the ILD and I was concerned about his role in Barney's new club. I agreed to help Barney, whom I liked and respected, but I hoped that his club would not be branded by his brother's political associations. I remember asking Sam where Barney had gotten the name for his club, Cafe Society.

"From Clare Boothe Luce," Sam said. An editor of *Vogue* and wife of publisher Henry Luce, Clare and "Cholly Knickerbocker" (Maury Paul), the Hearst columnist, had been using café society to describe the New York night club elite. Barney Josephson had copyrighted the phrase for his club.

I wanted Cafe Society to succeed. It would be a place where I could put new jazz talent, a place where blacks and whites could hear the best music in the city. Although Barney invested $16,000 to open the club, by the second week he was out of money. Benny Goodman, Willard Alexander, and I each put up $5,000 to keep it going, and from then on it made money. We all got our investment back.

Barney Josephson used to come to rehearsals for the *Spirituals to Swing* concert, and I remember him saying after one rehearsal, "I don't have to look anywhere else for talent. It's all here." And it was. We put in a mixed band. Dinner cost $1.50 and there was no minimum at the bar adjacent to the bandstand, so people could sip a 75¢ beer and listen all evening to the best jazz talent in New York. Barney hired several performers from my concert to appear at the club, as well as Hazel Scott, whom he had heard at the Hickory House, and who became a fixture at Cafe Society and its uptown counterpart during the 1940's.

One of the early performers at Cafe Society was Lena Horne. One day, while she was appearing at the Apollo with Charlie Barnet's band, I got a frantic call from her. "Can't you do something?" she cried. "I'm sick of being chased up and down the corridors of the Hotel Theresa by musicians. Can't you get me a job as a single?" I thought Lena was a beautiful, if not a particularly good, singer and certainly not a jazz singer. She had never worked with a small jazz band, and my interest in the club was best served by giving performers like her a chance to be heard with the best accompaniment.

When Barney met Lena he was overwhelmed. He took her hand between his and said, "Miss Horne, I have to tell you something. You're so beautiful, you have such class, we can't let you be called Lena Horne. Would you mind if I changed your name to Helena Horne?" So Lena opened at Cafe Society as Helena Horne.

Lena sang with Teddy Wilson's group at Cafe Society and of course she sang better than she ever had before. She was a hit at the club, and because she was going around with Joe Louis, Joe was at the club often, which could only help business. During her appearance, however, she took on a new manager, Harold Gumm, who immediately decided she should be making much more money than the $150 a week Barney was paying her. Gumm took her to Hollywood, where she appeared on the Sunset Strip and, of course, did make more money, as well as a few films. But her career really began at Cafe Society, where a sympathetic accompanying group helped turn her into the fine singer she became.

I couldn't wait to bring Billie Holiday to Cafe Society. It was the perfect place for her to sing to a new audience with the kind of jazz players who brought out her best. Unfortunately, her appearances were not the success they could have been, and they proved to be the end of my association with Billie's career. She was heavily involved with narcotics, and she had hired as her manager a woman from a distinguished family I knew well. I was concerned that she and her family might be hurt by unsavory gossip, or even blackmailed by the gangsters and dope pushers Billie knew.

It was one of the few times in my life when I felt compelled to interfere in a personal relationship which was none of my business. I told the manager's family what I knew and what I feared. Soon afterward the manager and Billie broke up, and Billie never worked at Cafe Society again. I think she never forgave me for what she suspected was my part in the breakup, but the woman who managed her is still my friend and I think she realizes now the complications which could have arisen.

While Billie was at Cafe Society she worked for a time with a composer, Arthur Herzog, who was a staff writer for E. B. Marks, the music publishers. Billie brought Arthur a title and an idea for a song which turned out to'be "God Bless the Child," inspired by her grandmother. I remember going to Arthur's apartment on Seventh Avenue, between 12th and 13th Streets, while he and Billie were working on the song. Arthur supplied the music and fleshed out Billie's lyric idea, and the song became one of the very few for which Billie Holiday will always be remembered.

After 1940 Billie's addiction to drugs made it too dangerous for Barney Josephson to hire her. She continued to work other uptown clubs, such as the Onyx and the Famous Door, until she was finally arrested and sentenced to a drug-rehabilitation institution. She finally went to Decca, lured by the promise of recording with large orchestras with string sections, an irresistible desire many jazz artists have succumbed to, usually with disastrous results. Before she left Columbia, however, she did a bizarre and successful record, "Strange Fruit" and "Fine and Mellow" for Commodore. Because Columbia felt that the lyrics of "Strange Fruit" were too strong for its distributors to handle, particularly in the South —the fruit, of course, being the body of a lynch victim hanging from a tree—she was released to record with my full approval for Commodore. I never liked "Strange Fruit" myself and I urged Columbia to have it recorded elsewhere. In many ways I think the song hurt Billie as an artist, although there is no doubt that its shock value helped her career.

Cafe Society continued for a decade to be the club I

had hoped it would be. It became in a way an extension of my *Spirituals to Swing* concert, a place where known and unknown performers could be heard, where jazz and blues and gospel were blended, where all my favorite performers could appear, where Negro patrons were as welcome as whites. For a man who knew only how to sell shoes, Barney Josephson deserves lasting credit. He was a pioneer who remained true to his principles and, incidentally, prospered because he did.

By 1939 Columbia Records had a new owner, CBS, a new president, Edward "Ted" Wallerstein, and its first new employee, John Hammond. Ted asked me to come back to Columbia as associate director of popular recording and I accepted at once. He had formerly run RCA Victor (incidentally bringing Benny Goodman to the label long before he was popular with record buyers) and he was counting on me to persuade Benny to return to Columbia. He also wanted Basie, as well as other artists whose careers I had had something to do with, realizing that the largest market for records was among teenagers and college students, groups the American Record Company, Columbia's former owners, had not been able to reach with any success. He knew my passion for searching out new talent and encouraged me to continue. He also knew my strong preference for Columbia throughout its years of turmoil and of my deep respect for him as the best record executive in the business. I was ready at last to accept the responsibilities of full-time employment with a company determined to overtake RCA Victor as Number One.

In December of 1938 Wallerstein had urged Ike Levy, vice president of the CBS Radio network, to persuade the CBS board to buy the American Record Company. Levy's relative by marriage, William Paley, had been familiar with the Columbia name in records since the mid-1920's, when he bought the skeleton of what was to become CBS. Paley's original radio network had been a subsidiary of the Columbia

Phonograph Company, and Kate Smith's early broadcasts for La Palina were sponsored by the Congress Cigar Company of Philadelphia, owned by Paley *père*. The reason Levy wanted CBS to purchase American Record was that he was on the board of the Philadelphia Orchestra. After talks with Wallerstein, who was his neighbor in Haddonfield, New Jersey, he felt that if CBS bought the Columbia label and entered the record business, the Philadelphia Orchestra would have a better opportunity to record the choice repertoire being denied it by RCA Victor. Levy's suggestion turned into one of the more successful purchases in the history of corporate diversification, and Ted Wallerstein became the new president of Columbia Records.

While Wallerstein kept many former American Record employees, he hired as vice president in charge of popular recording—and thus my immediate boss—a former Philadelphia stock broker and MCA employee, Manie (for Emanuel) Sachs, a close relative of Ike and Leon Levy, who, with Paley, were founders of CBS. Manie's recording experience was minimal, but he was a master at negotiating artists' contracts, at wooing artists to the label and seeing that they were kept happy. He was a bachelor who commuted between his home in Philadelphia and the Columbia offices in New York, and had a Goldwynesque flare for fractured bon mots. Explaining to Alec Wilder that he wanted arrangements neither too modern nor too square, he said, "Alec, just hit a happy nucleus." Thanking me for taking his cousin Dick Levy out on the town, he told me, "I just can't thank you enough for what you did for Dick. He was really incensed." When he and Goddard Lieberson shared responsibility for Columbia's recording, they made a trip to Hollywood. Noting a large body of water as they drove west on Sunset Boulevard, Manie asked Goddard, "What ocean is that?" His supreme accomplishment was persuading Frank Sinatra to become a recording artist on his own.

Wallerstein's own contributions to the rise of Columbia, however, can be best appreciated with some knowledge of the history of this famous name. Few companies have swung so dramatically between preeminence and extinction. War, mismanagement, depression, and the invention of the radio all contributed to Columbia's tremors, but because my own career in recording began, as it will end, at Columbia, this is an appropriate place to review its complex history.

Columbia Records started in 1889 as the American Graphophone Company. Six years later it became Columbia Phonograph. The earliest Columbia records were wax cylinders of the type invented by Thomas A. Edison in 1877. Edison, however, became diverted by the problems of electric lighting and the many subsequent improvements of the phonograph were the work of other inventors. Alexander Graham Bell, whose invention of the telephone arose from his life-long interest in speech transmission and deafness, was an experimenter with the Edison machine. And Emile Berliner, a German-born American, made several fundamental contributions. He invented the disk record, the matrix from which multiple copies could be pressed, and the shellac compound from which nearly all records were made until the introduction of acetate. Perhaps most importantly, he devised the method of transmitting the sound fluctuations of needle and tone arm to the sides of a spiral groove of uniform depth. (Edison used a variable-depth, "hill-and-dale" groove.) Columbia introduced its first disks in 1898 or 1899. They were seven inches in diameter and designed to rotate at 80 rpm. At that speed they offered a minute and thirty-five seconds of music. They retailed for fifty cents.

Edison, somewhat stubbornly, held to his cylinders long after the flat disk was introduced and most phonographs were being built to accommodate it. The Wizard did most of his record business with penny arcades, where for a penny or a nickel you could listen to a cylinder through two rubber ear tubes. Columbia continued to manufacture cylinders until 1912; I can remember listening to them in a penny arcade as late as 1917. When Edison finally switched to the flat disk he had his made of Bakelite, a nearly unbreakable synthetic resin, half an inch thick. Kids used Edison records as wheels for their wagons.

Eventually, Columbia and the Victor Talking Machine Company entered into a patent pool which effectively eliminated competition in the lateral-groove disk until 1920, when the Brunswick-Balke-Collender Company (makers, among other things, of Bakelite billiard balls) acquired a patent that opened the field to competition. Thereafter, anyone's records could be cut laterally rather than hill-and-dale. Most companies promptly leaped at the chance.

Despite the limited frequency range and minimal overtones of the early records, there were ambitious efforts to capture the best music of the time. The first opera—Verdi's *Ernani*—was recorded on forty single-side disks in 1903. Double-sided records came on the scene in 1904, and the first complete symphony—Beethoven's Fifth—was recorded by the Berlin Philharmonic in 1909.

Columbia entered the classical-music field in 1903. It got an exclusive contract with the Boston Opera Company and such stars as Jean de Reszke and Lillian Nordica. Victor, however, had the contract with New York's Metropolitan Opera, which meant access to such superstars as Enrico Caruso, Feodor Chaliapin, and Ernestine Schumann-Heink. (It also had one of the great promotional notions of all time: the cocked-head terrier sitting before a phonograph listening to "His Master's Voice.") Outclassed, Columbia quit the opera field in 1906.

Columbia's principal product during these years was the popular record. Its catalog contained some surprising performances, including records by the Fisk Jubilee Singers, a Negro octet from Fisk University in Nashville, Tennessee. These were recorded in the late nineteenth century and intended for the white record market in England and America. Columbia also recorded "coon" songs—that is, whites imitating blacks—comedy records such as *Cohen on the Telephone*, and an enormous amount of military band music. Columbia's big artist here was Arthur Pryor. John Philip Sousa, the "March King," became an exclusive Victor artist after originally recording for Edison.

During World War I, Columbia destroyed its entire

catalog of German artists and composers, including its entire Wagnerian repertoire, in a fit of "patriotism."

At about this time DuPont and Widener interests acquired Columbia Phonograph, and by 1923 the company was bankrupt. British Columbia Graphophone reorganized it a year later, and Louis Sterling, a Brooklyn boy who had founded this independent Columbia entity in 1917, took charge of the American label. American Columbia had its own British subsidiary in 1900; it was later judged to be in everyone's best interests to allow British Columbia to take over American Columbia's English branch.

Louis Sterling returned to America to run Columbia until 1925, when he concluded a deal with Western Electric for the first electrical—as opposed to "acoustic"—recordings. (Electrical recording is essentially what we have today. A magnetic pick-up converts sound vibrations to electric waves which move through pre-amp and amplifier, and are reconverted to sound by the mechanical vibrations of speaker diaphragms.) Sterling then returned to England to run the parent company, leaving one H. B. Cox in charge in the United States; it is his signature that appears on the Bessie Smith contracts beginning in 1926. I first met Sterling—later Sir Louis—in 1933, when I made my deal to record American jazz for the English market.

With the huge popularity of radio, beginning in 1927, and the distress of the American Depression, beginning in 1929, the record business plummeted and English Columbia found itself with a lemon on its hands. It looked desperately for a buyer, finally finding one in Grigsby-Grunow, manufacturers of America's most popular console radio, Majestic. Grigsby-Grunow bought American Columbia in 1931, but the Depression was too much for it, and a year later it, too, was operating in receivership. It was kept alive for two more years by the English, European, and Japanese affiliates' demands for American records.

In 1932 Columbia Records was selling about one hundred thousand units a year, hardly as much as a single hit record sells today. Labels included Columbia Masterworks for classical music, Columbia for popular records, and Okeh for country music and anything by and for the Negro. Harmony, a twenty-five-cent label, was a variety of names for such outlets as McCrory's, Kresge's, Grant's, and other chains.

Columbia was put up for sale again in 1934. Among several prospective buyers was E. R. Lewis, an Englishman I had first met in London in 1931, when he took over English Decca. Lewis wanted to buy Columbia in partnership with Herbert Yates, the head of Consolidated Film Industries, one of whose subsidiaries was the American Record Company. Yates had entered the record business after the first talking picture, *The Jazz Singer*, starring Al Jolsen and produced by Warner Brothers, became a hit. The sound for that film and other Vitaphone films of the era was recorded on sixteen-inch, 33⅓-rpm disks. The next year Fox invented a device which enabled motion-picture sound to be recorded and synchronized on film. With sound films established, Warner Brothers believed it needed a record company to produce the disks for their talking pictures. It bought the Brunswick label. Yates, whose Republic Pictures subsidiary produced B pictures and Westerns, decided he also needed a record company for sound production. He bought up several labels manufactured for the chain-store market, including Perfect-Pathé and Cameo. He consolidated them into a holding company called Scranton Button, a manufacturer of plastic buttons and phonograph records in Scranton, Pennsylvania. Yates called his producing unit the American Record Company, and made records on a variety of labels.

In 1928 Warner Brothers became discouraged with the record business. It retained the Brunswick label, headed by Jack Kapp, later the president of American Decca Records, but in 1931 leased it, and the Vocalion and Melotone labels and catalogs, to American Record without a down payment but with a pressing fee for a period of ten years. Brunswick thus became the top popular label for American, a seventy-five-cent record. Vocalion sold for thirty-five cents. Perfect and other special labels sold for a quarter.

Yates and E. R. Lewis agreed to buy Columbia on a

fifty-fifty basis, including the factories in Bridgeport, Connecticut, and Hollywood, California, for about a quarter of a million dollars. But while Lewis was en route to America to complete the deal, Yates decided to eliminate him from the partnership. Lewis was Welsh, a stranger, and incomprehensible. Yates simply decided he didn't need him.

Lewis was able to salvage something. When Warners leased its Brunswick label to Yates, it still had a plant in Muskegon, Michigan, with good manufacturing facilities. Lewis, with Jack Kapp of Brunswick, E. F. Stevens, a former sales manager of Columbia, and my friend Harry Kruse, the promotion manager of Columbia, formed the American Decca Company in the summer of 1934. They moved much of the equipment from Michigan to 619 West 54th Street in New York. The first products they released were among the worst ever pressed by an American record company. Decca, however, was fortunate enough to start at the beginning of the jukebox era, a tremendous market for popular records. It also went into business with Guy Lombardo and Bing Crosby, lured from Brunswick, and sold Deccas for thirty-five cents while all other important popular labels were selling for seventy-five.

American continued to release Brunswick and Vocalion, but Yates had no real feeling for the record business and left the operation to executives who, however, had little authority.

To keep the Columbia name alive, one or two popular records were released each month. Classical repertoire was imported from English Columbia, and the principal artists under contract to American Record recorded on Brunswick. These included the wishy-washy band of Kay Kyser, the handsome society pianist Eddy Duchin, Ben Bernie, Ruth Etting, Cliff Edwards, and others—all important and popular musicians at the time. But weak management and the deteriorating quality of the disks was reducing the famous Columbia name to minor status in the industry.

This was Columbia's condition when CBS bought it in 1938. It would be a natural adjunct to the CBS radio network, by then reflecting a growing interest in cultural programming and fine music. Paley paid $750,000 for the American Record holdings, including labels, artist contracts, and factories. Ted Wallerstein had suffered a heart attack shortly before he left Victor, but he accepted Paley's offer to become Columbia's president. He inherited completely inadequate offices at 1776 Broadway and miserable studios at 1776 and 1780 Broadway. Neither could compete with Victor and Decca facilities, so Ted moved into the old Brunswick-Balke-Collender building at 799 Seventh Avenue, where Decca had studios until it moved to its own building on 57th Street, and where Irving Mills had operated his music-publishing companies when I worked for him. Wallerstein took the two top floors: the sixth for offices, the seventh for studios. He also used the auditorium at Liederkranz Hall on 58th Street, a CBS radio facility and acoustically one of the finest recording spaces ever to exist in New York. It was at Liederkranz that Paul Whiteman recorded "Rhapsody in Blue" for Victor. Wallerstein also made a deal with the World Transcription Company, at 711 Fifth Avenue, for its studios, originally used by NBC. All of these outside studios were far better than those at 799 Seventh Avenue. I recorded most of my Columbias at either Liederkranz, at 711 Fifth Avenue, or a Broadway theater later used by CBS for the Ed Sullivan Show, actually the same building in which the old Billy Rose Music Hall had been located. It was in this theater, for instance, that I recorded a marvelous series of records by the Claude Thornhill band.

In August of 1939 Wallerstein revolutionized the record business. Victor classical records had been selling for from $1.50 to $2 for a twelve-inch, 78-rpm Red Seal. Victor and Brunswick popular records sold for seventy-five cents. Wallerstein believed these prices were too high for the market. He reduced Columbia Masterworks, including records by such artists as Szigeti, Walter Gieseking, and, through an arrangement with English Columbia, Sir Thomas Beecham, considered at that time the greatest conductor after Toscanini, to $1. Columbia popular records, with the same artists who had previously appeared on Brunswick, were reduced to fifty cents. Vocalions (now to be released on Okeh) remained at thirty-five. The move caught Victor unprepared and it put Columbia back into the competitive record market.

Victor, with its virtual monopoly of recorded classical music, was in a position of having too many artists, including every major symphony orchestra in this country. Wallerstein undertook a campaign to improve Columbia's lineup. He first signed the New York Philharmonic Orchestra, a comparatively easy accomplishment because it already was under contract to the CBS radio network. Not long afterward he took the Philadelphia Orchestra away from Victor.

His biggest success came in expanding the promotion of André Kostelanetz, who had been recording with only slight success on the Brunswick label. Wallerstein saw in Kostelanetz' interpretation of semiclassics the great middle-brow music of America. He gave him an unlimited budget for a large orchestra, better studio facilities, and, as a result, a surpassingly lush sound. Kostelanetz, still with Columbia to this day, has probably sold more records than any instrumental artist in the history of the record business.

Ted Wallerstein was also shrewd enough to realize that the 78 speed was not adequate for longer recorded works. As far back as 1939 he began to prepare for the long-playing record by hiring two engineers from the Muzak company to experiment with the 33⅓-rpm speed, and by ordering every Columbia record to be recorded simultaneously on the regular 78-rpm lacquer disk and on a sixteen-inch 33⅓ acetate disk on which the music was recorded flat, that is, without peaks. Sound curves could be added later when Wallerstein's cherished dream of a long-playing record became a reality. This foresight provided Columbia with a complete library of music when, in 1947 and 1948, the long-playing Microgroove Record finally was developed and introduced.

Despite the expertise of producers and the farsighted management of men like Wallerstein, the hit record which makes the difference in a company's survival is often unexpected and unpredictable. In Columbia's case luck came early in Wallerstein's regime when an obscure Midwestern band led by Orrin Tucker recorded a song called "Oh, Johnny, Oh," with a vocal by an unknown girl named Wee Bonnie Baker. The record sold half a million copies, an incredible sale for those days, and it put Columbia into the popular-record business to stay. Kostelanetz began to outsell the most famous of Victor's classical artists, and there has never been a year since its purchase of Columbia that CBS has not earned back at least its initial investment.

When I joined Columbia in 1939, its popular-recording sessions were being supervised by Joe Higgins, an employee of American Record whom Wallerstein kept on. Joe, who worked for the company until the day he died at the age of seventy-three, was beloved by music publishers, a valuable asset in the record business which pays royalties to publishers on every record sold. One of Joe Higgins' first contributions to Columbia's rejuvenation was to persuade publishers to reduce their royalty from 2¢ to 1½¢ per side when Columbia reduced its popular-record price to fifty cents. He was the only man in the business who could have accomplished this, and the fact that the wholesale price of a fifty-cent record was about twenty-three or twenty-four cents meant that the half cent saving was crucial. The royalty on a thirty-five-cent record, usually about 1¼¢, was usually paid only on one side. The other side would be a song in the public domain or whose copyright was owned by the company itself. Joe worked under Manie Sachs, as I did, and we shared the responsibility for producing Columbia popular records, along with my friend Morty Palitz.

Morty got into the record business in the mid-1930's because he was the nephew of Dick Altschuler, then president of American Record. He met Alec Wilder through Yella Pessl, the harpsichordist who recorded for American. With Wanda Landowska, she was among the first harpsichordists to perform on records, and it is her harpsichord—on loan—that can be heard on Alec's first Octet records. It was the Octet's audition in Yella Pessl's apartment, a chamber-music group which included Mitch Miller playing oboe, which provided Palitz with his first supervising job as a record producer.

Alec, now a legendary figure in the music business, was and is a distinguished composer both of chamber music and many great popular songs. His songs made him a hero to all singers, for while few were hits—his greatest hit was *It's So Peaceful in the Country*—all are classics. Wilder, the quiet bachelor recluse and permanent guest of the Algonquin Hotel on 44th Street, has always been a jazz fan. It was he who introduced me to Goddard Lieberson, and it is his book on the American popular song that is the accepted bible among students of this uniquely American art form.

Morty Palitz was a good musician with perfect pitch, and while he got his first job through Altschuler he earned the respect of every band and every soloist who worked with him. After CBS bought American, Ted Wallerstein kept Morty on to show Manie Sachs the techniques of recording, a lesson Manie never learned despite his considerable skills as a handler of Columbia's popular talent. Palitz was soon frustrated by Sachs and left Columbia to work for Decca while I was in the Army.

I continued to see Morty during the 1940's. He went to work for a while with Jerry Blaine at Jubilee Records. Finally, he was offered the job he wanted most, recording director for Frank Sinatra's new record company, Reprise. He died on his way to California to assume his new job and will be missed always by all of us who knew him.

As associate recording director, my own position was in some ways difficult. Every six weeks or so I made trips to Chicago to record regional, or "territory," bands like Frankie Masters, Dick Jurgens, Lawrence Welk, Tiny Hill, and Ray Herbeck. I was also called upon to supervise sessions in New York with such bands as Horace Heidt, Eddy Duchin, and Kay Kyser. I had been particularly scathing in my *Down Beat* reviews of Heidt, for instance, which made our relationship so strained that finally he ordered me out of the studio. I also recorded a bandleader named Jack Marchard, whose first session incidentally, featured an unknown singer from Pittsburgh named Vaughn Monroe.

I had great difficulties with Kate Smith, who had a sharp tongue and was not unwilling to use it. I had always respected Kate both as a singer and a dancer in the 1920's, but her musical director, Jack Miller, used good musicians to play excruciating arrangements and I could do nothing to improve them. To be called upon to work with artists for whom I had little enthusiasm, many of whose previous records I had blasted in my reviews, was not easy for them or for me. Worse, to be called upon to write liner notes when I found nothing praiseworthy about their records was hypocritical. It was no longer possible to be candid; to be dishonest was painful; still, I had accepted a full-time job in the commercial world of recorded music. I could no longer record only my favorites.

I did have my satisfactions. One of the first was persuading Benny Goodman to leave Victor for Columbia, which he did early in 1939. I almost lost Basie a second time, however, when, Jack Kapp sent an emissary to the Apollo Theater with $1,000 to re-sign with Decca. Although he needed the money, Basie, fortunately for me, rejected it. I simply did not think in those terms. Basie had followed Willard Alexander to the William Morris agency, a move which did not work out for Willard and one which my friendship with Bill Morris, Jr., partially set in motion. The Morris office, seeing the success of MCA's band department, wanted to add bandleaders to its roster of stars. It hired Willard away from MCA, assuming that Benny Goodman and Basie would follow. Basie did; Goodman didn't, a shock for Willard, who soon found no real interest at William Morris for bands and who, after the war, resigned to form his own agency.

Jack Kapp failed to convince Basie to remain at Decca and the band came to Columbia, where it recorded on the Okeh label for a while before switching to Columbia's. This meant I was responsible for recording both Basie and Benny, a pleasure which easily made up for the uncomfortable hours I devoted to recording lesser lights.

XXIV

About three months after joining Columbia I persuaded Ted Wallerstein to allow me to make an extended trip through the South looking for talent. This was one of my favorite activities and because it often had produced results, as Ted was well aware, he let me go. I set off with a friend in my Hudson convertible, stopping first in Memphis, Tennessee, where the only Negro band in town was playing a Chinese restaurant. An excellent trumpet, Johnny Hampton, was leading the band and Phineas Newborn's father was on drums, but overall they were not good enough to sign for Columbia. I continued to Texas, where I heard many lively bands, though, again, nothing quite good enough. One of them, a group in Beaumont, had Eddie Vinson, later known as "Cleanhead," playing sax. At that time he still had hair.

I also became friendly with the legendary—and tantalizing—Peck Kelley, who was playing piano in a small place called the Dixie Supper Club in a style not too dissimilar from Jess Stacy's. Peck was much admired in Texas, virtually unknown outside it, and content to leave things that way. Although Texas musicians such as Jack Teagarden and Harry James had been touting Peck for years, no one had ever heard him. He wouldn't leave the State and was too shy to record. Didn't think he could justify the build-up. I left several hundred dollars with a local radio station, hoping it could persuade him to record. No luck. I never received any acetates from the station, and thus never heard him on records until a few years ago, when a fan sent me some. By then, sad to say, it was obvious that he was past his prime and not good enough to release.

From Texas I drove to Oklahoma City, where I had heard there was a great band led by Ernie Fields. Indeed, it did include two magnificent players: Hobart Banks, a pianist, and Amos Woodruff, a trumpet. I was sufficiently impressed to wire Willard Alexander, who met me in Wichita, Kansas, where we signed the band to come to New York, represented by Willard and recording for Vocalion. (This was before Vocalion artists had been switched by Wallerstein to the Okeh label.) I recorded a tune called "T [for Tulsa] Town Blues," which was a minor hit. Unfortunately, Hobart Banks refused to accompany the band to New York. He didn't believe it had a future.

One record ringing up moderate sales was the only result of my first talent search for Columbia. It was not an impressive beginning.

One of the early sessions I supervised was the Mildred Bailey date with her Oxford Greys. As I mentioned earlier, this all-black band included Mary Lou Williams, the pianist for Andy Kirk's Clouds of Joy. Andy was playing the Apollo about that time with—to my horror—an electric-guitar player who used a metal bar to produce what has come to be called the Hawaiian guitar sound. After hearing him I asked Mary Lou, "How can you stand that horrible guitar?"

Mary Lou shrugged. "If you really want to hear an electric guitar played like an acoustic guitar," she said, "you've got to go to the Ritz Cafe in Oklahoma City, where Charlie Christian works. He's the greatest electric-guitar player I've ever heard."

I was scheduled to travel to the West Coast to record Benny Goodman's first Columbia records. I promised Mary Lou I would make a detour to hear Christian.

Because of the side trip I decided to fly rather than drive to California. I arrived in Chicago, where there was a six-hour delay before I boarded a single-engine plane to Oklahoma City, with intermediate stops at Wichita and eight other scenic stations along the way. When we finally landed there was one of those old pregnant Buicks with six Negroes inside to meet me. Until then I had been getting along well with my white fellow passengers—passing for white, you might say—but when they saw my welcoming committee they were quickly disenchanted. I was driven to the Humboldt Hotel, where I was told Charlie Christian's mother worked as a maid, so I met her first.

The members of the band wanted me to come to the Ritz that afternoon. The band only worked three nights a week for $2.50 per man per night, and they were off that day. At the Ritz I met Charlie Christian, a tall young man, thin, dark, and wearing a purple shirt and bright yellow shoes. I listened to him and knew immediately. He was great. He was unique. To begin with, he phrased like a horn, which no other guitar did in those days, and he had been influenced by Texans like Ben Webster and Herschel Evans. He was endlessly inventive, although he needed equally big talents to stimulate him. As with every other great musician I have "discovered," there was never a moment's doubt. I could hear the singularity of the sound. Always this quality seems so obvious. Lights flash. Rockets go off. Where is everybody? Why don't they hear it? This has always amazed me. Holiday sounds, Basie sounds, Wilson, Stacy, Hampton sounds—they issued forth as if waiting for me to hear them. I know part of it has been my enthusiasm for black musicians; I go anywhere to hear them, and, to be sure, I've never seen anyone from the white record industry there ahead of me. But Benny isn't black, and as for Basie and Wilson, all anyone had to do to "discover" them was sit on his butt and listen to the radio. Or perhaps there is another factor. As years have passed and I've gained experience, I know I am also aware of potentiality. It isn't entirely what's happening now, but also what might be, how the sound will develop, how it will respond in other settings, in combination with other musicians.

I knew immediately, for instance, that Charlie Christian belonged in the Goodman small group. I was on my way to join Benny; what could I tell him that would convince him? I called California. "I've just heard the greatest guitar player since Eddie Lang," I told him. "He plays electric guitar and. . . ."

"Who the hell wants to hear an electric-guitar player?" Benny interrupted.

"I don't know," I admitted, "but you won't believe him until you hear him. You've got a budget for the Old Gold show for contingencies like this. There's enough to fly him to California so you can hear him."

Goodman's first recordings for Columbia had to be made in an independent studio, West Coast Recorders, whose facilities were so poor I wondered when I saw them whether he would wish he had never left Victor. *Swingin' on A Dream*, the all-black version of *A Midsummer Night's Dream*, in which Benny was to appear as the only white act, was due to open in New York in the early fall and it was important to record the hit song, "Darn That Dream," in time to release the record for the opening. Goodman was scheduled to open at the Victor Hugo restaurant in Beverly Hills the night of the record session, so we had to use the Coast studios, poor as they were. Fletcher Henderson had written a great arrangement of Mendelssohn's "Spring Song" for the record date; it would be an important debut on Columbia both for Benny and for me.

In the middle of the first afternoon session Charlie Christian walked in wearing a large hat, his purple shirt and yellow shoes, lugging an amplifier and his guitar case. Benny took one look, his eyes steely behind those glasses, and went back to business at hand. The band was unusually good at that time. I had raided Lawrence Welk to steal a fine saxophonist named Buff Estes. Both Fletcher and Lionel Hampton were in tow and despite the studio things were going well. Benny had a lot on his mind when Christian walked in and he was anxious to get some rest before going to work at the Victor Hugo opening.

The moment the session ended Benny prepared to leave, paying no further attention to Charlie. "Won't you at least listen?" I begged him. "He's come all the way from Oklahoma to play for you."

"John, I've got things on my mind," Benny said impatiently. He paused, glanced at Charlie, and agreed. "Okay," he said, "chord me on 'Tea for Two'."

Charlie never even had a chance to plug in his amplifier. Benny, of course, was not impressed and the audition ended.

I left with Artie Bernstein, who was Benny's bass at that time. Charlie Christian left with Fletcher and Lionel for a hotel in the Watts section of Los Angeles, a city as segregated in those days as any in the Deep South. I told Charlie to meet me in the kitchen of the Victor Hugo at eight-thirty, the time Goodman was to conclude his first set. I then called a dozen musicians. "Benny doesn't know it," I told each of them, "but it's not going to be the Goodman Quintet tonight. It's going to be the Goodman Sextet. Be at the bar by eight-thirty."

While Benny was having dinner, Artie and I carried Charlie Christian's amplifier into the restaurant and set it up on the bandstand, where it would be ready when the moment came. The Goodman Quintet at that time included Fletcher on piano, Lionel on vibraphone, Nick Fatool on drums, Artie Bernstein, and Benny. When the time came for them to play, Charlie Christian, still wearing his only costume, appeared through the kitchen door. Goodman watched Charlie approach the bandstand, looked around the room until he spotted me, and zapped me with the famous Goodman "ray." For candlepower I think this one has never been surpassed. Benny's way of reacting to a musical boo-boo, or other infraction of his standards and procedures, was to glare at the perpetrator, his face expressionless, his eyes boring like laser beams, a devastating, silent reprimand which no recipient has ever forgotten. But before the opening-night audience there was nothing he could do but go along at least for one tune. He chose "Rose Room," a standard familiar to Goodman audiences, though one he assumed Charlie would not know. This would be Benny's revenge for my interference.

I am reasonably certain Christian had never heard "Rose Room" before, because it was a West Coast song not in the repertoire of most black bands. No matter. Charlie had ears like antennae. All he had to do was to hear the melody and chord structure once and he was ready to play twenty-five choruses, each more inventive than the last. Which is what happened. Benny would play a chorus or two, Lionel would answer him, and their talent would inspire Charlie to greater

Benny Goodman Sextet in full cry, 1941: Georgie Auld (tenor), BG, Charlie
Christian (guitar), Artie Bernstein (bass), Cootie Williams (trumpet).
Drummer (behind Benny) probably was Harry Jaeger.

improvisations of his own. Before long the crowd was screaming with amazement. "Rose Room" continued for more than
three quarters of an hour and Goodman received an ovation
unlike any even he had had before. No one present will ever
forget it, least of all Benny.

It is a fact that despite Benny Goodman's talent as an
improvisor and ensemble musician, he did need new inspiration every few months, the introduction of a new player with
fresh ideas. He had no difficulty attracting new stars because
being in the Goodman band and the stature it provided was a
career boost for any sideman.

Early in my new career at Columbia the Meyer family reen-
tered my life. Kay, the attractive daughter of our Mount Kisco
neighbors, had gone to Vassar and then worked briefly as a
reporter for the San Franciso *News*. She also had met a young
newspaperman named Phil Graham, whom I liked immediately. He had been born in Tampa, Florida, and I believe
his father was rather well off. Kay and Phil both became reporters in San Francisco, and both were fascinated by Harry
Bridges, the militant waterfront labor leader who headed the
International Longshoreman's and Warehouseman's Union
and was the West Coast director of the CIO. They were
amazed to discover that I knew him. "He's a jazz fan," I explained. "Every time he comes to New York I take him to
Cafe Society to hear Teddy Wilson and Billie Holiday, or to
Harlem to Smalls' Paradise, and I'm on the board of the Trade
Union Service which publishes a paper for the ILWU." Harry
was an Australian, a funny, dour man, and I believed him to
be thoroughly honest. Many thought he was a Communist
and at one point the Government tried to deport him. Harry
survived, happily, and I always felt the violence of the attacks
on him had at least as much to do with his strong and effective
labor leadership as his politics.

This was at the time of the Nazi-Soviet pact, when the
Communists had done another about-face. I can remember
Phil Graham derisively predicting that as soon as Hitler in-
vaded Russia all the phony peace organizations then sprouting

up in the United States to justify the Stalin-Hitler alliance would do another flip-flop. I was one of those taken in by some of this peace propaganda and Phil Graham was absolutely right: I felt like a fool when the turnabout came.

Jack Kahn's Profile, "Young Man with A Viola," had appeared in *The New Yorker*, which earned me a $50-a-week-raise from Ted Wallerstein. By that summer I suppose more people knew what I had been up to than ever before, and Eugene Meyer told me that if I ever needed a reference for the FBI he would be delighted to vouch for me. I think he was only half kidding.

Phil and Kay became engaged and soon married while Phil waited to enter the Army. After a time with the Office of Strategic Services (OSS) he wound up working for Jimmy Byrnes, the director of War Mobilization, who later became a Supreme Court justice and a bellicose cold-war proponent. Phil's work in Germany after the Nazi defeat turned him into a violent anti-Communist and a disciple of Byrnes', but we continued our friendship. He was so knowledgeable and so convincing I could not argue with him.

Eugene Meyer meanwhile had purchased an ailing Washington newspaper, the morning *Post*. It had an antiquated plant and conservative policies, and a short time after Phil got out of the Army he persuaded his father-in-law to buy the opposition *Times-Herald*, run by Eleanor Medill "Cissie" Patterson. The *Post* then became Washington's major newspaper, with Phil as editor.

Phil and Kay continued their empire-building by buying radio station WTOP, later the CBS television affiliate. Phil's persuasiveness revitalized the Meyer family. Agnes, the strong Republican boss in Westchester County, turned abruptly left, espousing the New Deal and devoting her lusty energies to every liberal cause. The family enterprises were becoming so successful that by about 1953, when Phil suggested buying *Newsweek*, then running a poor second to *Time*, Meyer money was again invested, again profitably.

Unfortunately, Phil felt under severe strain and began to suffer delusions of persecution. I saw evidence of this in conversation with him, although there was nothing I could say or do to ease his mind. Eventually he shot himself.

Few believed that Kay would be able to take over the Meyer-Graham empire, particularly in the face of her mother's enormous strength and involvement. But, of course, she did. She became a most acute and successful publisher, courageously backing her editors on the *Post* and making weekly trips to New York to handle *Newsweek*'s affairs. We have kept in touch throughout it all and remained friends. It is ironic to realize that despite the enormous Meyer energy, so apparent so long ago, it took Phil Graham, a funny, brilliant, and tormented man, to inspire them to the actions which were to change their lives.

In about 1946 the Meyer family invited the Hammond family to dinner. My mother and father and my wife and I were there, as well as Clare and Henry Luce. The guest of honor was General Omar N. Bradley. Kay and Phil were there, and perhaps one other couple. As the time for this very formal dinner neared, the Luces still had not arrived. At eight o'clock we all marched in to dinner without them; they appeared as we were on our second course. Agnes Meyer would not hold dinner even for Clare and Henry Luce, which made me admire her all the more.

I managed to get into a political argument with Clare Luce that evening over the Bridgeport *Herald*. Clare was then a Congresswoman from Connecticut, and the *Herald*, a social-democratic Sunday paper which I considered only mildly radical, was attacking her regularly. Clare insisted that the paper followed the Party line.

"Excuse me, Mrs. Luce," I had to say, "but that is just not so." When Columbia's record factory was organized by the United Electrical and Radio Workers, the *Herald* had supported the anti-Communist International Electrical Workers. I told her I knew the editor and publisher of the *Herald* and that it was inconceivable to me that he or his paper could be pro-Communist.

Our argument lasted ten or twelve minutes. Clare steamed, and every now and then Phil would pat me on the back. "Keep it up, John," he would say. "You're doing fine." That was the night I also told Clare of the one thing on which we did agree. "If it weren't for you," I said, "a marvelous night club in Greenwich Village would never have gotten its name, Cafe Society."

She was pleased.

XXV

Charlie Christian never told me he had had tuberculosis and Benny did not find out until a year later in Chicago, when Charlie began to cough a lot. Benny made him go to the Michael Reese Hospital for a checkup and a spot was discovered on one lung. Charlie was warned to take good care of himself and assured that if he did he could lead a normal, healthy life. Of course, that was impossible for Charlie to do, but Charlie Christian had become very important to Benny.

He was also the innocent cause of the first serious falling out between Benny and me. It happened at the second *Spirituals to Swing* concert, held on Christmas Eve, again in Carnegie Hall. This time Professor Sterling Brown, Howard University poet and authority on the blues, was the master of ceremonies, so I did not have to assume that role. And there were other changes. From Charlotte, North Carolina, I had brought the Golden Gate Quartet, four exciting black singers of spirituals who were much more commercial than Mitchell's Christian Singers (although this did not make them better). Ida Cox, a better singer than Ruby Smith, appeared in heavy make-up and false eyelashes, not exactly what I thought a blues singer should look like, but she was a hit. After the concert I recorded eight wonderful sides with Ida singing with two different bands, including Fletcher Henderson or James P. Johnson, Lionel Hampton, Charlie Christian, J. C. Higginbotham, Artie Bernstein, and Lips Page.

The second concert also included Benny Goodman's Sextet. That made the concert an integrated one, which the first *Spirituals to Swing* had not been, so Benny's appearance was important to me. Benny was scheduled to close the show. Without thinking much about it, I sneaked Charlie Christian in ahead of Goodman to play with Buck Clayton and Lester Young in the Kansas City Six, something I had done in a studio with happy results, though never before the public. Benny was furious. I had used his star with another group, thus—he thought—weakening his own appearance in the finale. Actually, as it turned out, Charlie's previous appearance in no way diminished Benny's. Benny couldn't have been better and the response to the Sextet was wildly enthusiastic.

The 1939 *Spirituals to Swing* concert was not the success the previous one had been. It was staged by Joe Losey and in some ways better performed, but it lacked the audience-performer rapport of the earlier concert. It was sponsered by the Theatre Arts Committee, a left-wing organization, although by then I was very happy to have some politics inserted. Hitler was on the march.

Charlie Christian, like Lester, had little interest, intellectual or amorous, outside music. When the Goodman band reached New York, Charlie would go to jam sessions at Minton's Playhouse, on the ground floor of the Hotel Cecil at 118th Street. There he became the new King of Harlem. As soon as Benny finished his night's work at the New Yorker Hotel, Charlie would take off for Minton's to join Dizzy Gillespie and Charlie Parker in experimenting with the various harmonic and rhythmic variants that produced the music of the bop era.

During this period the Goodman Sextet records on Columbia also revolutionized jazz. There was a time in 1941 when Benny's rhythm section included Mel Powell (piano), Sid Catlett, John Simmons (bass), and Charlie Christian. There has never been a rhythm section like it in a white band; without question it was the best Benny ever had.

Good things don't last long, not, at least, when they involve people as volatile and undisciplined as Charlie Christian. In 1941 he was popped into Seaview Sanitarium on Staten Island. Goodman's slipped disc was acting up and he was not feeling well himself. He was persuaded to have an operation at the Mayo Clinic, one that doctors these days try to avoid and one that did not solve Benny's problem. In the meantime, Charlie was in the hospital, and Staten Island before the Verrazano Bridge was built was a difficult place to get to. I used to visit him whenever I could, and Sam McKinney, a wonderful Harlem doctor and Christian fan, went to see him every week or two. The one person Charlie wanted most to see was Benny, but he never heard from him.

Charlie was forever grateful to Benny for rescuing him from obscurity. He was a sweet, loving man, as Lester Young was, with few defenses against the world. His only resource was his music and when he was unable to play he was unable to live.

I returned from California in 1942 to learn how sick Charlie really was. By then it was too late to do anything for him and he died alone at Seaview. There was a very simple ceremony for him in Harlem. He was buried in the cheapest coffin available.

Charlie enjoyed a brief two years of stardom in the jazz world, considered by all one of the great natural musicians in jazz history. When I first heard him he was nineteen years old. He died at twenty-three. At least he had those years.

I should have been aware of Charlie's final illness sooner than I was and visited him oftener, yet I too had something on my mind. During a flight to New York in 1940 with Paul Robeson, he turned to and said, "John, I have just the girl for you. I know her sister, who is married to a friend of mine, and this girl is beautiful and talented. She's for you."

I asked Paul what her name was.

"Jemison McBride," he told me. "And I know where she lives on West 58th Street with Fra Heflin, Van Heflin's sister. When we get back to New York, I'll see that you meet her."

XXVI

Jemy and I met at a party in honor of Paul Robeson given by Frieda Diamond, a vice president of Bloomingdale's. She was staggeringly beautiful and I was overwhelmed by her. I had never felt this way about a girl before. We couldn't wait to leave the party. As soon as we could we headed for Harlem and backstage at the Apollo, where a wonderful show was going on.

Jemy was born in Toronto, the younger daughter of parents who had emigrated from Belfast to Canada during World War I. While she was still a tot they moved to the United States, eventually settling in Batavia, a manufacturing community in upstate New York. Here her genial, hard-working father founded and ran the McBride Steel Plate Construction Co., which made snow plows, boilers, and other heavy metal products. Her mother, like mine, was a devout Christian Scientist, an enthusiasm Jemy did not share. There were three other children: an elder sister Micki and two younger brothers, Jimmy and Bobby.

Jemy had attended Antioch, where in her third year her artistic talents had caused her marks to slip, but after a year at Ohio State with straight A's she returned to Antioch. When we met, Jemy was twenty-three and I was twenty-nine, and almost immediately we knew we would marry. The fact that her mother was a Scientist seemed to help my mother accept her, and my father thought her the most beautiful girl he had ever seen. All parents were in favor of our marriage. The question was where and how. I could not face a church ceremony. When I did attend church I would not recite the Apostles' creed. I censored every response, reciting only what I believed and remaining silent when I did not believe. I took my convictions very seriously and Jemy felt much the same way. Moreover, neither of us was comfortable with the prospect of a large, fancy wedding with platoons of relatives in attendance.

Lester Young's tenor (held, as usual, at Prez's favored angle) and
Buck Clayton's trumpet were two of the all-time great sounds of jazz.

Jemy had met Edgar Siskin in New Haven, so I called to ask whether he would marry us in a civil ceremony. "Well," Edgar said, "I don't know how the congregation will take it, but maybe if we do it quietly there won't be any trouble. Would my apartment be all right?"

Of course.

"You'll have to choose the music," he said.

I agreed: a movement from Beethoven's last string quartet, Opus 135. There were very few guests: Cecilia Ager, Benny, my sister Alice, and Jemy's sister and brother-in-law. That was about all. Mother and Father were not there. I stopped off at 91st Street just before I picked up Jemy for the drive to New Haven. Mother said, "John, I'm so glad Edgar is marrying you. I hope he says a prayer, even if it's in Hebrew."

"Mother, I'm sure he will." I preferred, since we could not endure the elaborate ceremony Mother would have preferred, that no parents be present.

Jemy and I were married on March 8, 1941, and moved into my Sullivan Street apartment. Later, because it was too small, we took the whole top floor of the same building. I suppose I must add that I was a virgin on my wedding day, still the most inhibited young man there ever was and not at all prepared for marriage. Jemy appeared to accept me as I was and certainly we had much in common, sharing both convictions and friends.

I remember one evening in the winter of our courtship when we took Paul Robeson to dinner. "Let's go to Cafe Society," he suggested. "I know everyone there."

"Not at all," I said. "I think the best restaurant in the Village is Charles'."

"For God's sake, John," Paul said, "use a little sense. Don't try any games. It'll only embarrass you. It won't bother me because I'm used to it."

"I think you're being oversensitive," I said, and we went to Charles', on Sixth Avenue between 10th and 11th Streets. As we entered, someone politely took our coats. "Round one," I whispered to Paul.

The captain approached to ask how many in our party. Three? We followed him to one of the best tables in the room. "Round two," I said to Paul.

The captain lingered and finally said, "Mr. Robeson, I recognize you, and I wonder if you could tell me about your experiences in the Soviet Union."

Knockout!

Of course, what I realized and Robeson did not was that the restaurants organized by Local #1 of the waiters' union, a quite left-wing union, were likely to be safe. I knew the waiters' union, whose newspaper we published at the Trade Union Service, and I knew there would always be someone in a place like Charles' who would see to it that a Robeson would not be humiliated. I was not taking the chance Paul thought I was, and we continued to go there often.

The first year of marriage was a happy one, as well as a year of comparatively normal life for me. I continued at Columbia, I lived in the Village, and enjoyed for the first time the combination of a satisfying regular job and a home life filled with mutual interests and friends. It was too good to last.

Pearl Harbor propelled the United States into World War II, and the prospect of military service confronted me. James C. Petrillo, president of the American Federation of Musicians, chose 1942 to pull his members out to strike. Now that the record industry was beginning to thrive through radio broadcasting, jukeboxes, and record-playing at home, more and more musicians were in demand for studio work. The strike brought recording to a virtual standstill. Those of us who produced records had nothing to do. I could not sit idly in my office during the many months of the strike, and I knew that my time as a civilian was short.

I took a leave from Columbia to start a new magazine called *Music and Rhythm* with a former editor of *Down Beat*, Carl Cons, and Dave Dexter, a writer and jazz critic. *Music and Rhythm* was to be a monthly, a combination trade and fan magazine about jazz. I also intended to use the magazine to voice my protests against the discrimination in the record and broadcasting businesses. At last I could say whatever I pleased, and I wasted no time in doing so. One of my early articles concerned the deteriorating Benny Goodman band:

"Benny is still a great musician, but he is no longer an innovator or a musical radical. Instead of forming popular tastes he is bowing to them, and following the path laid down by his own imitators. . . . He no longer defies convention by breaking down racial barriers, and thinks primarily of the commercial appeal of his music."

Benny took my rap with good grace, in part perhaps because he now was my brother-in-law. Alice had divorced Arthur Duckworth and in 1942 she and Benny were married. Mother and Father liked Benny. They thought he was a marvelous musician and they gave their blessing.

In my monthly editorials I took on the AFM for its discrimination against Negroes, James Petrillo for his clumsy handling of public relations during the musicians' strike, and every complaint I had about record companies, jazz performances, and the music business in general. I also made one of my first campaigns the rampant discrimination in radio broadcasting. At that time NBC owned two networks, the so-called red and blue, and CBS had established a prosperous third. Larry Lowman, who was married to my cousin Kathleen Vanderbilt, was then a vice president of CBS, as well as a jazz fan.

I told Larry that there was not one Negro musician on the staff of any radio station in the city, or, I believed, in the entire country. Many stations, and the networks, employed musicians on a full-time basis, a situation which no longer exists except for live telecasts such as *The Tonight Show*. I thought that the obvious discrimination, particularly in war time when musicians not in uniform were becoming increasingly difficult to find, was outrageous.

"I think I can be of some help," Larry said. "Raymond Scott is putting a studio band together and he wants to use black musicians."

"I'll get him the best," I assured Larry.

For Raymond Scott's CBS band I got Cozy Cole

(drums), Emmett Berry (trumpet), Benny Morton (trombone), Israel Crosby, all told a scant half dozen out of the sixty-five musicians then on the CBS payroll; at least six of the best were black. I wrote an editorial about this situation in *Music and Rhythm*, adding that NBC's two networks had never employed a single Negro on staff. "This is particularly interesting," I wrote, "because David Sarnoff has just been appointed to the President's Fair Employment Practices Committee, the FEPC, which was established to end the very sort of discrimination practiced at NBC." The only thing NBC had ever done was to broadcast bands from the Savoy Ballroom, unsponsored programs like all remote broadcasts in those days, and to air a program called *The Chamber Music Society of Lower Basin Street*, which did use black players, but not regularly employed staff musicians. How, I asked, does David Sarnoff justify the discriminatory practices of his networks with his position on the President's committee?

I had the good sense to send an advance copy of my editorial to Sarnoff. At 9:05 the following morning, my phone rang. "This is David Sarnoff," a gruff voice said. "I read your editorial and it's a pack of lies."

"Mr. Sarnoff," I said, "it is not a pack of lies. I've researched the facts very carefully. I've investigated every ramification, and I know how many musicians have applied to NBC for work and have been told that there was no work. Jazz musicians who applied were told they would have to qualify for the NBC Symphony. There has been a consistent pattern of discrimination and you've never hired one Negro."

"I'll make you a proposition, Mr. Hammond," Sarnoff said. "This afternoon, if you like, or tomorrow, if it's more convenient, we'll set up a meeting with Samuel Chotzinoff, Mark Wood, Frank Black, and the contractors for both networks."

"I can't wait," I told him. Samuel Chotzinoff, a former accompanist for Jascha Heifetz and music critic, was then Sarnoff's assistant at NBC. Mark Wood was president of the blue network and Frank Black was musical director of the red network. It was a group I looked forward to meeting.

All the Cats Join In. A few of the folks around a table in Chicago, c. 1940: JH (2nd left), Earl Hines (4th), Helen Humes (bottom-right corner), jazz journalist Dave Dexter (4th right), Basie, Goodman.

Sarnoff called back and that afternoon we met in Mark Wood's office. Wood turned out to be a provincial from South Carolina. He opened the meeting by asking, "Mr. Hammond, are you by any chance Jewish?"

"What," I cried, "has that got to do with this meeting?"

The faces in the room dropped.

"Excuse me for asking," Wood continued, "but Larry Lowman always refers to you as his cousin."

"That's right. His wife is my cousin Kathleen Vanderbilt Cushing."

"Oh," said Wood.

I had already won. They went on to remind me of the Savoy Ballroom broadcasts, appearances by the Ink Spots, and that sort of thing. This was not the point and they knew it.

"There are six Negro musicians on the CBS staff," I said. "You don't have one on either network. This must be very embarrassing to your boss, who is on the President's committee to end discrimination in employment. What are you going to do about it?"

They hemmed and hawed, and finally agreed to employ Bill Dillard, John Simmons, and one other Negro on a trial basis. They were used sparingly during the summer of 1942, and the week I went into the Army all were promptly fired.

So much for my first encounter with David Sarnoff. Later we were to meet. When we did neither of us referred to our first conversation.

XXVII

John Paul Hammond, middle-named for Paul Robeson and forever afterward nicknamed Jeep, was born in November, 1942. No sooner had I settled down to become a father than I received the news that I had been classified 3-A and would join the Army early in 1943.

But there was an unexpected delay. Billy Rose and Oscar Hammerstein had recently obtained from Max Gordon the rights to a script he had been trying to produce for two years. It was *Carmen Jones*, the story and music of the opera translated into a contemporary Southern setting with an all-black cast and a new libretto by Hammerstein. Rose and Hammerstein, both firmly established in the Broadway theater and planning for a fall production, faced an enormous problem with casting. Opera required talent not then common among Negroes, who could expect few opportunities in the legitimate music profession and therefore rarely undertook to train for it. Paul Robeson and Marian Anderson, for instance, never appeared on the Metropolitan Opera stage in their entire, distinguished careers, and there were no black players in any major symphony orchestra in the nation. There was little incentive for a Negro to attend a conservatory, learn the operatic repertoire, or be qualified for a production like *Carmen Jones*.

Billy Rose decided that if anybody could cast the show I could. When he heard that I was about to be drafted, he and Oscar requested the Washington Square district draft board to defer me until *Carmen Jones* could be cast. My draft board was headed by a New York University sociologist, Professor Henry Pratt Fairchild, an unusually enlightened man.

I had no part in the request. I considered it a poor excuse to get out of the Army. Rose and Hammerstein felt otherwise. They had a large investment in what would be a most expensive production and they were insistent and influential men. Billy Rose intended to put me on his payroll during the casting period, which began in the spring of 1943, but I refused. I felt that if I were not employed I would have greater freedom and that Billy, if he received my services for nothing except expenses would be more likely to appreciate my choices. That was the way it turned out. When *Carmen Jones* opened in Philadelphia prior to Broadway, there was a gratifying program note to the effect that had it not been for my efforts the show might never have been produced.

The talent search took me to twenty-five college campuses, where music departments, choirs, glee clubs, and other singing groups might be expected to have trained voices with stamina. I visited Howard, Spelman, Talladega, Fisk, Tuskegee, and went as far west as Texas. Muriel Smith, who played the title role, was found in a camera store in Philadelphia. The role of Escamillo was sung by a six-foot-seven-inch cop from New York City. We had to hire alternates for the three principals, so that none would have to endure the unaccustomed strain of singing more than five times a week. The dancers came from Karamu House in Cleveland, a settlement house with great creative verve. By August we had our cast. By October *Carmen Jones* was hailed as a smash hit and I was headed for the Army's indoctrination center at Fort Dix, New Jersey. I joined a sorry bunch of draftees in Grand Central Station, filled with uncertainty about what lay ahead. I suffered some uncertainty myself. Jemy was six months pregnant with our second child when I left her, a terrible time for us to be separated.

By coincidence, Buck Clayton of the Basie band had been drafted the same day. I saw nothing of him during the trip to Fort Dix or for the first few days of processing. White draftees, in contravention of announced Government policy, were literally forbidden to socialize with Negro draftees at Dix. War Department directives to the contrary, we were told by our sergeant that certain places were off limits. The Negro barracks was one of them.

Being an adventurous soul, I lost no time in finding out where they were located and set off to find Buck. I found him easily enough and ran into a couple of members of the Four Keys, a drummer named Rudy Trailer, and many others I knew. I managed to sneak back and forth between the white and black sections of Fort Dix without ever being caught, and my personal war with the United States Army, although I did not realize it then, had begun.

After three weeks we were reassigned. The bulletin board told me I was going to Fort Belvoir, Virginia, to become a combat engineer. I had no idea where Fort Belvoir was, but at least it was not the Deep South, or an even more remote place where the rest were being sent. What I did not realize was that combat engineers were roughly comparable to marines and that we were destined for a basic-training period longer and tougher, we were told, than for any other branch of the Army. I wondered if someone had again confused me with John Hays Hammond, the inventor and engineer. Or, if not him, some muscular type better suited to the vigorous life. The question went unanswered, and like the rest I took what I was given.

Belvoir, some twenty miles from Washington, lived down to its reputation in every way. I was a ripe thirty-two and trying to keep pace with youngsters between eighteen and twenty-four. Nor was I in the best of shape to face a daily march averaging seventeen miles. The camp, of course, was completely segregated, the nearest Negro unit a couple of miles away, and for about nine weeks the monotonous routine of basic training continued without a single diversion.

There was a telephone, however, and I kept in touch with New York. I learned from Willard Alexander, now booking the Basie band from the William Morris office, that Bill was set for a week at the Howard Theater in Washington. I was also assured that the band would be willing to come to Fort Belvoir to play a show for us. I tried to pass this intelligence on to the Information & Education officer. No luck. He was too busy informing and educating to bother with a private. His assistant I knew: Lincoln Kirstein, long associated with the Shakespeare Theater at Avon, a ballet enthusiast and artist. Kirstein reminded me that the camp was segregated. "It would be impossible for the band to play for an audience of black and white troops."

"Then they shouldn't come at all," I said.

He suggested separate shows for whites and Negroes. "This is basic training, John, and I wouldn't press the issue. If both races trained together, that would be one thing. But the camps are separated."

"How will the band be treated when it gets here?" I asked.

"They'll eat in a Negro mess hall somewhere."

I was disgusted but determined and the band did come. As Kirstein predicted, they were transported in an old Army truck and fed in a black mess hall or kitchen somewhere. I m.c.'d the show, and black soldiers did appear, although they sat by themselves. Basie was wonderful and his performance was the only entertainment at Fort Belvoir that year.

Our second child was due in February. Jemy was by herself in New York. I had to see her somehow, so I broke a personal rule and took advantage of family connections to call my brother-in-law, now General Jack Franklin. Like many other businessmen he had accepted an officer's commission to serve the war effort. Jack was staying at the Shoreham Hotel and he was anxious to help. On the day Jemy arrived in Washington, he called the commanding officer at Fort Belvoir. In a gruff, no-nonsense voice he said, "I want Private Hammond for dinner tonight in Washington. It's very important."

I was driven to Washington in a chauffeured car to join Jack and Emily and Jemy for dinner. It was the only time I saw Jemy during basic training, and I was very grateful to Jack for arranging it.

When I entered the Army I weighed one hundred and seventy pounds. From that day my weight began to drop. At Fort Belvoir we carried an eighty-five-pound pack on our daily marches, and I continued to lose weight and to feel run down. Although we were not expected to fall out of ranks for sick call, there came a day when I could no longer make the hike. I went to the camp dispensary with a bad cold and totally exhausted. I was given a couple of pills and told to return to barracks. The next day I was worse, running a high fever, and was rushed to the camp infirmary with double pneumonia.

A few days later a young Negro corporal appeared at my bedside. He worked for the camp dentist, Captain Milton Greenberg, and had been sent to ask if I was the same John Hammond who was associated with the *Protestant Digest*?

Yes, sirree! *Protestant Digest*, even though a church paper, was probably the most controversial publication I was ever involved with. It was jointly edited by Pierre van Paassen and Kenneth Leslie, and I lent my name to it as a trustee in 1939 because I agreed with its strong stand against bigotry, particularly anti-Semitism which it excoriated as "a Christian sin." Neither Protestant nor Catholic churches were spared its tough-minded criticism. Since it courted unpopularity, it always amazed me in later years how many approving people had noted me in its masthead.

"Are you the same man who had something to do with Benny Goodman and Count Basie?"

"I am."

"My name is Rufus Smith."

So in the wilds of Virginia I found a friend. During the two weeks I spent in the hospital Rufus visited me often. Captain Greenberg turned out to be a fine man who now practices in Arlington, Virginia. I still see him. Corporal Smith was all I could have hoped for as an Army friend. He was a graduate of Florida A & M, a fine pianist, and at ease with white people. He and Milton and I had long discussions about the race question, and my recovery turned out to be a pleasant intermission between crises at Fort Belvoir.

I was discharged from the infirmary the day before my unit was scheduled to set off on maneuvers. I invited Rufus to my barracks for one last night of relaxation, hoping to enjoy myself before what I knew would be a difficult physical strain. Rufus arrived, and so did a sergeant, an Alabama cracker steeped in prejudice and drunk to boot. Young as he was, he had been a straw boss in a Georgia prison camp and boasted of the number of niggers he had killed; he hated me. I had made the mistake of mentioning one day that my grandfather had been a general on Sherman's staff in the Civil War. The sergeant had overheard, so I was in for it no matter what I did. He ordered Rufus out of the barracks and me to report to K.P. on the double.

"You can't do that," I told him. "There's nothing in the Army regulations to prevent a Negro and a white soldier from talking to each other. I refuse to be punished because of your prejudice."

The sergeant turned purple. "I'll have you court-martialed," he shouted.

I called Captain Greenberg. He said, "John, whatever your principles are, you can be court-martialed for insubordination. You report." So I reported. The soldier in charge of the kitchen was sympathetic. He told me to stick around for a couple of hours, then return to my barracks. But I had begun my defiance, my well-ingrained refusal to go along when the situation conflicted with my own convictions of fairness. I could never quite remember that I was Private Hammond in a military hierarchy whose patterns of behavior had nothing to do with my principles.

Just before we departed on maneuvers I called New York to learn that our new baby son had been born. Jemy had had a scare and an amusing rescue. Her labor pains had started at two in the morning, not an easy time to find a taxi, even when one lives across the street from a night club, as we did. This was Jimmy Kelly's, a Village spot of some note whose owner, a totally un-Irish Italian, was a political power in the district and a dispenser of favors. Jemy, alone and beginning to worry, sensibly decided to ask him for one: Could you help me get to the hospital? Not everything one heard about Jimmy was wonderful, but this night he was a gent. Two of his gorillas pounded up the stairs to our fourth-floor apartment, carried Jemy gently down to the street, and chauffeured her to LeRoy Hospital, at 61st Street, in Jimmy's limousine. The baby appeared ten minutes after she arrived—a fine little boy who would be named Douglas.

Meanwhile, we set off on maneuvers. I weighed one hundred forty-five pounds and still felt very weak from my bout with pneumonia. I told the Alabama sergeant that I had just recovered and was not feeling strong. "Tough shit," he said. "You report, and if you don't report I'll see that you're court-martialed."

We started off and for about the first ten miles I managed to keep up. An eight-minute break was called at that point. I sank down next to a corporal I knew, one of twins from some small town in New Jersey, both jazz fans and especially Basie fans. "I'd like to stay close to you until the next break," I told him. "I'm afraid I'll pass out and I don't want to keel over in the middle of the road." We continued for another mile or so, but I was staggering and the corporal was doing his best to hold me up. Just as the captain came to find out what was going on, I passed out. I was out cold for forty-five minutes, the one time I have ever lost consciousness.

This threw a scare into the captain. He was a young man from Ohio, not a bad guy, only intent on maintaining discipline. He had me taken back to the barracks by truck. I crawled into bed and slowly managed to come out of it. When I could I called Jemy. "Where have you been?" she cried. "We've been frantic." In his eighth day Douglas had suddenly developed an infection and his condition had rapidly become critical. He had been transferred to the Babies Hospital of Columbia Presbyterian Medical Center. "The Red Cross wired you to come home," Jemy said, "but we've not had a word from you."

At that point I was summoned to the captain's office and given a three-day pass to New York. The doctors at Presbyterian had told me I could not see my son that night anyway, so I took the sleeper train from Washington. Father joined me and we went together to the hospital, arriving a half hour before the baby died. He was a beautiful baby, the only dark-haired son in our family. Out of spite or carelessness I had never received the Red Cross telegram in time.

The effects of this tragic episode were shattering. Jemy was distraught after a difficult pregnancy, alone at the worst moment in her life, and I was not to be found. Both of us took it very hard.

When I returned to Belvoir I asked the captain why he had not told me sooner about the Red Cross message. He had no idea it was serious, he said. He apologized. The Army simply shrugged it off as one of the small tragedies of war. Our son Douglas was gone, and Jemy was again alone to recover.

Three weeks later I completed basic training and was given another three-day pass. It was hardly time enough for Jemy and me to find our way out of the tragedy together. I was ridden by guilt. I felt I had failed both Jemy and Douglas. I was unable to console her and certain to be sent even farther away.

I returned to Fort Belvoir to await the Army's plans for me.

XXVIII

I continued to see Rufus Smith despite feeling that my position on the race issue had contributed to the treatment I had received. Now that the worst had happened I was determined to behave as I pleased. Rufus, who later joined the staff of the NAACP as a field secretary, accompanied me to Washington several times to listen to jazz at the Bengasi Club, and usually we were stopped by MP's who examined our passes and gave us as difficult a time as possible. I visited Ted Poston, a Negro friend and fellow member of the Newspaper Guild who later worked as copy chief for the New York *Post*. He was then in the Office of War Information. I also saw Tom Williston, a Washington doctor who had a marvelous record collection, and I visited Kay and Phil Graham. It was during a visit to Kay and Phil that I learned of Agnes Meyer's new political career and her changed convictions on the race question. While Washington was still a hopelessly Jim Crow town, she was leading the *Post* toward a more enlightened racial policy, writing editorials of protest and wielding her considerable influence.

Early in March of 1944 I received orders to report to the Port of New Orleans Embarkation Center for duty in the Information & Education section. The implication in the set of orders seemed to be that I would be assigned to a special project for the War Department concerning Negro troops in the area. The only explanation I could think of for this unusual assignment was that I had a cousin by marriage, Major General Fred Osborn, head of I & E, who was interested in achieving just treatment for Negro troops. Fred knew of my work with the NAACP and of my experience in the entertainment field. It appeared that I was to be given the opportunity to use it.

I received permission to drive my car, a 1942 Hudson convertible, to New Orleans. If I was to scout the territory for entertainment a car would be necessary. It was a couple of days before I could report to the officer I was assigned to, and when I finally did see him he knew nothing about my orders. He was pleasant enough, he simply had no idea why I was there. Shortly, I was sent to Camp Plauché, which was about fifty-two per cent white and forty-eight per cent black. The blacks, of course, did most of the dirty work of digging trenches, picking up garbage, and other menial tasks before being shipped overseas. Some were being sent to Europe. Most were being shipped to the Pacific, after brief duty as clean-up troops.

Plauché was a barren-looking camp and Captain Bob Schaub, the entertainment officer, was a bit bleak himself. Formerly assistant manager of the Montgomery Ward store in Pottsville, Pennsylvania, he was one of those wonderful people who know everything. He knew all about entertainment. He knew all about sound systems. He knew all about Negroes. He was quite a man to work for. Camp Plauché, of course, was segregated and it had been a trouble spot for some time. The night before Negro troops were due to be shipped out they would wreck the recreation area of their camp, perhaps as a farewell gesture to the place.

The low morale of black soldiers was understandable. White soldiers had three excellent service clubs, a good library, and other Army luxuries. For Negroes there was one miserable PX and a Class C service club where they could buy ice cream and sandwiches, but not eat a meal. A recent camp directive had banned Negro newspapers because, whenever they had the chance, they discussed racial discrimination in the armed forces. Such reading matter might stir up the troops.

I felt that this was a serious mistake. While it was true that the Negro press quite properly highlighted abuses, it was also a fact that it glorified black achievements, raising the Negro's morale and making him feel that he was an important part of the war effort. Banning Negro papers at Plauché had obviously helped no one.

Freely interpreting my orders, I spent a great deal of time in the Negro area of the camp. I met a black lieutenant who worked for Schaub and who was a sensitive and intelligent young musician from Chicago. We trusted each other and he gave me the lowdown on everything that was going on. It seemed that until a couple of months before I arrived there had been a good deal of mingling between white and black soldiers, particularly in sports. The new commanding officer of the camp had put a stop to that and immediately morale had dropped. I met Bill Polk, who had worked for MCA in Chicago, a man capable of providing entertainment and without racial prejudice, although defeated by Army regulations.

I was determined to find a way to bring talent from New Orleans to the camp. First, we had to arrange facilities. There was no theater, segregated or otherwise, where shows could be put on. A fairly enlightened officer in the I & E section, a Middle Westerner, got around this by winning approval for an outdoor theater. Most of the troops would have to stand, and theoretically they would be segregated. The officer and I accepted this; we felt segregation would be difficult to enforce.

In a matter of weeks the theater was ready. I wrote Jemy, telling her of the conditions at the camp, the segregation policy, and my intention to write to Walter White at the NAACP about what was going on. I also called her every two or three days. During one of our conversations she told me that my letter had been opened and stamped by the camp censor. "It was the letter in which you talked about alerting Walter White," she told me. "You'll probably be hearing about it."

"I probably will," I agreed.

It didn't take long. The following morning there was a note on my desk from Captain Schaub ordering me to report immediately to G-2. I was quaking in my boots by then, thoughts of court martial, the stockade, and other terrors filling my mind. I reported to a lieutenant hailing from Birmingham, Alabama, about the most unfriendly human being I have ever encountered. He hated me so intensely he could not even look at me. "What do you mean by writing all this trash home?"

"It's not trash," I answered. "It's true."

"What are you," he asked, "a Red or something?"

Certainly not. "I happen to think that the abuses I described in my letter to my wife are against Army policy."

"Well, you're in for it," he promised. "Go in and see the captain."

"Yes, sir," I said, saluting smartly.

The captain was quite another man. He had been a newspaperman in a country town in Iowa and was not so emotional on the race question as his lieutenant. We could talk. He was aware that Negro morale in camp was terrible, that the conditions of the Negro section were a disgrace. We discussed it all for an hour or so. Finally, he said, "You know, you're in the Deep South here. The camp commander is from Texas and you're not going to change anything."

Again, I told the captain that I knew that camp segregation was against the official policy of the Army. "It's true there is a local option which allows camp commanders to establish certain rules," I said, "but there are very distinct Army directives to the effect that treatment of Negro troops, even if separate, must be equal. And they're not equal in this camp." I specified service clubs, PX's, and particularly the library. "I was sent here to help the situation," I added.

"How do you know all this?" He asked.

"Because my cousin General Osborn has told me," I answered, deciding to throw a little weight around. If family or other connections could serve as weapons, I would have no hesitation about using them.

There was a stunned silence. Why, with such connections, hadn't I gone to officers' training school? Why had I allowed myself to be drafted as a private?

"I think for me to do anything about the situation I'm better off as an enlisted man," I told him. "I don't think I'm better than anyone else. I want to go through the same experiences they do."

The interview ended with the captain's asking me if I would like to work for G-2, making weekly reports on the conditions of the Negro troops.

"In other words, you want me to be a stool pigeon."

"Well," he hesitated, "I don't like to call it that, but we'd like to know what the tensions are here."

"Thanks, anyway," I said. "I've been working in the field of race relations for a long time. I don't want to lose the confidence Negroes have in me, even for the privileges I might get in such a role." Aside from anything else, I was certain that whatever recommendations I made would be ignored, despite the captain's good intentions. I preferred to continue in the I & E section, getting shows for the camp, trying in my own way to raise the morale of the black troops.

I knew that if I were to quote anyone's grievances, he would be shipped out immediately, that whoever I talked to would automatically be incriminated. I had had experience before with stool pigeons. I didn't want to be one. All blacks felt strongly about the inequities at Camp Plauché. All would be in trouble.

Curiously enough, while I spoke this way to the captain I knew also that he was an honorable man, that he would not use what I told him against me or anyone else. And a few changes were made after our talk. Within a week Negro newspapers were again allowed to be sold in the camp. Negro service-club facilities were improved, and what intermingling there was only reinforced my conviction that segregation, whether practiced in the Army or in any other place, never works. It achieves nothing. It solves nothing. It is no safeguard. It never builds the Negro's morale, nor does it help the white's position. And separate but equal is fiction, impossible to create, impossible to believe.

My insistence that I could best serve the camp by providing entertainment was one thing. Now the problem was to persuade the black entertainers I knew to perform before segregated audiences. Perhaps my mother's example helped. Whatever she decided to do she did. I was determined to equal her if I could. I enlisted Bill Polk, for between us we knew just about every important artist who played New Orleans. The best source was the St. Charles, a variety theater run by Abe and Harold Minsky of burlesque fame. There was no burlesque at the St. Charles. It presented white name, and seminame, bands, such as Orrin Tucker, and all-girl bands led by Ada Leonard and Ina Ray Hutton.

I came to know the Minskys fairly well: Abe and Mrs. Minsky and son Harold, who, despite his occupation, was a Ph.D. from City College of New York. I explained to them that I was trying to find entertainers for camp shows, that the shows would be for both Negro and white audiences, and that I would appreciate their cooperation in allowing the talent they booked to come to Camp Plauché. They were with me all the way. Meeting the Minskys also gave me the opportunity to talk show business, to reminisce about the old times on the burlesque circuit, when Abe had operated the Eltinge and the Gayety theaters in New York. Abe was show business itself. At one time or another he had employed most of the great comedians. We talked about Mayor LaGuardia's banning of burlesque in New York when Negro bands played for white strippers.

Abe was a brother of Billy, the most famous of the Minskys, who had operated the National Winter Garden Theater in Houston Street, the first burlesque I ever went to. Billy also ran the Republic on 42nd Street and was the king of burlesque in New York. Abe's shows were always a little more vulgar, but they had more vitality than Billy's. When Abe died, Harold continued to run the burlesque theater in Newark, and we remained friends long after the war ended.

About the time I approached the Minskys for help, an all-black show was due in New Orleans featuring Ella Fitzgerald, the Ink Spots, and Cootie Williams' band with a young man named Bud Powell at the piano. It was a package show with dancers and comedians, just the sort of show that would be in demand at camps everywhere. The troupe had just arrived from Atlanta, tired and unahppy with the accommodations in New Orleans. I had lunch with Ella in a miserable black hotel· while she told me her troubles, and I remember one terrible moment when I said, "Well, now Billie . . . !" It was a slip of the tongue and Ella laughed about it. Ella was wonderful, but I had always thought that Billie Holiday was better and I had said so in print. Ella had not forgotten.

The show played the open-air theater at camp, and judging by the response it was the best show the guys had ever seen. The Negro troops moved up front. There was no segregation whatsoever. We had our problems. Lighting was inadequate, particularly in the beginning; we solved that by putting shows on in the afternoon. And we could never be sure of the unpredictable Louisiana weather. Captain Schaub was finding me a thorn in his side because I insisted that either all the troops saw the show, or there would be no show. He accepted my condition with ill humor.

Orrin Tucker played for us. Jan Garber came at a time when he had a very swinging band. He was appearing at the Southland Ballroom, a gambling joint outside New Orleans, and had some good musicians. He was not echoing Guy Lombardo and hiding his musical talent under a commercial bushel. Ada Leonard, who had been a stripper at Harold Minsky's Rialto Theater in Chicago, brought a band to camp. She was absolutely beautiful and her band was good. Gene Gifford, who had been with the Casa Loma band, was her chief arranger and somehow he got her band to swing. I was fascinated to find a couple of Negro girls in the band, passing as Orientals. Naturally, Ada's bunch was one of the biggest hits we ever had.

Not a week went by without at least one show. One marvelous night the late Louis Jordan, who began as a saxophonist in Chick Webb's band and in 1935 formed the famous Tympany Five, appeared. Louis accomplished the nearly-impossible in the late 1930's by becoming the first Negro band to attract an enormous white audience. Although he was playing at Lake Charles, some two hundred miles from New Orleans, he was willing to come to Plauché if we provided transportation. I persuaded the camp officers that Jordan was worth the effort. We used my old Hudson and one camp vehicle.

The band was a sensation. Louis was tired, as all entertainers who traveled the South were in those days of gas rationing and separate-but-unequal accommodations, but he couldn't have been more cooperative. He had a fine young trumpet player, Aaron Izenhart, whom I remembered hearing some five years earlier in Fort Wayne, Indiana. A kid then, now he was a star.

We seemed to have licked the segregation problem, and when we got a new recreation officer, Lieutenant Ralph Metcalfe, the Olympic sprinter from Marquette, things really started to hum. Ralph had good connections higher up in the chain of command. I think he came in over the dead bodies of all commanding officers. Suddenly there was an integrated athletic program. Everything which had been separated was mixed. Seeing integration finally become a reality at Camp Plauché was a high point in my Army career. Segregation was demolished by sports and music.

By the time Metcalfe joined us, however, there were far fewer Negro troops in camp. It was the end of 1944 and General Osborn and the I & E section in Washington had taken a firmer stand against discrimination. There never was any segregation in the officers' training schools. By that time, too, a voluntarily unsegregated outfit in France had distinguished itself in battle. The lessons were beginning to filter down.

As Lieutenant Metcalfe's programs began to take effect, I had to do more with our musical programs. We had a splendid Negro band in camp which included pianist Willie Anderson from Detroit, Joe Comfort, who later joined the King Cole Trio, Calvin Ponder, a fine tenor saxophonist, Dick Davis, from Chicago. Dick is dead now; I had known him in civilian life when he played with Sunset Royal, Doc

Wheeler's old band in which Sy Oliver had also played. That was where Tommy Dorsey first heard Sy and hired him as his chief arranger.

There was also a good white band at the Air Force camp at Lake Pontchartrain, some ten miles away. Mundell Lowe, the guitarist, was in it, and Jack Green, one of the three trombone-playing Green brothers. I used to put sessions together using the best white and black musicians in the service bands. We had open house for all the troops. This enraged Captain Schaub. Perhaps he hated jazz. Having put up with the professionals, he saw no reason for mixing service bands.

Schaub told me he had requested my transfer. So far, nothing had come of it. There must have been someone in Washington who agreed with him, however, because in January of 1945 I got my orders. They could not have come at a more inopportune time. I had just arranged for the fantastic Billy Eckstine band with Dizzy Gillespie, Howard McGhee (trumpet), Charlie Parker, Gene Ammons (tenor sax), Johnny Malachy (the best pianist in Washington), and Tommy Potter (bass) to appear at Camp Plauché. The vocalist was a new singer named Sarah Vaughan.

Billy Eckstine was due to appear on January 17, 1945. Three days earlier I was on my way to Muskogee, Oklahoma, to Camp Gruber, more familiarly known as Camp Gruesome. I heard from friends that the band was a smash. I could face Muskogee with some satisfaction. I left Camp Plauché a much different camp than I had found it, but Private Hammond's war with the Army was by no means over. In fact, the fiercest skirmishes were still ahead, and with each transfer I seemed to face a more determined enemy.

XXIX

Muskogee, Oklahoma, was always a fascinating town for me because I had known several good musicians who came from there. There was singer Lee Wiley, bass-player Aaron Bell, guitarist Barney Kessel, and Hobart Banks, the pianist I had heard with the Ernie Fields band. I was hoping that while I was at Camp Gruber I could at least find some of the Oklahoma musicians around Tulsa.

At Gruber I was assigned to a ski-troop outfit, the 90th Infantry Division, which had been stationed in Alaska and was scheduled to be sent on to the Pacific area somewhere. As luck would have it, my Form 20 was read by an officer who was a record collector. He had all of Columbia's reissues with my name on the album notes, so he put in for me to be assigned permanently to the 90th Infantry, and because for the time being the division was going nowhere I had free time to leave camp.

I drove into Muskogee to look around and found there was going to be a dance at the American Legion Hall. It was for whites, but playing the music was a five-piece Negro band, with Claude Williams, the violin-playing guitarist I had replaced in the Basie band with Freddie Green; Claude seemed to bear me no ill will. At the piano was Hobart Banks, the man I had hoped to find. Claude and Hobart told me I ought to go to the Negro dance hall, where Sonny Boy Williams was appearing with a six-piece band. Sonny Boy had had some big records, so I thought the chances of bringing good entertainment to Camp Gruber were pretty fair after all. There had been no entertainment of any kind at the camp for more than a year.

Accompanied by three musicians from the 90th, I went to the Negro section of town. I knew nothing about camp regulations, so I assumed there would be no problem. I walked up three flights of stairs to the dance hall and stood beside the bandstand, having a fine time. It was not a very good band, but it was entertaining and that was enough.

Suddenly the room was filled with military police. It seemed that the man taking tickets downstairs had been frightened by the sight of four white soldiers and had called the MP's to get us out. No one knew me. We were taken in a patrol wagon to the Muskogee jail, where we were questioned by a surly MP from South Carolina. I explained that I was on official business to bring Sonny Boy Williams to camp. If I knew nothing about off-limits regulations, I did know by 1945 that there could no longer be racial reasons for such restrictions. I was both tractable and polite. One of my friends, however, a bass player from Philadelphia, when asked why he was in the Negro part of town, said: "Quite obviously because they're much nicer than the white people in Muskogee." The MP did not appreciate that at all.

After a couple of hours word came from Camp Gruber that we were to be released. An official complaint was filed with an imperturbable, old-time Regular Army master sergeant. "What are you trying to prove?" he asked. "Why get in trouble? You've been here two days. We're keeping you here instead of sending you to Japan as an infantry replacement."

"Sergeant, there's a principle involved here," I told him—or Mother and I, speaking in unison. "If I can do anything to see that Army policy is translated into action Oklahoma crackers will understand, I'd like to do it."

I had heard that there was an extraordinary chaplain with the outfit, so I went to see him. My celebrity had preceded me. He'd seen my name in the *Protestant Digest*.

"Well, my name is Arne Lundberg," he said. He turned out to be a Unitarian minister from Boston, delightful in every way and as strongly committed as I was. Together we composed a complaint to the War Department, requesting an investigation of the policies of Camp Gruber which had led to the incident in which I was involved. We got action, though of no benefit to me or to the ski troops at Camp Gruber. We were again transferred to another Godforsaken Southern camp.

Permanently attached to the 90th Infantry, I assumed I would be in Muskogee for a while. I had not seen Jemy since a trip she had made to New Orleans, a trip during which our son Jeep managed to imprison himself in a restaurant locker while Jemy was in the ladies' room. I decided to rent an apartment in Muskogee, so Jemy and Jeep could be near by. But a few days after we had made arrangements I was ordered to Camp Rucker in Ozark, Alabama, by reputation the most dismal Army camp in the entire country. I drove to Ozark, about one hundred miles south of Montgomery, near the Florida state line. It was the most depressing terrain I had ever seen in the Deep South, an area of leached-out soil, abject poverty, and no hope.

For a few hundred soldiers in a ski-troop outfit to be transfered to Camp Rucker in the middle of February seemed illogical, but the Army does have its way of doing things. In any event, it was beginning to look as if the war was about to end and that at least we would not be going overseas. Ozark was a town of some six thousand people, much swollen by the nearby Army camp. The nearest city was Dothan (Pop.: 50,000) and there was the Hotel Houston. I discovered this vital information from a trombone player in the post band, Hank Schooley, who had been stationed at Rucker for months. We had virtually nothing to do at camp, and in the Army when there is nothing to do you make something happen. I became good at that, if at nothing else, as a soldier. The unit commander was a colonel, a former member of the Alcoholic Beverage Board in Los Angeles and a bright and sensitive man. He agreed that the camp should have some entertainment.

I drove into Dothan, looked into various service clubs and churches, and went to a synagogue with an excellent recreational center. A local Jewish merchant showed me around, insisting that a soldier's religion or race meant nothing to the people of Dothan. He had just shown me a perfect spot with pool tables, table-tennis tables, and a juke box, and I was ready to believe it was all too good to be true when my guide noted, "Of course, we don't allow any niggers." I asked him why not, and he told me in very specific terms, as if I were not quite bright enough to understand that there were limits to tolerance.

I had already experienced this paradox in the South long before I reached Camp Rucker. While at Plauché I had read Richard Wright's recently published book, *Black Boy*. One of my friends in New Orleans was the editor of the New Orleans *Item*, Clayton Fritchey, and through him I met many community leaders. Through these friends I was asked to come to the YMHA to discuss Wright's new book in relation to the general racial problem nationally. Of course, I accepted. The usual audience for such evenings, I was told, was very small. That night there was a crowd.

I began by discussing the problems of Negroes in general, and expected a sympathetic reaction from a Jewish audience in the Deep South. Suddenly, a large, mink-coated woman stood up. "Private Hammond," she observed, "you seem to be awfully friendly with Negroes. Tell me, would you let your wife dance with a Negro?"

"Of course," I answered. "Not only would I. She has." I then related an incident which had taken place at Cafe Society when Jemy and I had gone there with Paul Robeson. Being no dancer, I was relieved when Paul, who was very good, asked Jemy to dance. Suddenly, we heard a scraping of chairs. A party at the next table had asked for the check and was leaving the club. Barney Josephson told me the people were Southerners, and that one man had asked: "Do you allow niggers in here?"

"The New York State laws are very specific," Barney explained. "We cannot discriminate against people because of race. We allow anybody in here who is well-dressed, well-behaved, and who looks as if he can pay the check."

"Well, I don't get it," the customer continued. "Look at that. Do you allow niggers to dance with white women?"

Barney looked at Jemy and Paul. "That's Mrs. John Hammond and Mr. Paul Robeson, and Mr. Hammond is sitting at their table. He doesn't seem to disapprove."

The Southerner persisted. "Would you let your sister sleep with a nigger?"

"I don't happen to have a sister," Barney said patiently, "but if I did and my sister and Mr. Robeson wanted to sleep together, I would be happy to make the bed."

That was the story I told the YMHA audience. There was a gasp, one of those orchestrated gasps you rarely hear. About a third of the audience, led by the mink coat, left the room. After the door slammed there was a moment of tension. Then we all broke up, laughing. The audience which remained comprised soldiers from Northern states, members of the local Jewish community, and working people. There were also a few representatives of the Southern Conference on Human Welfare, a white organization which has made significant contributions to integration in the South. We held a frank discussion, with questions and answers about the camp, the morale problems of black soldiers, the Negro press, and the strange role of the Communists—demanding the suppression of Negro rights and aspirations for the good of the war effort.

There were repercussions. I always have wondered whether my getting transferred—again—so soon afterward might not have been connected with this little meeting. I felt, however, that my opinions had been constructive, not subversive, and that they needed to be expressed. In Dothan, discrimination by those who had once been targets of discrimination themselves was socially acceptable.

The only place I found in Ozark where I could enjoy myself was the Negro USO. The woman who directed it had a Ph.D. from the University of Chicago, and I found it the simplest way to keep in touch with the Negroes at Camp Rucker. My car with its New York license plates would be parked outside the building, giving the MP's fits. One night while I was talking to the USO director the military police broke in and hustled me off to the guardhouse. I immediately called the colonel, who ordered me released and wrote a letter to the camp commandant telling him I was to go wherever I wished in Ozark and Dothan, that I was acting for the benefit of the camp and the Army. He even issued me a pass specifically authorizing me to enter Negro areas.

I found a restaurant called the Silver Slipper, across the state line in Tallahassee, Florida, some forty miles from camp. We were always searching for a decent place to eat, and the Slipper had very good food. One night after payday I went there with three other soldiers, two sergeants from the South and a private from the North. While we were in the restaurant I asked our waiter quietly whether or not there was an NAACP chapter in town. He looked uneasy and said nothing. In about five minutes he returned with another waiter, a handsome fellow tall enough to be a basketball player. What did I want with NAACP? "That's just a middle-class, Uncle Tom organization," he said. "Out on the A & M campus we have a fine Southern Negro Youth Congress chapter, and I'm the head of it."

"I used to be on the board of the Southern Youth Congress," I told him.

"You were? What's your name?"

"John Hammond," I said, "and I think the NAACP is doing a hell of a lot better job than the Southern Youth Congress with its ties to the Party line."

I suddenly remembered that we had two Southern sergeants at the table and decided it might be better to end the conversation. The tall waiter gave me his dormitory room number on campus and asked me and the private to see him the next day.

The only thing I knew about Florida A & M, the leading Negro university in Florida, was that my friend Rufus Smith from Fort Belvoir was a graduate. The next day we visited our new acquaintance.

He was the vice president of his class, captain of the basketball team, and had escaped the draft because of a punctured eardrum. He had been a longshoreman in Jacksonville, and he had a stack of *Daily Workers* in his room. We listened to him sound off.

He was also a Baptist preacher who went around to small churches on Sundays. It is a curious fact that Southern

Negroes can be both religious and radical at the same time. We saw each other every couple of weeks, talking in his dormitory and going to the one Negro restaurant in town where he could take me. The last time I was in the area, in 1949, I looked him up and found that he had become the athletic director of the Dothan high school. He was delighted to see me and introduced me to the school principal.

He and the USO director were about the only Negro leaders in the area whom I knew while I was at Camp Rucker. I felt that it was wiser not to get involved with Negro soldiers at the camp because it might get them into trouble. I never wanted my association with them to be held against them by their unit commanders.

I did manage to bring two shows to camp while I was there. One was the Billy Eckstine band, whose appearance involved an unexpected performance. There was a handsome, opinionated, conceited Southern sergeant from Blytheville, Arkansas, named Jim Parks. We had already clashed on the race question, but he was interested in music and enjoyed my records. He considered himself a singer, so when Eckstine came to camp I told him it might make life a little easier for me if he would allow Parks to sing one number with the band. Eckstine agreed. Parks sang—not too badly—and after that we became friends. He was college-educated, and although very prejudiced he became somewhat converted through our friendship. After I was discharged I had occasion to visit Blytheville, where I stayed with Jim Parks, by that time assistant to Sid McMath, the new, liberal governor of Arkansas. He was in excellent physical shape and becoming a power in the State government. Some six months later I heard he had died of a heart attack. The one Southern convert I ever made in my Army days was gone.

I also brought the Eckstine band back to Camp Rucker after Billy left to become a single performer. Dizzy Gillespie was leading it. The colonel insisted that there be no segregation for the Gillespie appearance, the first, and perhaps the last, time that ever happened. The band had a beautiful shake dancer, Lovey Lane, but when it arrived Lovey was not with them. They had decided to spare her the ordeal of a two-hundred-and-fifty-mile round trip. She had sent photographs ahead, tantalizing shots posed in a brief costume, and the colonel had arranged a dinner in his quarters for the band and, especially, Lovey Lane. He was very upset by her failure to appear.

The Air Base in Dothan had a band led by Dean Hudson, an old friend. I was able to bring the Hudson band to camp, and it was excellent. Even in those days Dean's band was a proving ground for the Tommy Dorsey orchestra. Tommy used to raid it regularly. Of course, Dean and Tommy were friends and in return for a good player Dorsey would send Dean a few arrangements. The night Dean came to Dothan there were posters advertising the appearance for one night only of Snookum Russell's band at the Cotton Club. Nobody could—or would—tell me where this was. I had to find it for myself. By walking the streets I eventually came to an old building in a decrepit part of town with a small sign identifying it as the Cotton Club.

I arranged to go there with Dean, who was a Southerner and knew his way around. I realized that here we would be dealing with city police and that Hudson would be a good man to be with. I had heard about the Snookum Russell band, booked by a Negro agency called Ferguson Brothers in Indianapolis. Their acts played all the small towns. We entered the Cotton Club, which could comfortably hold about three hundred people, and found at least five hundred. I made my way to the bandstand, where I heard a marvelous bass player, a very young fellow, and after the set I asked him his name. It was Ray Brown.

The following day I called Billy Shaw, the New York agent, and told him he ought to do something about Ray Brown. I took great pride later when Ray joined the Dizzy Gillespie group. I assumed that my call to Shaw had resulted in Ray's chance to play with the kind of musicians he deserved to work with. It came as a shock to learn that Ray had known someone in Dizzy's band from Pittsburgh and had gotten the job himself! I also heard Charlie Carmen, a tenor saxophonist, in the Russell band that night. I recorded him later with the Eddie Vinson band.

XXX

Midway in my stay at Rucker orders suddenly appeared for me to report to New York to assist in the production of a film for the Office of War Information. It was to be a movie in which jazz would play a major role and it allowed me to go home for a six-week visit, an unheard-of privilege for a private.

During the filming I lived at home, reporting every day to the studio on 45th Street, where the script was being written. I was asked to choose a jazz club which would be typical of any in the country. I picked the Open Door on West 3rd Street, a terrible place, quite suitable for what the director, Irving Lerner, wanted. It might as easily have been located in Kansas City, but the acoustics were not bad and it looked right. I was also assigned to put a small jazz group together, a much more difficult job with most of the best musicians in the service by then. I did get Edmund Hall, the veteran clarinetist, and a few others. Most of the six-week leave was devoted to the script; the actual shooting took only two or three days, and although I tried to have my temporary assignment extended, I was soon sent back to Ozark. The film, as I later heard, was never released.

The temporary duty did allow a reunion with Jemy, a chance to make up for the months I had been away since Douglas died. I returned to Alabama believing that our marriage had revived, that I would return for good before the war destroyed it.

Back in Ozark there was nothing to do. To keep from going stir crazy I occasionally drove to Tuskegee, some ninety miles away, to visit Teddy Wilson's mother, Mrs. Jefferson, the librarian at the university. During one of my visits she old me about an Air Force sergeant, a dedicated record collector, who was anxious to meet me. This was Victor Hodge, originally from Oklahoma City, where he knew Charlie Christian and other musician friends of mine. After we became acquainted, Victor took me to the air base, where one of the more disgraceful military performances had occurred. In order to keep from training Negroes for first-class opportunities in the Air Force, the segregated air base had been established at Tuskegee. It was not even large enough to accommodate the larger planes in use at the end of the war, so Negro pilots received only meager training.

During one of our talks Victor Hodge told me about a lynching which had taken place in Union Springs, a town about eighteen miles from Tuskegee. The victim was a black man who had succeeded in life. He owned a small store and recently had purchased a car, an accomplishment in 1945 when cars were very scarce. People in Union Springs decided the man was getting too big for a Negro, so a night or two before I met Victor they had raided his store and shot him on the spot. The black community in Tuskegee was furious. It was the main topic of conversation that weekend. I said, "Why don't we go over there?"

Victor was nervous. "We'll have to go in my car," he said. "We can't go in yours with New York license plates. If we are even seen together in the Negro section of town it's the end of my career in the Army and probably the end of your life."

I wanted to go anyway. We drove to Union Springs, found the house, and after looking around carefully to make sure we were not seen we went to the front door. A young woman opened the door and asked what we wanted. Victor explained that we were there to help in any way we could. As he talked she took a second look at me. "John Hammond! What in God's name are you doing here?"

Then I remembered her. She was the wife of Walter Johnson, the drummer in Fletcher Henderson's band. It had been her father who was killed, and she had come down to help her mother. We went into the house and stayed for about an hour and a half. I got the whole, appalling story and called Clayton Fritchey, my friend on the New Orleans *Item*. I told him the story and asked him to get it on the Associated Press wire.

"No chance, John," he said. "It happens every day in the South."

Knowing no NAACP representative in the area, I called the Southern Conference on Human Welfare, thinking they might do something to get the truth to the public. But, as had often been the case with the Southern Conference, they simply passed it on to the Communist Party for propaganda purposes. The murder of Mrs. Johnson's father was simply not that important as news.

My war ended at Fort Benning, Georgia, where at last I had a good job in the I & E section and reason to feel my role in the service was finally meeting with understanding as World War II drew to a close. Fort Benning was, of course, a large and quite sophisticated military base. Still, in my view, it maintained the most rigid policy of segregation of any Southern Army camp. Although the commandant seemed to like me and knew something of my career in music, even he was not prepared for my racial convictions.

Soon after I arrived at Benning, Dorothy Maynor, the great Negro concert artist, was scheduled to sing at the camp. The colonel in charge of I & E asked me where we could put her. "The only place is the nigger barracks," he said.

"Colonel," I protested, "this is one of the three or four greatest black artists in the world. She's very famous and she has many white fans."

The colonel saw no way of allowing separate concerts. Not enough whites would show up for the white concert, he thought, and none could attend the black one. So Dorothy Maynor sang for the black troops only. She took it well. She had been born in Atlanta and knew what to expect. I was not at all satisfied. I wrote the details of the whole affair to Walter White at the NAACP headquarters in New York, adding a few other horror stories about segregation at Fort Benning.

The following week the Adjutant General of the Army

arrived and there was hell to pay. No one could figure who could have provided the information to Washington and I was never reprimanded. As a result of that official visit segregation was ended at Benning. Dorothy Maynor, who headed the Harlem School of the Arts, later discussed her concert and its results, and I believe she returned to sing to an integrated audience before the war ended.

No one at Fort Benning ever dreamed that a mere private had caused the wheels to turn in Washington. It was my last contribution to World War II.

I was discharged from the Army on January 20, 1946, from Fort Dix, nearly three years after I had arrived at that infamous indoctrination center and gone in search of Buck Clayton.

I returned home to a son I did not know, to a wife with problems—and, to be sure, good reasons for them. Another baby was due in a month and I faced responsibilities I felt unable to cope with. I was a stranger in my own home and I knew I needed help.

XXXI

I turned, as I often have, to my friend Cecilia Ager for advice. I thought I should see an analyst. I was not functioning well, I told her, at a time when I needed all the patience and wisdom I could muster. She told me about a man she described as the greatest Freudian analyst in the world. I went to see him. I knew immediately he was wrong for me. He spoke with a thick accent and seemed more interested in my family background and the rather spectacular life I had led than in understanding the crisis I had reached. He was the wrong man, I decided, for my problem.

Jemy's sister, Micki, now divorced, had married our family doctor, a delightful, thoughtful, and equable man who is the chief psychiatrist at Bellevue Hospital. He told me about an analyst he respected. Dr. Bernard Robbins, he said, was busy-busy, but might be interested in me because he had analyzed Teddy Wilson, something I had never known. I took to Bernie as soon as we met and he agreed to help me. Rather than offer advice, he made me face myself and examine the content of my problems. One of the first things he said was, "I just want you to know, John, that when I was first starting out as an intern twenty years ago, I was working at a hospital outside Philadelphia. One of my patients was your cousin, Henry Schieffelin. You don't have to tell me about all the hang-ups in your family. I know them already." That was good enough for me.

Jemy and I had bought a house on MacDougal Street in the Village in a block which was a sort of intellectual and artistic commune, although a very conservative one. Everybody knew everybody. When I returned from the Army Jemy had joined two other women isolated from their husbands by the war for afternoon sessions of mutual sympathy. One of her friends' marriage had already ended in divorce. The other was equally unhappy, and Jemy's mood fitted into this unfortunate circle of loneliness and frustration. By the time our third son, Jason, was born in February, 1946, Jemy felt depleted, distressed, and adrift. Her needs, as nearly as either of us could define them, were not ones my own restrained nature could easily or sufficiently meet. The kind of generosity I was used to giving was not the kind being asked for. It was a difficult time and I coped with it only moderately well. I don't know how I would have managed without my three visits a week to Bernie Robbins.

The music scene also seemed strange to me and took some getting used to. Bands in the vanguard of American popularity were Stan Kenton's and Woody Herman's. Basie, Ellington, and the Dorseys had managed to keep their bands together; otherwise the swing era was pretty well muted. The personnel of many noted prewar groups had been scattered by the long American Federation of Musicians' strike, which was finally settled after a year and a half with agreement by the record companies to pay a royalty on every record sold into a union fund to benefit unemployed musicians. Benny Goodman had no regular band, and I found that my often-unwelcome advice to Benny was even more unwelcome when we met again. Alice had astounded the Goodman family first by producing one daughter, Rachel, and then another, Benjie. With five daughters I think Alice felt she had had all the children she should, so there were no more Goodman offspring.

The record industry had also changed dramatically. Suddenly, there was no longer a shortage of shellac from India, as there had been during the war years, and with a new consumer market long deprived of luxuries, many companies, particularly those in the electronics field, turned to the manufacture of records. Columbia, Victor, and Decca, the only companies before 1941, found themselves faced with competition from innumerable smaller firms. Capitol Records, which had been started in 1941 by the composer Johnny Mercer, Glenn Wallichs, a Los Angeles record dealer, and Buddy Da Sylva, another famous songwriter, using the old Scranton Button Company factory as a pressing plant, and with an early hit in "Cow-Cow Boogie," was now a major West Coast competitor.

I returned to Columbia Records as soon as I was discharged from the Army—with reservations. I did not want to devote as much time as I had before the war to producing records by commercial bands and singers. I did, of course, want to continue to record jazz and I also hoped to do more classical recording. This put me in an awkward position. While I had brought the Budapest String Quartet to Columbia and had also recorded Joseph Szigeti, Goddard Lieberson, whom I had helped bring to Columbia, was now in charge of Masterworks recording. Goddard, who knew that my musical tastes were eclectic, that I was thoroughly familiar with classical repertoire and capable of recording it, preferred to handle this segment of Columbia's recording himself. I should stick to jazz.

In June I was asked to join the board of Keynote, a small, new record company specializing in jazz and folk music. It had been started by Eric Bernay, my *New Masses* friend who had sponsored the first *Spirituals to Swing* concert. By 1946 Bernay owned a small record store called The Music Room, on West 44th Street, and he had persuaded a Wall Street brokerage firm to float a $300,000 stock issue to purchase Keynote from its original owners. On the new board were several distinguished Wall Street financiers and Paul Robeson.

I considered the invitation to join the Keynote board perfectly compatible with my position at Columbia. Columbia was a very large, commercial company, too large to divert its manufacturing and sales energies to the sort of off-beat recording Keynote intended to market. I could do there what I could not and was not expected to do for Columbia. Ted Wallerstein, for whom I still worked at Columbia and whom I still thought to be the best record executive in the industry, was furious that I would even consider joining Keynote's board of directors. We argued and could find no way to resolve our differences. There would come a time when Columbia Records would encourage me to devote my energies to jazz and to other special-market music, but it was not then. There was nothing for me to do but resign, which I did.

At this time Ben Selvin, the former recording director for Columbia in 1932, when I first recorded Fletcher Henderson and the rest, had become a vice president of Majestic Records. Majestic Radio and Phonograph Company had risen from the ashes of the old Grigsby-Grunow Company, Columbia's one-time owner, and Majestic Records had taken its place among the new postwar upstarts. The president of Majestic, interestingly enough, was that old songwriter and somewhat tarnished ex-mayor of New York City, Jimmy Walker. Gene Treacy, a former Hearst employee and a most conservative man, ran the record division. They owned a factory in Newark, New Jersey, and had studios and offices on West 57th Street. Ben Selvin persuaded Treacy to offer me a job as recording director at a salary about double what I had been receiving from Columbia.

Treacy, although suspicious of my Keynote association

and what he had heard of me, obviously hoped I could bring Majestic some major artists. I had a few hopes and fears myself. It was not rewarding to record The Three Suns and Morton Downey. It was less painful to record Eddy Howard, whom I liked, and Jane Morgan. It was pleasant to record Mildred Bailey and the Ray McKinley band. And I did expect to sign some important artists of my own.

Still on the Keynote board, I accepted Ben Selvin's offer. I had never worked before for a small company, one whose policies were not yet formulated, whose distribution and selling organizations had to rely on independent wholesalers throughout the country. On the other hand, I thought I could learn aspects of the record business I did not know, which proved to be true, and Majestic needed the sort of established artists I had been working with for years. One of the first I set out to sign was Ella Fitzgerald. Ella had been under contract to Decca ever since she sang "A-Tisket, A-Tasket" with Chick Webb's band back in the 1930's, and she had not been receiving from Decca the sort of treatment I believed she deserved. I did my best to persuade Moe Gale, Ella's agent, and Gene Treacy to bring Ella to Majestic. Gale asked for an annual guarantee of $40,000 for Ella, more than three times the amount she was getting at Decca. I thought she was worth it, as did Treacy, yet for reasons I never understood Gale ended up re-signing her to Decca at the same $15,000 guarantee she had been receiving all along. It was a hard blow.

During the summer, just after I joined Majestic, Jemy and I rented a house at Ocean Beach on Fire Island with two MacDougal Street neighbors, Will and Sherley Roland. Will had been Benny's road manager for a spell before the war and was now about to enjoy a large success as producer and musical director for the Arthur Godfrey show, the most popular and most profitable radio program of the time. He and I stayed with my cousin Fred Field in his Village house on 12th Street during the week and joined Sherley and Jemy at Ocean Beach on weekends. Paul Robeson, who was trying to escape his own marital difficulties at that time, rented our MacDougal Street house.

Despite my personal gathering storm that summer was in many ways delightful. Of all my Vanderbilt cousins, Fred Field is a favorite. He and his brother Osgood, whose enthusiasm for Hotchkiss convinced me to follow them there, are both colorful and interesting men. Fred, particularly, has always fascinated me. About six years older than I and extremely handsome, Fred was school tennis champion at Hotchkiss and president of the *Crimson* at Harvard. Both brothers are expert mountain climbers and Fred is a recognized archaeologist. When he was first in Mexico, for instance, he and a friend from the museum noticed a strange configuration in the hills outside Mexico City. Diggers subsequently unearthed near the town of Tlapacoya a pyramid older than any other in Mexico.

After leaving Harvard Fred became a disciple of Norman Thomas and joined his Socialist Party. In the middle thirties he turned to Communism. His mother had died, leaving Fred, his brother, and two sisters in control of extremely large trust funds, far larger than any in my own family. Fred has always been financially independent, although I am sure he would have been the same unusual and courageous individualist without a dime. His Communist ties led to his being jailed. He and Dashiell Hammett were trustees of the bail fund for the Civil Rights Congress, a Communist-front organization. When some of the leaders of the Communist Party skipped bail in 1951, the Civil Rights Congress funds were forfeited. The Government was furious and demanded from the trustees the names of the contributors to the bail fund. They refused to reveal the information, maintaining that the names could in no way help the Government find the Communist fugitives and could only lead to loss of jobs and neighborhood harassment for several thousand contributors. Fred and Hammett were charged with contempt and sentenced to nine and six months respectively. The names eventually were released by the trustees to the New York State Banking Commission under a pledge that they would not be revealed to any other Government agency, a pledge that was honored.

Fred has always been sartorially perfect. He abhors filth of any kind, and he has a macabre sense of humor. Once when he was in Las Vegas, which he still visits periodically for a spot of gambling, he bought one of the original Ford Thunderbirds, a gleaming red beauty, second hand because it had belonged to Lewis Strauss, head of the Atomic Energy Commission. The price he paid was such a bargain he wondered whether perhaps the car had been exposed to atomic radiation, although he was so amused at the idea of owning Strauss' car he was willing to put up with a spot of contamination!

Fred moved to Mexico City by choice and married Diego Rivera's favorite model, a beautiful Mexican girl. Fred and Nieves have three dark and lovely daughters, and it appears that Mexico will be Fred's permanent residence. During his early years in the country his every move was noted by the FBI and CIA, an activity he found ridiculous. He is economically untouchable, after all, and afraid only of germs.

The summer Will Roland and I stayed with Fred we argued constantly about politics. Fred is not a jazz fan although he is fond of Baroque music and he and I have never agreed politically, so our breakfasts on those summer mornings were lively, controversial affairs. Our paths seldom cross anymore. If we can be said to share the Vanderbilt guilt, Fred has lived with it magnificently.

My major objective after I joined Majestic was to bring Basie with me, and I persuaded Gene Treacy and Ben Selvin to offer him a very good contract. It guaranteed him $25,000 a year for three years with a minimum of sixteen sides and albums included. It also included the provision that if I should leave the company, the contract could be cancelled. It was an excellent contract for the times, and since Majestic needed Basie it would surely promote him.

Basie was still being booked by the William Morris Agency, although Willard Alexander had left. The agent who ran the office and called the shots for Basie was Sam Weisbord. Basie's personal manager was Milt Ebbins, a man with whom I did not get along too well because I never felt he had Basie's best interests at heart.

To this day I have no idea what took place between Ebbins and Weisbord. All I know is that I went to California with the Majestic contract to meet with Weisbord and Basie. When I reached the Morris office I found Basie had already signed with Victor. I knew that RCA Victor would not promote him properly, that it was the end of the Basie band on records, and I said so. But whether Basie was in debt at the time, or Ebbins and Weisbord considered Majestic no place for him, I never discovered the reason for his refusal to sign our contract. Within two years Basie no longer had a band. He was reduced to a sextet with Buddy de Franco, the ghastliest combination Basie ever had.

The next night Basie and I were on a radio program together. As we left the studio Basie turned to me and said, "John, I've never been so ashamed of myself in my life." He was in tears, and because of the frustration I felt, so was I.

Yet it was simply a matter of personal regard. Bill Basie owed me nothing. I have always tried to be careful about my relationships with the talented people I like and admire so much, particularly in instances where I have been able to lend a hand—or, to put it bluntly, a dollar. I can remember that my mother's generosities—and there were many, to many people—unfortunately had a price tag: gratitude. Lady Bountiful's payoff was thanks. I don't know how I knew, but even as a kid I knew that stank. And that eventually a sour breath of hatred leaked out of the people from whom too many thanks had been extracted.

I've never felt I was buying anyone or putting anyone under obligation. Whatever help I've been able to give has been given freely. Money given simply represented opportunity, a chance to get something done that deserved to be done and that might not otherwise get done. Seeing it happily and successfully done was all the reward I ever wanted.

Anyone who wants anything more, anyone who wants

gratitude from or credit for a talent that already exists, is a pain in the ass. If I expected Bill Basie to come to Majestic because I was there and wanted him, then I was a pain in the ass, too.

Oddly, as things turned out for me and for Majestic, it probably was just as well that he didn't come.

The failure to sign Basie, my inability to persuade Gene Treacy to add the English Decca classical line, and new line of excellent phonographs, and, curiously, Treacy's discovery that I was under analysis, a "discovery" which alarmed him and aroused his suspicion that I might be mentally unstable, all contributed to my leaving Majestic Records after seven months.

Once again I had lasted only briefly at a regular job. In Treacy's view I had failed. My own feeling was that whatever my own failures, I could not continue happily at Majestic, and my domestic situation was worrisome enough. If a job in the record business could offer no compensating satisfaction, I was better off out of it.

A week after I left Majestic I was asked to become president of Keynote Records. The original underwriters had seen most of their money go down the drain and Keynote was all but bankrupt. I tried to hire Simon Rady, then the producer of children's records at Decca. Rady had recorded for a small label one of the spectacularly successful children's stories of all time, *Tubby the Tuba,* and although he could not make up his mind to join Keynote, he did introduce me to a Detroit record distributor, Max Lipin, who became our sales manager.

A look at Keynote's books revealed that almost all the money originally available to Eric Bernay had gone into an unprofitable factory in Los Angeles, an unrealistic location for a company whose primary market was on the East Coast. One of my first moves was to attempt to close the West Coast factory to improve our cash flow and enable Keynote to enter the classical-music field. To head the classical department I brought in a bearded oboe player named Mitch Miller, who had been a staff musician at CBS and was a great friend of my ebullient friend Alexander Schneider, the second violin of the Budapest String Quartet.

With Mitch at Keynote we made some extraordinary recordings, including Igor Stravinsky conducting a small orchestra of about twenty musicians in his *Dumbarton Oaks Concerto.* We also recorded two oboe concerti with Mitch, and the de Falla harpsichord concerto with Ralph Kirkpatrick. These were actual concerts, fully rehearsed, so that the costs to Keynote were lower than they would otherwise have been. My intention was to give Keynote a prestige market with recordings of works not available on the major labels. But we had problems. While our recordings were excellent, the quality of our pressing was not. This kind of technical flaw could destroy our reputation as a prestige label offering fine music.

Enter Irving Green, president of Mercury Records, a Chicago company, and a friend of Max Lipin. Green had decided to buy the Keynote plant in Los Angeles to supplement the Mercury factories in St. Louis and Chicago. He did not pay cash, however. Instead, he paid off by pressing Keynote records in his Mercury factories until the full price—$60,000 —was paid. Green's purchase of the plant helped Keynote out of a difficult situation and within a few months Green and I became friends.

Mercury Records was growing fast. Its financial resources were strained and it made sense to Irving and me that Mercury and Keynote should merge. This would bring to Mercury a classical line of great value and to Keynote the potential of a growing business in the popular field. In 1947 Mercury took over Keynote and I became vice president of the combined company.

My life with Jemy did not improve. I felt I was gaining insights into myself through the analysis. Yet, as anyone who has ever run the course knows, one does not overhaul oneself quickly, totally, or easily. One is not transformed. It is not even like shedding one's skin to accommodate new growth. All new acknowledgements and new awarenesses occur within the context of the original person.

It was still mostly our original selves with whom Jemy and I had to deal, and certainly they were out of sync. I cannot say any more whether we both were hoping, expecting, or waiting for the other to change into more acceptable versions of ourselves. The fact is that we ran out of time in which to try.

The second summer on Fire Island Jemy met and fell in love with a man I thought was my friend. He was a top executive of an advertising agency, an attractive, pipe-smoking bachelor. I was preoccupied with resurrecting Keynote, joining my family only on weekends, and had no idea of what was going on until Jemy asked me for a divorce. I refused. I did not want to leave the boys, then two and five years old; I did not want this man as their stepfather. Nor, for that matter, was I entranced with the notion of him as Jemy's husband. As it turned out, he did not persist in the relationship, and neither of these concerns became a reality. But the situation did bring our marriage to an end. I had hoped we might find solutions to our problems. I was not ready to admit defeat, but Jemy felt otherwise. She was determined to divorce me.

When my father heard the news he was heartbroken. He had always had the image of Jemy as the most perfect, as well as the most beautiful, wife and mother. I told him that it was not I who wanted the divorce. Father could not understand it. He did ask his law partner to handle the divorce as fairly as possible. He felt as I did that, no matter what the circumstances, my sons should stay with their mother with unlimited visiting rights for me. Jemy would continue living in the MacDougal Street house, receive generous alimony and child support, and be treated fairly in every way.

Our sons were upset by the separation. Jeep felt I had deserted him. The impact on Jason was less. Fortunately, he was still too young to understand fully what was going on. He had, however, suffered a painful accident some months before, pulling a pot of scalding coffee over onto himself, and was a long time recovering from the shock.

I wanted to hide, to see no one. I moved into the oldest apartment house in Greenwich Village, at 106 West 13th Street, a seven-story walkup, where I lived in a top-floor furnished room for $50 a month. When matters were arranged I drove Jemy and the boys to the airport for a flight to St. Croix. There Jemy got her divorce, returned a free woman, and never married again.

When Mercury bought Keynote, Irving Green left me in charge of Keynote's New York offices at 522 Fifth Avenue. Most of Mercury's recording at that time was being done in Chicago, where the company's headquarters were located. But I felt that to hold its own in the competitive field of popular music, Mercury should also record in New York. One of my first decisions was to put Mitch Miller, in whom I had complete confidence, in charge of popular recording in New York. Mercury's roster of popular artists included Vic Damone, Patti Page, Frankie Laine, Eddy Howard, and others with strong potential. Mitch gave them all hits while he worked for Mercury.

By this time Majestic was in receivership, but its new studios on East 40th Street, under the supervision of an excellent new engineer, Bob Fine, were available to outsiders. Mercury became Majestic's principal customer, bringing about a vast improvement in the quality of its records. In 1948 Majestic finally went out of business, and Bob Fine moved to the Reeves Sound Studios, on East 44th Street, the most modern ones in the city. Mercury continued with him at Reeves until 1952, a period in which the long-playing record was developed by Columbia, and in which wax disks were supplanted by magnetic tape for original recording. These innovations revolutionized the art of recording.

I made two trips to Prague: for Keynote in 1947, for Mercury in 1948. It made little sense for Keynote to compete in the popular-records field. Its best chance for success was to offer a classical, symphonic catalog, plus jazz and folk music. There were no small classical labels competing with Columbia and RCA Victor. With no more than $50,000 left of the original $300,000, there was no possibility of financing domestically recorded classical music, except for small chamber-music ensembles. Through my lawyer I discovered that the German Telefunken catalog had been seized by the Czechs in 1946 as war reparations. This was more easily accomplished than other seizures because the Nazis in the final weeks of the war had stored the original metal parts, the molds from which records are pressed, in Prague. It seemed to me that this offered an unique opportunity to acquire the American rights to a superb line of classical records, including performances by the Berlin Philharmonic and some of the most distinguished soloists in Europe, all recorded by advanced techniques and available for pressing by the Czechs from original German masters.

Among the Telefunken items were performances by Erna Sack, the brilliant soprano, who had an extraordinary range. She had long been a top seller in Europe, but had never been heard in the United States. Performances by the Czech Philharmonic, conducted by Vaclav Talich and by Rafael Kubelik, also were available. If I could persuade this orchestra to record standard classical repertoire, Keynote could offer competition even to Toscanini.

When I reached Prague in 1947 I found that the Czech Gramophone Works had been nationalized. The Czechs were not certain of their legal rights to the Telefunken catalog, but felt they had absolute rights to it within their own country and possibly rights to export it to the rest of the world. About sixty per cent of the German catalog had been transferred to Prague, and I believed it was well worth taking the chance to distribute these records in America. In September the deal was signed with the full knowledge of the local American authorities. Soon afterward the Czechs began to send us both their own and German recordings. By January, 1948, Keynote was issuing on 78-rpm disks the first of this foreign material, as well as Czech popular and folk music.

The next month the Communists staged a coup d'etat in Czechoslovakia, and in March Jan Masaryk, foreign minister and vice-premier of the Czech government-in-exile, was reported to have committed suicide by jumping from a window of his office. The Communist explanation was received with doubt and consternation around the world. Whatever the truth of the matter, we had grave doubts that Mercury could continue any sort of commercial tie-up with the new regime. In April I returned to Prague to size up the situation and see whether reciprocal arrangements could be made with the new management of the Czech Gramophone Works.

I brought with me David Hall, a well-known authority on classical recording, whom I had hired to handle the considerable job of cataloging the Czech and German material. He was known and respected by the Czechs, who were interested in establishing an international records archive. David would be an asset in delicate negotiations.

Josef Hasa, a very decent man, had been put in charge of Gramophone by the Communists, but I found a tremendous difference between the Czechoslovakias of 1947 and 1948. As far as a visitor could learn, there was no longer any personal freedom. Either the Czechs subscribed to the Communist regime, or they did not work or eat. Foreign press reports of the purges in the country evidently had been exaggerated, yet there was no doubt the Soviets were in firm control of the country.

David Hall and I stayed in Prague for nine days, meeting often with Mr. Hasa. In the Czech catalog in 1948 were recordings by such Soviet artists as Dmitri Shostakovich playing the piano with violinist David Oistrakh and a wonderful Czech cellist. Oistrakh had become a magic name throughout the world after winning the international competition in Brussels in 1939, and when I heard his records in Prague I agreed that he was the best. Such artists as these gave us very distinguished records to offer American buyers. We also had two serious complaints. The Czechs had been shipping to America thousands of 78-rpm records, many of which had a considerable political content. Some concerned the International Youth Festival of 1948, for instance, a Communist-sponsored gathering. Our contract with the Czechs specifically excluded any kind of political material and we felt we had been taken advantage of. We refused to pick up the records at Customs. The Czechs protested, but we remained adamant and they promised to send no more such material.

We were equally upset to find that manufacturing techniques were inferior and not improving. The Czech studios were the equal of our own, but the German equipment had not been well maintained. Materials for record manufacture were also scarce, all of which meant that the quality was not first class. We were assured that with a new factory these objections would be overcome, although it was not clear when the new regime intended to build one.

I returned from Prague with the contract still theoretically in force, but I warned Mercury that I did not feel we would be able to continue to do business under the Soviet-controlled government. Although our own jazz records were selling well in Czechoslovakia, it also appeared to me that the Russian view of jazz as bourgeois and degenerate would prevail. I was not optimistic.

Later in the year Capitol Records made a deal with the War Reparations Board in Berlin for the Telefunken catalog, and soon Capitol began to release many of the same records Mercury was selling. Capitol sued Mercury to prevent its distributing the German records, and although Mercury earned an impressive minority opinion by Judge Learned Hand in the U.S. Court of Appeals, it eventually decided to settle and withdrew the Telefunken catalog from its classical line. The Capitol versions of the Telefunken records were pressed from duplicates, while the Mercury versions were pressed from the original masters in Czech possession. The judge spotted the difference in quality and realized that the Mercury records were superior. The court action took years, during which Mercury was outselling the Capitol versions, but the Soviet takeover had effectively ended Mercury's contract with the Czechs in any case.

My two visits to Prague offered me the opportunity of my life to see what could happen to a country which had once been free and which was now a totalitarian satellite. Whatever political convictions I have held in my life, the one overriding concern I have always had is for individual liberty. Individual liberties in Czechoslovakia had vanished between one year and the next. There was little jazz, no foreign musicians, and no recent issues of American magazines, as there had been in 1947, when I recorded a Czech jazz band led by Karol Vlach and had heard the flashy, Maynard Ferguson-style trumpet of Dunca Broz. Czech newspapers all parroted the same political line, and circulation, I was told, had dropped in a year by seventy per cent.

Nonetheless, we did meet proud and fiercely nationalistic Czechs. One was Emanuel Ugge, a great jazz fan with a daily one-hour radio program in which he played and discussed jazz records from all over the world. He was also the managing editor of a Marxist literary magazine called *Art and Culture*, and he came from bourgeois family which had been the largest sausage manufacturer in the country.

The editor of *Art and Culture* was Emil Burian, a prominent composer, a former jazz musician, and the head of the experimental theater. He was also a Marxist, but he was a Czech first. The dominant characteristic of the Czechs we met was this national pride and the conviction that Czech culture was far superior to Russian. There were in 1948 many evidences that Czech Communists were extremely disillusioned, and, if a free election could have been held, the outcome would not have favored the Soviets.

XXXIII

One day in early 1949 I received a call at Mercury from Esmé Sarnoff, the wife of Robert Sarnoff, the son of General David, RCA's board chairman. Somehow she had persuaded the General to allow her to produce a jazz television show for NBC, a remarkable feat even for the daughter-in-law of the boss. It was hosted by Eddie Condon and so far had featured Louis Armstrong, Ella Fitzgerald and many other prominent jazz musicians. She had heard of a phenomenal jazz organist named Bill Davis, but was having trouble locating him. Could I help?

It so happened that I could. Bill Davis had been the pianist in Louis Jordan's Tympany Five, and some months back had asked me if I were any relation to the Hammond organ people; he wanted a Hammond and thought I might be able to help. I was still no kin to the organic Hammonds, but while I was in Chicago recording for Mercury I looked Bill up and made some very good sides with him. The day Esmé called he was making his organ debut at a place in Harlem called Joe Wells' Chicken Shack, between 132nd and 133rd Streets. When I told this to Esmé she suggested that we go hear him together.

I was staying with my friend Irving Townsend* on East 28th Street. I was feeling lonely and depressed by the divorce and the frustrations I was encountering in the record business, and I was winding up my analysis with Bernie Robbins. It was a time for company. Irving, a mutual friend, George Hayes, and I drove to Esmé's house on East 81st Street, picked her up, and headed for Harlem to hear Bill Davis.

Joe Wells was the Republican boss of Harlem. He served chicken and waffles, and offered the sort of music which would not offend anyone. We arrived at his Chicken Shack about nine-thirty; Bill Davis was appearing with a trio. Esmé thought he was perfect for her show and signed him up that night. I was delighted with Davis' organ playing, and even more amazed to find a girl who was both knowledgeable about jazz and blessed with a taste for good jazz. Her life style embraced the highfalutin New York society I had avoided, but her favorite musician was Fats Waller and she had a large record collection. I could not have been more approving. I also learned that she intended to divorce Bob Sarnoff.

Having satisfied myself that seeing Esmé would in no way encourage a marital breakup, that her mind had been made up before we met, I continued to see her. I found her fascinating: I enjoyed her quick sense of humor, abundant common sense, and lack of the social mannerisms I had learned to expect from former debutantes. I found too that we had much more in common than her background would have indicated. By spring I hoped that we would marry. When Jemy's divorce became final, I felt I could never marry again, but before Esmé left for Reno the following summer I had discussed it all with Bernie Robbins, met Esmé's daughter Rosita at her fifth birthday party, and felt accepted into her family.

* I have known Irving since John McChesney brought us together at Hotchkiss as youngsters interested in jazz. Irving followed me to Columbia, preceded me at Keynote, moved to a house near me in Connecticut, so that we became neighbors, and returned to Columbia in 1951, serving under Goddard Lieberson in various capacities from advertising manager to executive producer of popular albums. We have been close friends, share many of the same enthusiasms in jazz and many personal friends in and out of the record business. Few people have known me as long and well as he has, and his collaboration on this book is a natural one.

The following weekend I spent in Mount Kisco. My father was still shocked by my divorce, disillusioned, though he hated to admit it, with Jemy, though determined as I was to be completely fair to her. Mother was away, so father and I were alone. He had been practicing golf shots to prepare for a tournament the next day, and as he fired away I said, "Father, I've found a really wonderful girl."

"Who is she?"

Not very well, because one never does, I tried to describe Esmé's wit, beauty, love of jazz, and—importantly— her acceptance of me despite some fairly vast differences between us. There were some things I told him reluctantly. "Her grandfather was Judge Morgan O'Brien," I said, wondering what Father's reaction would be.

"Oh, he was a fine man," Father said. "I know he was the head of Tammany Hall, but everybody told me he was an honest man. What is Esmé doing now?"

"She's in Reno getting a divorce from Bob Sarnoff," I had to say, seeing a cloud come over my father's face. "The important thing is that I think we will be happy together."

The following day, as he was lining up a putt on the tenth green during his tournament, Father suddenly toppled. He never got up. He was seventy-eight years old and had never spent a day in a hospital. I was in my Mercury office when I was told of his death. At least, I had told him about Esmé. I know they would have loved each other.

Esmé returned to New York from Reno at the end of August, and I was at the airport to meet her. There was all sorts of hullabaloo about us in the press. The *Daily Mirror* had called my mother to ask if Esmé and I were going to marry, and Mother was tricked into telling all. It hit the papers, and I remember being told that when the news reached General Sarnoff he claimed never to have heard of Father or me. This was an interesting lapse of memory, considering that he and Father had served together on the National Industrial Conference Board (Father as its president). Somewhat more understandably he chose to ignore our 1942 conversation about my allegations of racial discrimination at NBC.

As Esmé and I wanted to marry with as little publicity as possible, I called Bernie McQuaid in Manchester, New Hampshire, for help. Bernie and I had met as reporters on the Portland *Evening News* twenty years before. More recently I had backed him in his share of the purchase of the New Hampshire *Sunday News,* a statewide paper. His two partners in this venture were Ben Bradlee, later to become famous as executive editor of the Washington *Post,* and Blair Clark, now editor of *The Nation.* Although the new owners of the *Sunday News* claimed to be liberals, I was not particularly pleased with their editorial stand in support of Truman for President. I was for Henry Wallace; I certainly did not expect them to be, although I thought they had not been sufficiently critical of the blunders in our foreign policy. Bernie also wanted financial help to buy a Vermont Sunday newspaper and I thought I could provide it, but I found I could not touch the principal of my trust funds and had to turn him down. He was disappointed, I know, and when I had to refuse further help a while later, Bernie sold the *Sunday News*—and his talents—to William Loeb, one of the most right-wing newspaper publishers in the country.

Bernie suggested that we could avoid the press by going to his little home town, Candia. "I can keep the story away from the wire services," he promised, "and I know a Congregational minister who will marry you in his study."

Esmé and I both wanted to be married by a minister, and the Reverend C. Leslie Curtice sounded fine. When we met he asked, "You aren't by any chance the same John Hammond who is on the board of the *Protestant Digest*?"

The perennial question. I told him I was.

"Isn't that a wonderful paper?" he exclaimed. "You really exposed anti-Semitism among the Protestant hierarchy." Once more I had discovered a man who shared my views in an unlikely place. I was even more pleased that we had driven to Candia to marry.

Esmé and I spent the first night of our honeymoon in my grandmother's house, Elm Court, in Lenox, Massachusetts. We slept in the same bed my mother and father had used during our many summer visits to Lenox in my childhood. The second night we spent in Weston, Connecticut, where Esmé's mother lived in one of the houses on the Alice De Lamar estate. Alice De Lamar is the daughter of a notable Wall Street speculator. She was an only child, with enormous taste in the arts, particularly the ballet, and had as much as anyone to do with the introduction and popularization of ballet in America. She, E.M.M. Warburg, and Lincoln Kirstein were responsible for bringing that invaluable cultural asset, George Balanchine, to the United States. Alice purchased a large piece of land in Weston, where she built a country home. The many old houses on the estate she rented at nominal fees to her friends, of whom Peggy O'Brien was one. It was all very strange to me, this artistic country commune, but in a short time another of the houses on the estate became *our* country home and remains our retreat from the city to this day.

Esmé did not want to live in the Village. I preferred New York's West Side; Esmé would have no part of that, either. We stayed in her mother's 57th Street apartment until one morning when Esmé noticed people moving out of the apartment house across the street. We rushed over, fell in love with the vacated apartment, and moved into it within a week of our marriage. It is where we continue to live, comfortably and conveniently, today.

For most of our friends there could hardly be two people less well matched than Esmé and I. She had been brought up a Catholic by Peggy, who married at fifteen, had her marriage annulled in order to marry Esmond O'Brien, and was herself a convert. Catholicism was a big factor in Esmé's life. She had been brought up in convents in France by nuns whom she liked enormously, and from whom she acquired a sincere and deeply felt commitment to religion. After she married Bob Sarnoff, and especially after she married me, she could not take the sacraments, but Esmé is blessed with a mind of her own, as well as a tolerance for differing points of view. If I loved her, she said, I would understand her faith.

My own attitude toward religion, at least toward the beliefs of others, had undergone considerable tempering over the years. I was no longer the intolerant agnostic. My changing relationship with my father had a tremendous influence on me, and I realized that integrity and convictions sincerely felt are to be respected and admired, even when they differed radically from my own. While my stand on organized religion remained unchanged, I had come to understand why others believed as they did. My friends have included Jehovah's Witnesses, Muslims, Catholics, even Fundamentalists. Whatever their faith, it has contributed to what they were as people I came to like. I could accept Esmé's faith as once I never could have, and could tolerate it even as she could understand my skepticism.

Esmé's family was also religiously divided. Her mother's ancestors were Northern Irish protestants; Peggy O'-Brien herself had been born in Moline, Illinois, and brought up in Davenport, Iowa. Esmé's father Esmond was Irish Catholic, born in New York City, the son of Judge Morgan O'Brien, the Tammany leader. He had gone to Hotchkiss and Yale; the money had come from Esmé's grandmother, a Crimmins, a member of an influential New York family in the construction business. Esmond O'Brien was a stock-market plunger, a friend of Mayor Jimmy Walker, and a business failure. Redeeming all this, he loved Harlem and the great entertainers of the 1920's. One of Esmé's earliest memories was a party at the family house with Eddie Condon's Mound City Blue Blowers playing. Esmé had met Eddie in 1927, long before I knew him. She had met George Gershwin. She knew Gladys Bentley, one of the most colorful blues singers ever. And she played the piano well by ear. She first heard Duke Ellington when she was thirteen at a Paris concert which—oddly enough—I had also attended. She had been a record collector for years, and wherever she and Bob Sarnoff lived she combed the record shops for jazz classics.

Esmé's mother was the opposite of my own mother. She was small and very stylish, with beautiful taste in clothes, in part a result of her having worked for Hattie Carnegie, the fashionable couturière. She had an eye for good furniture, an Irish wit, and all the social graces. Esmé's taste in clothes, her love of jewelry and bright colors, her own flair as a hostess, and her comfortable place in New York's social circles were partly a result of her mother's influence. Esmé had been the debutante of the year following the social emergence of Brenda Frazier, and she had been the darling of "Cholly Knickerbocker" and the rest of the society columnists and social gossipers.

Esmé's enthusiasms in these directions were not precisely mine, probably because Mother, having neither interest nor taste in any kind of decor, had not prepared me. The first anniversary present I bought for Esmé was a painting by Robert Motherwell, a strange-looking picture. I have never had much knowledge of art, although I have always liked the paintings of Stuart Davis and a few others, and now and then when something catches my eye I buy it. Esmé never liked the Motherwell painting, so I finally decided to sell it and contribute the proceeds to the Northside Center. A Parke-Bernet representative came to our apartment to appraise the painting and told me it was worth between $10,000 and $20,000. I had paid less than $1,000 for it. Still, after one look at the Motherwell, Esmé said, "John, I like jewelry." She told me about a jeweler named Seaman Schepps. "Go see him," she said.

I ambled into Schepps' store with *The Nation* and the *New Republic* under my arm, and the proprietor cried, "Ah, you read good things." Schepps dealt in the semiprecious stones Esmé loved, and he had a unique sense of design. After that I knew where to buy my wife a present.

For all her love of beautiful things, Esmé had had little wealth in her background and she was married to Bob Sarnoff at a time when he never made much money. Esmé asked no alimony and accepted only modest child support for Rosita. She had no ambition to be rich, only the rare talent for living gracefully and spending whatever money she had on her friends and herself with taste and originality. When we married, she realized that I was making very little money at Mercury, that I had heavy responsibilities toward Jemy and my two sons, and that I was under considerable financial strain. I even had to borrow money from my mother to handle the financial demands of a second marriage and a completely different life style.

Esmé had her doubts about me. She was a little terrified of my political past, having been told that I was an ex-Red, and, while she believed me when I told her my political views, she was always very sensitive to criticism of me. She also became a frustrated pianist. Once when she was playing I told her she'd got a chord wrong. She was furious. "That's what I get for marrying a critic," she said, and she has never played in front of me again. But she handled my own family beautifully, particularly my mother. She knew Mother did not approve of lipstick, makeup, colorful clothes and jewelry, and on first meeting Esmé settled matters once and for all. "Mother Emily," she said, "you've got to take me as I am. I like lipstick, and there it is." Mother did accept her as she was and loved her.

Esmé also had misgivings about my meeting her friends. One, for instance, was Elsie Sturgis Tailer, married to Tommy Tailer, an amateur golfer, card expert, and Newport socialite. Tommy was prejudiced against Negroes. Elsie's grandfather, however, a man named Morefield Storey, had been one of the founders of the NAACP. After Elsie died tragically of cancer, I came to know Tommy through Elsie's nurse, Dolores Martin, a girl I had cast in *Carmen Jones*, and later the wife of Dave Martin, Cafe Society's bandleader. Dolores changed Tommy's whole attitude about blacks, and he eventually made a large contribution to the NAACP legal defense fund.

One of Esmé's uncles was an Iowan named Ambrose Ralph Powers. He was a cartoonist and printer in Des Moines, and Esmé was worried about how we would get along. When we visited Uncle Ralph I discovered that his cartoons appeared in the *National Farmers' Union*, representing the most radical farmers' group in America. Uncle Ralph turned out to be much more radical than I, both of us black sheep in our families. Uncle Ralph subscribed to the *National Guardian*, a Marxist publication I did not approve of at all. "How can you like the *Guardian*?" I asked. "There is only one good radical paper in America, *I. F. Stone's Weekly*."

"I don't know that one," Uncle Ralph admitted.

I sent him a lifetime subscription to Izzy Stone's *Weekly*, and Ralph wrote to tell me how grateful he was. I think Esmé was somewhat annoyed to find her radical husband and her radical uncle getting along so well, but we did. Uncle Ralph had trained a pet rabbit to go to the refrigerator when he was hungry, press the foot lever which opened the door, and find his own dinner. Ralph Powers was one of the prizes of my life that I owe to Esmé.

Another of her close friends from Des Moines was Lois Cowles, the former wife of Gardner "Mike" Cowles, who published *Look* magazine. In Des Moines Lois ran a place called Willkie House, a sort of rehabilitation center for blacks. She was also an excellent newspaper woman, and when she came to New York I introduced her to the NAACP. Within a few months Lois became the treasurer of the NAACP Legal Defense Committee. I also introduced her to the Northside Center for Child Development, the only private psychiatric center in Harlem for black and Puerto Rican children, where she is still involved.

One friend of Esmé's who best illustrates what she and I found in common is jazz impresario Norman Granz. Esmé first met Norman in 1945 at his second *Jazz at the Philharmonic* concert. Esmé was in California to meet Bob Sarnoff returning from the Pacific, and she and Norman liked each other immediately. In fact, Norman would gladly have married Esmé after her divorce and has never felt that I am really good enough for her. Norman, whose career in jazz and whose musical tastes in many ways match my own, was also in a sense a competitor, a proud and independent man aware both of my accomplishments and failures. He is a business man, which I am not, a self-made millionaire through his shrewd management of jazz artists and the company he established to release records of his concerts, and I imagine that in his opinion there are few, if any, who qualify as good enough for Esmé.

Norman and I first met when he was releasing his records through Mercury. He has done more to improve the lot of jazz musicians than anyone. Like me, he is politically radical, a discoverer of jazz talent, and a record producer. After Esmé and I met, but before her divorce, she and Norman often had lunch at Henri Soulé's Le Pavillon restaurant. Even when Norman was almost broke he loved to eat in gourmet restaurants. He appeared one day to meet Esmé wearing a huge Henry Wallace button which he refused to remove, much to her embarrassment. At Le Pavillon Norman enjoyed filling his pockets with petit-fours, and more significantly, he managed to break the restaurant's rigid color line by bringing Ella Fitzgerald, whom he manages, and other jazz stars to lunch there. Norman's wedding presents were typical of him. To Esmé he sent a beautiful chess set from Hong Kong. To me he sent a set of dumbbells.

Our marriage, then, began with the discovery by Esmé that many of her friends approved of my political and racial viewpoints. While Esmé never has agreed with me politically, the experience of meeting each other's friends has taught us both tolerance and has vastly enriched our lives. I recall at times the happy marriage John and Molly McChesney had, despite their own differing viewpoints on so many subjects, so I have always felt Esmé and I could be happy together. But our marriage also came at a low point in my career. Mitch Miller had left Mercury for a much more lucrative job at Columbia, and there was very little to fulfill me at Mercury. Finally, I faced serious family problems. I needed Esmé's help, her companionship, her gentle strength to solve many personal and professional problems. My new marriage began at a critical time.

XXXIV

When Father died in the summer of 1949, Mother's life took a turn for the worse. Since about 1934 she had been associated with Dr. Frank N.D. Buchman's religious organization known either as the Oxford Group or Moral Re-Armament. MRA had been successful in obtaining large sums of money from rich widows shortly after the deaths of their husbands.

Mother and Father had sold the 91st Street house and moved into a modest, sixteen-room apartment which occupied an entire floor of 778 Park Avenue. Mother had never lived in an apartment, but she managed. And from this new headquarters she began dealing forthrightly with her affairs.

After Father's death she gathered my sisters and me together to see whether we wanted to take over Dellwood. We discussed the possibility at length, ultimately deciding we simply could not afford to maintain it.

"If that's the case," Mother told us, "I'm going to give it to Moral Re-Armament."

We were horrified, though powerless to stop her. She had title to the property, she had money, and, although approaching seventy-five, she was still perfectly capable of making her own decisions. The women in our family live well into their nineties. My grandmother died at the age of ninety-four. My Aunt Florence Twombly died at ninety-eight, and there was reason to assume Mother would live another twenty years. The only thing we could do was to insist that the Moral Re-Armament people maintain a wing at Dellwood for Mother's exclusive use.

As soon as Dr. Buchman's disciples took control of Mother's affairs, they persuaded her first to give up all her charities, so she could concentrate her money and her time on their interests. They took over Dellwood, promising us that there would be a wing for Mother and her maid and that they would keep certain employees at Dellwood to look after the farm, which they continued to operate.

In 1949 Mother was still president of the Three Arts Club, her inexpensive Manhattan haven for young girls. At the urging of the Buchmanites, however, Mother resigned as president and put Esmé in charge of the club. Esmé handled the job brilliantly, bringing in some young members on the board, and, when a couple of black girls applied, announcing herself in favor of admitting them. Mother was upset, believing blacks would cause trouble. Moral Re-Armament finally got her to close the club down. It was a deficit operation which needed donations of about $100,000 a year to keep going. Mother and various friends made up the annual deficit.

Esmé was most unhappy at the decision. She had worked hard, was making progress, and believed in the objectives of the club. It made no difference. Mother was now traveling around the world with the MRA forces, going to India and the Far East, underwriting the expenses of the group. Esmé was left to close the club, giving up a difficult, rewarding job and admitting defeat, as all of us were doing in the face of the MRA's ultimatums.

(Small-scale as it may have seemed, Three Arts was in fact a going concern and nearly $200,000 was realized on the disposal of its assets, much of it in cash. Esmé and her vice president had some nervous moments trotting to the banks with large rolls of bills in their purses. These funds, incidentally, did not find their way to the MRA. They were given to various nonprofit institutions in the arts.)

My sisters and I estimate that MRA received well over $3,000,000 from Mother. My sisters' objections to all this were less serious than my own. They felt Mother had a perfect right to do whatever she chose with her money as long as her gifts did not draw on funds previously intended for children and grandchildren. I felt differently, not because I expected to receive any of the money myself, but because I believed Mother's first consideration should have been for socially useful causes.

Another disastrous financial crisis arose concerning Mother's controlling interest in W. & J. Sloane furniture stores. By the mid-1950's there were Sloane stores in New

York, Palm Beach, California, and the Midwest. The chain was operated by Jack Sloane, my mother's first cousin and a charming gentleman. Jack had occasion to make a three-month trip to Africa. While he was away, Mother was approached to sell her stock in the corporation for about three times its market value. We—my sisters and I—urged Mother not to sell, but she let her interest go for something more than $1,000,000. All of the money went to MRA, and the Hammond connection with W. & J. Sloane ended.

As the 1950's passed, Mother dipped more heavily into trusts supposedly reserved for her grandchildren. Finally, in about 1960, I got together with a couple of brothers-in-law and suggested some kind of family agreement, so that Mother would not be allowed to use up all the family capital. They asked whether I had any ideas. I did. I thought we should have a legal statement prepared which specified that we—the family—would not object to Mother spending her income in any way she saw fit, even including gifts to MRA, if in return she would promise not to apply capital to MRA support.

The MRA people objected, but they realized they could not afford to take on the entire family. Neither could Mother. Confronted by this united expression of family feeling, Mother decided to change her will, which at that point made MRA the beneficiary of half her capital. Now, and henceforward, it would get nothing. The trusts for the grandchildren were salvaged and I believe that by our efforts we were able to save them about a million dollars.

Mother died in her ninety-sixth year, and until about the age of ninety when she became senile, she continued to believe in the principles of Moral Re-Armament. She loved her family and respected my accomplishments, but her responsibility to save the world with the resources she had been given was always her special concern. She did much to be proud of, and my sisters and I loved her and understood her need for a personal commitment to good works. That she was often misled, especially after my father died and could no longer provide some measure of wise counsel, we understood and forgave, and for myself I felt that the bond between

Mother and me was never broken. I think each of us knew how much alike we were.

Esmé and I became stepparents as well as parents, never an easy role in second marriages, but one we were determined to assume with as little animosity and friction as possible. Rosita had been brought up as Esmé believed she should be. When we were married, Rosita was five and attending Miss Hewitt's classes in New York City. She lived with us in the 57th Street apartment until she was old enough to go away to a preparatory school. Her father, I believe, thought it advisable for Rosita to go to a boarding school and I was able to get her into Farmington through my sister Rachel, who was the head of the alumnae board.

Indeed, several generations of the family have attended Farmington and hold it in affection and regard. It was, of course, very Wasp, and for the first time in Rosita's life she had to face the fact that being half-Jewish could be a problem. In her first year she was assigned a room with another half-Jewish girl, but Rosita had chosen Farmington herself, and she handled this first slight wisely and patiently. She continued to be an excellent student. She was accepted by the other girls and she decided to be the first in the school's history to go to Swarthmore, among the more difficult colleges in the country to enter. She graduated from Swarthmore, an accomplishment which made us all proud, and chose a career in educational television.

Of my own two sons, Jeep had most trouble with the new marriage. He could not understand my living separately, nor the fact that Rosita lived with us and he could not. Jason, born a month after I got out of the Army, was only three, so he was able to accept his new stepmother easily and with great love, settling into both households without difficulty.

Jemy and I did not want too structured an education for our sons. We wanted them to have as much freedom as possible and to come to know as wide a cross section of children as possible. In the 1940's public schools in Greenwich Village were out of the question because of the poor quality

of their education. We chose instead the Little Red Schoolhouse on Bleecker Street, around the corner from our house
on MacDougal. There were excellent teachers there, as well
as some inadequacies. Jeep, whose ear was unusually good,
was unable to study any foreign language because the school
did not believe in language instruction before high school.

The fact that Rosita was receiving a fine education and
my sons were not created problems for me, because I did not
want to fight with Jemy. I went along with Little Red for
about three years, then, when Jeep was about nine, I took
him out and put him in Collegiate School. From a relaxed
school atmosphere, where students called their teachers by
their first names, he entered a structured situation, although
one offering excellent academic instruction. Perhaps the
change was too abrupt and too great. Jeep hated his teachers,
developed a stutter, while at the same time finding a superb
art teacher and learning how to study.

Both Jeep and Jason were natural athletes and I found
it difficult to communicate with them as their interests and
talents began to diverge from my own. I could not explain to
either one the exact circumstances of my divorce, that their
mother had fallen in love with someone else and that it had
not been my wish to divorce. Looking back, I realize it was
a mistake not to tell them what they needed to know, but
hindsight, especially for parents, is always easy.

One Washington's birthday I decided to take them to
the Concord Hotel in the Catskill Mountains. Both boys were
good swimmers and Buster Crabbe, of Tarzan fame was the
swimming coach there. Neither Esmé nor Rosita went along.
This was to be a weekend for the three of us to be together.
We arrived on a Saturday afternoon in time for lunch. Jeep
and Jason ordered shrimp cocktails, which in keeping with its
semikosher status the Concord did not serve. After lunch I
started to light a cigarette only to be reminded it was the Sab-
bath and that smoking was not allowed in the dining room.

That afternoon there was a swimming meet for boys
under twelve. Jeep was eleven and Jason eight, and of the
twenty boys in the race Jeep was the tallest and Jason the

shortest. Jason, therefore, was given a headstart of a couple of lengths. Needless to say, Jason won the race with Jeep coming in second. Buster Crabbe was so impressed with Jason that he singled him out to demonstrate the free-style stroke to the other boys. He told me that Jason could get a swimming scholarship to any college: "I urge you to consider it, because I haven't seen any boy like him."

Jeep, who was a faster swimmer than Jason, was less than overjoyed at his brother's success. Both, however, received gaudy trophies and altogether we enjoyed ourselves. If they never did get over substituting kippered herring for scrambled eggs and bacon, the swimming and skiing were marvelous, and we returned home much closer to each other.

By the time Jeep was fourteen he wanted to leave Collegiate in the worst way and I wanted him to leave the city entirely. I sent him to Hotchkiss summer school, which he thoroughly hated. What next? George Milmine, who ran the summer session, gave me a clue. A new school called Marvelwood was opening in Cornwall, Connecticut. It was run by Robert Bodkin, one of the fine English teachers in this country. Jeep was in Marvelwood's first graduating class and from there was accepted at Antioch, his first choice and the college his mother had attended. Marvelwood recognized Jeep's ability as a painter and sculptor, and an arrangement was made with Hotchkiss to send its art teacher over twice a week to teach an art class.

Antioch, however, was not the right place for him. It had the worst art department possible, although neither Jemy nor I realized it at the time, and Jeep arrived there having completed a summer as the youngest pupil ever at the Skowhegan Art School in Maine.

By the time Jeep got to Antioch he was already interested in music. He was born with perfect pitch, a gift which helped him to be a far more natural musician than I ever was. He came to me with his discovery of Elvis Presley, assuming I would be appalled. "I know how good Presley is," I said, "but I'd like to take you to the Apollo Theater to hear the man Presley learned all he knows from. His name is Bo Diddley."

In a single show at the Apollo Jeep heard not only Bo Diddley, but Muddy Waters and another blues singer named Howling Wolf. After that we went backstage to meet them all. I never heard Jeep mention Presley again. A couple of weeks later he came to our house in Weston with records by Bo Diddley, one of which was called "I Am A Man," and records by Chuck Berry, who has influenced him more than any singer of the rock era.

In 1958 I took Jeep to the Newport Festival blues show, which included Berry, Big Maybelle, and some wonderful jazz players. I had booked the show to demonstrate the links among jazz, blues, and rock, although with Chuck Berry's gyrations and the hard-rock sounds the audience went wild. There nearly was a riot and the police had to be called. That night's performance was preserved in the motion picture, *Jazz on A Summer's Day*, and it was one Jeep never forgot. By the time he reached Antioch he was already a blues aficionado. This new interest was to determine the course of his career.

Jason also went to Little Red Schoolhouse. Again I had reservations and wanted to move him to a better school. Jason did not agree, however. He persuaded every kid in his class to sign a petition asking me not to remove him from school. Jason was an operator even then. He once came to me to ask why he could not be bar mitzvahed like everyone else in his class. "Because you're not Jewish," I explained. He asked me if he had to be Jewish and I told him that at least in this particular instance he did.

Jason managed to graduate from Elizabeth Irwin High School, although I'll never understand quite how, and he went on to New England College, in New Hampshire. This was in the mid-1960's when pot was everywhere, and everywhere illegal. Jason was asked to leave the college because, he told me, the authorities had found a girl in his room. When I went up to investigate, however, I was told the real story, that he had been caught with marijuana. Soon afterward he was in the Army. Jason always thought himself a runt because his brother was six feet two. Actually, at five-ten he is of normal size and a fine athlete. At Camp Gordon in Georgia Jason was the catcher for the All-Southern U.S. Army baseball team.

Again, however, a few grains of marijuana were found in his field jacket and he was discharged from the Army. Jason claims that as company clerk he typed out his own discharge papers. Because I loathed the Vietnam War and because Jeep managed to escape the draft, I must confess I was not unsympathetic. Jason's career, as unexpected and as rewarding as his brother's, was about to begin.

XXXV

One of the consistencies of my life has been my long association with the NAACP. I joined its board in 1935, convinced at last that our stands on racial equality were in agreement, and although I remained part of a minority which felt that a strong policy was the only effective method of achieving integration and true justice for blacks, we were a militant minority and often persuasive. The guiding force in the twenty years following my election to the board was Walter White. Although surrounded by many reactionary executives, Walter was a strong leader and showed his courage time and again in his term as executive secretary.

In 1949, however, Walter White divorced his wife Gladys, a woman I liked, even if her favorite band was Guy Lombardo's, and married Poppy Cannon, a white woman and a very well-known one. Walter's skin was actually paler than Poppy's, but she was white and he was black and there was an immediate uproar in the ranks of the NAACP hierarchy. Poppy Cannon was a gastronomic expert with a column in the New York *Post,* and after she married Walter she began a food column in the *Amsterdam News* and other Negro newspapers. The reactionaries of the NAACP board decided that Walter White should no longer serve as executive secretary. Although it took about five years to accomplish, Walter White eventually was outmaneuvered. By 1954 he was out and Roy Wilkins was in as executive secretary.

A case came to the NAACP in 1948, however, while Walter was still in charge, that created a crisis on the board and led to precedent-setting decisions in the following years. It involved school integration and opposition to the law of the land as defined in an 1896 decision of the Supreme Court called Plessy versus Ferguson. This decreed that separate-but-equal treatment of blacks in railroad trains, schools, and so forth, was constitutional. It was the position of many of us on the NAACP board that "separate but equal" was unconstitutional, that there was no equality in the kind of separation blacks had endured in the half century since Plessy-Ferguson.

The case involved farmers in Clarendon County, South Carolina, who had applied to the Federal judge in Charleston for a separate-but-equal high school to be built for black children who constituted a majority of the student population. They directed their petition to J. Waties Waring, who had been born in Savannah, Georgia, moved to Charleston early in his career, and married a prominent Charleston woman. Judge Waring had been "a good old boy" in Southern politics for years and had served as the campaign manager for Senator Ellison Duran "Cotton Ed" Smith. Waring was a Southern gentleman, with all the prejudices the phrase implies. In 1942 he was appointed by President Roosevelt to a lifetime Federal judgeship at the instigation of "Cotton Ed" and Jimmy Byrnes, the other senator from South Carolina. After his appointment, however, things began to change. He got a divorce, which was unthinkable for a South Carolina judge. Then he married a volatile, explosive, divorced woman from Michigan, Elizabeth Hoffman. It also turned out that his daughter, who was married to a friend of Esmé's and mine, had a number of black friends.

Judge Waring's first action was to open up the white Democratic primary in South Carolina to Negroes, threatening to jail any sheriff who did not comply with the Federal court order. This, of course, shocked the Establishment. When the Clarendon County farmers came along on the question of separate-but-equal schools. Judge Waring told them their proposal was useless, that their best move was to challenge the whole idea of segregation and bring the case before the Supreme Court. "I'm one of three members of the Court of Appeals here," he said, "so at worst you'll get a minority opinion upholding your stand."

The farmers then came to the NAACP for help in challenging Plessy-Ferguson. The NAACP board had a fit. I was at the meeting when Thurgood Marshall told them there was no way of getting the case through the Supreme Court. The NAACP had been pecking away at "separate but equal," for years, he said. Medical and law schools had been opened up, access to graduate schools had been gained, but it was not the right moment to confront the whole issue head-on.

There were about six of us on the board who strongly opposed Marshall's view. We hammered at the majority stand for months, arguing that it was fruitless to predict what the Supreme Court might do when no one could be certain who would be on it when the case was presented, and that in any event the NAACP should take a position against the legalized inequality of Plessy on principle. Eventually we won out.

In 1951 the first of several trials took place in Charleston. Tom O'Connor, managing editor of New York's struggling liberal-radical tabloid, *The Compass*, and a friend, decided I should cover the story for him. Earlier, Esmé and I had met Judge and Mrs. Waring while visiting friends in Charleston. We simply went to their house one night and knocked at the front door. By then it was being stoned regularly; the Warings were in fear for their lives and under Government protection. Elizabeth Waring came to the door. I introduced ourselves, saying I was on the NAACP board and a great admirer of the judge. We wondered whether there might be anything we could do to help. We were invited in and soon we all were playing Canasta. By the time I covered the trial for *The Compass* I had a friendly relationship with the Warings and was invited to stay with them, rather than at a hotel.

Pleading before the three-judge court, Thurgood Marshall was dismayingly nervous, uneasy, and not at all effective. Things went so badly Judge Waring wondered whether Thurgood was sabotaging the case! Of course, he wasn't. He was a fine trial lawyer and had always been proud of his ability to get along with even the most reactionary Southern whites. He was worried, though. Plessy *was* the law and Thurgood didn't have many legal legs to stand on, or helpful precedents to push.

I was careful not to be too critical of Thurgood's performance in my *Compass* articles, and fortunately, like Judge Horton in the Scottsboro case, Judge Waring intervened to score a few points from the bench. Thurgood's one inspired move was to bring in Kenneth Clark, professor of psychology at City College of New York (and an old friend from the Northside Center), to testify that enforced segregation caused psychological damage to both black and white children.

After considerable wrangling, a two-judge majority ruled against the plaintiffs. Judge Waring's dissent became the basis of the appeal which finally was heard by the Supreme Court. And Kenneth Clark's argument was the keystone of the Warren Court decision striking down Plessy.

The Supreme Court action took place in 1954 and I was privileged to watch the proceedings. Setting forth the arguments Thurgood Marshall was brilliant. Not only is he one of the fine legal minds of the country, he has no physical fear. He has been threatened with lynching, but this was his opportunity to make a big step and he came through. The victory was an enormous one both for the NAACP and for Thurgood Marshall. I am sure his performance weighed heavily in his eventual appointment to the Court.

Although it was a victory for those of us on the NAACP board who had pushed for the confrontation leading to the decision, I was not renominated. After twenty years of service, this was a bit of a blow, although I don't believe there should be anything automatic about membership on any board, or that long service should necessarily be rewarded with longer service. I became a vice president, keeping my post on the all-important Branch Committee, which maintains liaison with the organization's thirteen hundred branches. I could still attend board meetings. I could talk as much as I wanted to—always a pleasure. And I remained vice president of *The Crisis*. So, on the whole, I did not feel chastened.

There was, nonetheless, an ideological power struggle going on within the NAACP, and it was my proposal in 1955 that E. Franklin Frazier, head of the sociology department at Howard University, be appointed to the board that precipitated the next internal convulsion.

Ed was an extraordinary man, president of the American Sociological Association and the first black to be so honored. He was a former dock-walloper from Baltimore, fiercely independent, afraid of no one and nothing. He literally had been run out of town for his militancy when he was at Atlanta University, as well as at Fisk, in Nashville. Invited by mistake to attend a luncheon at segregated Vanderbilt—ah, there!—University nearby, he had accepted and appeared in the cafeteria on schedule. Jaws dropped and the sheriff was called. He ate his lunch, anyway.

He was a contributing editor of a Marxist monthly called *Science and Society*, although he despised the Communists for their stand on self-determination in the black belt. He felt that this was a contradiction of everything enlightened people who believed in integration should support.

When I proposed him for the board, Roy Wilkins was running the meetings with what seemed to me an iron hand. I made an impassioned plea for Ed as a brilliant man in tune with NAACP principles. Attractive as I made him sound, there were things about him that worried some of the board. For instance, Ed had recently published a book called *Black Bourgeoisie*, a devastating critique on the black middle-class which, he argued, mirrored and intensified the faults of its white counterparts. (It also slammed his wife's social friends in Washington, D.C. Although Ed was happily married, he hated poker, bridge parties, and the chitchat that went on in his house when he was trying to work!) First published in France, it was a sensation. When it appeared in America it outraged all the middle-class Negroes I knew, including, of course, the NAACP board. Thurgood Marshall, Henry Lee Moon, even Ted Poston thought the book too critical to be printed.

Wilkins allowed the discussion of the nomination to proceed until it appeared Frazier would be approved unanimously. He then announced in his temperate way that if Frazier were elected he would resign as executive secretary. Ed represented the kind of independence Roy could not control, and knowing that he was virtually irreplaceable Roy gave the board a choice of either-or. Ed Frazier was not elected. We needed his kind of soaring intellectual freedom, but we never got it.

Roy Wilkins had ability and he knew how to manipulate the levers of power. He had been a successful newspaperman on the Kansas City *Call*—his had been among the black editorial voices raised in protest against the shilly-shallying of the NAACP in the early stages of the Scottsboro case—and had been an assistant editor of *The Crisis* under the great W.E.B. DuBois. He was an effective speaker and he piled up credits by his tireless campaigning for various board members.

Organizationally, Roy had powerful props on two sides. One was Kelly Alexander, an undertaker from North Carolina, a most personable fellow whom I always enjoyed. But he had the heart of a businessman who profited from segregation, as indeed he did. It is a perverse fact that in an unsegregated society a black mortician will do less well. He will lose the monopoly that a segregated society bequeaths: No—or almost no—white undertaker will have anything to do with a black corpse. Accordingly, the black undertaker is not above exploiting every scrap of fear and race consciousness in the black community. For Roy, Kelly and his cohorts ran NAACP conventions with a rigid hand on the tiller. Progressive platform planks proposed by young—or even by aging—Turks were almost invariably defeated.

The other was Kivie Kaplan, the white president of the NAACP. Kivie was a prominent Boston businessman—the Colonial Leather Company—who had been involved with the NAACP since the late 1930's. Kivie, who had perfected his fund-raising techniques in the United Jewish Appeal and other black and white charitable organizations, told the NAACP it should promote more life memberships. He suggested putting pressure on every community and awarding prizes to the branches which produced most life members. Further, he said, there should be junior life memberships for children under fifteen. When I joined the NAACP I was the thirtieth life member. Now there are forty or fifty thousand. Life memberships, of course, bring in large amounts of money immediately, but each life member no longer pays annual dues and receives all NAACP publications automatically. My son Jason is a junior life member.

Kaplan eventually succeeded Arthur Spingarn as president of NAACP. I knew Arthur, a wonderful old man with one of the world's finest collections of books by Negro authors. Soon after World War II the Spingarn Award, the highest honor the NAACP pays to distinguished blacks, was awarded to Duke Ellington. It was presented at a large banquet at the Roosevelt Hotel in New York, where Arthur spoke of Ellington's many achievements and his many famous compositions, including "Mood Indigo," "Black and Tan Fantasy," and "Take the Train!" Several of us in the audience shouted "Take the A Train," to no avail. Duke was not only credited with Billy Strayhorn's famous theme for the Ellington band, but the whole point of the title was lost. No surprise. The NAACP never was known for its knowledge or appreciation of jazz!

Kivie Kaplan was a more aggressive president than Spingarn. He went along with whatever Roy Wilkins wanted, however. When I urged a stand on the Vietnam War, when I said the NAACP was more interested in finding organizers with college degrees than with jail records for defying Southern segregation, Kaplan backed Wilkins completely and my protests were muffled. Kivie's contributions to the NAACP continued until he died of a heart attack a few years ago, and financially his leadership was good for the association. But his support of Wilkins' refusal to move leftward, as the NAACP should have done in the interest of the majority of its members, in my view hurt its effectiveness.

XXXVI

I returned home one day to find two FBI investigators waiting for me in the lobby of my apartment house. I was about to be subpoenaed, I was informed, for testimony regarding my connection with the Metropolitan Music School. This was in the early 1950's, when every American liberal was suspect; certainly my own activities over the years must have filled a fat file somewhere in Washington. Though why my distant connection with a music school should come under Justice Department scrutiny I had no idea.

One of my former neighbors on Sullivan Street, Wallingford Rieger, was chairman of the board of the Metropolitan Music School. Teddy Wilson had taught there and it was the only school in the city which recognized jazz as a suitable subject for an educational curriculum, as well as one of the few which did not discriminate against black students. My agreement to join its advisory board was freely given, although I had never actually visited the school. The FBI agents accompanied me up to the apartment and the questioning—with Esmé hovering nervously in another room—began.

"What are you doing on the board of the school?"

"Very simple. The school has no racial prejudice."

"How did you get involved?"

"I've been on the board of the NAACP since 1935. I've had a lot to do with music."

"What sort of papers have you written for?"

"I've written for the Brooklyn *Eagle,* the New York *Times,* the *Herald Tribune.* I covered the Scottsboro case for *The Nation* and the *New Republic.*"

"You did what?" one of the agents cried.

"I covered the Scottsboro case," I repeated.

"My God," he said. "I did my college thesis on the Scottsboro case."

The official ice was broken. The hostility I had felt toward me was thawing rapidly. The agents suddenly became human. I told the story of the *Daily News* reporter Tom Cassidy, who became radicalized by the Scottsboro trials and as a result organized the first Newspaper Guild unit in New York. His conversion caused the *Daily News* to become the first newspaper in the country to sign a closed-shop contract with the Guild, a CIO union. The agents were fascinated, though not about to be converted.

"What about these *Spirituals to Swing* concerts?" the second agent asked.

"I produced those concerts in 1938 and 1939," I said. "They were something I had wanted to do for years. They simply showed the sources of black music and its evolution into today's jazz." I explained my fruitless attempts to get the NAACP to sponsor them, and how the middle-class values of the NAACP not only put jazz and blues outside its experience, but made it look down on both the music and the Negroes who performed it. "I went to the International Ladies Garment Workers' Union, which produced *Pins and Needles*," I continued, "but they and their membership were not interested, either." So when the business manager of the *New Masses* finally offered its sponsorship on my condition that there would be no politics mentioned in the promotion, I had agreed. "There was no other way to get the concerts produced."

The questioning continued. I wondered where it was leading, what was the point of the whole interview. Finally, it came. "Now we have to ask you the $64 question: Are you or have you ever been a member of the Communist Party?"

"I'm going to pause before I answer that," I told them, "because it's really none of your damned business. I think it's important to tell the absolute truth, because not only was I never a member of the Communist Party, nor would I be a member of the Communist Party, nor am I a member of the Communist Party, I could not be because I am interested in civil rights and it is not. Throughout the years the Communists have done flip-flops, and if I had been a member of the Party I could never have made the kind of waves I did.

"If you're expecting me to plead the Fifth Amendment, I won't. I'll simply say I was never a member of the Communist Party and that since I have not been a member it is impossible for me to tell you who was. Only Party members would know."

The district attorney's office withdrew the subpoena. I was never called to testify.

Eventually, I withdrew from the School's board; it

simply was not an operation to which I could give much time or attention. As far as I am concerned it was and is a good music school. I know I found a fine trombone teacher for Jason there.

It was not the last time I was attacked for my activities and associations. During the 1960's the John Birch Society waged a telephone campaign of defamation against me, announcing themselves on their calls. They ran ads in newspapers and on some small radio stations urging people to call a certain number and learn about the Communist conspiracy going on at Columbia Records. Callers heard a stream of villification against me, going all the way back to my association with Cafe Society in 1939. By the 1960's I was associated with several recording artists who also were targets of the Birchers, so through me, it was claimed, the Communists were taking over CBS. I finally managed to have the telephone campaign stopped. CBS, I am proud to say, was never overly concerned about having a subversive in its ranks, and, even more remarkably, was tough-minded enough not to worry about possible effects either on record sales or the company image.

XXXVII

In February, 1953, Benny came to me with an offer to manage a six-week tour of his original band, or at least as many of the original members as we could get together. He had already made arrangements with Joe Glaser to include Louis Armstrong's group as a second act. This decision was made after he failed to get Harry James, who wanted fifty per cent of the tour profits. Louis was to receive fifty per cent of the gross, too, but his was going to be a much more substantial contribution to the show than Harry's would have been.

Esmé and I discussed Benny's offer very carefully. I had not wanted to become involved with him again, either musically or in a business way. He was now a part of my family, our relations in the past had often been strained, and my contributions and suggestions, once so welcome, now struck Benny as interference. It seemed wise to restrict our future relationship to a merely personal one. Still, the offer was a challenge. I loved the original Goodman band and I thought it would be fun to get it together again. With the success of the Carnegie Hall concert recordings* released by Columbia in the early 1950's, and followed by other recordings made in the late 1930's which Benny somehow acquired and leased to Columbia, there was a new public eager to hear that band in person. After thinking it over, I told Benny I would accept his offer, which included an advance of $300 a week for expenses against twenty per cent of his net profit.

The tour was scheduled to begin in April, giving us two months to assemble the band, arrange bookings throughout the country, and secure the kind of guarantees a group this expensive would require. The payroll would be enormous, for many of the original players, like Ziggy Elman and Teddy Wilson, had become stars in their own right. Further, ex-employees of Benny's usually felt they had been underpaid in the glory days with him and were determined not to allow it to happen again.

We began by getting Gene Krupa and Teddy Wilson. For bass we hired Israel Crosby, not an original, but as fine a bass as there was in the country. Benny wanted Allan Reuss on guitar; happily, we got Steve Jordan from Ray McKinley's old band. We got Ziggy, and Helen Ward, Benny's first vocalist. Helen was not an artist of the stature of, say, Billie, yet in songs such as "Goody Goody" and "You Turned the Tables on Me" her honest, straightforward, gently swinging voice undeniably contributed to the sound of the original band. We hired Georgie Auld on tenor, if not an original at least a graduate of a later Goodman aggregation. We found Vernon

*Incredible as it may seem, no arrangements were made to record this extraordinary event. It was preserved for posterity through the foresight and good will of Albert Marx, then Helen Ward's husband, who recorded it live at Zeke Frank's commercial studio on Carnegie Hall's third floor. He never got a cent of the proceeds of this most successful two-LP album, or even a line in the notes acknowledging his rather important contribution to its existence. In 1977 I was awarded a gold plaque by the National Academy of Recording Arts and Sciences for having produced these memorable records. Honored, but remembering who had saved these sounds for us, I sent the plaque to Albert, with thanks.

Brown, one of the early trombonists.

Some of the replacements actually were better than the originals. The marvelous alto, Willie Smith, joined us, as did trumpeter Charlie Shavers, both jazz stars of the first rank. I had to talk several of the men into rejoining the band because of past fracases with Benny. On the other hand, the money was good and we had all those superlative Fletcher Henderson arrangements.

About a week before the tour was to begin Benny became alarmed about starting the show without a couple of break-in engagements far enough out of town so none of the New York critics would hear the band before it was ready. One of the secrets of Benny's success as a leader has always been his insistence on rehearsals, on complete preparation before he is heard by critics. I decided one of the safest places would be Manchester, New Hampshire, where Esmé and I had escaped the gossip columnists when we were married. I also found that Charlie Shribman, who had booked the first Goodman band in New England in 1935, would handle the New Hampshire date. We opened on a Friday night in a drenching rain that discouraged no one. There were well over two thousand people in the small ballroom and the band played well. Benny, returning as a bandleader after several years of only intermittent appearances, none of them too successful, was under considerable strain. He was not playing with the ease that was his hallmark in the old days. Still, all appeared to go satisfactorily.

The following night we were booked in Portland, Maine, another stamping ground of mine. I knew the local newspapermen and the promoter was still Charlie Shribman. I think we broke every record at the Portland Armory with a wildly enthusiastic crowd of over three thousand people jammed into the hall. Benny relaxed and played as I had not heard him play for years. The band was like a bunch of kids, happy to know that the old music still had a public, that they had not been forgotten.

I drove back to New York after the Portland engagement. I took Gene Krupa with me because he wanted to make an eight o'clock mass in Yonkers, which would have been impossible if he had returned with the band. I got him there at ten minutes past seven. We made the trip from Portland to Yonkers in less than six hours. The following day, Monday, was the first time Louis Armstrong and Benny met since the tour had been booked. That turned out to be a serious error on Joe Glaser's part. He had made the booking without filling Louis in, or seeing to it that Louis and Benny discussed the tour themselves. Benny was rehearsing in a hall on 48th Street and things were going well. Benny was all business, auditioning a couple of last-minute players. Suddenly, the door burst open and Louis and his group and some of their wives, as well as many hangers-on, marched in.

Louis was, of course, a gregarious man, so everybody greeted him and there was bedlam for some twenty minutes. Benny stood it as long as he could, then asked Louis if he would mind sending his entourage out so the rehearsal could continue. Louis took offense. He considered himself a co-star in the show, although actually Goodman was the boss. After a brief conversation with Benny, Louis left. The next day, when he was supposed to show up for another rehearsal, he didn't appear.

The tour was booked to open on a Wednesday at the New Haven Arena. We arrived about two o'clock in the afternoon, giving the band time to rehearse. Armstrong's band bus arrived about five o'clock. There were more words between Benny and Louis, who by this time was feeling put upon. Louis decided that his part of the show was going to be just as long as Benny's, so Louis went on and did his regular vaudeville act. He was on for an hour and twenty minutes. He was supposed to be on for forty. Benny was boiling. The show was supposed to close with Armstrong joining Benny in a finale with the Goodman quartet. Benny announced, "Now, ladies and gentlemen, I want to present Louis Armstrong." There was a horrible pause. No Louis. Benny was left hanging on stage.

I rushed to Armstrong's dressing room to plead with him to come back on stage with Benny. Louis refused. The following day Benny tried to heal the breach by asking Louis to have dinner with him. Louis couldn't make dinner. He promised instead to meet Benny in Newark that night an hour before the show at the Mosque Theater. I drove to Newark with Benny and Virginia Wicks, the excellent publicist who had been hired to promote the tour. We arrived well before seven-thirty. No Armstrong. At eight-thirty Benny, in a rage, rearranged the program and began the show himself. Louis arrived at ten of nine, the first time I can ever remember him being late. He apologized, saying he had been held up in traffic driving from his home on Long Island.

After the first set Benny walked into the dressing room, picked up a glass, and smashed it on the ground. Georgie Auld, one of the wits in the band, asked, "Who do you think you are, Benny, the Jewish Marlon Brando?" a reference to Brando's violent movie performances. Benny gave Georgie a "ray," then swallowed his anger and laughed. He and Louis did perform together after that. It began to seem that the Carnegie Hall concerts next on the schedule would not be fiascos after all.

The Carnegie Hall dates produced the largest grosses of any jazz concert ever played up to 1953 and in both Benny played atrociously. The *Times* and *Trib* sent their top music critics, who knew little about jazz, and both raved. According to the Saturday papers it appeared that Goodman had returned in all his glory. Those of us in the audience who knew better, who had seen Benny stagger a couple of times on stage, and who knew the arrangements and his own immaculate playing, recognized that his performance was less than glorious. Benny is such a perfectionist, so uniformly flawless as a musician, that even the slightest deviation from the norm is immediately noticeable.

The tour next played the Met Theater in Providence. This was a date which had given me a great deal of difficulty because the day after, a Sunday, the tour was booked for Symphony Hall in Boston. The Providence theater insisted on two shows, the first to start at two-thirty in the afternoon, a physical impossibility for a band which had gotten off stage of Carnegie Hall at two in the morning. It would have meant leaving New York at dawn. After much discussion we scheduled the first show in Providence at four-thirty to be followed by the regular evening show. The band still would have to leave New York at ten in the morning with very little sleep.

I drove to Providence, so I could return to see my family. I had been on the road for two months prior to the tour setting up bookings and promotion, and I wanted to get home. I reached Providence in the rain to find the house a quarter filled. The theater management was frantic and Benny was furious. He played the afternoon show. He was not playing his best and knew it. Afterward Benny and I went to the Providence Biltmore for dinner in his room. As we sat down Benny said, "John, do you realize I haven't confirmed any of the tour dates beyond two weeks from now?"

I did. "And the theaters and promoters are screaming," I said.

"You know why?" he asked.

I didn't.

"We don't need Louis Armstrong," he said. "The attraction is the revival of the old Goodman band."

"I thought that from the start, Benny," I told him. "But I don't think you can be too tough on Louis. Don't forget that Joe Glaser has never even shown Louis the contract."

"Oh, I'm not blaming Louis," Benny said. "I'm blaming Joe Glaser entirely." Benny continued to talk, upbraiding Glaser, sipping cognac, repeating his conviction that it was Benny Goodman's band the people were coming to hear. I thought he had a point.

At the evening show in Providence both Benny and the band played well. After the show Benny asked me to drive to Boston with him. "I hope you don't mind," I said, "but I must see my family. I haven't seen anything of them for two months. I'll rejoin you in Boston tomorrow."

I packed my suitcase and left Providence after the intermission. There was a fog that Saturday night which only New England and Old England can produce. By midnight I reached Manchester, about ten miles north of Hartford. I realized I was too tired and that it was dangerous to continue. There were no hitchhikers on the road to keep me company and I was falling asleep at the wheel. I found one room left in a highway motel and took it. I awoke at nine, called Esmé, and told her to expect me in New York by noon.

I arrived at our apartment about fifteen minutes before noon. Esmé met me at the door. She was ashen. "You're flying to Boston on the one o'clock plane," she told me. "Benny has had a heart attack. He's very ill. He's in an oxygen tent and nobody can speak to him."

I was filled with guilt. All I could find out from Virginia Wicks was that Benny was having difficulty breathing, that his condition was serious. Virginia and I caught the plane and were at the Ritz-Carlton Hotel by two-thirty that afternoon. The concert was scheduled for four and there were regular radio announcements that Benny would not be appearing. No one was allowed to see him. Alice, whom I reached by telephone, said Benny had left Providence at midnight, driving with someone, and had reached Boston at about four in the morning. He arrived at the Ritz-Carlton, where Alice and his secretary, Muriel Zuckerman, were waiting for him. There he collapsed. The hotel doctor was called, and because of his breathing difficulty he was put in an oxygen tent. Then various specialists were called.

My friend Ed Winer, the owner of the hotel, told me he did not believe Benny was very sick. Winer thought the collapse was a result of tension, the difficulties of the tour. His own doctor could find nothing wrong. The afternoon concert at Symphony Hall was a sellout. Gene Krupa took over direction of the band. Louis m.c.'d the show and was marvelous. He was obviously trying to help Benny as much as he could, certainly feeling guilty about all the misunderstandings between them.

I spent a sleepless night at the Ritz-Carlton. As manager of the tour I was called constantly. At two-thirty in the morning the United Press asked confirmation of a report that Benny had passed away. It was the sort of rumor which circulates whenever anyone prominent in show business is ill. I devoted the rest of the night to denying rumors and reassuring callers. Unable to see Benny, I flew back to New York the next day. Benny had a cardiogram scheduled for Monday or Tuesday and for the next few days at least would not be able to rejoin the tour.

Monday night the show played Bushnell Auditorium in Hartford. Tuesday was a day off for the musicians. I drove to Hartford on Monday—Benny was still incommunicado in Boston—and while there were few refunds there was an audience letdown. I returned to New York Tuesday morning with many things to do. The promoters, naturally, wanted to know whether Benny would rejoin the tour. If not, other financial arrangements had to be made, advertising changed, and so on. The next five dates were being booked by the Washington promoter, Irving Feld, who was convinced Goodman would be back with the show and who refused to change the advertising to drop Benny's name. I told Feld that as far as I knew, Benny would not be with the show, though of course, there was always a chance that he could be.

Tuesday I spent an hour with Benny's attorney, Sidney Kaye, to find out if I could what Benny's intentions were. I told Kaye about my conversation with Benny in Providence, about not needing Louis Armstrong on the tour. Sidney said, "But, John, not after the way Louis has filled in for Benny."

I agreed with Sidney that the whole picture had changed. I also agreed that up until then Benny had every right to get out of his contract with Armstrong, even though the problems were not Louis' fault. I felt much better after Sidney agreed that it would be unthinkable to drop Armstrong from the tour. The band was booked to play Wednesday in Reading, Pennsylvania, a concert promoted by Irving Feld. Arriving there I found pandemonium. All day people had been asking for refunds because Benny, despite Feld's advertising, evidently would not appear. Out of four thousand people who had purchased tickets, two thousand demanded and received their money back. Feld was panicky. I had heard the day before that Benny's cardiogram was satisfactory, that he had not had a heart attack, so I sent him a wire saying that, even if he had to be wheeled on stage, it was necessary for the sake of the tour to appear. I realized that my telegram would stir him up, that he would be upset with me, and that perhaps a little adrenalin flowing at my expense was just what he needed to get moving again. I also felt that if he let this crisis defeat him it would be years before he played again.

There had been considerable conflict over the tour between Benny and Alice. Alice has been the most wonderful wife any man could ask for, but because of Benny's slipped disc in 1941, which had not been corrected, she had wanted him to work less, to be home more often with their children, and to avoid the rigors of the life of a bandleader. I felt that Alice would now encourage him to forget the tour for the sake of his health, a normal attitude perhaps but in my opinion the wrong one. I went to Harrisburg for the next night's concert, one where Benny's absence had been announced. Although it was not a full house it was a profitable date. I went to every radio station in Harrisburg to explain Benny's absence and to praise Armstrong's great work in substituting for him. Louis could well have asked for a larger percentage of the grosses, because he was the star attraction. It wasn't in him to take advantage of the situation. He never said a word about money.

Returning to New York, I called Benny person-to-person at the Ritz-Carlton. I knew he had spoken by telephone to Sidney Kaye and also that he had talked to Charles Wick, formerly of the William Morris band department. The hotel operator told me Mr. Goodman had checked out and gone home to Stamford, Connecticut. I wondered why I had not been informed, and was also surprised that he was well enough to drive home. A call to Stamford revealed that he was not expected. Esmé and I decided there was nothing to do but wait for someone to solve the puzzle for us.

Shortly after midnight our telephone rang. It was Benny calling from Boston. "Hey, John," he asked, "did you get my wire?"

No. "Where are you?"

"I'm at the Ritz."

"That's funny. We called you. Everybody said you were on your way home."

"That's what we told everybody," Benny said. "I wired you in Harrisburg." When I explained that I had left Harrisburg late in the afternoon he said, "Well, I'm just as glad you didn't get it. It was a very disagreeable wire. That was a terrible telegram you sent me."

"I didn't think it was, Benny. When are you coming back? The tour needs you, and you need it, too. I know you can play."

"John, I'll tell you," he said. "I have every intention of coming back. I'm having a complete physical examination on Monday. If it's okay, and I'm sure it will be, I'll be back on the tour."

"That's the best news I could hear."

"I want to tell you," he continued. "I've gotten a new manager, Charlie Wick, who is going to be my booker. You're still my personal manager."

That was fine with me, if rather surprising that he had acted so quickly. Again Benny assured me that I was still in the picture and that all would be well. "Okay," I said. "The thing that makes me happier than anything else is to know you'll be back playing again. I know it will be good for you."

From here on the story becomes part melodrama, part farce. I have to say we all overreacted: high dudgeon, pronunciamentos, operatic threats. We were a sextet singing all at once and not harmoniously. Looking back I even find it funny. There were hard words and injured feelings, however, and unfortunately those are part of the memories, too.

The following morning the telephone rang. It was Joe Glaser returning my call. "Joe," I said, "I have good news. Benny told me last night he has every intention of rejoining the tour."

"He has?" shouted Glaser. "I've just been told by Charlie Wick to cancel the tour completely, not to honor any dates where the contracts have not been signed. I'm going to call Petrillo." James Petrillo, czar of the musicians' union, was powerful enough to take action if he decided to.

I was dumfounded. I told Glaser of my conversations with Benny and with Sidney Kaye. On Saturday I received a long telegram from Benny firing me as his personal manager. By telling Glaser Benny would rejoin the tour I had, in all innocence, scuttled Benny's intention, or bluff, to cancel the whole deal. He was furious. I was furious. I had been caught in the middle of Benny's feud with Glaser and his desire to get Armstrong out of the show.

Cooling down, I realized that things were getting out of hand. When I told my sister Emily that I was considering a suit, she said, "But, John, you can't sue your own brother-in-law! You'll hurt Alice and create a family scandal."

Of course, she was right. Despite the wide differences of opinion existing among my multitude of relatives, particularly my own social and political disagreements with various kin, we all have managed to see the best and put up with the worst in each other—and avoid taking disputes into the public arena. We have managed to remain fond of each other and civilly respectful of each other's benighted views. When Emily reminded me of the gossip a lawsuit against Benny would create I knew I couldn't go through with it. Benny was now as much a member of my family as his wife was.

I received a check from Benny a couple of months later for my expenses up to the point of being fired, and I accepted it. I decided I would never again have anything to do with Benny in a business way. I was not happy, but we would be friends. We live near each other in Connecticut and we are very fond of each other's children. That would be the extent of our relationship in the years to come.

Or so I thought.

XXXVIII

Nearly two years went by before my sister Alice called on Benny's behalf. She had a request. "Universal Pictures is going to film Benny's life story. The script only goes as far as the Carnegie Hall concert," she told me, "and your part is very sympathetic."

As it should be, I thought.

"All you have to do," Alice went on, "is to sign a release and you'll be paid $3,000 for the use of your name."

"Alice, I couldn't sign anything until I've read the script," I told her. I was perfectly willing to cooperate on that basis.

"All right. This isn't the final version, but I'll send it over by messenger. I'm sure you'll approve it."

I read the script that night and was horrified. Benny's life had been rearranged to create a romantic follow-up to the successful *Glenn Miller Story*. All the Hammonds in the script, however, were portrayed as schnooks. Alice was shown proposing to Benny. I was a rich dilettante attempting to help Benny, although he made all the decisions. Much more serious, the role I was to play was that of Benny's manager, something I had never been; either officially or unofficially. And there was no mention of Willard Alexander, who actually served as his manager and booker during the early days of the band. Willard's role in Benny's success was as important as anyone's, and even in a Hollywood version of the Goodman story he should not have been ignored.

I went to my lawyer. "What shall I do?" I asked him. "I hate the script anyway, but I'm given credit for what Willard did for Benny on the business level. The artistic contributions I actually made to his career are not even mentioned. I can't sign the release unless this is straightened out and Willard receives the credit due him."

My lawyer checked around and found that the only precedent applicable to the situation we faced was *The Ruth*

Etting Story, in which Colonel Gimp, Ruth's manager, was treated unsympathetically in the script. Gimp asked and received $50,000 for allowing himself to be so roughly portrayed. "I'll probably never get it," I told my lawyer, "but that's what I'm going to ask. And I think I'm perfectly justified." I had never received a dime from Benny in the old days, nor had I expected to be paid. Still, the memory of the Goodman-Armstrong tour lingered, and in 1953 I had needed the money. The new marriage, heavy demands for support of Jemy and the boys, and little, if any, income from the record business left me unable to meet my obligations from my own income. I had to borrow from my mother to keep going.

Universal Pictures, hearing my asking price, decided to write me out of the script. That was fine as far as I was concerned, but the studio and the scriptwriter were now in trouble with Willard, who had found out he was not even mentioned. Hollywood's solution was to change my name to Willard Alexander! This was too much for Willard. He explained to Universal that he had not introduced Alice to Benny, that he had had nothing to do with the concert at 91st Street. "I was Benny's booker," he told them, "and I won't sign a release unless John Hammond's proper role is included."

This put Universal on the spot, though no more so than me. Benny was my brother-in-law and another family crisis loomed. What could I do? Universal finally raised its offer from $3,000 to $5,000. I still did not want to sign, and, if I did, I wanted to add another stipulation. I knew how bad the sound stage at Universal was. They would never re-create the sound of the old Goodman band. I was itching to be given the musical supervision, but Benny would not hear of my having anything to do with the picture, so that was out. The script was changed so that both Willard and I played barely recognizable versions of our actual roles in Benny's career, and while I believed the picture would be a disaster, I signed the release.

Although *The Benny Goodman Story* finally made its investment back after several years, it was as bad as I had expected it to be. Valentine Davies, the scriptwriter, directed the film, which was no advantage. Steve Allen, who looked a little like Benny, was not the actor he should have been, certainly not as good as Jimmy Stewart, who had played the role of Glenn Miller, and the sound track was so distorted that not only was the Goodman band sound totally absent, the dynamics were lost. Benny himself, still not completely recovered from his "illness," did not play well, and the story was patently false. But peace was restored between the Hammonds and the Goodmans. I gave Esmé the check I received from Universal.

I discovered that one of my favorite screen stars was a neighbor a few floors above us. Judge Waties Waring's daughter, Anne Warren, who was then in charge of cultural events at the Brooklyn Academy of Music, had decided to have a symposium on the role of the Negro in the arts, and had persuaded her father, then living in New York City, to be the moderator. Anne asked me to help enlist a panel. I got my friend Nat Ash, then sports director for radio station WNEW, to talk about the Negro in athletics. I planned to do Negroes in music, and Anne wanted Arthur Miller for Negroes in theater. I knew Arthur from the years when we both served on the board of the *Protestant Digest*.

I called him one evening: "Do you mind if I discuss something with you?"

"Not at all, John. Come on up."

I explained the deal and asked him to join us.

"Well, John," Arthur began, "I don't think there is any chance for the Negro in the theater. I don't believe the public will stand for black actors in white roles."

Marilyn Monroe Miller, who was listening to our conversation, suddenly jumped in. "What do you mean, no chance for Negro actors?" she cried, shrilly.

"The theater is the art of making people suspend disbelief," Arthur said, "and it's impossible to do that with black people playing whites."

"You believe that the theater lags behind the opera?"

I asked, for by the mid-1950's opera was handling the challenge of black singers in white roles most successfully.

Miller would not budge and he did not join the panel. Marilyn and I argued with him for more than an hour. Neither of us could make him change his mind. Marilyn was marvelous. To see her was a treat. To hear her passionate expression of views made her seem even more beautiful.

I saw Arthur Miller at the premiere of a revival of *Death of a Salesman* some twenty years later. George C. Scott played Willy Loman, and the neighbor and his son, originally played by whites, were now black. During the intermission I met Arthur. "Times have changed," I said. He grinned. "Yes, John."

XXXIX

My association with Mercury ended in 1952. During the last years I was neither as active as I wanted to be, nor very happy. Jazz in the late 1940's and early 1950's was undergoing strange and, to me, often unhealthy changes. The bop period I considered a dead-end street, a wrong turning for jazz. I was not enthusiastic about the music and, except for one unfortunate session with Lennie Tristano, whose piano interpretations I did not like, I recorded none of the early bop artists.

Bop lacked the swing I believe essential to great jazz playing, lacked the humor and the free-flowing invention of the best jazz creators. In their place it offered a new self-consciousness, an excessive emphasis on harmonic and rhythmic revolt, a concentration on technique at the expense of musical emotion. It defied the jazz verities without improving on them. Boppers gave a nod to Lester Young, to Charlie Christian, and to other real innovators, without actually absorbing what they had to give. Instead of expanding the form, they contracted it, made it their private language. I extend this critical judgment even to such giants as Bird Parker, Thelonious Monk, and John Coltrane. The superlative Miles Davis is exempted.

While I'm at it, I may as well say I just didn't dig the new breed of drummer, either. Max Roach, Philly Joe Jones, even Art Blakey were too loud, too eccentric, too everything for my taste.

Heretical as it may sound, those who became big sellers were not players I wanted to record. For me there was more jazz feeling in the gospel singers, the young rhythm-and-blues performers, than in the cerebral gymnastics which passed for modern jazz.

Grumble, grumble, grumble. I know how plaintive this sounds. Actually, I won't back away from anything I've said. These *were* my feelings about fifties' jazz. At the same time, I *was* a generation removed from what was happening and I did feel out of it, perhaps more than at any other period of my life in music. Fortunately, I have been able to respond with a fresh ear and enthusiastic spirit to the changing sounds of the two subsequent decades. To the fifties I seem to have been tone deaf. However justified I felt, it was not pleasure, I can assure you.

Further, Mitch Miller accepted an offer from Columbia Records to become director of popular recording. Mitch had the ideal talent for picking hits, songs which fitted a particular popular artist on the label and which, with amazing regularity, reached the top ten best-selling records in the country. This is a rare and valuable asset, one which I have never had to any degree. Mitch produced hits for every Mercury artist. He went on to do so even more spectacularly for Columbia. Mercury felt that I was partly responsible for Mitch's leaving, which was, of course, ridiculous. Mitch left Mercury at the call of his old friend Goddard Lieberson, then vice president of Columbia, because it was the top job in the record business, and because he was offered more money than any employee of any record company was making. Nonetheless, his leaving crippled Mercury as far as commercial recording in New York was concerned and I was not equipped to fill in for him.

It seemed important to forget about trying to be a commercial-record producer and get back to recording the music

I loved. Many of the records I had produced in the past became hits, but I had hardly ever produced a commercial hit which was not first an artistic performance I believed in. And it is possible to become so involved in the routine of searching for commercial hits that one's basic objectives, tastes, and honest enthusiasms are lost. This was what had been happening to me ever since 1946, when I joined Majestic. I decided to wait until the right opportunity was offered, one which would allow me to record the kind of music I liked, regardless of what happened to be selling. Happily, I did not have to wait long.

From 1951 to 1953, therefore, I did a considerable amount of writing about jazz. I missed being in the recording studio, yet jazz no longer interested Mercury as it struggled to compete in the popular-record market. I recognized that no company could afford to specialize in jazz, though there seemed no reason to let it die of neglect. To anyone who looked, it was clear that jazz was becoming an unwanted stepchild in the catalogs of most large companies, poorly recorded and indifferently marketed. In November, 1953, I wrote a long article for the New York *Times* in which I discussed what was wrong with jazz recording. I pointed out that engineers with the highest technical standards for classical recording ignored their own criteria on jazz dates, putting microphones all over the studio and producing a completely artificial sound. I predicted that the first company to take the same care in recording jazz that it devoted to classical music would make a tremendous impact on both the record dealer and the buying public. This, after all, was the era of high-fidelity recording and the public was being sold on quality. My own standards for good jazz recording have always included a belief that the musicians should balance themselves, that when a man plays softly the engineer in the control room should not turn up the volume, distorting the balance and the musician's intention. Conversely, if a player is attempting to achieve a crescendo the engineer should not reduce its effect by twiddling knobs.

About two days after the *Times* article appeared I received a call from Seymour Solomon of Vanguard Records, a small, classical-record company. He wanted to know whether I would be interested in making a series of jazz records along the lines I had recommended in the article. I knew Seymour as a fellow student of Ronald Murat, the violin teacher I continued to study with until the late 1950's. His proposal sounded like fun to me, so I agreed to join him and his brother Maynard at Vanguard.

We began our series in December, with records by Mel Powell, Buck Clayton, Vic Dickenson, and Sir Charles Thompson, a pianist who had long been an enthusiasm of mine, and whose knighthood was a modest effort to keep pace with the counts and dukes of the jazz realm. I also recorded a group from the Basie band led by Joe Newman, my favorite of the contemporary band trumpet players. The first Vanguard jazz records came out in early 1954 and made a tremendous impression. Whitney Balliett gave them a most welcome and impressive three-page review in *The New Yorker*. The first albums we released were ten-inch LPs, a form which eventually caused difficulty for Vanguard because the major labels were switching their popular and jazz albums to twelve-inch disks. I warned Seymour that the ten-inchers were passé, to no effect. I believe he thought jazz was not important enough to deserve the larger, higher-priced records. When Vanguard finally converted, it was too late to take advantage of the industry-wide change, and much of the ten-inch material became obsolete on dealers' shelves long before it should have.

On one important issue, however, Seymour and I were agreed: both jazz and classical music should be recorded in a studio with concert-hall acoustics. Accordingly, Vanguard used a Masonic temple in Brooklyn with an auditorium which seated about four hundred people and had a superb sound. It became a studio superior to any in Manhattan, and because the mid-1950's was a time when sound quality was being stressed by every company Vanguard's superiority was recognized by both critics and public.

Although I had been in the record business for more

A high-quality session at Vanguard, 1955: Sir Charles
Thompson at the piano, Emmett Berry (trumpet), Benny Morton
(trombone), Earl Warren (alto), Steve Jordan (guitar),
Coleman Hawkins (tenor), Aaron Bell (bass),
and Bobby Donaldson, a cousin of Fats Waller's (drums).

than twenty years and thought I knew manufacturing techniques inside out, I had seen nothing until I watched the Solomon brothers work. The music was first recorded on magnetic tape, introduced in the late 1940's and by the early 1950's universally used in all recording. From the taped performance a lacquer master was made and a test pressing run off. The test pressing was then brought to the laboratory, where it was played on the finest sound equipment to make certain it exactly matched the quality of the original tape. Often more than a dozen test records were rejected before the required quality was achieved. Even so, each shipment of records from the factories of the companies which pressed for Vanguard was spot-checked. After five thousand records were pressed, the stamper, or mold, was destroyed and a new one made from the original master. Vanguard was assured that every record pressed had the same high fidelity. This rigid quality check, unprofitable for a large company to maintain, made Vanguard records unique. The Solomons' devotion to quality was a revelation to me and a most welcome one.

The records I produced for Vanguard during the four years or so I was associated there included many of which I am extremely proud, as well as the usual quota that should have been better. A record producer, particularly one who produces jazz, can expect a batting average no better than about .250. Three out of four records are almost certain to have frayed edges emotionally or an unexpected production snafu. Musicians do not always feel right the moment the tape machines are turned on. Or if they play well one day they do not necessarily play well the next.

The best recorded jazz involves a gamble. It is this element of risk, even more than a carefully planned ensemble of players, that offers the possibility of memorable performances. Musicians too used to hearing each other are not inspired. The producer, unlike the bandleader, can hire new members for each session. This is his edge and he should use it as imaginatively as he can.

I loved the element of surprise and it often worked well for me. The *Jo Jones Special* I did for Vanguard was a case in point. I had Jo, Freddie Green, and Walter Page, three quarters of the old Basie rhythm section, plus Nat Pierce on piano, Emmett Berry on trumpet, Lucky Thompson on tenor, and Benny Green on trombone. We recorded at the Masonic Temple, and things were going well, if not spectacularly, when in walked Basie himself. I had told him about the session and invited him over for a listen, but it was all pretty casual and I hadn't thought for a minute he'd come. So what was more natural than that Basie sit in? Nat moved out gracefully and the Basie rhythm section, which had long since gone its separate ways, was reunited. Not unexpectedly, a few of those choice Basie notes and the pace picked up. We did a "Shoe Shine Boy" and that was so good we did another "Shoe Shine Boy." And I was so pleased I kept them both on the record. Emmett and Lucky and Benny were blowing beautifully and the rhythm swung lightly and delicately and yet so decisively. It was sheer delight. And as one of the takes wound down with a few plink-plunks from Basie and a few rat-tats from Jo, Benny Green broke into a yuk-yuk-yuk laugh that was so infectious we kept it on the record, too.

Now I had some lovely takes and no contractual right to Basie's services. Who did? My good friend Norman Granz. I didn't need dumbbells this time, but a real favor. And, sure, it was all right with him. Record producers are used to making these accommodations for each other and don't regard them as anything special. I've done them, too. But it's one of the gracious and generous aspects of a not very gracious or generous industry, and I've always been a little surprised and a lot grateful when it happens.

Among other Vanguard productions, I have always been fond of the sides I made with Mel Powell, an intellectual who swung. Mel was an academically trained pianist who studied with Paul Hindemith and Nadia Reisenberg, and who eventually left jazz to teach composition at Yale. More recently he has been dean of music at the California Institute of Arts. While he was with us in the jazz world, however, he played fine piano—as much like Teddy Wilson as anyone—and even did a turn with the Goodman band.

Jo Jones: "I have recorded him off and on since 1936 and I think he can do more things superlatively well than any drummer I ever heard."

Ellis Larkins and Ruby Braff were a marvelous combination, Ellis another classically trained piano and Ruby the self-taught cornet. Both had warm and mellow tones and a subtly swinging style. They made beautiful music together.

I also put Ruby with Mel and Paul Quinichette, the splendid tenor who so resembled Lester in style and tone that he was often called "Vice Prez." I've always felt their collaborations were far ahead of their time.

The records by Vic Dickenson and Sir Charles were highlights, and the albums I produced by blues singer Jimmy Rushing are, I believe, among the best he ever made.

Altogether, it was a most satisfying period for me creatively and personally.

At Vanguard I also had a part in the classical recording, and again the small company presents the record producer with a challenge. First of all, most major American orchestras are under contract to major record companies. Secondly, the cost of recording them in the United States is more than a small company can afford. Major artists are also under exclusive contract, making it necessary for companies like Vanguard to search for new talent—although that was never a worry for me.

One such artist whose American career I became involved with was Friedrich Gulda, a young Czech pianist brought up in Vienna, the son of teachers and winner at sixteen of the international music competition in Geneva. He began his career as a concert pianist and toured the world. I heard in Gulda's classical playing the potential of a jazz artist, just as I once did in the playing of Walter Gieseking, who I later discovered had gone to the Grand Terrace in Chicago to listen night after night to Earl Hines. I heard in Gulda's playing a rhythmic line I recognized as the essence of superior jazz playing, even though he was performing classical repertoire.

Gulda wanted to play jazz. He formed a group in Vienna which in many ways was better than the group I assembled for him when he visited America. He had no pretensions. He simply wanted to play jazz. He was a highly nervous young man, with enormous hands and thick horn-rimmed glasses. He was very tense, except at the piano. He also seemed arrogant when he spoke to audiences in the United States, a result, I think, of insecurities. On a panel at one of the Newport Jazz Festivals he was critical of several American classical pianists, and as a newcomer to jazz speaking to jazz fans and critics he was considered presumptuous. Yet I was with him when he listened to Teddy Wilson for the first time in person. Tears came to his eyes and he said, "I didn't know there could be this kind of perfection in jazz."

Gulda wanted more than anything to play at Birdland, the jazz mecca of the mid-1950's. He told me he would rather play for, and be appreciated by, Birdland listeners than an audience at Carnegie Hall. I was able to arrange a two-week stint for him and his band. He was overjoyed. Most interestingly, every morning at 4 a.m., when the joint closed up, he would sit alone at the piano playing Bach for any hangabout musicians who remained and for the waiters and busboys cleaning up.

One of the major Vanguard albums in which I was involved, and certainly one which led me into the field of commercial recording during the 1960's, was the recording of the 1957 Newport Folk Festival.

The idea of a festival at Newport, Rhode Island, reached me in an unlikely way, involving once again an old friend turning up in my life. Sylvia Marlowe, whom I had known as Sylvia Sapira, the staff pianist at radio station WEVD in 1932, and who was also a friend of Esmé and her mother, called out of the blue to say that Louis and Elaine Lorillard wanted to start a jazz festival in Newport and would like to discuss the idea with me. Stuffy old Newport, that bastion of entrenched wealth, seemed the least likely place on earth for a jazz festival, so the notion intrigued me and I agreed to listen.

Sylvia arranged for us to meet for cocktails at her apartment on East 60th Street. The Lorillards were extremely attractive people, although it was clear that Louis knew nothing about jazz and Elaine only a little more. They had no experience dealing with musicians, either. But they did have an idea nobody in America had ever had before.

Jazz had long since reached the concert hall, beginning with Benny's concert in 1938 and my own *Spirituals to Swing* concerts. Norman Granz had inaugurated his highly successful series, *Jazz at the Philharmonic.* Even jazz clubs like Birdland had demonstrated that jazz could fill a room with listeners instead of dancers. But a jazz festival implied a series of concerts performed over a number of days to essentially the same audience, something no one had tried before.

Louis Lorillard was one of the heirs of the Lorillard tobacco fortune. His family is an old and socially prominent one in Newport. Elaine came from a quite different background. She was a Bostonian, the grandniece of Lillian Nordica, the noted American operatic soprano of the late nineteenth century. She had lived in Greenwich Village for a while, had listened to jazz, had the vitality and the determination to stir up Newport as it had never been stirred before.

The Lorillards told me they had worked actively with a Newport music committee which imported members of the New York Philharmonic to play concerts every summer. These were open-air affairs, sparsely attended, and the Lorillards didn't think they were ever very good. They liked much better the idea of a jazz festival.

"Well," I began, "I don't know much about Newport. I've had a number of relatives who lived there, however, and I wouldn't say the people who summer in Newport are very sympathetic to jazz."

"Nor," I added, "are they very broad-minded on the race question." I remembered that Newport had frowned on Jews, and if a large influx of blacks was to occur, as would happen for a jazz festival, I would expect the colony to react rather violently. "I'd be happy to be associated with such a festival," I said, "but accommodations for Negro artists and Negro patrons would have to be arranged first. Unless that is established there could be no successful jazz festival anywhere."

The Lorillards gulped, thinking, I suppose, of some of their Newport friends. They thought nonetheless that it could be done. They asked me if I knew George Wein, who ran a small night club in Boston and also played jazz piano around the Boston area. No, but I had heard good things about him. George, it turned out, was the Lorillards' choice to run the show. Marshall Stearns, a professor of literature at Hunter College and founder of the Institute of Jazz Studies, a repository of jazz memorabilia, was on the board with him. I served on an advisory committee.

The Festival made a modest beginning in 1954 with a two-day concert series on the grounds of the Newport Casino. As I expected, the town split pro and con over the influx of musicians and jazz fans, and old residents were startled by the number of photographers and reporters who arrived from everywhere for this incredible story of an explosion of jazz in the sacred precincts. We also had bad luck with the weather, which was stinko.

Fortunately, the music was marvelous: the Oscar Peterson trio (Barney Kessel, guitar, and Ray Brown, bass), Ella Fitzgerald, and Eddie Condon's Chicago-style group, among others. There was no budget for a big band, but Wein was to use Stan Kenton as M.C. The atmosphere was relaxed and amicable, the audience of some 10,000 was reasonably well behaved, the race problem was not a problem, and the worldwide publicity was enormous. At the end there was a small profit—a thousand or two—which was donated to Professor Stearns' Institute. The Lorillards were pleased. They did not think the local resistance was widespread or serious enough to be troublesome. And they seemed ready to make the Festival an annual event.

The board of the Newport Casino had some second thoughts, however. It announced that the thousands of folding chairs set up to accommodate the crowd had damaged and would continue to damage its carefully tended grass tennis courts, and it declined to be the arena for such festivities again.

What to do? Leonard Feather and I were named to a

committee to consider the problem. Despite our success, it was clear that Newport was less than ideal as the site for a big event. The place was a bottleneck. Getting there was difficult in the best of circumstances. With traffic from all over New England backed up at the Newport ferry landing and cars inching through the streets of the town, it was a mess.

The simple answer to that was a shift to some big city, preferably New York. On the other hand, Newport could be charming in an elderly, somnolent sort of way, and in early summer we would be the only act in town. The lovely incongruity of Newport and jazz rubbing elbows had given us favorable publicity that would not transfer easily to another location. I also felt that by breaking down racial barriers in what was certainly one of the snob communities of this fair land, we had achieved something that should not be abandoned. Finally, the Lorillards were the driving force behind the whole idea, willing to make up a deficit if there should be one, and they wanted the Festival to remain in Newport. We would never find such eager sponsors elsewhere.

We thrashed around for a while and then decided, when all was said and done, to return to Newport. If the Casino wouldn't have us, Freebody Park, a town facility, would.

The second Festival had a splendid array of talent—the bands of Count Basie and Woody Herman, the Dave Brubeck Quartet, and Louis Armstrong All-Stars—and a number of serious problems. George Wein tried to serve as talent booker, producer, stage manager, artist's rep, and occasional pianist, and it became more than any one impresario could handle. The sound equipment was the worst I have ever heard at an outdoor concert. It was complicated by an echo from the speakers produced by the concrete stands, and, ironically, the higher the ticket price, the worse the sound. A shell had been built in which all the sound equipment was tilted toward the sky. People in helicopters could have heard more of the music than the audience in the park. A pity, for the music was grand.

I became a full member of the Festival board in 1956 and served until 1970, a period in which this lively event grew to maturity as the most exciting celebration of jazz in America, as well as one of its most heartening demonstrations of the ability of black and white to mingle in a mutually shared and enjoyed experience. Mahalia Jackson also gave the Festival a great boost of respectability in 1956 by her unprecedented appearance and glorious singing at a Sunday morning service in Newport's unassailably white Trinity Episcopal Church.

By the following year it was clear that folk music was sweeping the country and competing strongly with jazz for the attention of college audiences and record buyers. This inspired us to launch a Newport Folk Festival, and those parts which were available were recorded and released on the Vanguard label. The success of this album was an indication of the direction young America's musical taste would run for the next two decades.

The high point of my years with Vanguard came with its decision to release the *From Spirituals to Swing* concerts on records. Fortunately, all those fine sounds had been preserved. I had arranged for both events to be recorded on acetate disks. Vanguard paid all the musicians involved for the right to release their performances, and I was given a royalty of fifteen per cent of the retail price of the two-record package containing the best moments of both concerts.

This looked pretty good to me. I had averaged about $600 a year in salary at Vanguard, an amount hardly worth describing as a salary. Of course, my job was not full time and involved producing only certain records of my choice. As usual, I preferred freedom to money. With the exception of my full-time jobs at Columbia, Mercury, and Majestic between 1939 and 1952, I had never sought any other arrangement. The Vanguard album of *Spirituals to Swing* eventually sold more than one hundred thousand copies, and I must have made between $25,000 and $30,000, the most I'd ever received from a recording project.

Yet the greatest of Vanguard's many gifts to me was the patience and care Seymour Solomon and his engineer, Jack

Beaumont, lavished on my scratched and worn acetates to give the *Spirituals to Swing* album the quality and integrity of a Vanguard product.

XL

The 1950's were years of transition for music in America, years in which jazz achieved perhaps its greatest commercial acceptance among record buyers, while at the same time undergoing painful identity crises. Discrimination against Negroes virtually vanished from the music industry. Mixed jazz groups became the rule rather than the exception. Jazz itself was recognized as a legitimate subject of study and the jazz student became part of the academic scene. There was a negative side, too. These were years when even the word jazz was put down by many of its practitioners. Musicians as various as Duke Ellington and Miles Davis protested that the word segregated and circumscribed their music, and that they were penalized economically because jazz was somehow thought to be outside the mainstream of music and therefore inconsequential. Some jazz players attempted to reject the uniqueness and heroic past of jazz, or to intermix it with other musical forms so that its simplicity, its improvisatory excitement, and its swing were lost in complexities. It was also a period in which many dominant figures of the jazz world were advancing into middle age and feeling themselves discarded, feeling that their contributions to this personal, volatile music were no longer welcome. To some extent this may have been true. To some extent it was the pressure of upcoming generations, pushing into the limelight before their predecessors were ready to leave it. As always, there were more musicians than opportunities to play.

And, as in any period, there were the inevitable personal tragedies. By the mid-fifties Billie Holiday's voice had been ravaged by years of abuse, although her heart and her impeccable musicianship were still in working order. Billie's last years as a performer were hard ones. She was unable to sing in New York clubs because of the infamous cabaret-card rule by which the police were empowered to license performers and could bar anyone convicted on a narcotics charge, as indeed Billie had been. Norman Granz kept her alive as a singer. He found bookings for her in Europe. Although her voice was failing and her need for drugs increasing, she became a box-office star as fans rushed at the opportunity to hear this now-legendary performer in person.

Norman went his own way through the 1950's, ignoring new trends and recording many of the best and, ironically, least well known of the older jazz stars. As impresario he assembled casts of memorable players from the 1930's and 1940's, including Ella Fitzgerald and Oscar Peterson, who were under his personal management, putting on concerts in the finest halls and seeing to it that everyone who worked for him was well paid, well treated, and well appreciated. Through his record company, Verve, he released a huge catalog of jazz albums, including his live concerts. To work for Norman was a full-time job for many who, like Billie, might not have worked at all without him. While albums by Dave Brubeck and Miles Davis were actually at the top of the charts of popular bestsellers, Norman was releasing albums by Art Tatum, Count Basie, and other giants of a previous generation.

In the late fifties, Granz suddenly sold out his record interests to MGM for more than $2,000,000 and invested the proceeds in Picassos. He continued to manage Ella and to produce occasional jazz concerts in Europe; now, in the recent seventies, he has returned to the record business with his Pablo label, recording the jazz players he likes—such as the inspired pairing of Basie's piano and Zoot Sims' tenor—ignoring popular trends and the musical tastes of any but himself. I couldn't approve more.

The final records made by Billie Holiday were included in a Columbia album called *The Sound of Jazz*, a recreation of the television show produced on CBS for John Crosby by Nat Hentoff and Whitney Balliett. The show was one of the last times Billie was seen by the American public, and, fittingly, she was accompanied by the best—Gerry Mulligan, Lester Young, Buck Clayton, Vic Dickenson, and others.

I remember being at the recording session at Columbia's 30th Street studio. It was there that I had my last conversation with Lester Young. Prez had been in poor health for years. Between takes he came up to me to say, "John, I've got an awful lot to thank you for, and I'm sorry we haven't seen more of each other in recent years."

It was the first time Lester Young had ever said anything remotely personal to me in all the years of our association. I was both touched and scared. It suddenly occurred to me that Lester might be aware that time was short, that he wanted to say something while he could. Within a few months Lester was dead.

After the funeral service for him I went down in the elevator with Billie. I think she realized that part of her own life ended with Lester's death. They were an odd, aloof pair, not much at ease in the world, and they had found much comfort in each other's company. Their perceptions of each other were apt. A younger, happier Billie had nicknamed him Prez, and he had given her the title Lady Day. The voice of Lester's tenor can be heard lending exquisite support to her own rich sound on some fifty records. There had been estrangement, too, but a quiet reconciliation before the end. Within a few months of Prez's death she too was gone.

Mildred Bailey's life also ended in the 1950's. Except for recording sessions at Majestic in 1947 I had seen little of her for years. Now, in 1958, Irving Townsend asked me to assemble a Mildred Bailey memorial album for Columbia. He knew Mildred personally, but he also knew that I had been closely associated with her recording career and that I could find and select her best work for her last album.

I managed to get permission from Diners Club, which owned the bankrupt Majestic Records, to use the sides Mildred had recorded for them. I also got permissions from English Parlophone, from Brunswick, and half a dozen other defunct labels.

Listening to that clear, lilting voice, hearing it as it had been twenty, twenty-five years earlier, I realized this was my first retrospective album. I was moving back in time, not forward. My contemporaries were no longer the wave of the future. Vanguard's *Spirituals to Swing* had been a revival, of course, an oldie, yet new in the sense that it had never been heard on records before. Mildred's reissued songs were all there would ever be of her. It gave me a turn. I was captivated nonetheless. Mildred had a naïve, little-girl quality in her voice; I always felt she tried to create an illusion of sounding slenderer than she was. For all that, her voice was a superb swinging instrument blessed with what someone has called "the jazz quaver," and she was a musician of extraordinary taste and sophistication. If I haven't said it before, I will say it here: She was the finest white jazz singer I've ever known.

I produced a three-LP set that Columbia eventually issued in 1960, a good album I was happy to have done. Even better, it led to Goddard's hiring me as a full-time employee and producer, an assignment that led to a completely new phase of my career in records.

XLI

Goddard brought me back to Columbia at a salary of $10,000 a year, less than I had made at Majestic in 1946. This did not bother me. It was a pleasure to be returning to Columbia; it was where I wanted to be. It appeared that I was going to be able to record the kind of thing I loved and would not be asked to record the commercial junk that bored me, so I did not ask for more money. I was treated handsomely in any event. As the years went by, my salary was doubled and finally quadrupled—a sufficiency, if not the foundation of a new Vanderbilt fortune.

Columbia had become the largest record company in the United States, surpassing RCA Victor at last, and its very size opened up opportunities of a sort I could not have found

Goddard Lieberson (c. 1954) was a brilliant
executive, a prescient picker of musical
and theatrical winners, a witty and
sophisticated companion, a loyal friend.

elsewhere. The top artists on the popular label were Mitch Miller, Johnny Mathis, and Ray Conniff, and there was a large staff of producers to take care of them. I was to supervise the program for reissuing records from Columbia's old catalog, then in the process of being transferred to LP's. I was also charged with finding new talent for the label, a responsibility I always seek, and had the latitude to record a certain amount of jazz and special material particularly appealing to me. Goddard knew me well, my weaknesses as well as my strengths. He did not think me much of a business man. He knew that my standards for judging talent were, and are, based primarily on artistic rather than commercial potential, although in many cases the two go together. What I liked might well prove to be profitable, as it often had been in the past, but I was not expected to turn new artists I found into commercial stars by recording them for the commercial marketplace. If that was to happen, others would do it.

My first five acquisitions for Columbia were Ray Bryant, Pete Seeger, Aretha Franklin, Carolyn Hester, and Bob Dylan.

Ray was an extraordinary young pianist I was sure could also be commercially successful. He had started as an organist for his mother, a preacher in the Holiness Church in Philadelphia, so he had good gospel roots. I signed him to a Columbia contract in 1959 to make single records like "Little Susie" and "C Jam Blues," records for juke boxes and for the Negro market. The postwar boom had put some money into black pockets, too, and this lucrative and growing slice of the total market for records had hardly been touched by Columbia. We also went in this direction with Ray's first album, *It's Madison Time*, which capitalized on the popularity of the Madison, a new dance originating in Baltimore.

Pete Seeger, of course, was not a find. He'd had a distinguished career as a folk singer for years. There was nobody like him at Columbia, however, and I was sure the growing interest in folk music in the United States would make him popular with young people. I included a clause in his contract to the effect that if he wanted to record material Columbia could not use, he was free to take it to a smaller label. Pete still was being blacklisted for his political views, so before I signed him I wanted to be certain that Goddard and CBS would not be vulnerable. "It was hot for you around here when you were attacked by Westbrook Pegler," I reminded Goddard. "I don't want Pete to be an embarrassment without assurances that CBS is fully aware of the situation."

Goddard called Richard Salant, a corporate vice president who later became head of the CBS news division. "I've got a question in a delicate area. It's Pete Seeger. Can we use him?"

"We don't need him and he's not welcome on CBS television," Salant said.

"We want to sign him to Columbia Records."

Salant asked if we though Seeger would sell.

"I wouldn't be calling you if we didn't," Goddard replied.

"Well, we're big boys now," Salant decided. "Do what you want."

So, Pete Seeger was signed and I did a lot of good recording with him.

One day Curtis Lewis, a black composer, arrived at my office with a demonstration record of various songs he had written. The fourth one particularly caught my ear, partly because it was a good song, partly because it sounded familiar. It was called "Today I Sing the Blues" and performed by a young woman who accompanied herself on the piano. I couldn't recall when or where I might have heard it; in any event, I was distracted by the singer. Her name was Aretha Franklin, and even at first hearing, on a poorly made demo intended to sell songs rather than the singer, she was the most dynamic jazz voice I'd encountered since Billie. I wanted her for Columbia.

Curtis told me she was from Detroit, the daughter of a Baptist minister. Like so many of the best jazz performers she had her roots in the church and its free-wheeling gospel singing. Coincidentally, Sam Cooke, then a star on RCA Victor, had also been a member of the Reverend Franklin's choir

Aretha Franklin and Ray Bryant:
"Both have strong roots in the
gospel music I think is the starting
point of so much good jazz."

and road show.

Shortly thereafter, Mrs. Jo King, who owned a small recording studio at 1697 Broadway, called. "I know you're interested in Aretha Franklin," she said. "If you want to meet her, she'll be in my studio today."

I wasted no time. I went to the studio, heard Aretha sing, and was convinced she would be a star. I knew exactly how I wanted to record her: keeping as much of the gospel feeling in her voice as possible, while using material which would attract jazz fans. Although Aretha's great popularity came in the rhythm-and-blues field, I was not particularly interested in that market, nor, at that time, was Columbia. I had been told by Mrs. King that Sam Cooke was determined to sign Aretha to RCA Victor, and that information was all I needed to convince Columbia to offer her a top royalty contract with a small advance, unusual for an unknown artist.

Early in 1960 Aretha signed her contract and I recorded her in our 30th Street studio. I made Ray Bryant the musical director, because Ray had also started in the church. We recorded her with five or six musicians, and although Aretha always insisted on having a rock drummer, she wanted only good, solid jazz players behind her. The first records impressed the Columbia sales and promotion people, so much so that a young man named Dave Kapralik, in the artist and repertoire department of Columbia's subsidiary label, Epic, got in touch with Aretha's father in Detroit and signed Aretha's sister Erma to an Epic contract. I did not learn of this till later. Aretha said little about it; nonetheless she was upset to have her sister competing with her in the same company. Although I had had nothing to do with Erma's deal, this incident proved to be the beginning of the end of my association with Aretha.

When Esmé and I returned from a vacation in Europe in 1961, I found that Aretha had been assigned to another producer to make popular singles. I was to record her only for albums. It was the feeling among the young A & R producers at Columbia that, while I might be able to find a potential star, I was not able to produce the sort of commercial single records that became hits. Aretha had quite a lot of money in accumulated royalties, because her first records had been inexpensively produced and had sold well. It had been decided while I was away to use the unpaid royalties (record artists receive royalties every six months as a rule) to record her with large, commercial backgrounds. I watched her go from one producer to another while these lavish single records did little to increase her sales and nothing to enhance her career.

When her five-year contract with Columbia ended I was not unhappy to see her go to Atlantic. I knew Jerry Wexler, who would produce her records there, and was sure he would return her to the gospel-rooted material she should be recording. After she left Columbia and became an instant hit on Atlantic, however, it was decided to sweeten the records I had made with her by adding strings and brass. I was heartily against it, which cut no ice. Aretha was equally against it, which did. Believing that Columbia had violated her contract by altering the original accompaniments of her records, she sued. The out-of-court settlement cost the company lots of money.

The musical misuse and eventual loss of Aretha as a recording artist disturbed me greatly, not least because her career since leaving Columbia has fulfilled every confidence I had in her. She had every musicianly quality I thought she had. All she needed was to hold to her roots in the church.

Recently, Helen Humes, the singer I wangled into the Basie band, said, "John, do you remember that song I wrote a long time ago called 'Today I Sing the Blues'? I don't know what ever happened to it. I sure never got any royalties."

Of course I remembered. I'd recorded it with her at Mercury in 1947! I'd heard her sing it. Helen had written it with Curtis Lewis, who simply failed to credit her on his demonstration record. No wonder Aretha's vocal had sounded so familiar.

I wanted to continue signing folk singers. I passed on Joan Baez, whom I had heard at the Newport Folk Festival, because she was asking a great deal of money while still a rela-

Bob Dylan, 1966: "He helped shape the attitudes of a generation, and God knows his unique and uncompromising albums transformed Columbia Records!"

tively unknown artist. Vanguard signed her instead. I decided to look further. Carolyn Hester, a Texas girl with a good voice, was in town, so I went to one of her rehearsals and heard a kind of folk music I knew nothing about. One member of her group was Dick Fariña, a writer *(Been Down So Long It Looks Like Up to Me)*, poet, and lyricist who was killed a few years later in a motorcycle accident. There were two other guitar players. One, a young fellow wearing a cap and a harmonica holder, was a friend of Fariña's. I watched him for a while and found him fascinating, although he was not particularly good on either guitar or harmonica.

Bob Dylan—I learned his name and that's about all. After Carolyn's rehearsal I invited him to our studios to discover whether he could sing and to listen to the kind of songs he was writing. As it turned out, he had few songs of his own. One was enough. He sang "Talking New York," a social commentary on life in Manhattan that knocked me out. "Bobby," I said, "I don't know what Columbia is going to say about this, but I think you're absolutely wonderful and I'm going to sign you." Bob said he wanted to record for Columbia because we had signed Pete Seeger and allowed him to do whatever he wanted. "I think this is the place for me."

I asked him how old he was. Twenty. "That means you have to have your mother and father sign the contract, too. The New York State laws don't allow a minor to sign a legal agreement without his parents' approval."

"I don't have a mother or father," Dylan said.

Did he have any relative who could sign for him?

"I've got an uncle who's a dealer in Las Vegas."

"You're trying to tell me you don't want anyone to sign for you, aren't you?"

"John," Dylan said, "you can trust me."

And I did.

Bob Dylan is a superlative artist and a most complex human being. He lives, I think, in a fantasy world which he is powerful enough to impose on the real one the rest of us inhabit. He has created his own persona and put it to the service of his art. The combination is irresistible.

Its superficial aspects are not the important ones. Dropping out of the University of Minnesota, assuming part of Dylan Thomas' name, losing track of his family, bumming around the country in the footsteps of Woody Guthrie—all of this is part of the legend, the aura, but not integral to the man.

His genius has been the acuity of his vision of American life, his ability to internalize his observations and experiences, and his artistry in retelling them in a penetrating and dramatic poetry that overwhelms his hearers. With persistence and intensity he has opposed war profiteers, lynchers, racists, and all forms of injustice, most notably the celebrated case of Rubin "Hurricane" Carter, in whose innocence he passionately believed. He helped shape the attitudes of a generation, and God knows his unique and uncompromising albums transformed Columbia Records!

As I look back, I think it was his air of being willing to take on the world that grabbed me. It was bold, it was witty —for all his somber moods Dylan has a saving humor—and it was very attractive. And I confess he twanged a responsive chord in the young part of me which shared his ambitions to change the world.

When Dylan made his first album for Columbia there was only one other person who recognized his potential, who thought he was as good as I did. This was Billy James, a young man in the publicity department, who really went to work to give Bob a boost. He managed to get features in *Seventeen*, *Mademoiselle*, and other magazines read by young people. This was before the days of rock and folk papers like *Rolling Stone* and *Crawdaddy*, so it was not easy to publicize an unknown.

Meanwhile, Dylan was having a thin time of it. I had been lending him money, and I knew that until something happened he had very little to live on. Bob wondered whether it would be possible to get him a publishing contract. I called Lou Levy, the owner of Leeds Music. "We've got an extraordinary young artist on Columbia named Bob Dylan.

He has an album about to be released. Could you give him a publishing contract?"

Lou, formerly the manager of the Andrews Sisters, was a most successful song publisher. A writer whose songs were about to be heard on a record was a sure thing, as far as he was concerned. He signed Dylan to one of his firms—Duchess Music-BMI—with an advance of $500 which Bob badly needed.

The first album sold eight or nine thousand copies—not bad, not good, certainly not much profit for Columbia. Dylan was now in that most ambiguous, most vulnerable position for a young artist, when the people who have his fate in their hands have to make a cold-eyed assessment of his talent and decide whether to push him further or cut him loose.

Reactions at Columbia were mixed. At the A & R department's weekly meetings, during which new records were played and evaluated, Dylan impressed a few, not many. Everyone acknowledged that his songs had content that could not be ignored, but almost everyone was put off by his mediocre playing and raspy voice. Generally, he was known throughout the building as "Hammond's folly."

By the time I cut a second record with him, some six months had passed and people were running out of patience, in particular Dave Kapralik, the ambitious young head of Columbia's popular recording. "We're going to drop Dylan," he told me one day. "I don't see any future for him."

"You'll drop him over my dead body!" I said.

Happily, for a while at any rate, my dead body was not hostage for Dylan's future. Among other things, it happened that in the second album was a song called "Blowin' in the Wind." I knew it was a fine song, although, frankly, I never guessed it would become the hit it did.

Now the Dylan story becomes infinitely more complicated. Inevitably, I guess, for as no one really needs to be told the music business now involves such enormous sums of money that no artist controls his career for himself. The familiar army of agents, managers, lawyers, and other assorted advisers, flunkies, and friends now intervenes between the artist and his art. I have no complaints about efforts to preserve, protect, and defend the artist from exploitation. It is my fond hope that every deserving artist may become as wealthy as my great-great-grandfather. But I also feel that things are getting out of hand. Too much rides on the success or failure of a record, on guessing the future of a singer or a song. Too many voices have too much to say about too many artistic decisions. And fear is making musical impulses more cautious than they should be.

The old days were not better. I could cry when I think how little recognition or reward so many fine musicians achieved. Yet a very precious musical freedom they had. Just listen to them. You can hear it. Fortunately, it wasn't worth anyone's time or trouble to tell them to do it differently.

Back to Dylan. He sang "Blowin' in the Wind" one night in a Greenwich Village joint before his record was out. Peter, Paul and Mary happened to hear it, liked it, and took it to their manager, Albert Grossman, to arrange for recording it in their next album for Warner Brothers Records. *Their* songs were being published by Artie Mogull of Warners, and when he heard "Wind" he wanted it. Of course, Dylan told him that Lou Levy had already signed him for all his songs. Mogull said he thought he could take care of that. "How much advance did they give you?" he asked. "Five hundred," Bob said. Mogull handed him $1,000. "Why don't you go find out if you can buy your contract back?"

Well, why not? Not a wheel had turned in the months since Dylan had joined Duchess. Evidently the feeling was mutual. Levy was out of the office when Bob showed up, but one of his executives, knowing that the first album had made very little money and hunching that Dylan wasn't going to make it, took the opportunity to get out of the contract. Leeds kept only the songs in the first album.

Warners then signed Dylan to its publishing company. Peter, Paul and Mary's recording of "Blowin' in the Wind" became a gigantic hit. And because Warners happened to be affiliated with the American Society of Composers, Authors, and Publishers, the venerable ASCAP was suddenly plunged into the marketplace of rock and folk songs.

Al Grossman obviously wanted Dylan under his management. Bobby wondered what I thought. I told him I could get along with Al, although I didn't expect a smooth ride. Al had promised Bob $2,000 for doing a film for the British Broadcasting Corporation, money he would welcome. And gradually people were discovering that Dylan was an original and beguiling performer, as well as an effective songwriter. They were also discovering the word for what he had—charisma. He still was the shaggy-haired, unprepossessing figure I had first heard with Carolyn Hester, seemingly oblivious to the commercial world of hit records, and altogether puzzling to Columbia's staff of sales and promotion people. But somehow when he stood alone to sing, to puff into his harmonica on its holder, to accompany himself with all but inaudible guitar chords, eyes and ears were riveted upon him. His attitude in front of an audience seemed both shy and defiant, as if he couldn't care less what response his performance received. For record salesmen, of course, he became all the more puzzling and challenging.

As soon as Dylan signed a management contract with Grossman, Columbia received a letter which began, "In view of the fact that I was a minor when I signed my contract with Columbia Records, I hereby demand the return of all metal parts, masters, tapes, etc. and declare this contract null and void." The letter, of course, was signed by Dylan.

The Dylan letter was turned over to a new, young lawyer at Columbia named Clive Davis, who called me to ask whether or not I was aware that Dylan was underage when he signed his contract. I told Davis I did know it, that Dylan had told me I could trust him, and that I had never yet been double-crossed by any artist I had helped before. "I have just one question," Davis said. "Has Dylan been in the studio since he became twenty-one?"

"At least six or seven times," I said. His birthday was in March, and by this time it was August, a year and a half later.

"Well, if that's the case," said Davis, "he has already confirmed his contract and this letter is nothing."

"Clive," I interrupted, "I want you to prepare something for Dylan's signature which will repudiate this letter and add two more option periods to his contract. A year and a half of his three years have gone by, and I think we deserve more."

Davis agreed. Dylan agreed, too. He was not what I would call enthusiastic, but he signed.

Over the years I probably have not paid as much attention to contractual considerations as I should have. In this case, however, my insistence on additional time to work with Dylan—which I think we were in every way entitled to—enabled Columbia to develop, and benefit from, more of his sensationally successful albums.

Al Grossman and his assistant now began showing up at recording sessions, interfering, volunteering suggestions, criticizing my supervision, even telling Bob where to stand when he sang.

This kind of flak is met with in all recording studios these days. Producing used to be a fairly simple intermediary function which involved getting the musicians to play the way you wanted them to play and insuring that the engineers preserved the sounds faithfully. If everyone did his part diligently you were likely to emerge with a nice record.

Today so much rides on every record that even the most trivial opinion is impelled to express itself and, worse, may even have to be listened to. In the bad old days, when jobs were scarce, any musician who got a record date automatically assumed that the producer who arranged it must have his best interests at heart. Today musicians—big-money artists—are not so sure. The producer also gets a lot of heat from his A & R department head and, in highly competitive situations, from colleagues who are not reticent to suggest that they could do better with their friend's stable than he can. The A & R head, whose every waking hour mingles artistic concerns with their potential contribution to the corporation's bottom line, has become a man of respect. The emphasis is always upon sales. Hit records become the final measurement of an artist and his producer. Artists may be shifted from one producer to another by the department head, and in the multimillion-dollar record industry the key men, with dozens of artists under their control and hundreds of releases each year to promote, have become expert marketers and powerful star makers. Such was the young, ambitious, and tireless Dave Kapralik with whom I clashed so frequently over Aretha and Dylan. Presumably we sought the same objective—good records to serve the greater glory of Columbia—yet our views of how to achieve it were widely divergent. Eventually, our professional antagonism kept us from being the personal friends we started out to be.

All this being so, artists can be forgiven for wanting someone in their corner, too. Hence, the personal manager, the adviser, the whisperer and head-shaker, the pain in the ass whose job gets in the way of my job. I finally threw Grossman's assistant out of the studio one night and my relations with Al are at about the tension of an E-string. I've been around while beautiful music was being made by some very fine-tuned temperaments in my day, and I don't need lessons in mike placement from committees.

Dave Kapralik of course came around to the view that Dylan was indeed a talent and I was slowly eased out of the picture as his producer. I did manage to have Bobby record with Bob Johnston at Columbia's Nashville studios, where I felt the atmosphere and the accompanists would be right for him. *Nashville Skyline, Highway 61*, and several other platinum albums resulted.

Dylan left to make two albums for Asylum Records—both, unhappily, bombs—then returned to sign a new Columbia contract in 1974. Nostalgically, he decided he wanted to record in the studio where he had made his first three albums between 1961 and 1963. Through CBS no longer owned the premises, we arranged it. Our first record date happened to fall on the Jewish New Year. Promptly at sundown Bobby brought out a Bible and some wine, and we drank a ceremonial toast. A year after that, to my surprise, he appeared on the television show, *The World of John Hammond*, not because I had asked him, but because he wanted to be there. I was very pleased.

Incidentally, Bob has parents living in Hibbing, Minnesota. Whether or not he has an uncle dealing in Las Vegas I never found out.

Important as he was, Bob Dylan did not take up all my time. In this period I also produced one legitimate stage musical for records and had the usual run of successes and failures.

Cast albums of theatrical shows have been a long-standing tradition at Columbia. Its all-time hit, of course, was *My Fair Lady*, a triumph for everyone connected with it, not least Goddard Lieberson, who had the wit and the prescience to involve CBS as sole angel for the show as well as producer of that lovely album. (For Columbia's recording of the recently revived *My Fair Lady*, he was called back from retirement to supervise the production.)

Goddard's awareness and creativity were always at work. One small, effective trick: Knowing that the voices of a cast that has been singing all week may be tired by the time they are called upon to record in a studio, he always kept an arranger and music copyist on hand to lower a key, if necessary.

My own venture into this area was considerably less glamorous, though fun. In 1960 there was an off-Broadway musical called *Ernest in Love*, based on Oscar Wilde's *The Importance of Being Earnest*. It had an excellent score by Lee Pokriss, a cast of less than ten, and a five-piece orchestra led by an accomplished young woman. For the recording we expanded it to ten pieces. The remarkable thing to me was that the total cost of re-creating this show was less than $11,000, a very low figure. Musicals are particularly expensive to record, because the entire cast, orchestra, and chorus must be paid, sometimes a week's salary, and composers, lyricists, and arrangers must be paid for recording rights. The recording must be completed in a single day, perhaps a Sunday, when the cast is not performing. So we did rather well on costs and the album enjoyed a modest success. It was my first and last experience with this kind of recording. I'm glad I tried it once.

One of the most satisfying projects I took on was the recording of Alex Bradford and the Abyssinian Baptist Choir in Newark, New Jersey. This was a black gospel chorus of more than one hundred voices which sang in a church in the heart of the Newark ghetto. As with all large productions there were problems. To begin with, Alex Bradford, the conductor, was under contract to Savoy Records, so that he was not allowed to sing on our record, although he could—silently—conduct the choir. The songs we recorded were all composed by him and they were great.

The recording was a remote, which is to say that we took our equipment to the site and set up a sort of portable studio in the church basement. The congregation was present and we recorded its responses. The Columbia engineer and I were the only white people there. I even hired a black photographer to take pictures of the choir in action. Later I found out that one other white was present: Herman Lubinsky, president of Savoy, showed up to make sure his star, Alex Bradford, did not open his mouth during the session!

The album was a sensation. Rock star Clyde McPhatter's brother Willie was the pianist, and a young woman, Pola Roberts, played the drums. She was first class in every respect. I remember that after one session I went up to Smalls' Paradise; Ms. Roberts had got there ahead of me and was sitting at the bar. The album sold well. The sound of that huge choir in stereo, the shouts and clapping of the congregation, and the presence of the church atmosphere made it a unique recording.

One of the Hammond failures during my first years back with Columbia was Nikki Price, a singer with an incredible three-plus octave range. She was a good musician, but one of our first records was a very poignant ballad in which she insisted on going up two octaves on the last note. I protested. She would not change it. I told her about "Wouldja for a Big Red Apple?" the song I heard Billie Holiday sing at Monette Moore's Harlem Club. I could never persuade Billie to sing it for records, but Nikki searched the ASCAP files and found it. It was by Johnny Mercer, the second song he ever wrote lyrics for. When I called the publisher, Herman Starr, he was so pleased we had found a song he never knew he owned that he offered me a penny rate—that is, one cent instead of two cents royalty per record sold. Nikki Price's album, however, was pretentious and did not sell. There seemed no way I could point her in the direction of success.

XLII

In 1962 I had a severe cold and went to a doctor for treatment. He prescribed a drug from which I developed a rash that itched so badly over the next two years that often I could not sleep. It was a miserable time. I don't like popping pills, so between the itch and the lack of sleep I became rather run down. In March of 1964 I went to a rehearsal of an African choir at St. Clement's church on 46th Street, between Ninth and Tenth Avenues. I listened; the group was not all that good; I left. As I was crossing Ninth Avenue on my way back to the office, I felt a tremendous stab of a pain in the middle of my chest. I had no idea what had hit me. I kept walking, staggering east on the long blocks between Ninth Avenue and Broadway until I came to a Bingerino parlor, where I sat down to rest.

I continued on to the Columbia offices at the corner of Seventh Avenue and 52nd Street, arriving shortly before noon. My friend Ken Glancy, then in charge of the A & R department, took one look at me and asked if I had had a kidney attack. "I never saw you with such a color," he said. "You better get home fast."

I went down the back stairs of the building and luckily found a taxi. "Please keep talking to me," I told the driver, "because if you don't I'm afraid I may pass out." The driver drove and talked all the way to my apartment building just as Esmé was leaving for lunch. She called the doctor, who had me wrapped in a blanket and sent for an ambulance. "Give him a slug of bourbon," he told Esmé.

We went by ambulance to Lenox Hill Hospital. I was given a shot that knocked me out. When I woke up I was in an intensive-care unit. The man in the next bed, who turned out to be Maria Callas' father, was screaming and in terrible pain. The noise in the room was incessant. "Do I have a doctor?" I asked the nurse. "And what's his name?"

"His name is Claps," she told me, "like the disease."

My doctor was Francis Xavier Claps, a fine heart specialist.

I had suffered my first and worst heart attack, and at the moment my condition was critical. I could expect to be out of action for six months. If I recuperated satisfactorily and learned to take things easier there would be no reason I couldn't go back to work. I determined to get back on my feet as soon as I could.

It took six months, just as the man said. I returned to Columbia in September. My regimen required that I be careful, take daily walks, play golf, and rest more frequently. To the extent that I did so I could go on making records. My enthusiasms, my curiosity, my urge to see and hear all the world offered were no less strongly felt. I was and am incapable of giving in to physical restrictions that might change my life. Back at Columbia I had no sooner entered my office than I received a call from Bob Bach, once the co-host with Leonard Feather of a jazz show called *Platterbrains* and for the last fifteen years coordinator of *What's My Line?* "No matter what else you do, John," Bach told me, "go to the Canadian Broadcasting Company's New York office and ask them to run a film for you on the Montreal poet Leonard Cohen."

Cohen had written a fascinating novel, *Beautiful Losers*, and was considered to be one of the finest poets in North America. I went to see the film and was amazed to discover that Cohen, a dark, gloomy sort of man, had an absolutely magic attraction for kids. They followed him from coffee houses to pinball parlors to all the young people's haunts in Toronto. Mary Martin (not the actress) was Cohen's manager in New York, and after talking to her I decided it would be important to sign him for Columbia. At this point Goddard Lieberson had been moved to a senior vice-presidency of CBS, and Clive Davis was about to take over running the record division. Davis, however, had not yet taken active control, and Bill Gallagher, formerly the head of sales, was making artistic decisions. I brought the Cohen idea to him. "A thirty-two-year-old poet?" he cried. "Are you crazy, John? Besides, he wants a lot of money."

That was one reaction. Cohen was published by an old friend of mine, Tom Guinzberg, at Viking Press. I saw Tom at lunch. "I'm about to sign one of your writers," I told him. "Leonard Cohen."

"Well," said Guinzberg, "you may be interested to know that we sold five hundred and forty copies of his last book of poems. You're really crazy, John."

"Didn't *Beautiful Losers* do well in paperback?" I asked.

"Yes, it's true. Its sexual imagery has a wide public un-appreciative of poetry, and it must have sold six hundred thousand copies by now."

"Doesn't that make you believe he has something?"

"Not really," Tom said.

Well, it made a believer of me. I was persistent and I got my way. Clive approved the contract and Leonard was signed. In the recording studio he got the jitters. He could not conceive of his voice being commercial enough to sell records, and was worried about the quality of his guitar playing. Actually, although he was a less sophisticated musician then the professionals later brought in to assist him, he was within his limitations a superb technician and a compelling artist. Simplicity was his great asset and we told him so. It was not what he wanted to hear. When he recorded he insisted that all studio lights be turned off. Then he burned enough incence to make the place smell like a Turkish bazaar. I finally located one musician, Willie Ruff, a black French horn player and bassist (now into electronic music at Yale) who thought Leonard was a genius. He quietly instilled in Leonard a confidence I don't think he'd ever had before. With Willie on bass and Jimmy Lovelace playing delicately on drums, he recorded an entrancing album of his own material.

When Leonard hear the records he decided they were not commercial. I was overruled and another producer brought in. He added strings and assorted pillows of sound for Cohen's voice to rest on. As soon as I heard the new tracks I knew they were wrong. Others at Columbia agreed with me. "Whatever spell you've created has been lost," I told Leonard. "This isn't you any longer." Furthermore, he was running a risk with the record buyers. A hundred times I've seen efforts to make a record more commercial simply turn the buyers off. Stand or fall on what you are, I tell my people. Be yourself. Even so, this never stops artists from looking for all the musical support they can get.

We removed as much of the sweetening as we could. It's like trying to take the sugar back out of the coffee. We must have succeeded. Leonard was a smash. He was an oddball who paid off because he was unique and because in that unpredictable decade he had something to say that was important to young people. I was not particularly interested in continuing to record him. As with Dylan, his success turned him from an original voice into a gold mine, and that factor would outweigh all others in his future work. Once again Bob Johnston in Nashville took responsibility for the subsequent albums, all of which were big sellers. In the seventies Leonard is still making albums and his books have boomed. Viking Press had a profitable poet after all.

The murder of Medgar Evers, one of the vicious crimes committed during the painful years of white Southern resistance to integration, shocked me and prompted me to what I now realize was both a foolish and dangerous response. I was very fond of Medgar, our best NAACP board member from the

South, and felt I should attend his funeral in Jackson, Mississippi. My decision, impulsively arrived at, as many of my reactions have been, involved Jason and Esmé, making it all the more thoughtless and naïve. Esmé considered it a flamboyant thing to do, totally unnecessary under the circumstances and unfair to the family.

But I was determined to be there. The timing, too, was significant. It was June 15, 1963, a time of turbulence and disillusionment for blacks and for all who fought for their cause. Thurgood Marshall had not yet been appointed to the Supreme Court, and the victories so dearly won in the courts during the 1950's were being vitiated by resistance to their application throughout the South. This was especially painful for me because I was no longer so active or effective in the affairs of the NAACP as I had been. Attending Evers' funeral would be a small way of reminding myself—and others—of my presence and my continuing militancy. I have never paused long to weigh the consequences when I felt impelled to do something. Like my mother, I see my duty and I move toward my goal, thinking, perhaps like her, that while others may not agree with me at the time their good as well as my own will be served. That is enough for me.

Jason and I flew to New Orleans, where we boarded a plane to Jackson and found ourselves sitting next to Ralph Bunche. When we arrived in the Jackson airport we noticed that all the seats had been taken out of the lunch counter. Ralph laughed. "You know, John," he said, "if you're sitting down it's integration. If you're standing up it's accepted!"

We walked into town from the airport, feeling reasonably safe, although it was clear from the angry talk in the air that the mood of the town was ugly. The funeral was held at the Masonic temple, where about a thousand people had crowded in with no more than half a dozen white faces among them. Outside afterward a march was forming, and it was then that I finally felt that the situation could be dangerous and that bringing Jason into it for the sake of my gesture to Medgar had been foolhardy. We left. Shots were fired during the march, but by then Jason and I were on our way.

Medgar Evers was a giant. He had died on a battlefield I knew well in a war far from over, despite the encouraging progress made since I had first traveled to the Kentucky coal fields.

By the mid-1960's black supremacy and black nationalism were being shouted by such leaders as Stokely Carmichael. We were back to separation of the races rather than the integration I still believed most strongly to be the only viable long-run solution. The cries of the separatists were unbearably loud in my ears. Like many idealists of my generation, I had been taken in more than once by those who spouted agreement for self-serving reasons. Because I believed I had no personal ax to grind I had often failed to notice other axes around me. I sought the agreement of all I talked to, persuading and arguing, supremely satisfied when I felt I had made a new disciple, whether in jazz or in social reform.

I was now being forced to withdraw to some extent, both by black leaders I disagreed with and by physical limitations of my own, though neither could blunt my enthusiasm or my conviction. The sharp corners of the keystone which holds a man erect in his own eyes, I discovered, are not blunted by his being put to pasture.

In 1965 I was still less than happy with the directions jazz was taking. It still was being intellectualized. It was not honest and unpretentious. Despite gaining complete respectability, it was not selling as well as rock, folk, and rhythm-and-blues. The artists I liked particularly—Ray Bryant, Buddy Tate, Basie and his veterans—seemed of little interest to young listeners, whose notions of jazz derived from the jazz-rock mixture purveyed by several best-selling groups. And the new-found intellectual complexity of jazz was having a strange effect on young jazz musicians. Educated, technically far more proficient than the generations preceding them, they nonetheless lacked the feel, the natural talent, the self-inspired expressiveness of older jazzmen. Jazz was defined, composed, studied, and dissected, not *played*.

And every now and then someone came along to make

my point for me. George Benson, for instance. I got a letter one day from Jimmy Boyd, the manager of a number of r-&-b artists (and the father of a New York City policeman), who said he had a guitar player greater than Charlie Christian. "You better come up and hear him" Jimmy wrote. "He's opening at the Palm Tavern on 125th Street next week."

I took Esmé with me. George was playing with organist Lonnie Smith, and after hearing a couple of sets we agreed he was indeed the best since Charlie. There was not a facet of the guitar of which he was not a master. Even Charlie never had George's technique, and furthermore George combined it all with control, good taste, and—one thing poor Charlie never had—good health. Good health invigorates one's music, freshens one's spirit, exhilarates one's head. Half dead, Charlie Christian could outplay most musicians he met. But George combined talent and strength. He was a genuine pleasure to hear.

I thank Jimmy Boyd for tipping me off. Still, I should have known about George before. He had played in Jack McDuff's organ trio; if I hadn't disliked jazz organ so much I probably would have heard him months earlier.

I signed George for Columbia and, after learning that he had started out as a nine-year-old rock singer on Victor's "X" label, I had him sing a couple of tunes—"Summertime" and "A Foggy Day"—on his first album for us. Jimmy Lovelace sat in on drums. I also recorded him with Lonnie Smith, and with King Curtis and Blue Mitchell. King was a tenor-sax star in the r-&-b field until he was killed a few years ago, and Blue Mitchell still is a widely respected trumpet player. I guess "It's Uptown" is my favorite of the albums we did together.

Eventually, George left Columbia, accepting the offer of a $30,000 advance from Verve Records when his option ran out. Then he moved to A & M Records for $35,000 up front. Finally he signed with Creed Taylor at CTI. Creed was the founder of the Bethlehem label and producer of the hit records of the late Wes Montgomery. At CTI George succeeded Wes, a little commercial now for my taste, yet undeniably the biggest-selling jazz artist in America in the late seventies. Like Charlie Christian, George Benson has found his path crossing Benny Goodman's. On the *World of John Hammond* show they played together. Unlike Charlie, however, George does not need Benny. In 1975 he signed with Warner Brothers Records and had platinum albums in the following two years. He won a Grammy award for "This Masquerade" as the best single of 1976, a record in which his guitar was backup for his hugely commercial voice.

While attending Antioch, Jeep became a musician. Already a fan of early blues, he learned to play the guitar from a boy in his dormitory. Jeep had an affinity for the instrument, a good ear, and he knew what he wanted to sing and play. I was preparing to reissue an album by Robert Johnson, the great blues singer who had died in the late 1930's, before he had become widely known (and before I could get him for *Spirituals to Swing*). I sent Jeep an acetate of the Johnson album and he was tremendously impressed. He had his musical hero at last and knew how he wanted to sing himself.

Under Antioch's policy of allowing students to take outside jobs in their second year, jobs which are supposed to fit their academic interests and add practical experience to their education, Jeep left to work as a handyman in Boca Grande, Florida. He bought a pair of blindman's glasses and a tin cup, and took to the streets to play and sing the blues. He felt that only by disguising himself would he be allowed to enter black taverns where he could learn more about singing the blues. Although I didn't realize it, my son had decided on a career and set for himself a very difficult goal. For a white boy raised in New York City to sing with honesty and persuasiveness the music of the Southern poor black, uncommercial music mostly unknown to his own contemporaries, was quite a feat. Nonetheless, it was his intention and his accomplishment.

Everything was going well in Boca Grande until my sister Adele's daughter and her husband happened to stay at the hotel where Jeep the handyman was working. Not only that, they saw him on the street with his guitar and tin cup. The news whistled through the family, setting off various reactions of shock and dismay, as well as of approval. Jeep, who, I am sure, cared not at all for our opinions, seemed on his way to being another wayward Hammond.

Jeep returned to Antioch briefly, where he appeared in a production of *Guys and Dolls*, which Rosita and I went out to see. He was very good, although Frank Loesser's Broadway tunes were not his dish of tea. At the end of the term he told me he was going to take a leave of absence. "That's a dangerous thing to do," I warned. "Nowadays it's important to get through college. You'll probably never go back."

"Dad," he asked, "how long were you at Yale?"

That ended the discussion. Jeep hitchhiked to Aspen, Colorado. He knew a few artists and managed to win a scholarship at a local art school, but he was much more interested in singing in the local coffeehouses at night. After a few weeks, for reasons I know not, he left Aspen and wound up working in a gas station in San Francisco. From there he went to Los Angeles, where he played every hootenanny he could find. I decided that if he was that interested in a career as a blues singer I would try to help. I took him to my friend Sonny Burke at Decca, who was impressed with Jeep's talent, though no one else there though him commercial enough. He was, after all, a young white boy singing rural Negro blues. Other people liked him, however, and I advised him to wait for the right opportunity.

The first place at which I saw Jeep sing was a club called The Insomniac, at Hermosa Beach in California. This was 1962. He wore a Dylan-type cap, made $25 a night singing seven nights a week, and my professional, as well as fatherly, assessment was that he sounded good. He looked down at his guitar too much. Shyness, or perhaps uncertainty about his ability to carry an audience along with him, seemed to prevent him from looking at his listeners. He would have to get over that.

From Los Angeles he made his way back to New York where a group called the Rooftop Singers discovered him. They took him to Vanguard to meet the Solomon brothers, who had no idea I had a blues-singing son. They signed him on. His first album, which cost almost nothing to record, sold well. He thought Vanguard was the wrong company for him, however, because it did not sell single records, so he made the mistake of joining Redbird. There, backed by some of the members of the Rolling Stones, he made his best album, but Redbird went bankrupt. The album was sold to Atlantic, which kept it on the market, and Jeep began to record for Atlantic.

I realized I should keep out of Jeep's career as much as possible. He wanted to make it on his own, and up to the time he started to record for Atlantic I had nothing to do with his decisions. I always hoped, of course, that because of my friendship with Jerry Wexler at Atlantic Jeep would get a better break, but he did not. Nor did he come to me for advice. Jeep wanted to sing simple country blues his own way, as directly and honestly as he could, and he has never been a commercial property. He doesn't write many songs, either, which these days is an important asset for all folk and blues singers. Still, he has never been without a job and he usually makes far more money than I do. He insists on calling himself John Hammond. This is reasonable enough: John, after all, is his name and he considers Jeep Hammond undignified. The result has been more confusion for me than for him. Now people ask me if I am the blues singer, instead of the maker of electric organs.

When Arthur Penn was about to direct *Little Big Man* for Cinema Center Films, a CBS-owned motion-picture division, he decided not to have Indian music on his sound track, but to use authentic Negro blues. In discussing this with me he said he thought a story of discrimination ought to have the *sound* of discrimination, and that even for a movie about In-

John Hammond, 1976: "I am very
proud of my son. He has made it on his
own in a rough business."

dians most people would expect that sound to be Negro.

"Fine," I said. "What sort of blues do you want?"

He described the sort of instrumental blues Leadbelly used to play.

"I don't think that's what you really want. I think you want the Robert Johnson sound, in which there are practically no lyrics, where there are whoops and hollers, and bottleneck guitar playing."

I played him the Robert Johnson album. Penn reacted immediately. "My God," he said, "that's just what I want. I hope we can get him."

I explained that Johnson had been dead for thirty years. Penn then asked about Jeep. He had heard of him from film editor Dede Allen, was curious about his style and sound, yet cautious about a commitment. "Listen for yourself," I suggested. I reached Jeep at the loft where he was living. He was about to leave for California. "You'd better get over here fast," I said, "and bring your National guitar." I had bought him one of those blindman's guitars for his twenty-first birthday and it was his proudest possession.

Jeep arrived in fifteen minutes and played for Penn and for Stuart Millar, the film's producer. They thought he was marvelous. They even gave him a couple of screen tests. These came to nothing, but they were absolutely sold on his performing the sound track.

Because *Little Big Man* was to be a CBS-owned motion picture and Jeep was an Atlantic Records artist, either Columbia would have to give up the sound-track rights to Atlantic, or Atlantic would have to release Jeep to Columbia. Clive Davis, now president of Columbia Records, took the position that unless all rights to the music became Columbia's property and Jeep signed an exclusive Columbia artist contract, there would be no deal. I called Jerry Wexler, embarrassed to be in such a position, as well as opposed to Jeep's becoming a Columbia artist at all. I asked Jerry to waive his exclusive rights to Jeep's performance in the picture and on records. "My son has a chance to do a very important score for a big-budget picture," I explained, "but he won't be able to do it unless he becomes a Columbia artist."

Jerry was cooperative, as always. "We haven't really done the job on Jeep we should have," he said, "and it's my fault because I've been so busy with Aretha and Roberta Flack. I'll see if I can't arrange it." Atlantic generously released Jeep from his contract without asking a dime from him or from Columbia, even though he still owed money on advances Atlantic had given him.

All of a sudden my son was a Columbia artist, something I felt would be wrong for both of us. Jeep's score for *Little Big Man* was a solo performance. He strummed his guitar and hollered away like Robert Johnson. If it was not the best, it was certainly one of the least expensive scores in the history of motion pictures. The film did not do well. It was something of a masterpiece and may yet earn its money back. That time is not yet. Meanwhile, its stiffish $9,000,000 cost was what persuaded CBS to get out of the motion-picture business.

Jeep made another album for Columbia before the picture was released; neither that nor the *Little Big Man* soundtrack album sold. Columbia's A & R director—by now Kip Cohen—then decided to cut an album with Jeep, Dr. John on piano, and Mike Bloomfield on guitar, each taking one third of the royalty. Recorded in San Francisco, it cost more than $100,000 to produce. By the mid-1960's this was not uncommon. Rock groups and singers use inordinate amounts of studio time, editing time, and costly multitrack recording equipment. Records often are experiments in feedback, sound layering, and other electronic combinations at company expense. In any event, the album sold well, the first one Jeep was associated with that turned into a commercial success. Jeep is his own man, however, While he enjoyed the aura of success, it was not the direction he wanted to go, and he was aware that it was Dr. John's name—well known to the rock audience, as Jeep's was not—which made the sales.

Jeep's first marriage ended in divorce. He and Dana had a fine little son who is much loved and enjoyed by Grandmother Jemy, as well as by Esmé and me. Jeep is now married to Peggy Scott, a vital young woman, a New England Quaker, previously married to an artist and with two children of her own. When they decided to marry, in 1975, I asked who would perform the ceremony.

"Well, Dad," Jeep said, "I think we'll be married in Grace Church."

"What?" I cried. "You've never been baptized and neither has Peggy, because she's a Quaker. You've both been divorced. Grace Church is very high Episcopal, and I don't think I'll ever see the day when two unbaptized, divorced people are married there."

"You don't understand," my son said. "Peggy's step-father was Bishop Moore's roommate at St. Paul's. We're going to be married in Grace Church because Peggy's mother wants us to be married there."

"That should be very interesting," I told Jeep. I knew Paul Moore very well because he and I had been on the board of the NAACP Legal Defense Committee for years. Esmé knew Paul even better than I because they had grown up together and helped to start Boys' Harbor on Long Island. I knew that neither Esmé nor I could have persuaded Paul to marry Jeep and Peggy. But they were married in Grace Church, just as Jeep said they would. We all gathered for a prewedding luncheon at Luchow's, on 14th Street, in a driving rainstorm. Three of my sisters came, as did my cousins James Clark and Gloria Vanderbilt, and Gloria's son Chris Stokowski, whose father had turned ninety-three the day before.

We arrived at Grace Church drenched. Then we were off to the reception at the Tiffany Room of the Gramercy Park Hotel. I had checked the piano the night before, found it hopelessly out of tune, and paid someone to have it put into shape pronto. George Benson and Ray Bryant played, along with a friend of Jeep's, the flutist, Jeremy Steig. The music was my wedding gift to the bride and groom, together with a portrait of Bessie Smith singing at the Alhambra Theater, done many years ago by Stella Block. The wedding guests were a strange mixture of Hammond relatives and friends of

Jeep's, including one man in a white suit who never took off his hat. He turned out to be Leon Redbone, whose first Warner Brothers album created such a stir in the summer of 1976.

Jeep and Peggy and their children live in an old house on several acres in East Hampton. They have put a lot of work into it, installing plumbing and so forth, and I think it is a setting and environment good for them all.

I am very proud of my son. He has made it on his own in a rough business. Even more impressively, he has succeeded in a musical form which demands simple, honest performance without the staging and electronic gimmickry that surrounds most of today's singers. He went back to the blues where I began, where jazz began, and where, if there is to be great jazz, it must always return.

XLIV

By the early 1960's I found myself in an increasingly compromising position in the NAACP. I was still vice president of *The Crisis* and a member of the branch committee, but I could not accept Roy Wilkins' leadership of the organization. Wilkins was feuding with Martin Luther King, Jr., because Dr. King was a pacifist and Wilkins in accord with the militant policies of Lyndon Johnson on the Vietnam War. Wilkins, in fact, later threatened to fire the leadership of any NAACP branch which officially opposed the war, a dictatorial and wrong-headed position considering the antipathy of most young black Americans.

The good people among the leadership were disaffected or dropping away. Constance Baker Motley, for years one of the top attorneys of the NAACP Legal Defense and a woman I hope will be appointed to the U.S. Supreme Court, had left to become a Federal judge in New York. Palmer Weber, my friend, was ousted. Judge Hubert Delaney had become ill and was no longer able to attend board meetings.

I still showed up, principally to talk to the dissidents,

although I saw no point in fighting any longer. We went nearly two years without a youth director, another year without a church director. Roy had advanced into his sixties without younger people designated to succeed him. I regretted I had not aligned myself with the Legal Defense Fund, which was then defending Martin Luther King, Malcolm X, Muhammad Ali, and other black militants anathema to Roy Wilkins. That seemed to me to be where the action was. It was too late for me to join the LDF, however; most of all it needed fund raisers. I could raise a lot of hell, not a lot of money.

In 1967 I resigned from the NAACP with a letter to Roy which I insisted be read to the entire board. I also sent a copy to the *Amsterdam News*, New York's weekly Negro newspaper, which printed it on the front page. Wilkins answered with a ten-page letter of his own which he justified as necessary for the record. It was a skillful letter. Roy has always been a good writer and a persuasive man. I didn't think he answered my charges. As far as I was concerned it set forth the philosophy of a man who had moved steadfastly in the wrong direction.

Leaving was a wrench. I have missed my associations at the NAACP and, as a matter of fact, whenever I meet Roy Wilkins we have long and friendly talks. I think he realized later that he'd been wrong on Vietnam. I never believed that the NAACP should be committed to either political party, or to any policy that did not bear directly on the condition of black Americans. I felt that the NAACP should play Republicans against Democrats, and vice versa, knowing full well that neither party really had the interest of the Negro at heart, although in my time Democrats have been better on the issue than Republicans.

My resignation from the NAACP ended my formal connection with all such organizations, except for the Northside Center for Child Development in Harlem. My convictions and my support for real justice for Negroes in America will never change. Today the catalyst for all my activity in the long battle is, as it has been, jazz and black music.

One marvelous experience was recording Eubie Blake in 1969. Eubie was playing ragtime in Baltimore in 1899 (!), and our two-record set, *The Eighty-six Years of Eubie Blake*, revived him as an artist and launched him on a new career which has lasted into his nineties. He has been equally long lived as a composer. His "Charleston Rag" was also of 1899 vintage and "I'm Just Wild About Harry" was the hit of 1921's *Shuffle Along*, the first Negro revue to make it big on Broadway. I brought in the late Noble Sissle, the bandleader, who was only a few years younger than Eubie and who collaborated with him on "Harry." Eubie played piano, sang, and reminisced to his heart's content, while Sissle sang along. After the session we celebrated Eubie's birthday with a party. A celebrity once more, he went off to make regular appearances on the college circuit.*

Another long-held dream was to reissue the records of Bessie Smith for a generation that had never heard her, although their songs sprang from the blues she sang. In 1969 Chris Albertson, who had done a lot of recording for Riverside Records, and who had been station manager of WBAI in New York, proposed the idea. He would undertake the prodigious job of transferring Bessie's catalog of 78-rpms to LP's, working in many cases from old, scratched pressings. I agreed, suggesting moreover that we do something never done before: issue every single side Bessie ever made. Columbia was the only company she had ever recorded for, so we were in the unique position of being able to put together her entire output. There were one hundred and sixty sides, enough for five double-LP albums.

The job of locating the original records, transferring them to tape, and eliminating as much of the surface noise as possible was enormous. Chris took nearly two years to complete the transfer and his accomplishment made him an au-

---

* In the summer of 1976 I recorded Eubie again in the Bill Bolcomb-Joan Morris album, released in early 1977. Bolcomb, a classically trained pianist, and his wife, Joan Morris, who sings vaudeville songs, celebrated Eubie's then ninety-three years with a record of more of his material.

thority on Bessie Smith. He later wrote her biography, with a flowery inscription in my copy as the man who made the whole project possible. But somehow he got the idea that, while he did all the work, I profited from the albums' success. Although Columbia producers do participate in a bonus plan based on sales of the albums they produce, the bonuses are never calculated on reissued records. Albertson's charges in his book were completely untrue, and Stein and Day, the publishers, deleted his unfortunate statements in subsequent European and paperback editions.

I have never been paid any incentive bonus for the many reissues of Columbia records I produced back in the 1930's. The reward for me in the reissue of these older records, particularly the Bessie Smith albums, has been to enable a generation of rock fans hear what I heard long ago, the basic strength and beauty of the blues, and to become a fan of Bessie Smith nearly forty years after her death.

XLV

The role of the record producer, after the musicians have been chosen, the songs picked and arranged, and all of the preliminary plans made, is one of supervising the transfer of live musical performance from the studio floor to the disk or tape spinning inside the control room.

The studio itself is usually a cold and barren room, functionally furnished with some chairs, music stands, microphones and cables, the in-house piano, and, once it is inhabited, with that most depressing of civilization's many throwaways—the paper coffee cup.

The musicians perform in a closed universe, under observation from behind a glass wall, their every sound being heard, with amplification, by the producer and the engineers. Communication is by microphone through huge speakers. The atmosphere is Orwellian. To put musicians at their ease, to coax them to play better than they ever have before (or sometimes just better than the last time), and to push them to produce their best within the several hours allotted for the session all are parts of the job. The producer must detect every mistake, stop and start the performance, ask for innumerable "takes" until he thinks he has what he wants, all without upsetting egos and often at ungodly times of day or night when the musicians are in no mood to play well.

Actually, of course, it's no different from any other human enterprise that depends on people pulling together. When they do it's a joy. When they don't it's exasperating and the product suffers. The technicalities of making records have advanced enormously over what they were when I was starting out. I have observed no similar advance by people. They're about what they've always been, if younger.

One of the best sessions I ever had anything to do with was a date for Vocalion in Chicago in 1936 with Count Basie and four of his musicians. The conditions were primitive. The studio was a small room—about twelve feet by fifteen—in an office building across from the Drake Hotel. It was too small for a grand piano and it lacked the acoustical paneling and soundproofing that are standard today. I had one engineer. He operated both the control panel and the recorder which etched the sound onto the wax master. There were only two mikes, of which I chose to use only one, and the acoustics were so poor that the thump of the bass drum, together with the resonance of the string bass, occasionally caused the needle to break the grooves of the disk.

The musicians were Basie, Walter Page, Jo Jones, Tatti Smith on trumpet, and Lester Young. Jimmy Rushing was on hand for a spot of singing. Jo, Tatti, and Lester had never recorded before. We began the date at ten in the morning, after the band had played all night at the Grand Terrace. I chose the time purposely, so that everyone, while tired, would still be stimulated by the night's work. Like other jazz producers, I have discovered that jazz players are better before sleep than after, and particularly following a night on the bandstand. We had to eliminate Jo's bass drum lest it shatter our equipment, so he played only a snare drum and cymbal. Basie had to play a baby-grand piano, and everyone was crowded. So what? They were ready, excited, and at ease with each other.

People who have seen Basie since he reached the serene plateau of mature professionalism may have a hard time visualizing him as anything but rotund, courtly, assured, like someone's amiable but slightly reserved uncle. That has been his image—give or take a few pounds and a few muttonchop whiskers—for the past thirty years or so. In that Chicago studio that day, however, he was a slender young man of thirty-two. There wasn't much meat on him; part of that was youth and part the malnourishment that black children endured, and still endure. (It's easy to assume that black musicians who die young—and there have been many—have been debilitated and overwhelmed by booze or drugs. Often they just didn't have the vitamin-enriched childhood of whites and grew up physically inadequate for the rigors of life.) Basie's face was lively and appealing in its eagerness. Already he had the mustache and the dimples, and the gentlemanly manner. His wrists and hands were slender, too, and if the fingers hit more notes faster than their master later thought necessary, they were learning economy. The taste was always there. Also the personal equilibrium; Bill Basie is a very solid man.

Walter was his burly self. Jimmy, too. Throughout the years Jimmy waxed but did not wane. He never became *less*. Tatti, Lester, and Jo were simply younger versions of themselves: Tatti small and dapper, Lester fey, Jo handsome and imperious. One advantage of having four trim musicians out of six was that we were certain to fit into that twelve-by-fifteen studio.

The group was so pleased with the first playback that there was never a breakdown. I made two or three versions of each of the four tunes we could record in our three-hour period, although each was cut without interruption, each a flawless performance. By one o'clock the date was over, the masters ready to be shipped to the Bridgeport factory, and the band on its way to bed. It was an intimate, exhilarating experience for us all, leaving that small studio bushed—as we used to say—yet knowing we had four little jazz masterpieces:

"Lady Be Good," "Shoe Shine Boy," "Evenin'," and "Boogie Woogie."* The label announced them as the work of Jones-Smith, Inc.

Technically, these were probably the worst records I have ever produced. The range of sound capable of being recorded did not go below two hundred cycles, nor above eight thousand, a narrow wedge of sound which eliminated the tops and bottoms of the actual waves we made. Still, these sides included the finest solos Lester Young ever recorded—if I say so myself. Even packed into that small room the band was free and swinging. All four sides have become classics.

For contrast, a record date in 1975 with the Bill Watrous band. Bill is an ex-Dixieland trombone player in his mid-thirties, a handsome fellow and a real showman whose sheer exuberance and tremendous technical facility are the equal of any I've heard since the melodious and artful Jack Jenney. This is high praise. I've always placed Jack, who died too early, at thirty-five, among the three best trombones ever.

Bill had a fourteen-piece band and liked to record on sixteen-track equipment—that is, sixteen separate channels on wide recording tape, each channel fed by its own microphones. There was a microphone for the reed section, four for the brass, and seven for the drummer, so that each drum, each cymbal, was miked to isolate its individual sound. It is also common practice to leave three or four channels open for overdubbing later. It also is possible to feed each mike into its own channel.

The capacity of modern equipment to record each instrument separately, followed by long hours in editing rooms, where the multiple tracks are reduced to two, where the balance of sounds is artificially blended, has made all record production extremely expensive. In the old days companies did not charge the artist for studio or editing facilities. Production costs were minimal. In the early 1960's, however, the brilliant Paul Simon and Art Garfunkel became fascinated by the

---

* It was, of course, in nostalgic celebration of this session that Basie launched into "Shoe Shine Boy" with Jo and Walter at the Vanguard reunion described on pages 331-32.

gadgetry of the recording process. The engineer who supervised their early sessions was able to link up two sixteen-track consoles to offer them thirty-two separate tracks on which they spread a cumulative performance, one track at a time. They managed to use every track, adding instruments, vocal parts, overdubbing themselves, with the result that "Bridge Over Troubled Water," for instance, required something more than eight hundred hours of studio and editing time.

This is expensive time. Engineers are paid by the hour, with various overtime payments for nights and weekends. A single reel of sixteen-track tape costs about $100. Now the expense of production is charged against artists' royalty payments—and all too often records do not earn it back. What began as a simple art form has become a needlessly complicated process. Worst of all, unless a performance is judged likely to sell hundreds of thousands of copies, no one will take a chance on recording it at all.

Columbia in New York offers the producer a choice among three types of studio. Thirtieth Street, formerly a church, is a large, live studio where natural reverberation is possible. A second is about thirty feet by forty, with a nineteen-foot ceiling and movable panels so that sound can be controlled. Third is a small studio, not much larger than the Chicago room where I first recorded Basie, although rather better equipped. Watrous recorded at 30th Street.

The complexities of recording determine procedures. The day before the session I had to provide the engineers with a floor diagram to indicate where each musician would sit, plus supplementary information on soloists and any special instruments required.

Half of Watrous' three-hour session was taken up with placing microphones, testing each for sound leakage into other tape channels, and balancing each in relation to the others. This makes me grind my teeth. Instead of rehearsals and musical balancing, we have prayerful inaction, waiting for the high priests of electronics to tell us our circuits are working. Fortunately, the tunes recorded by the Watrous band had been previously rehearsed. Even so, all the performances had to be assembled later in the editing room. And no amount of editing, rebalancing, splicing, and enhancing can make a performance great unless it was great to begin with. The Watrous band was less than great. The album sold moderately well, though not enough to recover its production nut of $50,000.

There was a further problem: the always-crucial, often-delicate artist-producer relationship. This exists regardless of recording methods, of course, although, as I have mentioned earlier, the number of options available today—the rationale for each album, the choice of each tune, the number of ways music can be made to sound, the artist's precarious hold on the upper rungs of his profession, and the recording company's heavy investment—all put pressure on the trust and confidence artist and producer should have in each other.

I had been warned that Watrous could be very assertive about the conduct of a session, and that getting along with him would depend on doing pretty much as he wished. I thought I could give him what he wanted if he would give me a few things I wanted. I felt, for instance, that he was better on ballads than on faster jazz pieces and insisted that he include a couple in his album. A tune I though would be perfect for him was Ray Ellis' theme song for the Today Show on which Watrous is featured. Bill refused. He also had a couple of favorite arrangers we didn't agree on, and the result of his choices made for loud, unswinging music.

I know this is a problem with more than one side. The age difference which now separates me from most record artists is a considerable one and can make it difficult to establish the sympathetic vibes that contribute so much to a good record. I think my taste is still contemporary, although it has evolved from many, many musical experiences and has been influenced by some musicians no longer among us. And, finally, I have an admittedly old-fashioned notion that it is the quality of the players, not the complexity of the equipment, which produces honest performance. Musicians who record on sixteen or twenty-four tracks will splutter at this. If music is bad it isn't necessarily the equipment that makes it so. It may just be bad ideas or bad execution. Well, sure. I just think there's more room to hide in a jungle of equipment. Knowing you have this out does not encourage you to be uncompromising about the quality of your performance. This is not, however, an argument I expect to win.

I'm not sure what Bill would say about me as a producer. Certainly it is difficult for a young jazz musician to take the advice of someone twice his age. I still am convinced that he is as good a trombone player as there is to be found. Just before he left Columbia he won the *Down Beat* poll as the most promising new star, the best trombone, and one of the three or four best bands. He runs college jazz clinics and has become as fine a teacher as he is a player. So I have had to look for some answers in myself as to why we didn't do better together.

I do feel, as I've had occasion to say once or twice before, that the best music comes from musicians clustered so they can hear each other, support each other, inspire each other. As far as mikes are concerned, less is more. Fewer are better. I'm not trying to turn back the clock. I only say that a drummer who can only hear the rest of the band through earphones, and who cannot himself be heard, cannot possibly provide the lift the band expects of him. Even such a modest effort as a recording I did with a twelve-piece band on four tracks without overdubbing made it necessary for so many musicians to wear headphones that the rhythm section was never quite together. At a second session I moved the group closer together, eliminated the headphones, and got a performance that required virtually no editing.

The kind of session I really love was one I arranged in 1975 around Helen Humes, who was then appearing at Barney Josephson's Cookery, with Ellis Larkins at the piano. It had been twenty-seven years since I last recorded her and forty-seven since she had made her first sides for Okeh as a girl of fifteen. I wanted to come as close as possible to the feeling of the old Teddy Wilson-Billie Holiday classics for Brunswick. That meant no arrangements, a minimum of musicians, and an intense intimacy.

I got the impeccable Ellis on piano, Major Holley on

bass, Oliver Jackson on drums, and the tasteful Buddy Tate on tenor and clarinet. As a fillip I added George Benson, and, indeed, his guitar contributed a special measure of imagination and interest.

The material was either blues or standard ballads. No specific track had instant commercial appeal as a single so that sales were not so great as the musical content deserved. But it was a beautifully balanced, beautifully blended session and Helen's sixty-two-year-old voice had a wonderful girlish quality that reminded me of Mildred.

This was a four-track recording made in Studio E at 49 East 52nd Street. It was a good, tight setup and we accomplished everything we set out to do in less than two three-hour sessions.

The recording of classical music is also worth mentioning. In the old days a sonata by violin and piano required perfect performances by each player. There was no way to eradicate mistakes. Nowadays the same sonata is likely to be a dishonest performance in which all errors, mis-hits, wrong notes, slurs, and so forth, are corrected or eliminated by splicing the tape.

In the early 1970's Vladimir Horowitz agreed to allow a Carnegie Hall performance to be recorded by Columbia. The producer wisely recorded rehearsals as well as the actual performance in order to have a choice of versions to insert where mistakes occurred. As released, the album was perfect. There is a record dealer in New York City, however, who makes it a practice to record notable performances himself, and who manages to make these homemade disks available to interested people, such as critics and collectors. In this case, a comparative playing of the Columbia and actual performances revealed rather large discrepancies which became the subject of a New York *Times* feature. Horowitz was furious at having his mistakes revealed and there was considerable hell raised at Columbia. Yet as long as human failings can be corrected and a false but perfect record released, all artists will continue to take advantage of splicing.

I was present in 1935 when Joseph Szigeti performed

the most difficult of the Paganini Caprices for unaccompanied violin. There were seventeen breakdowns which required Szigeti to begin all over again until he got it right. Szigeti's was a totally honest performance. What we have now is not. Whether one day the Federal Trade Commission will require suitable explanation of this fact I don't know, but record buyers should be aware of it.

In the prewar era microphones were so primitive that it was never possible to record the full range of sound frequencies actually produced by an orchestra. In 1947 English Decca introduced recording techniques which made it possible to duplicate sound from about fifty cycles to nearly twenty thousand, almost the full range of audible sound. Decca called its system Full Frequency Range Recording. The playback equipment of those days was also limited, however, so after two or three plays with a heavy stylus digging into the grooves the higher frequencies were scratched away.

With better turntables and tone arms which place less than one gram of weight on the surface of a record, it is now possible to reproduce the full range of sound, but again fidelity depends on the quality of the home equipment. Radio and television speakers are generally so poor that full sound is almost never achieved. I maintain that if anyone wants to hear honest music he should go to a concert or listen to a band in a room. The natural dynamics of a performance are heard, just as recording with a single microphone properly placed produces the room sound on records. Stereo sound theoretically provides one microphone and speaker for each ear, a natural extension of what is heard in a concert hall. Even a piano solo benefits from the use of two microphones, as I learned at Vanguard. One microphone is placed close to the instrument, a second farther away to pick up overtones.

I used to marvel at the English Columbia recordings of Walter Gieseking, whose liquid piano sound was beautifully reproduced. When I finally recorded Gieseking myself, I found how it was done. He was a large man with very small nostrils who played very vigorously. When he hit a chord there was always an accompanying snort. The only way to avoid his snorts was to move the microphone farther and farther from his nose; that distance was what gave his recordings the sound I so much admired.

For all the spouting about sound quality, for all the variety of expensive equipment offered to the public, and for all the fanatical preoccupation of the experts with stereo, quadraphonic, and other devices to sell recorded music, performance is still the only meaningful criterion, as it always has been. I have been a record fan and collector for fifty years, during which time record quality has been vastly improved. But to all of us who love records the important thing will always be that a moment in the career of a great artist could be preserved and offered to us all to listen to as often as we like. That was true when Sir Harry Lauder sang "Roamin' in the Gloamin' " for me long ago, and it is still the way I feel today when I hear, even on a pocket radio, a performance unlike anything ever played before.

XLVI

Between 1964 and 1974 I suffered four more heart attacks. Each was less severe than the previous one. Each followed a rugged plane trip without sufficient time to rest and recuperate. The second came in 1970, after Esmé's and my return from our first trip to Japan and the Far East. We traveled to Singapore, Bangkok, and Djakarta, and enjoyed it all, but I went back to Columbia too soon and faced too many assignments without rest. It will always be difficult for me to sit still, to wait a moment or a day before setting out to discover the world all over again. I am an early riser, among the first to buy each day's *Times*, and my daily armful of new magazines is as much my trademark as my crewcut. Since I first discovered Mr. Epstein's newsstand at 91st Street and Madison Avenue I have never missed an issue of any periodical with something to say. This compulsion to see, to read, to hear everything as soon as possible is as strong now as it ever was, and to be the first to know—or, certainly, never the last—is vitally important to me. To allow the events of a single day to reach me second hand, to miss my morning call at the newsstand, to drive without the car radio turned on, to pass by a marquee announcing a show or a movie or a jazz player unknown to me will never be possible. I try to be careful, but I cannot stop.

In the winter of 1973 I was stricken again, this time after our return from a midwinter vacation in Paris. As soon as we got home I was off to Max's Kansas City Club, where I climbed too many stairs, took subways instead of taxis, and felt the chest constrictions return. The fourth attack, the least severe, followed a strange combination of ailments Esmé and I both endured in Paris: a severely abscessed tooth for me, severe food poisoning for her. The combination of illnesses, the stress of the long flight home, and the immediate problems there brought on a minor heart attack.

Esmé made up her mind that we could never travel again, although we have and will continue to. I force myself to rest at the end of each flight and am careful not to schedule return flights too soon. Death has never frightened me. I have led a full life, one I have enjoyed, and when it ends it ends. I do not believe in an afterlife, but if there is one, fine. Like most good Catholics Esmé too has no fear of death, so by different routes we have arrived at the same conclusion and enjoy each day with peace of mind. Retirement for me is impossible. If I must walk more slowly, I will start out sooner.

Recently, a hernia has forced me to give up one of my lifelong addictions, pinball. I never have passed a pinball parlor without stopping for a game or two. For years my home court was two adjacent pinball machines in the Paramount drugstore in the Columbia Records building at 799 Seventh Avenue. There I played with Richard Himber, Tony Bennett, and other fanatics while we discussed record sessions and won free games. My pinball winnings over the years have kept me supplied with television sets, electric typewriters, and other prizes, and once Columbia presented me with a Bingerino machine I still have. These days, however, pinball in New

Top: Esmé O'Brien Hammond,
Jason Hammond & Rosita Sarnoff, 1977.

York costs 25¢ for two games, and the prizes are no longer worth the investment. Unable to stand in one place for long periods I have had to give up my favorite sport, but then pinball, like jazz, is not what it used to be.

So much for Hammond afflictions, except for the story of my son Jason's recent accident, a terrible ordeal, one which tells more about my younger son than his considerable accomplishments.

After Jason's discharge from the Army, a parting neither regretted, he decided to work with children. He had always been wonderful with kids and he hired on at Walden School, where he taught kindergarten children for about five years. Next, he and two friends decided to buy a one-hundred-and-ninety-acre farm in North Adams, Massachusetts, adjoining the Savoy National Forest. I believe their idea was to establish a riding camp there. The three boys had to raise about $30,000 apiece to buy the farm, but another of Jason's talents is carpentry. He began to work with wood, setting up his own shop, and he was very good at it.

For the past two years Jason has enjoyed living on his farm. He had had to learn to be a business man, to keep books and pay his debts, and if he has had difficulty he has not told me. In 1976, however, disaster struck. On St. Patrick's Day, Jason was alone at the farm working with a power saw. He was sawing a board with a knot in it. The high-speed saw jiggled and four of the fingers on his right hand suddenly flew off.

Jason's girl friend who had left the day before for New York, had warned him that in case of such an accident he must save all the pieces. Jason reached the telephone and called North Adams for an ambulance, but was told that because of bad roads it would be a while before help could arrive. He realized that if he waited for the ambulance he might bleed to death, so he made a tourniquet, wrapped the severed fingers in a towel, and set out to walk the three miles to the nearest country store. An hour after the accident he was picked up by the ambulance after having staggered to the store with only the thumb of his right hand still intact.

It so happened that at the hospital there was a trio of surgeons who had left New York Hospital for Special Surgery to establish a practice in North Adams. One doctor was a specialist in leg injuries and skiing accidents, another in facial injuries. The third, Kurt Winnecke, treats injuries to hands and limbs. Nobody called me at the time of the accident, but Jeep and Peggy came for dinner the following evening and gave me the news. I had a fit. Jeep assured me that Jason was under the best possible care, but that was not good enough to reassure me.

I have a cousin, Bill Vanderbilt, a former governor of Rhode Island, who lives close to Jason's farm. Bill was at his home in Florida, so I called him and asked if he had ever heard of Dr. Winnecke. "He happens to be my next-door neighbor, John, and my personal doctor. What else do you want to know?"

I asked Bill to do whatever he could, and when he called Dr. Winnecke the surgeon expressed guarded optimism about saving one or two of Jason's fingers. I drove to North Adams as soon as the operation had been done and the bandages removed. Jason's index finger had been severed in two places, but the finger had been completely reconstituted and functions today as well as it ever did. His little finger, completely severed, is in working order. He lost the tips of his two middle fingers, but when I visited him he said, "Now, Dad, I'll really have a good curve."

Jason has returned to carpentry. With complete use of both hands, he has since completed the construction of two houses and a barn.

I have enormous respect for Jason's courage and good sense, and I am very happy that he is the way he is. He remains devoted to Esmé and to all his family, and I think he likes me. He is a son to be proud of, just as Jeep is, and his life will be filled with friends and with satisfactions.

XLVII

One morning there was a note on my office calendar: Mike
Appel, 11:00. Who was Mike Appel? "He's a songwriter," my
secretary explained, "and he has an artist he wants you to
hear. He's very insistent about seeing you because he's tried
everyone else at Columbia and nobody will give him the time
of day."

Well, sometimes that's the way it is. So promptly at
eleven Appel and artist appeared. Appel took the chair on my
left, the young man with the guitar sat down in a far corner.
Appel cut loose. "So you're John Hammond, the man who is
supposed to have discovered Bob Dylan. I want to see if you
have any ears. I've got somebody who's better than Dylan."

This was rather more belligerent than the situation
seemed to call for and I bristled. "I don't know what you're
trying to prove," I said, "but you're succeeding in making me
dislike you. Now, I haven't got much time. Who's your boy?"

"His name is Bruce Springsteen."

I turned to him. "Why don't you take out your guitar,
Bruce, and start playing before I get any more irritated."

Bruce, who had been grinning easily while Appel and
I clashed, unleashed his guitar. It was tuned. He was ready.
Obviously he knew what he was doing. He launched into an
extraordinary piece filled with street imagery. I heard immediately that he was both a born poet and an extremely good
guitar player. I kept a lid on my excitement; I didn't want
Appel to see how impressed I was. I asked Bruce if he had
anything really far out.

"Yeah," he said, " 'If I was a Priest.' " It was a song
about the Virgin Mary running a whorehouse in the Old West
with Jesus as a customer. I had never heard such a song in
my life. "Bruce," I said, "that's the damnedest song I've ever
heard. Were you brought up by nuns?"

"Of course," he said.

It was a long-shot guess. I'd assumed from his name

Bruce Springsteen, 1974: "He has
learned his lessons and paid his dues. He is
in complete command of his craft."

that he was Jewish. Not so. He was three quarters Italian and one quarter Dutch. He'd had a parochial-school education and was both fascinated with and repelled by it. Hence, his sacrilegious song.

He played and sang for two hours. Finally I phoned Sam Hood, proprietor of The Gaslight, to ask whether I could get a live audition for Springsteen. He had never worked as a single anywhere and I wanted to see how he would perform in front of an audience. Sam offered to put Bruce on that night, before the regular performers began at eight-thirty. "There won't be many people here," he warned, "but there'll be enough for you to tell."

We went to the Gaslight and Bruce absolutely amazed his little audience. A noted guitar player who happened to be there asked me, "Hey, John, where did you find this guy?" What could I say? He'd just shown up in my office with his soft-spoken manager. It wasn't like finding Basie.

Now I thought I'd best get a few songs taped. I booked the small Columbia studio the following day and told Appel I wanted to be left alone with Bruce for the duration of the session. I let one outsider in: Jane Boutwell, a writer of "Talk" items for *The New Yorker*, who was planning a profile on me for the *Times* (which, incidentally, never got published). "I've found a new artist and I think something will happen with him, although it may take time. Come to the studio. I'd like you to hear talent when it's really raw."

In less than two hours that day Bruce recorded fourteen songs, every one of them better than anything he later recorded in his albums—in my view—because he was, and is, at his best by himself, playing guitar, playing piano, and singing. On the recording sheet, a log the company requires after all studio auditions, I wrote "the greatest talent of the decade!" or some such understatement. Clive Davis shared my enthusiasm and we signed him. That was in 1973.

He made one album and then appeared at Columbia's annual sales conference which was held that year in San Francisco. By then Clive Davis had been deposed as Columbia's president and Goddard Lieberson had been called back to run the company. Bruce's appearance before the convention audience was, oddly, a downer. He played with the excellent group he had assembled for his album, but their lyrics were unintelligible, and their listeners, including Goddard, became restless and bored. That this might be a problem had never occurred to me. But, of course, the lyrics had been printed in his album (and had gotten rave reviews), so those of us who had worked with him, and his record audience, reading along, were thoroughly familiar with them. And what you know you can hear, even if delivery or enunciation is not perfect. Without that advantage the Columbia audience froze. Bruce's debut was not auspicious.

(Dylan's, ten years previously, was worse. He decided the Columbia sales force looked too smug and comfortable, and launched—relentlessly—into every militant, red-hot, anti-Establishment, antiwar, antipollution, antiracist protest song in his repertoire. There were counterprotest shouts and boos from the audience which Goddard and other biggies did their best to ameliorate. It was then, I think, that Columbia realized it had a tiger by the tail. Dylan might be controversial, but he was one of the superlative audience-grabbers of all time. Like him or not, you couldn't ignore him.)

As with Dylan, Bruce was soon beyond my control. I had recognized his quality, corralled him, and pointed him in the right direction. I was not, however, producing his records. Mike Appel wanted that pleasure and responsibility.

Not surprisingly, I found Mike a difficult fellow, although I appreciated that he (and a partner) had such faith in Springsteen that they had invested almost everything they had to advance his career. I applaud that kind of faith. Still, once Bruce was signed with Columbia, Appel wanted no part of me or of what Columbia could contribute to the development of his star. Despite my interest Appel made it almost impossible to attend Bruce's recording sessions. He scheduled them in a studio in New Jersey. He scheduled them at midnight. And, worse, he began adding tracks and overdubbing Bruce's voice on prerecorded accompaniment, tricks I was sure would hamper Bruce's style.

The first two Springsteen albums did not do well, although the critics were warm. Jon Landau, writing for an underground paper in Boston and contributing to *Rolling Stone* and *Crawdaddy*, wrote after hearing Bruce live: "I have seen the future of rock, and his name is Bruce Springsteen." This ardent support led to his becoming the producer of Bruce's third album, which included "Born to Run." The result was a gold single and a platinum album, an incredible achievement for a young artist. After three years he was suddenly the hottest item in the music business. As everyone remembers, he even made the covers of *Time* and *Newsweek* the same week.

I'm fond of Bruce and I guess I know him as well as anyone in the business, although that isn't saying much. He's a very private person. He doesn't shut people out, the way Dylan can; despite the privacy he's very warm, considerate, generous. I think much of this comes from his stability. As youth likes to say, he has it all together. He feels no need to assert his celebrity. His star quality is not diamond-bright, but modest, natural. Watching him on stage, you can see how much he moves around, sharing the spotlight with his fellow musicians, breaking the focus of attention on him. This modesty also extends to money. He has made far less than he might have because he is content to share on a cooperative basis with the band, and to share himself and his songs quite liberally with Appel.

He is in complete command of his craft. He has learned his lessons and paid his dues. He has scuffled around with several rock groups, including Doctor Zoom and the Sonic Boom, as well as with another group which traveled the carnival circuit. He has crossed the country on buses, been stranded, seen a lot and thought about it. What he thinks is expressed with clarity and facility in the poetry of his lyrics. I find him an extraordinary phrasemaker, with an acute sense of imagery and rhyme. And musically—in folk or rock—he is brilliant. I wish I knew him ten times better than I do.

The World of John Hammond, 1975.
Red Norvo, George Benson, Benny Goodman,
Jo Jones (behind Benny), and Milt Hinton make music.
Discussion with Bob Dylan and brother-in-law.

When the producers of the television show about my career called Mike Appel to ask Bruce to appear, Appel would not even discuss it. "Bruce's never been on television. Why should he begin by performing for free for John Hammond?" he wanted to know.

The next time Bruce came to my office he asked me why he had not been asked to appear on the program. "I would love to have appeared on your show."

"You were asked," I assured him, "and the producers were turned down."

A week or so later a girl from Choate-Rosemary Hall School called to ask if I though Bruce might be willing to appear at their new art center. The school could only afford to pay him $5,000 she said, and I doubted that it could manage even that much. I agreed to ask Bruce. He had never performed at a private school and I thought it would be a good experience for him. The same week Willard Alexander's office called me to relay an offer of $35,000 for a one-night appearance in Texas taking place at the same time.

I sent a letter about the school to Bruce, marking it for his personal attention. Mike Appel opened it and promptly turned the date down. I then checked to find out whether Bruce had received it. He had not. When he saw it he overruled Mike, turning down Texas and accepting Choate. It's the way he is.

I have mentioned occasionally the television tribute called *The World of John Hammond.* It was one of the many surprising honors I have received in the past few years. The show was created and produced in Chicago. It was a three-hour tape for showing throughout the country on public-television channels. I was very flattered, very appreciative, although I told the producers I would not ask anyone to appear with me. Anyone who came would have to volunteer.

I was overwhelmed by the response. There was a small band led by Benny Carter and featuring Jo Jones, and George Benson, Teddy Wilson and Red Norvo joined in; so did Benny Morton and Milt Hinton, and Benny Goodman even traveled from Connecticut to appear. I was most grateful to John McDonough, who knew enough of my background to round up such long-ago friends as Helen Humes, the gospel singer Marian Williams, and Sonny Terry. Jerry Wexler was there, Mitch Miller, Leonard Feather, and Goddard—all good companions on the long road we have walked together.

Perhaps the biggest surprise was Bob Dylan's appearance. That touched me deeply. But it was everyone's willingness to come to Chicago to reminisce with me, and to play and sing for me, that made this a special event in my life.

The show was so modestly budgeted that no one could be paid more than expenses, and no retakes were possible. That may be one reason it was as good as it was. For—goofs and all—it was a warm reunion, and it has been repeated many times on the public television network. Since then I have frequently had the pleasant experience of being recognized by a stranger who hails me to say that he, too, lived through those years and loved the music.

XLVIII

I returned to Hotchkiss for my forty-fifth reunion in 1974. I found it difficult to come back to the school with John McChesney and George Van Santvoord gone, although there were even greater differences between the school I remembered and Hotchkiss today.

Each of us old grads was assigned a student to explain the changes in the campus and the curriculum and to answer, if he could, our questions. The young man assigned to me was the president of the senior class. He told me he had been accepted at Harvard even before his Hotchkiss graduation, enabling him to enter college as a sophomore. He came from Brooklyn and he was black. I asked him whether or not he had any interest in music. No, he told me, but he had a brother who played in a symphony. "I'm sure you never heard of it," he added. "It's called the Symphony of the New World."

"What do you mean, I've never heard of it? I'm its president," I said.

The boy looked at me, surprised. Perhaps he didn't expect that of an old Hotchkiss grad. But I looked at him with equal amazement, a black president of the Hotchkiss senior class.

There had been a boy in my class from Chattanooga, Tennessee, named Joe Johnson. He had been the class big shot, with every inherited racial prejudice a Southern boy in in the 1920's carried with him. Joe also returned for our reunion, his first visit to the school since we graduated. I asked him what he was doing now. "I'm the medical director of a large insurance company in Chattanooga," he told me, "and I'm very much interested in civil rights, John. I do a lot of work with the black community."

The new headmaster of Hotchkiss, Bill Olsen, told me of an experience the previous month. "We decided to ask Ernest Gruening to speak to the school," he said. "He was the only well-known Hotchkiss graduate we had never officially asked back."

I was delighted and very curious. Ernest Gruening had recently retired from politics after his defeat for reelection as one of Alaska's Senators. Gruening and Wayne Morse of Oregon had been the only two Senators to vote against the Tonkin Resolution. This had led to their defeat at the polls and to deeper American involvement in the Vietnam war. By then, Gruening (Hotchkiss '03) was more than eighty years old. Bill Olsen said that when Ernest was met at the school gate he told the boys he had not been back for seventy years.

"Senator Gruening's speech was the most popular event we've ever had at Hotchkiss," Olsen told me. "The auditorium was filled, people were standing, and many residents of the town had to be turned away." After the speech, Olsen asked Gruening to stay over. Gruening agreed and spent the following day talking to small groups of students, answering their questions, voicing his continued opposition to the Vietnam War, to Johnson and Kennedy, to Nixon, and telling them that the only really decent man we had had in the White

House was Dwight Eisenhower, who, Gruening acknowledged regretfully, was not smart enough to handle the presidency. The Hotchkiss boys loved him.

At one point in the day Gruening had asked about the new swimming pool. "I understand you have a wonderful pool here," he said, whereupon they took him to see it. Gruening stripped and swam three laps, then dressed and continued his discussions. Gruening left Hotchkiss the third day of his visit, and in his honor the school declared a holiday. Six weeks later Ernest Gruening died of cancer. He had summoned all his resources to return to the school. After his death I wrote a memorial piece for *The Nation*. He was a maverick, a great man who I am certain will be remembered in American political and social history. But he was more than that to me. Like John McChesney, Ernest Gruening taught me to find my own way.

In December, 1975, I reached the mandatory retirement age for employees of CBS. My salary had been increased and I received the retirement benefits accumulated over twenty somewhat scattered years of employment. It was time to leave, although much to my satisfaction, I was offered a two-year contract to produce records for Columbia as an independent. Esmé and I formed our own corporation, Snum Music (a family joke), with offices near Columbia's and a budget for future Hammond productions.

I welcomed the new agreement for many reasons. Principally, it assured me of continued involvement with Columbia and the record world, as necessary a part of my life as music itself.

Within a few months I was in pursuit of my newest find. He was Adam Makowicz (Ma-KO-vitch), an in-his-thirties young Polish pianist. Jan Byrczek, head of the International Jazz Federation, brought him to my attention. He sent me a solo record which amply displayed Adam's awesome technique and fascinating harmonic sense, as well as his originality as a composer. I was charmed, excited, and impressed.

It's never fair to an artist to say, "He's like. . . ," or,

"He'll remind you of. . . ." For this kind of quick identification becomes a label, and adherents of the one he's like immediately disagree and begin knocking him for his presumption.

So perhaps I should not say that Adam sounds a bit like Art Tatum, but he does, mostly in his rapid runs and arpeggios. Otherwise, he is his own man, classically trained, with a dense, complex style anchored by a very strong left hand. He likes to play a fragment of melody, then bend it, turn it under, obscure it, before letting it come out the other side, sometimes wreathed in dissonance, sometimes with right and left hands playing in different tempi, sometimes simply heading straight for home. Much of the time he plays with head bowed low over the keys, which would seem a bit cramping for his rush of notes but is not.

For all his pianistic complexity, he is an unpretentious man, respectful of the influences he has absorbed, yet not beholden to any and unafraid of exploring new directions for himself.

It took a year to get Adam to the United States. He made his debut—where else?—at Barney Josephson's Cookery, went on to play the Newport Jazz Festival with Earl Hines, George Shearing, and Teddy Wilson, and to record for Columbia. I think he'll hold his own.

So I have returned to a way of life which has always appealed to me, in which my days are filled with variety, with the time and freedom to do something about a lot of things. I can suit myself, go at my own pace, leave one thing for another when it is time to move on. My mornings start with early breakfast and catching up with the world since yesterday in newspapers and on the radio. I walk through Manhattan streets to my office, attend a record date or an audition, and lunch with a friend whose opinions fit or replenish my own. There is time for a meeting of a group with a social cause I can discuss to my heart's content, time to visit a record store, to drop in at Columbia, or to chat with an old friend on a street corner. There is time for dinner at a favorite restaurant, a preview on Broadway, the opening night of a favorite performer; and then to bed, earlier than when I was young, but

Recording session with pianist
Adam Makowicz at Columbia's 30th
Street studio in June, 1977.

with everything considered, nothing missed.

I am still a New Yorker who owns no house, who thrives on city weekdays and country weekends. I still would change the world if I could, convince a nonbeliever that my way is right, argue a cause and make friends out of enemies. I am still the reformer, the impatient protester, the some-times-intolerant champion of tolerance. Best of all, I still expect to hear, if not today then tomorrow, a voice or a sound I have never heard before, with something to say which has never been said before. And when that happens I will know what to do.

A Selective Discography

All records 78-rpm singles (popular 10″, classical 12″) until 1948. Thereafter, all records 12″ LPs unless otherwise specified. All records monaural unless specified stereo.
* indicates historically significant records.

Date	Artist	Selections	Label
11 Sep 1931	Garland Wilson	When Your Lover Has Gone/St. Joe's Infirmary	Not issued
2 Feb 1932	Garland Wilson	Memories of You/Rockin' Chair	Okeh
9 Dec 1932	*Fletcher Henderson Orch	Honeysuckle Rose/Underneath the Harlem Moon	Columbia
		New King Porter Stomp	Okeh
14 Mar 1933	Benny Carter Orch	Swing It/Synthetic Love/6 Bells Stampede/Love, You're Not the One for Me	English Columbia
18 Apr 1933	Spike Hughes Orch	Pastorale/three others	Eng. Decca
18 May 1933	Spike Hughes Orch	Arabesque/four others	Eng. Decca
19 May 1933	Spike Hughes Orch	Donegal Cradle Song/four others	Eng. Decca
22 Sep 1933	*Fletcher Henderson Orch	Queer Notions/It's the Talk of the Town/Night Life/Nagasaki	Columbia
26 Sep 1933	Joe Sullivan (solo)	Honeysuckle Rose/Gin Mill Blues/two others	Eng. Parlo-phone
29 Sep 1933	Coleman Hawkins Orch	Day You Came Along/Jamaica Shout/Heartbreak Blues	Eng. Parl.
2 Oct 1933	Joe Venuti Blue Six	Jazz Me Blues/In de Ruff/two others	Eng. Col.
3 Oct 1933	*Horace Henderson Orch	Happy Feet/Rhythm Crazy/Ol' Man River/Minnie the Moocher's Wedding Day/Ain't 'Cha Glad?/I've Got to Sing A Torch Song	Eng. Parl.
10 Oct 1933	Chocolate Dandies	Blue Interlude/I Never Knew/	Eng. Col.
10 Oct 1933	Teddy Wilson (solo)	Liza/Rosetta	Col. Not issued

Date	Artist	Selections	Label
6 Oct 1933	Benny Carter Orch	Devil's Holiday/Blue Lou/two others	Eng. Col.
8 Oct 1933	*Benny Goodman Orch	I Gotta Right to Sing the Blues/Ain't 'Cha Glad?	Eng. Col.
27 Oct 1933	Benny Goodman Orch	Dr. Heckle and Mr. Jibe/Texas Tea Party	Eng. Col.
24 Nov 1933	*Bessie Smith	Do Your Duty/Gimme A Pigfoot/ I'm Down in the Dumps/Take Me for A Buggy Ride	Okeh
27 Nov 1933	*Benny Goodman Orch	Your Mother's Son-in-Law (first Billie Holiday vocal on records)	Columbia
4 Dec 1933	Benny Goodman Orch	Tappin' the Barrel/Keep on Doin'	Columbia
8 Dec 1933	*Benny Goodman Orch	Riffin' the Scotch	Columbia
20 Dec 1933	Chick Webb Orch	On the Sunny Side of the Street/Darktown Strutters' Ball	Columbia
15 Jan 1934	Chick Webb Orch	If Dreams Come True/Get Together	Columbia
2 Feb 1934	Benny Goodman Orch (Vocal: Mildred Bailey)	Junk Man/Georgia Jubilee/two others	Columbia
23 Feb 1934	Benny Morton Orch (Vocal & trumpet solo: Red Allen)	Tailor Made/Gold Digger's Son/ two others	Columbia
14 May 1934	Benny Goodman Orch (Vocals: Jack Teagarden)	Moonglow/three others	Columbia
18 May 1934	Chick Webb Orch	Stompin' at the Savoy/three others	Columbia
7 Jun 1934	Chick Webb Orch	Blue Minor/Lonesome Moments/two others	Okeh
15 Aug 1934	Wingy Manone (with Jelly Roll Morton)	Never Had No Lovin'/I'm Alone Without You	Okeh rejected
16 Aug 1934	Benny Goodman Music Hall Orch	Bugle Call Rag/three others	Columbia
21 Sep 1934	Benny Goodman Modernists	Stars Fell on Alabama/Solitude/ two others	Banner
26 Sep 1934	*Red Norvo Septet	Old-fashioned Love/I Surrender, Dear	Columbia
27 Sep 1934	Louis Prima & New Orleans Gang	Stardust/'Long About Midnight/two others	Brunswick
4 Oct 1934	*Red Norvo Septet	Tomboy/Night Is Blue	Columbia
26 Nov 1934	Benny Goodman Music Hall Orch	Cokey/Music Hall Rag/two others	Columbia
23 Jan 1935	Reginald Foresythe Orch (with B. Goodman, Krupa)	Dodging A Divorcée/three others	Eng. Col.
25 Jan 1935	*Red Norvo Octet	Blues in E Flat/Bughouse/two others	Columbia
19 Feb 1935	Benny Goodman Orch	Original Dixieland Band/Night Wind/three others	Columbia
21 Feb 1935	Taft Jordan & Mob (Teddy Wilson, et al)	If the Moon Turns Green/Night Wind/Devil in the Moon/one other	Perfect
4 Apr 1935	Benny Goodman Orch	Hooray for Love/Dixieland Band/ two others	Victor
19 Apr 1935	Benny Goodman Orch	Always/Restless/two others	Victor
25 Jun 1935	Benny Goodman Orch	Blue Skies/three others	Victor
1 Jul 1935 (with Eli Oberstein)	Benny Goodman Orch	Sometimes I'm Happy/King Porter Stomp/two others	Victor
2 Jul 1935	*Teddy Wilson-Billie Holiday Orch	I Wished on the Moon/Miss Brown to You/What A Little Moonlight Can Do	Brunswick
13 Jul 1935	Benny Goodman Trio	Body and Soul/Who/After You've Gone/Someday Sweetheart	Victor

Date	Artist	Selections	Label
7 Oct 1935	Teddy Wilson (solo)	Liza, Rosetta, Every Now and Then/It Never Dawned	Brunswick
20 Oct 1935	Mildred Bailey Swing Band	Someday Sweetheart/I'd Love to Take Orders from You/When Day Is Done	Vocalion
25 Oct 1935	Teddy Wilson-Billie Holiday Orch	If You Were Mine/Eeny, Meeny/two others	Brunswick
19 Nov 1935	*Gene Krupa Chicagoans	Blues of Israel/Three Little Words/Last Round-up/Jazz Me Blues	Eng. Par.
21 Nov 1935	Meade Lux Lewis (solo)	Honky Tonk Train Blues	Eng. Par.
22 Nov 1935	Benny Goodman Orch	When Buddha Smiles/six others	Victor
22 Nov 1935	Teddy Wilson (solo)	I Found A Dream/Of Treasure Island	Brunswick
3 Dec 1935	Teddy Wilson-Billie Holiday Orch	You Let Me Down/Spreadin' Rhythm Around/two others	Brunswick
4 Dec 1935	Bud Freeman Orch	Buzzard/What Is There to Say?/Tillie's Downtown Now/Keep Smiling	Eng. Parl
13 Dec 1935	Bunny Berigan Orch	I'm Comin' Virginia/Chicken and Waffles/You Took Advantage of Me	Eng. Parl
6 Dec 1935	Mildred Bailey (with Teddy Wilson, Bunny Berigan, Johnny Hodges)	Willow Tree/Honeysuckle Rose/Squeeze Me/Downhearted Me	Eng. Parl
15 Jan 1936	Jimmy Noone New Orleans Band	He's A Different Type of Guy/Blues Jumped A Rabbit/Sweet Georgia Brown	Eng. Parl
17 Jan 1936	Teddy Wilson (solo)		Brunswick
30 Jan 1936	Teddy Wilson-Billie Holiday Orch	Life Begins When You're in Love/one other	Brunswick
13 Feb 1936	Albert Ammons Rhythm Kings	Nagasaki/Boogie Woogie Stomp	Decca
14 Feb 1936	Albert Ammons Rhythm Kings	Early Morning Blues/Mile or More Bird Rag	Decca
17 Mar 1936	Teddy Wilson (with Ella Fitzgerald)	Christopher Columbus/Melancholy Baby/All My Life	Brunswick
30 Jun 1936	Teddy Wilson (with Billie Holiday)	I Cried for You/Guess Who/These Foolish Things/one other	Brunswick
Aug 1936	Roy Eldridge	Christopher Columbus/three others	Decca rejected
24 Aug 1936	Teddy Wilson Orch (with Benny Goodman. Vocal: Helen Ward)	You Came to My Rescue/Here's Love in Your Eyes/two others	Brunswick
9 Oct 1936	*Jones-Smith, Inc. (First recording with Count Basie)	Shoe Shine Boy/Evenin'/Boogie Woogie/Lady Be Good	Vocalion
21 Oct 1936	Teddy Wilson Orch (with Billie Holiday)	Easy to Love/The Way You Look Tonight/With Thee I Swing	Brunswick
28 Oct 1936	Teddy Wilson-Billie Holiday Orch	Who Loves You	Brunswick
29 Oct 1936	Billie Holiday & Her Orch	A Fine Romance/I Can't Pretend	Vocalion
9 Nov 1936	Mildred Bailey & Her Orch	Sentimental Reasons/It's Love I'm After/'Long About Midnight/More Than You Know	Eng. Parl.
19 Nov 1936	Teddy Wilson-Billie Holiday Orch (with Benny Goodman)	Sailin'/I Can't Give You Anything But Love/Pennies from Heaven/That's Life I Guess	Brunswick

Date	Artist	Selections	Label
5 Jan 1937	*Teddy Wilson Orch (with Buck Clayton, Benny Goodman, Lester Young, Freddie Green, Walter Page, Jo Jones)	He Ain't Got Rhythm/This Year's Kisses/Why Was I Born/I Must Have That Man	Brunswick
8 Feb 1937	Teddy Wilson-Billie Holiday Orch	Mood That I'm In/You Showed Me the Way/Sentimental and Melancholy/Last Affair	Brunswick
1 Mar 1937	Teddy Wilson-Billie Holiday Orch	Carelessly/How Could You?/Moanin' Low/Fine and Dandy	Brunswick
1 May 1937	Teddy Wilson-Billie Holiday Orch	Yours and Mine/I'll Get By/Mean to Me/Son Showers	Brunswick
1 Jun 1937	*Teddy Wilson-Billie Holiday Orch	Foolin' Myself/Easy Livin'/I'll Never Be the Same/I Found A New Baby	Brunswick
9 Jun 1937	Mildred Bailey Orch (with Buck Clayton, Edmund Hall, Freddie Green, et al)	If You Should Ever Leave/Moon Got in My Eyes/two others	Vocalion
0 Jun 1937	Count Basie Orch (Savoy Ballroom air check)	Bugle Blues/Count Steps In/Swing, Brother, Swing/others	Columbia
5 Sep 1937	*Teddy Wilson Quartet (Harry James, Red Norvo, John Simmons)	Just A Mood 1 & 2/Ain't Misbehavin'/Honeysuckle Rose	Brunswick
2 Nov 1937	Teddy Wilson (solo)		
1 Dec 1937	Harry James Orch (with Buck Clayton, Vernon Brown, Herschel Evans, Dave Matthews, Jess Stacy, Walter Page, Jo Jones. Vocal: Helen Humes)	Jubilee/When You're Alone/Can't I?/Life Goes to A Party	Brunswick
1936–1937	Benny Goodman Trio	Six sessions	Victor
5 Jan 1938	Harry James Orch	Texas Chatter/One O'Clock Jump	Brunswick
6 Jan 1939	Harry James Orch	Song of the Wanderer/It's the Dreamer in Me	Brunswick
4 Feb 1938	Joseph Szigeti (with orchestra, Max Goberman conducting)	Mozart: Divertimento #15 B-flat Major	Columbia M322
23 Dec 1938/ 24 Dec 1939	*From Spirituals to Swing	Excerpts from two Carnegie Hall concerts	Vanguard
0 Dec 1938	Albert Ammons	Shout for Joy	Vocalion
1936–1938	Benny Goodman Quartet	Thirteen sessions	Victor
1936–1938	Benny Goodman Orch	Twenty-six sessions	Victor
8 Jan 1939	Mildred Bailey–John Kirby Sextet	St. Louis Blues/I Cried for You/two others	Vocalion
1 Feb 1939	Harry James & Boogie Trio (with Pete Johnson/Albert Ammons, Ed Dougherty, Johnny Williams)	Boo Woo—P.J./Woo Woo—A.A./Home James—P.J./Jesse—A.A.	Brunswick
6 Mar 1939	Mildred Bailey & Oxford Greys (with Mary Lou Williams)	Gulf Coast Blues/Arkansas Blues/Barrelhouse Music/three others	Vocalion
9 Mar 1939	*Count Basie Orch (first CBS session)	Rockabye Basie/five others	Vocalion
5 Apr 1939	Count Basie Orch	Miss Thing Parts 1 & 2/12th Street Rag	Vocalion
2 Apr 1939– 5 Apr 1939	Frankie Newton Cafe Society Orch	Tab's Blues/Frankie's Jump/four others	Vocalion

Date	Artist	Selections	Label
15 Apr 1939	Walter Gieseking	Debussy: Second Book of Preludes	Columbia M382
19 May 1939	Count Basie Orch (Basie on pipe organ)	Nobody Knows/one other	Vocalion
14 Jun 1939	Mildred Bailey (with John Kirby, Red Norvo)	Moon Love/Blowing Bubbles/ others	Vocalion
24 Jun 1939	Count Basie Orch	How Long Blues/three others	Vocalion
27 Jun 1939	Mildred Bailey (with John Kirby, Red Norvo)	Ghost of A Chance/three others	Vocalion
10 Aug 1939	Benny Goodman Orch	Stealin' Apples/Jumpin' at the	Columbia
11 Aug 1939	Benny Goodman Orch	Woodside/What's New/Night	
16 Aug 1939	Benny Goodman Orch	and Day/six others	
2 Oct 1939	*Benny Goodman Sextet (with Charlie Christian)	Flying Home/Rose Room	Columbia
10 Oct 1939	Stuyvesant String Quartet (with Laura Newell)	Bloch: String Quartet #2	Columbia M392
5 Nov 1939	*Count Basie Kansas City (with Buck Clayton, Dickie Wells, Lester Young, Freddie Green, Walter Page, Jo Jones)	Dickie's Dream/Lester Leaps In	Vocalion
8 Nov 1939	Redd Evans Orch (with Teddy Wilson)	Milenberg Joys	Okeh
22 Nov 1939	Benny Goodman Sextet	Soft Winds/Memories of You/ 7 Come 11	Columbia
31 Dec 1939	Ida Cox & All-Star Band (with Lips Page, J.C. Higginbotham, Edmund Hall, James P. Johnson/ Fletcher Henderson, Charlie Christian, Artie Bernstein, Lionel Hampton)	Four-day Creep/five blues: Deep Sea, Death Letter, Hard Times, Pink Slip, Take Him Off My Mind	Vocalion
4 Aug 1939– 24 Sep 1941	Count Basie Orch	Thirteen sessions (63 selections)	Columbia Vocalion/ Okeh
1939–1942	Benny Goodman Orch	Thirty-two sessions	Columbia
7 Feb 1940	Benny Goodman Sextet (with Count Basie)	Till Tom Special/Gone With "What" Wind?	Columbia
7 Feb 1940	Metronome All-Star Band (with Harry James, Jack Jenney, Jack Teagarden, Charlie Christian, Gene Krupa, et al)	King Porter Stomp	Columbia
7 Feb 1940	Metronome All-Star Band (with James, Punch Miller, Benny Carter, Teagarden, same rhythm)	All-Star Strut	Columbia
9 Feb 1940	Joe Sullivan Orch at Cafe Society	Low Down Dirty Shame/I Can't Give You Anything But Love	Vocalion
29 Apr 1940	Joe Sullivan Orch at Cafe Society (Vocals: Helen Ward)	I Cover the Waterfront/I Gotta Crush on You	Okeh
22 Mar 1940	Stuyvesant String Quartet (with Laura Newell)	Ravel: Introduction and Allegro	Columbia X 167
13 May 1940– 14 May 1940	Joseph Szigeti, Bela Bartok, Benny Goodman	Contrasts	Columbia X 178
4 Oct 1940	Eddy Howard & All Stars (Bill Coleman, Benny Morton, Edmund Hall, Bud Freeman, Teddy Wilson, Charlie Christian, Billy Taylor)	Old Fashioned Love/Stardust/ Exactly Like You/Wrap Your Troubles in Dreams	Columbia

Date	Artist	Selections		Label
1940–1942	Benny Goodman Sextet	Eight sessions		Columbia
7 Apr 1941	Teddy Wilson (solo)			Columbia
6 Oct 1941	Teddy Wilson Orch (Vocal: Lena Horne)	Out of Nowhere/one other		Columbia
1 Nov 1941	Paul Robeson (with Count Basie Orch)	King Joe, Parts 1 & 2 (By Richard Wright in honor of Joe Louis)		Okeh
3 Nov 1941– 7 Jul 1942	Count Basie Orch	Seven sessions		Columbia
6 Jan 1942	Metronome All-Star Leaders	(with Cootie Williams, J.C. Higginbotham, B. Goodman, B. Carter, Basie, Krupa, J. Kirby, C. Barnet)		Columbia
9 Jan 1946	Count Basie Orch	Four selections		Columbia
4 Feb 1946	Count Basie Orch	Lady Lady Blues/The King/two others		Columbia
8 Oct 1946	*Mildred Bailey & Ellis Larkins Cafe Society All-Stars	I'll Close My Eyes/Me and the Blues/Lover Come Back to Me/ At Sundown		Majestic
1947	Igor Stravinsky, cond.	Stravinsky: Dumbarton Oaks Concerto		Keynote (78) Mercury (LP)
1947	Mitch Miller, oboe	Cimarosa: Concerto for Oboe & Strings		Mercury
1947	Mitch Miller, oboe	V. Williams: Concerto for Oboe & Strings		Mercury
1947	Ralph Kirkpatrick	de Falla: Concerto for Harpsichord		Mercury
1947	Schneider, Horszowski, F. Miller, Katims	Brahms: Piano Quartets in G, A, C minor		Mercury
1951	Alfred Newman & Hollywood Symphony Orch	Gershwin: American in Paris/ Songs. Two records.		Mercury
1951	Alfred Newman & Hollywood Symphony Orch	Famous Ballet Themes/Famous Movie Themes. Two records.		Mercury
Dec 1953	Vic Dickenson Septet, Vols. 1 & 2	(with Ruby Braff, Edmond Hall, Sir Charles Thompson, Walter Page, Steve Jordan, L. Erskine)	10″	Vanguard VRS-8001/2
Dec 1953	Sir Charles Thompson	(with Pete Brown, Joe Newman, Benny Powell, Gene Ramey, Osie Johnson)	10″	Vanguard VRS-8003
Dec 1953	Mel Powell Septet	(with Hall, Buck Clayton, Henderson Chambers, Jordan, Walter Page, Jimmy Crawford)	10″	Vanguard VRS-8004
1954	Brother John Sellers	(with Braff, Sir Charles Thompson, Page, Green, Jones)	10″	Vanguard VRS-8005
1954	Sir Charles Thompson Quartet	(with Green, Page, Jones)	10″	Vanguard VRS-8006
1954	Joe Newman Band	(with Matthew Gee, Frank Foster, Frank Wess, John Acea, Eddie Jones, Johnson)	10″	Vanguard VRS-8007
1954	Buck Meets Ruby	(with Clayton, Braff, Benny Morton, Buddy Tate, Jordan, Aaron Bell, Jimmy Jones, Buddy Donaldson)	10″	Vanguard VRS-8008
1955	Sir Charles Thompson Band	(featuring Coleman Hawkins)	10″	Vanguard VRS-8009
1955	Urbie Green Band	(with Braff, Med Flory, Bell, Green, Donaldson)	10″	Vanguard VRS-8010
1955	Jimmy Rushing Sings the Blues		10″	Vanguard VRS-8011
1955	Vic Dickenson Septet Vol. 3	(with Braff, Hall, Shad Collins, Jordan, Thompson, Jones)	10″	Vanguard VRS-8013

409

Date	Artist	Selections		Label
1955	Sam Most Sextet	10″		Vanguard VRS-801
1956	Mel Powell Bandstand	10″		Vanguard VRS-801
1956	Don Elliott Doubles in Brass	(featuring Ellis Larkins)	10″	Vanguard VRS-801
1956	Nat Pierce Bandstand	10″		Vanguard VRS-801
1956	Sir Charles Thompson Quartet	10″		Vanguard VRS-801
1956	Ruby Braff and Ellis Larkins, Vols. 1 & 2	10″		Vanguard VRS-801 8020
1955	Mel Powell Trio	Borderline (with Paul Quinichette)		Vanguard VRS-850
1955	Mel Powell Trio	Thingamajig (with Braff)		Vanguard VRS-850
1957	Jo Jones Special	(Count Basie, Emmett Berry, Lucky Thompson, Morton, Page, Green, Jones)		Vanguard VRS-850
1956	Jimmy Rushing	Listen to the Blues		Vanguard VRS-850
1956	Braff & Larkins	Two by Two		Vanguard VRS-850
1957	Joe Williams et al	A Night at Count Basie's (live on location)		Vanguard VRS-850
1957	Basie Band, Moms Mabley, George Kirby, et al	A Night at the Apollo (live from theater)		Vanguard VRS-900
1957	Rolf Kuhn Quartet	Streamline		Vanguard VRS-851
1957	Bobby Henderson	Handful of Keys		Vanguard VRS-851
1957	Ronnell Bright Trio	Bright Flight		Vanguard VRS-851
1956	Jimmy Rushing and Band	If This Ain't the Blues	stereo	Vanguard VRS-851
1958	Jimmy Rushing and Band	Goin' to Chicago		Vanguard VRS-851
1958	From Spirituals to Swing	1938–39 live concerts at Carnegie Hall		Vanguard VRS-852
1958	Jo Jones Plus 2	(with Ray Bryant)	stereo	Vanguard VRS-852
1958	Mae Barnes	(with Clayton, Bryant, Jones)	stereo	Vanguard VRS-903
1958	Ben Ludlow Orchestra	Dancing in High Society	stereo	Vanguard VRS-904
1956	Bobby Henderson	Call House Blues		Vanguard VRS-901
1956	Freidrich Gulda	Live at Birdland		RCA Vic
1956	Buck Clayton All-Stars	Robbins Nest Hucklebuck All the Cats Join In Jumping at the Woodside		Columbia Columbia Columbia Columbia
Reissue	Mel Powell	Out on a Limb (collated from 10″ LPs)		Vanguard VRS-850
Reissue	Vic Dickenson Showcase Vols. 1 & 2	(Collated from 10″ LPs)		Vanguard VRS-852
Reissue	Nat Pierce-Mel Powell	Easy Swing (collated from 10″ LPs)		Vanguard VRS-851

410

Date	Artist	Selections	Label
reissue	Braff-Larkins	Pocket Full of Dreams (collated from 10″ LPs)	Vanguard VRS-8516
reissue	Most-Elliott	Doubles in Jazz (collated from 10″ LPs)	Vanguard VRS-8522
1960	Ray Bryant Trio	Little Susie	Columbia CS8244
1960	Ray Bryant Combo	Madison Time	CS8267
9 Apr 1960	Abyssinian Baptist Gospel Choir	Alex Bradford, composer & cond. Stereo	CS8348
1961	Jack Douglas	Live at the Bon Soir	CS8357
1961	Charles Bell	Contemporary Jazz Quartet	CS8382
1961	Nutty Squirrels	Bird Watching	CS8389
1961	Aretha Franklin	Aretha	CS8412
1961	Ray Bryant Trio	Con Alma	CS8433
1961	Pete Seeger	Story Songs	CS8468
1961	Crowell & Pokriss	Ernest in Love. Original cast album	OS2027
1961	Dukes of Dixieland	Breakin' It Up on Broadway	CS8528
1961	Carolyn Hester		CS8596
1962	Kay Ballard	Peanuts	CS8543
1962	Don Elliott & Orch	Love Is A Necessary Evil	CS8554
1962	Aretha Franklin	The Electrifying ———. Co-producer.	CS8561
1962	Bob Dylan	Bob Dylan	CS8579
1962	Dukes of Dixieland	Now Hear This	CS8593
1962	Peter LaFarge	"Ira Hayes"	CS8595
1960–62	Marlowe Morris Quintet	Play the Thing	CS8619
1963	Olatunji	Flaming Drums	CS8666
1963	Ray Bryant Orch	Hollywood Jazz Beat	CS8667
1963	Dukes of Dixieland	Hootenanny	CS8671
1963	Pete Seeger	Bitter and the Sweet	CS8716
1963	Paul Winter Sextet	Jazz Meets Bossa Nova	CS8725
1963	Pete Seeger	Children's Town Hall Concert	CS8747
1963	Dukes of Dixieland	At Disneyland	CS8766
1963	Bob Dylan	The Freewheeling ———	CS8786
1963	Olatunji	High Life	CS8796
1963	Paul Winter Sextet	Jazz Premiere	CS8797
1963	Carolyn Hester	This Life I'm Living	CS8832
1963	Dukes of Dixieland & Clara Ward Singers	We Gotta Shout	CS8842
1963	Paul Winter Sextet	New Jazz on Campus	CS8864
1963	Pete Seeger	We Shall Overcome	CS8901
1963	Illinois Jacquet	(with Sir Charles Thompson, Roy Eldridge)	Epic BA17033
1963	Herb Ellis All-Stars	Midnight Roll	Epic BA17034
1963	Herb Ellis	Three Guitars in Bossa Nova Time	Epic BA17036
1963	Herb Ellis-Stuff Smith	Together	BA17039
1963	Nikki Price	Nikki	BN26005
1964	Gene Stridel	This Is ———	Columbia CS8915
1964	Jeremy Steig Quartet	Flute Fever	CS8936
1964	Paul Winter Sextet	Jazz Meets Folk Song	CS8955
1964	Denny Zeitlin	Cathexis	CS8982
1964	Dukes of Dixieland	Struttin' at the World's Fair	CS8994
1964	Friedrich Gulda	From Vienna with Jazz	CS9051

Date	Artist	Selections	Label
1964	Paul Winter & Carlos Lyra	Sound of Ipanema	CS9072
1965	Pete Seeger	Strangers & Cousins	CS9134
1965	Denny Zeitlin Trio	Carnival	CS9140
1965	Friedrich Gulda	Ineffable	CS9146
1966	Bobbe Norris	The Beginning	CS9224
1966	Pete Seeger	God Bless the Grass	CS9232
1966	Len Chandler	To Be A Man	CS9259
1966	John Handy	Live at Monterey	CS9262
1966	Denny Zeitlin Trio	Shining Hour	CS9263
1966	Pete Seeger	Dangerous Songs!?	CS9303
1966	George Benson Quartet	It's Uptown	CS9325
1966	Dick Davy	You're A Long Way from Home, Whitey	CS9345
1966	Joe Masters	Jazz Mass	CS9398
1966	George Benson Quartet	Cookbook (with Lonnie Smith)	CS9413
1967	Malvina Reynolds	Sings the Truth	CS9414
1967	Clare Fischer Orch	Songs for Rainy Day Lovers	CS9491
1967	Lonnie Smith Combo	Soul Organ	CS9496
1967	John Handy Orch	New View	CS9497
1967	Pete Seeger	Big Muddy	CS9505
1967	Leonard Cohen	Leonard Cohen	CS9533
1967	Dick Davy	Stronger Than Dirt	CS9537
1968	Denny Zeitlin	Zeitgeist	CS9548
1968	Len Chandler	The Lovin' People	Columbi CS9553
1968	Pat Lundy	Soul Ain't Nothin' But the Blues	CS9588
1968	Willie Ruff	Smooth Side of Ruff	CS9603
1968	Don Ellis Orch	Shock Treatment	CS9668
1968	John Handy	Projections	CS9689
1969	Pete Seeger	Now	CS9717
1969	Addis & Crofut	Eastern Ferris Wheel	CS9746
1969	Don Ellis Orch.	Electric Bath	CS9845
1969	Roberta Peck	Extraordinary	CS9848
1969	Eubie Blake	Eighty-six Years of ———.	C2S847
1970	Pete Seeger	Young vs. Old	CS9873
1972	Jerry Hahn Combo	Brotherhood	CS1044
1972	Pete Seeger	Rainbow Race	C30739
1974	Pete Seeger	The World of ———	KG3194
1974	Horace Arnold Band	Tribe	KC3215(
1974	Bill Watrous Band	Manhattan Wildlife Refuge	KC3309(
1975	Bill Watrous	Tiger of San Pedro	PC33701
1975	Helen Humes (with Ellis Larkins & George Benson)	It's the Talk of the Town	PC33488
Reissue	Thesaurus of Classic Jazz (Dorsey Brothers, Miff Mole's Little Molers, Red Nichols & Charleston Chasers, Arkansas Travellers, et al)	Four records	Columbi C4L 18
Reissue	*Mildred Bailey—Her Greatest Performances 1929–1946	Three records	Columbi C3L 22
Reissue	Jazz Odyssey—Vol. 3— The Sound of Harlem	Three records	Columbi C3L 33

ate	Artist	Selections	Label
eissue	The Original Sound of "The Twenties"	Three records	Columbia C3L 35
eissue	*Thesaurus of Classic Jazz —King of the Delta Blues Singers—Robert Johnson	Crossroads Blues/Terraplane Blues/Come on in My Kitchen/ Walking Blues/twelve others	Columbia CL 1654
eissue	*Father of the Stride Piano—James P. Johnson	If Dreams Come True/Swingin' at the Lido/fourteen others	Columbia CL 1780
eissue	Stompin' at the Savoy— The Immortal Chick Webb	Let's Get Together/If Dreams Come True/ten others	Columbia CL 2639
eissue	*The World's Greatest Blues Singer—Bessie Smith	Down Hearted Blues/Do Your Duty/Gimme A Pigfoot/Down in the Dumps, etc. Two records	Columbia GP 33
.ve	The Legendary Son House-Father of Folk Blues	Death Letter/Pearline/ Preachin' Blues/six others	Columbia CS 9217
eissue	*Robert Johnson—King of the Delta Blues Singers, Vol. 2	Kind Hearted Woman Blues/I'm A Steady Rollin' Man/fourteen others	Columbia C 30034
eissue	*Bessie Smith—Any Woman's Blues	Two records	Columbia G 30126
eissue	Bessie Smith—Empty Bed Blues	Two records. Executive producer.	Columbia G 0450
eissue	Stars of the Apollo	Two records. Executive producer.	Columbia 30788
eissue	Bessie Smith—the Empress	Two records. Executive producer.	Columbia G 30818
eissue	*The Billie Holiday Story, Vol. 1	Two records (from C3L 21, The Golden Years, no longer available)	Columbia KG 32121
eissue	*The Billie Holiday Story, Vol. 2	Two records (from C3L 21 and C3L 40, The Golden Years, Vols. 1 & 2, no longer available)	Columbia KG 32124
eissue	*The Billie Holiday Story, Vol. 3	Two records (from C3L 40, The Golden Years, Vol. 2, no longer available)	Columbia KG 32127
eissue	*Precious Lord—New Recordings of the Great Gospel Songs of Thomas A. Dorsey	Two records. Executive producer.	Columbia KG 32151
eissue	*From Spirituals to Swing— 30th Anniversary Concert— 1967	Two records: George Benson, Count Basie, Joe Turner, Big Mama Thornton, et al	Columbia G 30776
eissue	*Solo Flight—The Genius of Charlie Christian	Two records	Columbia G 30779
eissue	*Billie Holiday—God Bless the Child	Two records: I Can't Pretend/ Jim/I'm All for You/Georgia on My Mind/twenty-five others	Columbia G 30782
eissue	*The Gospel Sound	Two records. Executive producer.	Columbia G 31086
eissue	*Nobody's Blues But Mine— Bessie Smith	Two records: Careless Love Blues/What's the Matter Now?/etc. Exec. producer.	Columbia G 31093
eissue	*Count Basie—Super Chief	Two records: Shoe Shine Boy/ The Moon Got in My Eyes/ twenty-six others. Exec. producer.	Columbia G 31224
eissue	Ethel Waters' Greatest Years	Two records (with Fletcher Henderson, James P. Johnson)	Columbia KG 31571
eissue	The Gospel Sound, Vol. 2	Two records	Columbia KG 31595 GA 31595
eissue	Teddy Wilson and His All-Stars	Two records	Columbia KG 31617
3 Jun 1977	Adam Makowicz	First U.S. album. Jigsaw/others	Columbia

Index

Page numbers in *italic* refer to illustrations.

DATE DUE